Introduction to German Philosophy

Introduction to

GERMAN
PHILOSOPHY

FROM KANT TO HABERMAS

Andrew Bowie

polity

The right of Andrew Bowie to be identified as Author of this Work has been asserted in accordance with the UK Copyright, Designs and Patents Act 1988.
First published in 2003 by Polity Press in association with Blackwell Publishing Ltd.

Editorial office:
Polity Press
65 Bridge Street
Cambridge CB2 1UR, UK

Marketing and production:
Blackwell Publishing Ltd
108 Cowley Road
Oxford OX4 1JF, UK

Distributed in the USA by
Blackwell Publishing Inc.
350 Main Street
Malden, MA 02148, USA

A catalogue record for this book is available from the British Library.

Library of Congress Cataloging-in-Publication Data
Bowie, Andrew, 1952–
Introduction to German philosophy : from Kant to Habermas / Andrew Bowie.
p. cm.
Includes bibliographical references and index. ISBN 0-7456-2570-3 (alk. paper) – ISBN 0-7456-2571-1 (pbk. : alk. paper)
1. Philosophy, German – History. I. Title.
B2521 .B69 2003
193 – dc21
2003004253

Typeset in 10.5 on 12 pt Times Ten
by SNP Best-set Typesetter Ltd., Hong Kong
Printed and bound in Great Britain by MPG Books, Bodmin, Cornwall

For further information on Polity, visit our website: www.polity.co.uk

CONTENTS

PREFACE

Einstein once said: 'Everything should be made as simple as possible, but not simpler.' He may not have been talking about explaining modern German philosophy, but the same principle probably applies. The present book offers an account of the German philosophy from Kant to the present which forms the often neglected background to much recent theoretical work in the humanities. My aim is to provide a comprehensible, but not reductive, outline of the major concerns of the German philosophical tradition for students and teachers in the humanities who need a text that can give them an initial orientation in this often rather formidable area. The book is also intended for those working in the tradition of Anglo-American 'analytical' philosophy who have realized that the rigid boundaries between their concerns and the concerns of the European tradition are breaking down in the light of the arguments of Donald Davidson, Nelson Goodman, Hilary Putnam, Richard Rorty, Wilfrid Sellars and others.[1]

Any such enterprise poses considerable difficulties, not least because of the size of the area to be covered. The texts which form this tradition are often written in a manner which puts off the non-specialist reader, and the interpretation of the texts remains controversial. Nietzsche, to take an extreme example, is regarded by some, including in certain respects myself, as a dangerous Social Darwinist

---

1 These thinkers share the conviction that we must give up the ideas that we can claim the world has an inherent 'ready-made' structure and that there is an infallible kind of access to that structure which provides reliable knowledge. Such ideas will become clearer to non-philosophical readers in the course of the book. See e.g. Davidson (1984), Goodman (1978), Putnam (1983), Rorty (1980), Sellars (1997).

with leanings towards the kind of ideas which later informed Nazi ideology, and by others, such as Jacques Derrida, as a valuable resource for feminist thinking. In relation to the first problem, I have generally tried to avoid extensive quotation, as this can lead to the need for lengthy commentary to explain the text in question. I have, though, on occasion dealt with a key passage of text in some detail. In relation to the second, I have tried to restrict my agenda to the kind of questions which interest people working in the humanities today, or which interest natural scientists who wish to reflect upon philosophical issues in their scientific practice. This approach has allowed me to avoid extensive engagement with the literature on the interpretative debates. Doubtless none of this will prevent the inevitable feeling for many readers that I am not doing justice to the complexity of the work of the thinkers in question. However, this feeling would be based on a misapprehension of what I am trying to achieve. The point of this book is to enable its readers to gain access to the primary texts which, when read without the help of such an introductory work, often seem wholly intractable. If I succeed in facilitating such access, any questionable judgements on my part can be corrected by a subsequent engagement with the primary texts.

The further methodological point here concerns the nature of the story I am telling. Some of the stories told in the Anglo-American philosophical tradition about the history of philosophy consist of the exposition of a series of philosophical arguments which replace each other as the preceding arguments are rendered invalid. Such an approach is valid for some purposes. However, it does little to show why philosophical positions become generally accepted in a wider community. The approach also fails to deal with the ways in which philosophical arguments are situated within historical and political debates that can affect their very nature, and, of course, vice versa. The simple fact is that philosophical arguments do not invariably determine the success of philosophical theories. It is not, however, that a plausible alternative general theory of what really does this is available. The success of theories in real contexts depends upon so many factors that it is only through particular research in an area that one can begin to arrive at more adequate judgements. My main concern is, then, with the role the major works of the German tradition play in philosophy and in theoretical approaches in the humanities today. A final point: the book is best read sequentially. This is because arguments and concepts explored in earlier chapters are often necessary to understand ideas that occur in later chapters. I have tried to give a basic explanation of unfamiliar philosophical concepts when they first occur (I have also appended a glossary). If the reader does not understand a concept used in a later chapter, they should consult the index, where the explanatory reference will be highlighted, or the glossary. At the end of each chapter there is a commented list of selected further reading on the author or topic. The works listed (all in English) offer some possibilities for exploring both the work of the philosophers and the movements to which they belong. The books also offer bibliographical information on more specialized aspects of the philosophers concerned, and they may be relevant for more than one chapter. I have included some books also cited in the references, if they offer a useful broader picture.

The completion of this book was assisted by an award from the Research Leave scheme of the Arts and Humanities Research Board.

INTRODUCTION

Why is German philosophy so central to our philosophical and theoretical culture, and yet also a warning of what can happen when ideas and historical reality interact in the wrong ways? Answers to this question can play a significant role in the contemporary situation in the humanities, where theoretical reflection has never before been so widespread. The theoretical developments that go under the headings of 'literary theory' and 'continental' or 'European' philosophy have brought about a rethinking of conceptions of language, subjectivity, science and art in most humanities subjects. However, it is too rarely acknowledged to what extent nearly all the new directions in the humanities rely upon the tradition of German philosophy which begins with Immanuel Kant's work from the 1780s onwards, and continues through German Romanticism, German Idealism, historical materialism, phenomenology, hermeneutics and Critical Theory, to the present day.[1] Michel Foucault's reflections on the way power is inseparable from knowledge, for example, rely on ideas which go from Friedrich Nietzsche's ideas in the late nineteenth century back to the work in the late eighteenth and early nineteenth century of Arthur Schopenhauer, F. W. J. Schelling, and J. G. Fichte, and even to the work in the earlier part of the eighteenth century of Gottfried Leibniz. There is these days also an almost universal adherence in all areas of 'theory', as well as in the Anglo-American tradition of ana-

1 I will generally either explain in the text the initial occurrence of any technical name for a kind of philosophy or any technical term that is required for my argument or I will include an explanation in a note. Many of these terms are also included in the glossary. The content of the terms referred to here is not part of the main argument and will be explained later.

lytical philosophy, to some version of a 'linguistic turn'.[2] The linguistic turn shifts the focus of philosophy away from the workings of the mind towards the role of language, and it too can be traced to origins within the Kantian and post-Kantian German traditions.[3] In some other areas of the humanities, like social theory, the influence of the German philosophical tradition is widely acknowledged. However, this still has not led to a broader philosophical examination of this tradition of the kind to be offered here.

In the light of Germany's dominant role in nearly all spheres of modern culture, the lack of attention to the broader German tradition in recent theory is particularly surprising. The work of Kant, G. W. F. Hegel, Karl Marx, Nietzsche and Martin Heidegger in philosophy, and of Mozart, Beethoven, Wagner and Schoenberg in music is frequently regarded as addressing the concerns of the modern world in ways not equalled by other cultural traditions. It is, though, hard to ignore the sense that these exceptional German intellectual achievements are also connected to what has been wrong with Germany in the modern period. This is one of the reasons why the role of German philosophy in much contemporary theory has been underplayed.[4] From the second half of the eighteenth century onwards the intensity both of philosophical activity and of musical creativity in Germany is linked to the failure of German society to transform itself politically, socially and economically in the way that countries elsewhere in Europe were doing. Historians often connect this initial failure to the disastrous way in which Germany then belatedly began to modernize during the second half of the nineteenth century. In this period traditional forms of feudal social and political organization were kept in existence along with new forms of production and exchange. The socio-political transformations required to make these forms part of German culture simply did not take place or took place too late for them to have a socially integrative and stabilizing effect. This disjunction is characteristic of modern Germany,

2 Suspicions that the linguistic turn may not resolve every question about meaning and the mind are, though, becoming common in both analytical and European philosophy.
3 The obvious example of theory where this is not immediately the case are feminist and gender theories, which can truly be said to have broken new ground. Even here, though, many of the conceptual resources now employed in such theories can be traced to Hegel, Nietzsche, Heidegger and others in the Romantic and post-Romantic traditions. There has been no lack of attention to specific thinkers in these traditions, like Nietzsche or Heidegger – on the contrary – but there has been a lack of attention to the broader picture and its implications.
4 A more contingent reason for this is the narrow agenda of much of German Studies in both the USA and Europe, an agenda which is now being broadened.

in which different aspects of society develop at sometimes very divergent rates. The writer Heinrich Heine, himself no uncritical admirer of German philosophy, already suggested in his *On the History of Religion and Philosophy in Germany* of 1834 that 'German philosophy is an important matter, which concerns the whole of humanity, and only the last grandchildren will be able to judge whether we should be blamed or praised for working out our philosophy before our revolution' (n.d. 615–16). It is clear that Europe would have benefited socially, politically and historically had the sequence been the other way round. However, this is not a reason to disregard what is offered by the German philosophical revolution for understanding our world.[5] Why is it, then, that modern philosophy developed in the most revealing ways in Germany?

Karl Marx's remark in the Communist Manifesto of 1848 that in capitalism 'All that is solid melts into air' provides a clue here. What Marx meant was that the new market economy undermined the idea of a fixed order of the world which was given by tradition. It did so by subordinating the value of objects for their particular use to their money value. The market economy made it more the case than ever before that the value of things depends upon the contexts in which they are encountered, rather than upon something intrinsic to the things themselves or upon their traditional or theological value. This change is echoed in other aspects of modernity, and Germany often has great trouble adjusting to these changes. It was therefore more likely that Germany would also produce more elaborated theoretical responses to them. There are, broadly speaking, five main interrelated dimensions in which previously established orders tend to disintegrate in modernity.

1 The old social, political and economic *hierarchies* are replaced by new, shifting hierarchies, in which values are no longer directly derived from existing tradition or from theology.
2 The idea that people have a stable *identity* which is a result both of their ascribed place in society and of their inherent God-given nature gives way to two opposed new conceptions. In the first, one can autonomously *make* oneself what one is, rather than be told what one is by a higher authority. In the second, one is *made* into what one is by the new historically shifting social and economic

---

5 The contemporary development of the Islamic world in a world dominated by modern science and technology seems to me to have worrying parallels with the German development. In both cases what Ernst Bloch calls 'non-simultaneity', the coexistence of modern techniques with pre-modern beliefs, has often devastating effects.

pressures, by the language into which one is socialized, and by other factors, such as one's early upbringing, one's unconscious mind, or one's place in the class structure, all of which are ultimately beyond one's control.

3 *Knowledge* based on theology and established authority handed down the generations is replaced by knowledge that changes at ever more bewildering speeds via empirical research in both the natural sciences and the humanities.

4 *Art*, which had been seen mainly as either entertainment for those in power or as connected to religious observance, comes to be seen as 'autonomous', subject only to its own changing rules and to the freedom of the artist. At the same time, however, art itself also becomes a commodity which can be bought and sold like any other commodity.

5 *Language*, which was previously conceived of as originating in God, and thus as the symbolic medium in which a pre-existing order of things is reflected, comes to be seen as in some way 'constitutive' of what there is in the world. It brings things to light by giving them a name which makes them what they are. Greater importance is therefore attached to the languages of poetry and of music, and a new interest emerges in the way that the languages of differing peoples can offer new perspectives on the world.

These five dimensions will play a major role in the chapters to come.

The changes in question here all involve aspects of a vital tension, the manifestations of which are particularly characteristic of Germany's responses to the modern world. On the one hand, the disintegration of traditional orders liberates technological and creative potential, giving rise to new and previously inconceivable possibilities. On the other hand, the – albeit often repressive – stability provided by traditional orders is lost. People therefore often anxiously seek for new points of reference within which to locate themselves, or try to sustain the old order against the destructive forces of the new. This tension between the destruction of existing orders of things and the need to establish new orders is vital both to modern Germany's history and to its philosophy. How much of a role this tension plays even now in Germany can be illustrated by the following observations on the effects of the disintegration of the German Democratic Republic in 1989. In the GDR: 'People were not allowed to decide anything because there was nothing left to decide, because history had already decided everything "up there".' After the fall of the Wall, the other side of the tension comes to the fore: 'Now, in freedom, they may and must decide for themselves; all the existing institutions have collapsed, all the old certainties are gone ... The joy of freedom is at the same time a falling into a void. Now let everyone look after himself. What are the rules? Who's in charge?' (Friedrich Schorlemmer, cited in Elliott 1999: 156–7). The worst aspects of the GDR were a result of an attempt to find ways of controlling the freedom which is inseparable from modernity, and this has been a major issue throughout modern German philosophy.[6]

In order to understand how the main elements of the modern German philosophical tradition came about, it is useful to consider a manifestation of the essential tension between the destruction and creation of order that is a frequent point of reference for the German thinkers we shall be examining. In two of the founding texts of the modern world, the *Discourse on Method* of 1638, and the *Meditations on First Philosophy* of 1641, René Descartes bids farewell to the medieval world-picture. He does so by deciding to doubt the veracity, both of all scientific truths derived from tradition – his and others' scientific researches suggest they often cannot be verified – and of all perceptual experiences – because he can never be completely certain that he is not dreaming or hallucinating. He is left with the sole certainty of his own existence as a thinking being, which he cannot doubt without removing the very possibility of doubting itself. There can be no doubt without something existing that can doubt. Every other aspect of experience is, he argues, potentially deceptive. Descartes aims to construct a new world-picture which will provide truths based on rigorous method, rather than on received wisdom, by beginning from whatever he thinks he can establish as indubitable.[7] Subsequent history would appear to confirm the positive aim of this enterprise. The natural sciences have provided more and more theories which enable us really to control the natural world for our purposes, rather than rely on mythical explanations. At the same time, however, the history of philosophy since Descartes has been a history of the failure to explain *why* it is that the sciences are so successful in providing reliable predictions. The sciences provide new conceptions, in the work of Newton, Darwin, Einstein and others, which enable more and more control of nature and of ourselves, based on predictive laws. What *explains* the predictive and explanatory success

6 Many of those ways were simply adopted from the authoritarian past: anyone who knew the GDR would always remark upon how 'Prussian' it was.

7 What Descartes wished to achieve is much more complex than this, and he actually relies on a further theological argument. What matters here is that he has been understood predominantly in relation to what he makes of 'I think, I am'.

of those conceptions remains elusive. Philosophy does not, as some
hoped, become the 'science of science'. Even more importantly, the
growth in the ability to explain and predict is not accompanied by a
similar growth in the ability to make rational decisions about what
should be done with the results of this ability.

Reflections on these issues have consequences both for modern
societies and for philosophy's relationship to the sciences and the rest
of human culture. Science may, for example, *be* nothing more than
the human activity of predicting the course of events in nature and
thus controlling nature, rather than being a true picture of the world
'as it really is'. This view of science as pragmatic control is often
associated with Descartes's claim that there is a firm foundation for
science in our thinking, which will enable us to become 'lord and
master of nature'. When seen in the context of the sometimes catastrophic effects of the application of modern science serious questions therefore emerge as to what science actually is. These questions
affect how the image of the world presented in the sciences relates
to the everyday world we inhabit, in which most of us rarely think in
terms of the scientific explanation of what is happening. Responses
to these questions have often gone in two opposed directions.

1   If science is indeed merely our way of controlling nature, it can
    become the object of a wider investigation of what it is about
    human beings in the modern world that can make their activity,
    from the atom bomb to the growing ecological devastation of
    large parts of the globe, so destructive of nature. Why does the
    human mind, which itself depends on natural biological processes,
    lead to acts which are so damaging to nature?
2   Giving up the idea that science truly represents what there is, and
    thus relativizing science's privileged position in relation to the rest
    of human culture, can offer an opportunity to make better deci-
    sions about what human beings want to do with themselves and
    their world. Such decisions are not dependent on invoking scien-
    tific criteria that are necessarily inadequate to the complexity of
    our needs, desires and ethical impulses.

The view expressed in (1) is often espoused by German thinkers
who are involved in the catastrophic history of Germany in the first
half of the twentieth century, although the beginnings of what led to
this view emerge, as we shall see, in the work of Schelling in the 1790s.
The view expressed in (2) is often that of contemporary American
pragmatists who live in a country which has not seen the kind of dev-
astation that has occurred in Germany and elsewhere in Europe.

These divergent responses to the understanding of science already suggest the way in which this issue impinges on how modernity is conceived. Is the main characteristic of modernity the disintegration of the new Enlightenment hopes for a better and more humane form of existence that develop out of the decline of feudal authoritarianism? Or does modernity still offer the potential for an opening up of major new possibilities for humankind in ways which are not necessarily destructive?

German philosophers react in a variety of ways to the centrality of the natural sciences in the modern world. These range from the attempt to make philosophy itself into a kind of science which would require the same degree of rigorous proof as well-confirmed scientific theories, to the claim that there may be, as Ludwig Wittgenstein says in the 1930s, 'nothing good or desirable about scientific knowledge' and that, if this is the case, 'humankind which strives after it is running into a trap' (1980: 56).[8] The divergence of these conceptions indicates how problematic this area can be. How, then, do such conflicting conceptions emerge from the same cultural milieu? It would be foolish to offer any kind of definitive answer to such a question. However, the tension we have observed, between the need to come to terms with new orders of things and the feeling that this can entail the destruction of indispensable cultural resources, clearly has to do with the coexistence of such opposed views.

The opposition just described has sometimes been characterized in terms of an opposition between 'Romanticism' and 'Positivism'. This opposition can establish a framework that the coming chapters will employ to clarify some complex issues. The opposition is often understood as between conceptions which concentrate on the subjective and expressive dimensions of human experience and conceptions which concentrate on the objective ways in which we can find out about the world and ourselves. In its most well-known guise in the English-speaking world the opposition was seen by C. P. Snow in the 1950s as involving 'two cultures', the artistic and the scientific. The resulting debate affected major aspects of British culture, and continues to do so. If the issue seems too abstract, think of arguments over the fact that the arts make more money for the British economy than the car industry, or look at the relative spending in university departments on the arts and the sciences. Another way of looking at this issue is to contrast the description of a human being by an evolutionary biologist, who sees us in terms of how we are determined

---

8 As we shall see in chapter 8, the earlier Wittgenstein has a view of philosophy less suspicious of the sciences.

by genes and by the need to adapt to an environment, and a novelist, who might see us in terms of our ability to be both self-determining and yet also prone to give way to baser determining impulses. How can one exist under both kinds of description at the same time? The very dissonance generated by the attempt to think of oneself both as a piece of causally determined nature like any other, and as someone who can care about others and the world, can suggest the kind of problem produced by the division between a 'Positivist' and a 'Romantic' conception of philosophy.

This division is obviously not just an abstract philosophical matter, because decisions about what is done in society depend upon which assumptions one adopts in this respect. Criminals are, for example, regarded very differently, depending on whether one thinks they are subject to their genes or are able to choose what they do.[9] One of the reasons why the German tradition is so important is that it offers extreme examples, both at the level of theory and at the level of real historical events, of the consequences of these issues. The contrast of the Enlightenment idea of human self-determination with the Nazi idea of a self predetermined primarily by its race evidently does not just come down to a disagreement about which theory is correct. Both Enlightenment thinkers and Nazis, however, tend to invoke science as a way of legitimating what they *do* with such descriptions.

The decisive point here lies in the way in which the scope of science is conceived. Until the nineteenth century what we term natural science was included under the wider umbrella of philosophy. Science up to and beyond Isaac Newton was termed 'natural philosophy'. Since the second half of the nineteenth century, however, philosophy has ceased to be the all-encompassing discipline which, along with theology, it was throughout the Middle Ages and the early modern period. We have now reached a point where many of those engaged in philosophy spend time pondering whether philosophy may not be at an end, because so many of the tasks previously allotted to it have been taken over by the natural sciences. This situation might seem only likely to worry professional philosophers, as their chances of getting a job diminish along with the scope of the profession itself. Indeed, this is what has already happened in professional philosophy, particularly during the second half of the twentieth century. As the sciences became more and more industrialized and became an ever greater source of wealth-creation, philosophy departments shrank in the face of the increased resources being pumped into the sciences.

9   Interestingly, this rarely seems to mean that those who think predominantly in terms of genetics are more forgiving of the failings of criminals; if anything, it is the other way round.

However, this 'Positivist' development also made possible a new explicit role for philosophy. This role is based on its link to 'Romantic' concerns about what science may obscure, that is therefore only accessible in other ways, such as through works of art. The very success of science, then, changes the perceived role of philosophy, either in the direction of its abolition in the name of science, or in the direction of a potentially critical role in relation to the sciences.

In the Anglo-American world the former view became more and more dominant until quite recently. The present renewed interest in the German tradition evident among the best contemporary American philosophers is not least a result of a reaction against 'scientism', 'the doctrine that natural science is privileged over other areas of culture, that something about natural science puts it in closer – or at least in more reliable – touch with reality than any other human activity' (Rorty 1998: 294). This academic change in the focus of major philosophers is not necessarily just a result of the fact that many of the arguments claiming to be able to get rid of philosophical problems by finding scientific solutions have been shown to be seriously flawed.

One aspect of German philosophy which has proved to be particularly durable is its concern to see things 'holistically'. Holism is the idea that no particular phenomenon can be properly understood in isolation, and therefore must be seen in terms of its contexts. The contemporary questioning of scientism within philosophy evidently relates to the wider *cultural* suspicion of the assumption that all human problems are best approached solely by using the methods and assumptions of the natural sciences. At its worst this suspicion can, though, lead in irrational directions. It sometimes results in an indefensible refusal to accept that in their own domain the natural sciences are capable of a precision and reliability absent in other areas of human life. However, it is precisely the fact that the sciences have their effects in social and cultural contexts that are themselves *not* susceptible to the same kind of analysis as the objects of science which is at the root of the demand for better philosophical responses to the ways science affects the modern world. Even today, philosophy oriented principally towards scientific methods dominates much of the academic world. The reappraisal of the more critical responses to natural science in the German tradition now taking place in Anglo-American philosophy is therefore an indication of a broader concern about the direction of the modern world. The problem in this respect is, of course, the Janus-faced nature of German philosophy, which, on the one hand, seems to offer critical resources lacking in some of Anglo-American philosophy, and, on the other, is associated with a

very disturbing history indeed. The fact that two of the thinkers in
Germany in the twentieth century who developed serious ecological
ways of thinking, Heidegger and Ludwig Klages, were, respectively, a
member of the Nazi party and a reactionary anti-Semite, makes clear
how difficult this area can be.

No assessment of this tradition is going to overcome all the
methodological difficulties involved in finding a focus which both
does justice to the arguments of the thinkers and takes proper
account of the historical developments within which their arguments
emerged. Modern philosophy is divided between (1) assessing arguments from the history of philosophy as part of the discipline of philosophical argumentation in the present, and (2) seeing philosophical
arguments as part of a wider historical field of research. In the former,
Kant becomes, for example, the source of key ideas in the theory of
knowledge which still affect debates over the nature of scientific
knowledge today. In the latter, Kant's theory of knowledge is part
of a broader historical shift away from established authority in the
direction of a new autonomy for human thinking which relates to the
French Revolution, Beethoven's music and a host of new phenomena in modernity. There is no necessary reason why these approaches
need be incompatible. The right historical interpretation of Kant
might turn out to be the truth about why scientific knowledge is valid,
and be independent of the fact that Kant arrived at his views in specific historical and intellectual circumstances which influenced how
he thought. However, the fact that this possibility seems implausible
indicates something important about the nature of philosophical
interpretation. A historical interpretation of Kant has no need to
come to an end, because the relevant contexts and the information
discovered by new research continue to grow, and what counts as
valid evidence changes as our conceptions both of philosophy and of
history change. How much of these contexts and information is significant for contemporary philosophical debate will alter, depending
upon the focus of that debate, a focus which continually shifts in
nearly all areas of philosophy.

Despite this obvious fact, manifestations of this tension between
the approaches are widespread in contemporary philosophy. Some
philosophers in the Anglo-American analytical tradition talk, for
example, of the 'philosopher they will call Kant', knowing that they
are simply employing certain very limited interpretations of Kant's
arguments for contemporary purposes. These philosophers will tend
to refer to what those involved in a historical approach are doing as
merely the 'history of ideas'. Others in the 'European' tradition are
horrified that such thinkers often have only read one or two books

by Kant and that they therefore have no ambition to understand the complexity of Kant's wider project, preferring instead to reduce his thought to being another means of combating what they think is wrong with 'empiricism'.[10] Neither of these approaches is satisfactory, and yet both are an ineliminable part of contemporary philosophy. I shall not attempt to resolve this tension here, because it is part of the story this book is concerned to tell. Philosophers must surely think that their own theory, because it seems to them to deal more effectively with the crucial problems, is a better account of the truth than competing theories. This leads them in the direction of a justified concern with the cogency and rigour of philosophical arguments. On the other hand, the history of philosophy shows that even the most widely held theories are eventually invalidated, albeit only to re-emerge in some new guise at a later date. They often do this because it comes to be thought that they have been inadequately interpreted. Philosophers working within a historical framework therefore have to focus as much upon why the theories were 'held as true', as upon whether they are true or not – although philosophers of this kind can tend to ignore the question of whether the theories are worth examining in such detail. German philosophy offers many examples of responses to this tension which are both historically and philosophically illuminating, and which therefore enable one to explore the tension between the 'argument-based' and the 'historical' approaches in a more reflective manner.

The tension just described is, of course, another version of the tension between 'Positivist' and 'Romantic' conceptions, which this time also maps onto the now more and more widely discussed division between 'analytical', and 'continental' or 'European' philosophy. Until recently this division was seen by many philosophers as almost unbridgeable, the one tradition being supposedly concerned to pursue argument with the utmost logical rigour by isolating problems and working on them in detail, the other concerned to explore the textuality and history of philosophy as much as the validity of the arguments in the texts studied. These approaches are, however, becoming much harder to separate, as it becomes apparent that the borders of each approach are not hard and fast. The style of argument among some 'continental' philosophers may differ from some of their analytical counterparts, but anyone now interested in Hegel would, for example, be ill-advised to concentrate solely on works on Hegel from one side of the notional divide. The very challenge such radically divergent approaches pose to contemporary thought seems

10 The reasons for this will be examined in chapter 1.

to me inevitable in the present situation. In what follows I aim to offer a way into what is at issue that might contribute to establishing a more creative future dialogue between the traditions.

SUGGESTIONS FOR FURTHER READING

Bubner, R. (1981) *Modern German Philosophy* (Cambridge: Cambridge University Press). *Good, if demanding, general account of the area.*

Habermas, J. (1987) *The Philosophical Discourse of Modernity* (Cambridge: Polity). *Classic overview of modern philosophy by German's leading contemporary philosopher and social theorist.*

O'Hear, A. (ed.) (1999) *German Philosophy After Kant* (Cambridge: Cambridge University Press). *A useful collection of essays on individual philosophers and on central themes in German philosophy.*

Roberts, J. (1988) *German Philosophy* (Cambridge: Polity). *Quirky, but readable, account of some key thinkers.*

Schnädelbach, H. (1984) *Philosophy in Germany 1831–1933* (Cambridge: Cambridge University Press). *Scholarly and philosophically acute account, which includes much important material on lesser-known academic philosophers.*

1

THE KANTIAN REVOLUTION

Accounts of the history of modern German philosophy generally begin with Immanuel Kant (1724–1804). However, exclusive attention to Kant's role can distort what was significant about German philosophy in the modern period. Concentrating on Kant produces a picture of the early development of modern philosophy in which the dominant factor is the analysis of the structures of the mind as the new post-theological basis of knowledge and ethics. This picture leads to the claim that the decisive contribution of the twentieth century to philosophy is the 'linguistic turn' – the turn towards the primacy of questions of language before questions of the mind – which some philosophers regard as invalidating much of what was attempted by Kant. An account of this kind fails, though, to show that a version of the linguistic turn is itself part of German philosophy in the eighteenth and early nineteenth centuries. In the work on language of J. G. Herder and J. G. Hamann from the 1760s onwards, which is taken up by the Romantics at the end of the century and developed by the linguist, Wilhelm von Humboldt, and the philosopher and theologian, F. D. E. Schleiermacher, the role of language in thought is regarded as essential. Many of the assumptions of the 'linguistic turn' are, therefore, already present much earlier than is usually thought. Modern German philosophy has always been concerned both with the mind and with language. However, even though Herder had already published his *Essay on the Origin of Language* in 1772, nine years before Kant's most influential work, it is still best to begin with Kant. We will look at Kant in more detail than many of the other philosophers because his innovations affect all his successors.

Making Kant Accessible

Many approaches in contemporary theory in the humanities involve questions about the nature of the self which demonstrably derive from Kant. Kant is, however, not easy to understand. Much of the notorious difficulty of Kant's thought is a result of the language he employs. His vocabulary often derives from philosophical texts of his era which are now neither easily accessible nor widely read. He is, moreover, writing at a time when there is no real precedent for writing philosophy in German: most philosophical texts until his time were written in Latin. Despite these obstacles, things are not as hard as they are sometimes made out to be. To take one example: the fact that Kant refers to what he is writing as 'transcendental philosophy' is enough to make many people think that he is concerned with something incomprehensible beyond the everyday world. However, what he means by 'transcendental' has nothing to do with anything other-worldly. Something is transcendental if it is, in Kant's phrase, the 'condition of possibility' of something. Thus it might be said that sex, at least until the advent of in-vitro fertilization, was transcendental in relation to pregnancy. Another example: the first part of Kant's first major work, the *Critique of Pure Reason* (the 'first Critique') of 1781, is called the 'Transcendental Aesthetic'. *Aisthesis* in Greek means perception by the senses, and this section of the work is simply concerned with the conditions under which perception takes place. Perception must be of something in a spatial location at a specific time. Kant's claim is that the conditions of perception are functions of the mind. Space and time are the prior framework – what he terms the 'forms of intuition' – within which we perceive objects, so they are not attributes of the objects themselves. Why is this so important?

The idea that space and time are functions of the mind remains one of Kant's most controversial doctrines. However, the idea is part of a series of contentions about the nature of knowledge which revolutionized modern philosophy. In order to understand a revolution one has to understand what preceded it that meant there had to be a radical change, rather than a gradual one. The thinking which Kant put in question can be summed up in a phrase used by the contemporary American philosopher, Hilary Putnam. Putnam refers to the rejection of the idea of a 'ready-made world'. This idea can be construed in a theological sense, so that Kant is understood as undermining the idea that God made the world. The real point of the idea, though, is that in a 'ready-made' world there is no doubt that the truth about what is the case is already 'out there' as part of the world itself.

Knowledge therefore entails establishing something which is the way it is completely independently of anything we do. Kant's contention is that we can no longer justifiably claim to be able to attain such a point of view, because what we know is known under certain unavoidable conditions. It is *not* that Kant is denying the validity of well-confirmed scientific theories, or that what we justifiably know *might* indeed be true of a 'ready-made' world; he is just asking what it is that makes theories reliable once previous assumptions about this reliability have been shown to be impossible to sustain.

The power of what preceded Kant's new claims lay in the idea that the world was held together on the basis of a pre-existing divine foundation which could not be shaken. There was a way the world really is because it was *made* that way. René Descartes (1596–1650) had already begun to shake the faith in this basis when he pointed out both how unreliable the senses could be and how much of the science of the ancients turned out to be mistaken. Along with his argument about the certainty of his existence as thinking being, Descartes did, however, also rely on the claim that he could prove God existed.

Kant not only shows in the first Critique that Descartes's proof of God's existence is invalid, but he also accepts aspects of an even more emphatic attack on the notion of a reality with an inbuilt rational structure, that of the Scottish Enlightenment philosopher, David Hume (1711–76). Hume's arguments threaten any claim to the effect that the universe is, so to speak, held together by theological glue. This glue is supposed to be apparent in the laws of nature, which reveal a regularity and necessity which we cannot escape or ignore. Hume's argument is simple. He asks how we in fact arrive at the knowledge of the laws that govern the functioning of nature, and insists that we require observation of phenomena for this. The phenomena come to us through our senses, and we can only know something if it is associated with other phenomena that have also come to us through our senses. If we think something is caused by something else, we therefore do so because we *habitually* see a conjunction of events of the same kind. However, the vital fact about what comes to us through the senses is that it is contingent. We never absolutely know what we will perceive next, and even when we think we are certain that we do know, we can be mistaken. Everything we know therefore has contingency built into it, because it is reliant on what we happen to have perceived in the past, rather than on anything 'out there' which is already ordered independently of ourselves. This 'empiricist' view made the world feel a very unstable place indeed.

What, though, of the fact that there did seem to be a kind of knowledge which was not subject to contingency, namely the a priori truths of mathematics, which could not be changed by experience? The 'rationalist' philosophers of the seventeenth and eighteenth centuries, like Baruch Spinoza and Gottfried Leibniz, had invoked these truths as a proof that there must be a pre-existing structure of things. In the light of the success of Newton's new laws of physics, the mathematically based view seemed highly plausible, but it was always confronted in actual scientific investigation with the empiricist reliance upon contingent observation. What was therefore required was a way to combine the empiricist and the rationalist positions, and this was what Kant tried to establish.

Kant refers to what he is initiating as a 'Copernican turn'. During the first half of the sixteenth century Copernicus had been the first modern thinker to oppose the view that the earth was the centre of the universe with mathematically based arguments. In the wake of Copernicus, at almost exactly the same time as Descartes was beginning to change the medieval world-view in the 1630s, Galileo gave more decisive evidence for what Copernicus had suggested, and was threatened by the Catholic Church with being burned at the stake for doing so. Here it becomes rather easy to see what might have been 'at stake' in challenging medieval religious authority: others had already been burned to death for doing so.[1] The odd thing about Kant's turn is that it can be seen as involving the *opposite* of Copernicus's turn, though it is just as revolutionary. Copernicus began to take us *away* from the centre of the universe, and thereby helped set in motion the development of the scientific image of the universe we now inhabit, in which the place of humankind is pretty insignificant. Kant, on the other hand, makes our thinking the very principle of the universe's intelligibility, thus putting the human mind at the centre of everything.

It should now be clear that something spectacular is afoot in what Kant proposes. The big question is how he is to be interpreted. On the one hand, he can be understood as demonstrating that reliable knowledge depends upon our ability to employ certain prior mental rules which cannot be derived from looking at the world. On the other hand, he also seems to be suggesting that nothing could be intelligible at all without the activity of thought, which becomes the 'light' that illuminates an otherwise dark universe. It is vital to

1   There is a kind of rationale for some of the opposition to such challenges, which is well illustrated in Bertolt Brecht's play about Galileo. In it the little monk suggests that what Galileo proposes is likely to render his peasant parents deeply unhappy because it threatens the stable world-picture that made sense of the harshness of their lives. This kind of ambivalence about science is crucial to modern German philosophy.

remember that, even though he has generally been read in the English-speaking world as a theorist of knowledge and of ethics, what Kant is ultimately trying to achieve is a map of our location in the world once we can no longer assume a theological basis for what we know and do.

Kant himself says that he is drawing the limits of knowledge to make space for religious faith, but it is now pretty clear that the modern world has been unable to fill that space. In the philosophy of J. G. Fichte, F. W. J. Schelling and G. W. F. Hegel, known as 'German Idealism', which begins in the 1790s, the space is often filled with aspects of what Kant proposes which are given a more emphatic status than Kant himself thinks possible. Fichte, for example, will make the activity of the I the source of the world's intelligibility in a way that Kant rejects.[2] Development of some of these thinkers' ideas will be germane to Schopenhauer, Ludwig Feuerbach, Marx, and Nietzsche, who, though, reject many of the central philosophical contentions of German Idealism. However, the structures which inform much of what these thinkers say still depend upon what might initially appear to be rather specialized aspects of Kant's philosophy. In the following I will primarily consider elements of the *Critique of Pure Reason*, the *Foundation of the Metaphysics of Morals* (1785)[3] and the *Critique of Judgement* (1790), with the emphasis mainly on the first Critique.

The First Critique

The *Critique of Pure Reason* seeks to come to terms with the fact that modern science has begun to progress so rapidly, both because of the new importance of empirical observation and because of its reliance upon the certainties of mathematics. The problem is that the first of these two sources of knowledge is changing and contingent, whereas the second is supposed to be unchanging and necessary. This problem has been around in Western philosophy at least since Plato, so the impact of Kant cannot just be explained in terms of his contributions to dealing with this perennial dilemma. Let us, then, look at how Kant tries to reconcile the apparently incompatible dimensions of observed empirical data and a priori knowledge. In previous

2 He does, though, seem to come close to Fichte in his final work, the unfinished *Opus Posthumum*.
3 I choose this in preference to the second Critique, the *Critique of Practical Reason*, because it is more accessible and its influence has probably been greater.

philosophy the realm of a priori knowledge, the realm of 'pure reason', had been the location of debates about the nature of God and being, which did not rely on empirical evidence. The title *Critique of Pure Reason* indicates Kant's desire to question the basis of such debates. The vital element in the first Critique is the establishing of a series of necessary – a priori – rules of thought for the classification of phenomena, together with the idea that these rules are based on the 'spontaneous' nature of the mind. For Kant something is spontaneous when it takes place 'of its own accord', rather than being caused by something else. It might seem odd that in cognition *spontaneity* functions in terms of necessary rules, but this is the crux of what Kant proposes. The idea is that the knowledge of natural necessity is only possible on the basis of something which is itself not necessitated. The borderline between deterministic nature, and human spontaneity, is the location of the most fundamental disputes in modernity about how human beings are to describe themselves. Kant's three 'Critiques' can be seen as concerning themselves with: in the first, how we arrive at natural laws and what that means for our descriptions of our place in the universe; in the second, how we understand human freedom; and, in the third, how we might connect the realms of natural necessity and freedom via the fact that we can also apprehend nature as beautiful and create beauty ourselves in art.[4] This threefold division has, in turn, led to the view that Kant maps out the ways in which modernity separates the spheres of natural science, law and morality and artistic expression, which had not been separated in pre-modern cultures (see the Conclusion).

Kant claims that knowledge must have two sources: 'intuition', what is 'given to us' in specific perceptual experience of the world, and 'categories' and 'concepts', the mental rules according to which we link intuitions together into judgements. The first source involves 'receptivity': it depends upon how the world impinges on us. The second source is spontaneous: it involves the activity of the mind. The way to understand what is persuasive about this is to ponder how we apprehend objects in the world. We have no choice but to do this all the time, although we can be mistaken about what we apprehend. In one respect the impact of the world upon us is just causal: physiological reactions in the brain and the rest of the organism take place when we perceive things. This does not explain, though, how an object which we may assume is the same object can be apprehended in very different ways. At this level it seems clear that there must be an active

4 All three Critiques discuss the relationship between freedom and necessity, but their primary focus is what is suggested here.

element of judgement in play. The very possibility of re-describing something cannot just be the result of how it impacts upon our organism, because we can so easily misjudge. This might be because the object has been located in the wrong context, as when a vegetable is classified as a fruit. It can also be because what were thought to be the boundaries of an object turn out not to be. This kind of confusion is apparent in the history of the chemical elements, in which things that are now seen as different were seen as the same, and vice versa. Immediate perception, then, is not the same as judgement: the former is passive and can take place with only a minimal active contribution by the mind, the latter entails the activity of the mind. The source of Kant's ideas here is Jean-Jacques Rousseau's 'Profession of Faith of a Savoyard Curate' from *Émile*. What Kant means is underlined by his claim that the 'senses do not judge', so they cannot be mistaken: mistakes occur when we judge what the senses provide us with in terms of concepts.

The use of concepts to describe perceivable objects inherently involves the possibility of re-describing what is perceived. However, in the first Critique, Kant is initially most concerned about how scientific laws can be invariably valid, despite Hume's sceptical objections. His contention is that there must be necessary kinds of judgement. These involve what he terms 'categories', or 'pure concepts of the understanding', by which he means forms of thought which cannot be derived from looking at the world. The difference between empirical and pure judgements is vital to his conception. If I assert that there is one red billiard ball on a table, my understanding of its being red comes from having learned to use the concept 'red' by seeing red things that have the same or similar attributes as what I now see. We learn concepts by repeatedly seeing things as related to each other. How, though, do we learn about 'oneness', which is a notion universally applicable to any single entity and is required for mathematical thinking, or how do we learn about 'sameness'? We cannot learn the notion of oneness from seeing lots of single things, because that *presupposes* the notion we are trying to learn. The categories of oneness and manyness are the basis of what Kant terms 'synthetic judgements a priori'. The judgement $2 + 2 = 4$, which is usually taken to be both a priori (not derived from experience) and 'analytic', in the manner of the analytic judgement 'all bachelors are unmarried men', is, he claims, really 'synthetic' (i.e. it adds to our knowledge).[5] This is because 4 can also be $3 + 1$, $4 + 0$ and an infinity of other combinations, such as 3.3333 recurring $+ .7777$ recurring. There can

---

5   We shall come back to this – questionable – distinction in chapter 8.

therefore be pure knowledge that can be increased without input from the senses, so this knowledge is also 'synthetic'.

A further pure concept is the notion of cause. If I see the billiard ball move because it is hit by another billiard ball, the movement is caused by the moving ball. What I see, though, are two balls moving in certain ways. I cannot *see* that one causes the other to move. In order to do this I must *already* possess the notion that if one thing *necessarily* follows from the other in time it is caused by it. Hume's alternative is that *any* event which is followed by another event would have to be seen as possibly caused by the preceding event, even though the events might be completely unrelated apart from the fact that I see one follow the other. To say something really *is* causal, then, means adding an element of necessity *in thought*. This necessity cannot be said to pertain in the world, because all our information from the world is subject to the contingency Hume highlighted.

Another element of Kant's thought can suggest why his argument should be taken seriously. For Kant, the essential factor in knowledge is the ability to say something is the same as something else. The problem here is that, as Leibniz had demonstrated by his principle of the 'Identity of Indiscernibles', it may be that no thing really is the same as anything else. Any two objects may appear to be identical in all respects, but they will always differ in some respect, even if it is only at the microscopic or even smaller levels (although there are now arguments that in the quantum domain this may not apply). A strict application of Leibniz's idea would mean that the only real form of identity is that of something with itself. As a result, all true statements would have to be tautologies, because they would simply explicate a particular thing's already existing intrinsic properties. Each thing would just be what it is, and would never be identical with anything else. For Leibniz this leads to the notion of a divine insight into the ultimate true nature of things, all of which are inherently particular.

Leibniz's conception of identity would, though, render all scientific knowledge based on observation liable to the sceptical objection that, because things are never really the same, one could not assert that they obey laws. This is precisely what Kant wishes to avoid. We therefore need a way of dealing with the fact that things may never *be* exactly the same. They may, of course, also *appear* to be completely different, even though they are the same with regard to the laws which govern them. Yet more problematic is the fact that subjective *experiences* are both contingent and also never identical, because we never receive precisely the same patterns through our senses at any two moments in our lives. Kant consequently argues that the identity required for informative knowledge must be a built-in function of our thought. In order for our thinking to function in this manner, there must, though, be a way of coming to terms with the fact that the sources of knowledge are of a different order from each other. One source receives endless particularity, the other actively subsumes this particularity into forms of identity. The vital factor here will be the identity across time of the subject that apprehends in terms of these forms, without which experience would merely disintegrate into random particularity.

The first Critique is divided up into three main sections. The first is the 'Transcendental Aesthetic', the theory of space and time as the 'forms of intuition'. The second is the 'Transcendental Logic', the account of the necessary forms of thought. The third is the 'Transcendental Dialectic', the account of what occurs if concepts that are only supposed to apply to the world of experience are applied to what is beyond the limitations inherent in experience. These limitations are: (1) that experience has to take place in a specific time and place, (2) that experience requires certain a priori notions to be intelligible at all. In this latter part of the Critique Kant is referring to what one does if, for example, one moves from using the notion of causality to explain a specific regular occurrence in nature based on empirical evidence, to asserting that the whole of nature is causally determined. The latter judgement would require infinite confirmation, because the evidence for it is only ever supplied when the law for a phenomenon is arrived at by experiment and observation. At the same time, without the *assumption* that all of the natural world functions deterministically, we would be faced with scepticism, because the particular part of nature under examination might in fact be an exception to the iron law of causality. Kant's attempt to deal with this situation has far-reaching consequences for his successors. The first Critique moves, then, from an account of the necessary framework of thinking, to considerations of what happens to the traditional questions of metaphysics, concerning God, the world, and freedom, in the light of the restrictions imposed by this framework.

The Transcendental Subject

The decisive aspect of the first two parts of the first Critique, which influenced much subsequent philosophy, is the role given to the subject, in the light of the 'Copernican turn'. The first aspect of the subject, which is dealt with in the Transcendental Aesthetic, is the fact that it can only perceive objects within a framework. The account of

the 'forms of intuition', space and time, is part of Kant's demonstration that our knowledge requires step-by-step elaboration, because
we are never able to grasp an object as a whole all at once. The ability
to know the whole of something at once would only be possible
for God, who actually brings the object into existence. Once it is
acknowledged that space and time should be thought of as belonging to how we must perceive things, rather than to the things themselves, we can achieve certainty within the limits set by how objects
can appear to us. We cannot know how objects are independently of
the form in which we must perceive them. Knowledge of 'things in
themselves' is therefore impossible.

The Transcendental Logic is Kant's account of what he calls the
'understanding', our capacity for law-bound knowledge. If it is the
case that experience has an irreducibly contingent element, there
must be an element in knowledge which overcomes contingency.
Experience takes place in time, and judgements of experience require
the linking of contingently occurring events as *necessarily* related.
Perceptions *must* be different from one another (otherwise they
would merge into one inarticulable whole), and they are not actively
produced by the knowing subject, because the subject receives them
in 'intuition'. What links them together must, then, itself be something
that remains the same. Cognition depends upon memory, and
memory depends upon a subject which itself remains identical
between different experiences and which can *apprehend* the experiences as the same. Furthermore, the subject must also be able to
apprehend the moments of remembered perception as belonging
to *it*. The moments must have a 'mineness' which means they can be
reidentified as part of my experience as a whole.

This essential requirement Kant terms the 'synthetic unity of
apperception'. 'Apperception' is Leibniz's term for the 'reflective'
awareness *that* one is perceiving something in the world. I think about
my partner, and then 'apperceptively' think about the way in which
I think about my partner. This kind of self-consciousness is essential
to being able, for example, to ponder whether one may have mis-
judged something. Kant's extension of the use of the term beyond
'empirical apperception', which occurs when I reflect on my awareness at a particular moment, to the 'synthetic unity of apperception',
is vital for his whole account of epistemology. Consider the 'synthetic
unity of apperception' as follows. If I am to remember later in the
day something I saw this morning, a whole series of perceptions, experiences and thoughts will have intervened between now and this
morning. Most of these experiences will not have occurred to me in
an 'apperceptive' manner: I will just have had them without reflect-

ing on their relationship to my consciousness. How, then, is it that I can connect to moments of awareness in the past as being part of my experience at all, unless there is a connecting unity of myself which makes this possible? I am not conscious of this unity in my general experience, because empirical apperception only occurs when I reflect on my perceiving, and this may be a rare occurrence. The unity does, however, seem to have to exist if I am to make sense of experience at all, especially 'experience' in Kant's strong sense of perceptions correctly judged according to rules. As Kant puts it, 'an "*I think*" must *be able* to accompany all my representations' (1968a: B 132).[6] Furthermore, if scientific laws are to be possible, the 'I think' which accompanies my experience must also be able to make necessary links between moments of experience. These moments are not subject to my will, even though the linking itself must take place via my 'spontaneity' in judgement.

The kinds of linkage which are a priori rules for organizing experience are termed the 'categories', or 'pure forms of understanding'. Kant lists twelve of these, under four headings: *Quantity*, *Quality*, *Relation*, *Modality*. These forms divide up how things exist in terms of ways of thinking which cannot be derived from observing the world. The forms have been argued about ever since, and we do not need to get embroiled in the detail of these arguments. Two points should, though, be noted. An important issue for subsequent philosophy is how these forms of thought relate to natural languages: do they remain the same even in languages which do not possess the same distinctions as Kant is making? The other point concerns how these distinctions came to emerge at all in human thinking. Kant does not concern himself with the genesis of the categories in the first Critique, but a significant part of German Idealism, and the work of Heidegger and others, will be concerned with the genesis of forms of thinking.

The next stage of the Critique, the 'Transcendental Deduction of the Categories', is about justifying the use of these a priori forms of thought in relation to objects encountered in the world. 'Deduction' is used in an old German legal sense, where it means 'legitimation'. This part of the Critique will give rise to some of the major questions in German Idealist and Romantic philosophy. We have already encountered the main argument in explaining the 'synthetic unity of apperception'. Kant insists that this unity is the 'highest point, to

6 The page references to Kant are, as is now standard, to the A and B versions of the Academy edition which are generally given in all editions of Kant. The A version is the original 1781 version, the B version is the extended version of 1787.

which all use of the understanding, even the whole of logic, and, following it, transcendental philosophy' (ibid. B 134) must be attached. The basic issue is how 'subjective conditions of thought can have objective validity'. They can only do so if there are necessary a priori rules of synthesis which make true judgements possible, and which are inherent in the thinking subject. For *this* to be possible, as we saw, there must be an underlying unity in the subject which is independent both of the contingency of its experience and of the different moments of its temporal existence.

The question which is vital to Kant's immediate successors, such as Fichte, is how the claims about the 'transcendental subject' can be substantiated. If knowledge comes about on the basis of the unity of this subject, how can the subject arrive at knowledge of *itself*? Knowledge must always be arrived at under the conditions of space and time, and of the categories, and these depend precisely upon the subject. The subject is therefore split. On the one hand, it is an empirical object in the world, namely its body. On the other hand, its body obeys laws that are *themselves* only possible because of the subject's *further* existence as something that is *not* in the world, namely as the spontaneous source of judgements. It is this issue which leads to radically divergent construals of Kant. Some of these go in an extreme Idealist direction, making the spontaneity of the I the ultimate key to the very intelligibility of nature itself. Others try to make out that this apparent necessary opacity of the thinking subject to itself need not invalidate Kant's claims about knowledge. A further crucial divide emerges here. Some thinkers, like Schopenhauer and Freud, claim that the problem of self-knowledge reveals an irrational basis for the rational aspects of the subject. This basis is the source of the subject's spontaneity, which is inaccessible to philosophical explanation and which must be explored by other means, such as art or psychoanalysis. We shall return to these issues in the coming chapters.

Judgement

Kant' describes knowledge in terms of a 'threefold synthesis', in which something is first 'apprehended' as affecting the mind, then is 'reproduced' in the imagination and finally is 'recognized' via a concept which classifies it. This all depends on the ability of self-consciousness to 'synthesize' identity from multiplicity. We order appearances by the 'power of judgement'. Judgement takes place when the rules of the understanding (categories and empirical concepts) are applied to intuitions. Even though the understanding is the source of rules, judgements applied to things encountered in the world cannot *themselves* be rule-bound. In order to judge in terms of rules whether a phenomenon belongs under a particular rule or not – is the object I see in front of me to be classified as a dog or a horse? – one would require a rule for deciding that this is a decision between dogs and horses, a rule for deciding between dogs and horses, a rule for applying that decision, a rule for that rule, and so on. Kant therefore claims that judgement is a 'talent' that cannot itself be acquired by rules. We are always going to be in situations where an indefinite number of rules could apply to a phenomenon, so that a regress of rules for rules would be ubiquitous. If someone is bad at judging, there is therefore no way in which they can improve their judgement by just learning more rules. Judgement involves an element of in-eliminable contingency, and yet is required in *any* concrete knowledge claim. The exception to this are the categories, which necessarily apply to objects a priori. If I am trying to judge how many x's there are (whether they be dogs or horses), I cannot even begin to do so if I do not already have oneness and manyness as a prior part of my thinking. I may make mistakes in judging the actual number of x's, but even to do this in an intelligible manner requires the ability to be able to count at all.

There is a further important stage in Kant's account of judgement, which makes things significantly more complex. The problem is how pure concepts can be applied to the world of the senses. This dilemma leads Kant to the notion of 'schematism'. He illustrates the problem when he says that 'nobody is going to say: this, e.g. causality, could also be intuited through the senses and is contained in appearances' (ibid. B 176–7, A 137–8). You can't point to a cause, saying 'Look at that cause!', and hope to be understood. All you can do is to point to two events and claim their connection is causal. Dichotomies between wholly separate domains always cause difficulties in philosophy, and the attempt to separate the a priori and the empirical is no exception. Kant argues that there must be a third, connecting term between categories and appearances, which must therefore be both pure and empirical. The argument is made more plausible by his example. Five points . . . . . are, he says, an 'image' of the number five. What, though, of a thousand points? The image of this, like the image of a thousand-sided figure, is quite easy to represent – it can be drawn without great difficulty – but it will not be perceptible *as such* to any normal person. The 'schema' of a thousand is, therefore, 'more the idea of a method' (ibid. B 180, A 140) of representing a thousand in an image than the image itself. The schema seems suspended between the empirical and the a priori. It does, though, make some sense of how it is that wholly accurate mathematical calculations about a triangle can be linked to the messy empirical object we recognize in a drawing.

The implications of the notion of schema are more far-reaching than it might at first appear. The schema is also what allows one to apply a general concept to a concrete particular in the world, such as a dog. A dog can look like a small, rat-like beast, or like something closer to a small horse. Without the schema any new, never-before encountered member of the species 'dog' could not be recognized as such. The empirical schema is what enables us to 'see something as' something, even if we have not encountered this version of the something before. Such an ability is crucial if one considers that the same object can be seen as a whole variety of different things, or can have an indefinite number of descriptions attached to it. Schelling will soon realize (in 1800) that there is therefore a link between what Kant seeks to achieve with the schema, and the working of language. Use of the same word for different things involves the ability to abstract from the particularity of the things to a general rule that applies to the type of thing, which governs whether the word is correctly applicable. The link between schematism and language will be central to Romanticism, and to the development of modern 'hermeneutics', the 'art of interpretation'.

Kant discusses the role of schemata with regard to the categories. All these ways of thinking about objects in the world depend on how the a priori category is applied to contingent intuitions. This application always involves some form of temporal ordering: 'Schemata are for this reason nothing but *determinations of time* a priori according to rules' (ibid. B 184, A 145). The schema of 'reality', for example, is therefore the 'existence at a specific time' of an object given in perception. For Kant, something's being real means that it can be given in perception, and this, as we have seen, can only be at a specific time in a specific place. The link between the schemata and temporality will be a crucial component in Heidegger's thinking. Heidegger argues that without the prior 'opening up' of a world where time reveals things as *different* the subject would not be in the position of bringing these forms of identity to bear on the world.

Kant makes a further distinction concerning the relationship between mind and world. He claims that we must think of objects of knowledge in two respects: as they appear to us, as 'phenomena', and as they exist independently of our thinking of them, as 'noumena'. The former allow one to form concepts of the object through the synthesis of intuitions. The latter, in contrast, might seem to demand their own form of knowledge, a knowledge of things beyond what can be apprehended by the senses. However, Kant makes a distinction between two notions of noumena. In the 'negative' sense the idea of the noumenon is what we arrive at by abstracting from the object as an object of perception. We assume it exists, but can say nothing specific about it, because all determinacy relies on perceptual input. In the 'positive' sense we assume a special kind of access to objects which does not rely on their being given in 'intuition'. This access, of course, is precisely what Kant regards as impossible. The first of these conceptions of the thing can be plausibly construed in terms of thinking about the totality of the aspects of the object. We can only ever apprehend an object piecemeal, but it is not contradictory to assume the object exists under all the different descriptions we could give of it, though the question of when a new description means an object is no longer the same object as it is under another description may arise here. The second conception suggests that the thing is now a complete mystery, wholly separate from anything specific we can think about it. Despite Kant's insistence on rejecting the positive sense of noumenon, other aspects of his thought will encourage people to think that he has built a complete barrier between ourselves and the way the world 'really is'. We shall return to this point later.

Reason

We now need to consider Kant's response in the Transcendental Dialectic to the consequences of the limitations inherent in knowledge. The understanding can only judge empirical data, and it is characterized precisely in terms of the limitations on what it has access to. Clearly, though, thinking involves more than making judgements about the laws governing specific things in the world. Even making the claim that the understanding can be *described* as being limited to such judgements means that thinking must be able to move beyond what the understanding alone can do. The further capacity of thought which makes the move beyond empirical judgements possible Kant terms 'reason'. Reason creates unity among the rules of the understanding, whereas the understanding creates unity among empirical data. The latter can rely on reality, in Kant's sense of that which is given in perception; the former runs the risk of falling back into what the whole of the first Critique is concerned to avoid, namely speculation about the ultimate nature of things based on concepts that cannot refer to reality. The problem is that the kind of notions involved in such unsustainable speculation cannot actually be avoided if we think about questions such as: 'Is all of nature causally determined, and does that mean that there is no free human action?'

Kant has no doubt that the nature given in perception is wholly determined by laws. However, he also thinks that rational beings must be able to exercise 'causality through freedom' when they decide to *act* in terms of rules they impose on themselves, rather than merely behave in terms of stimulus and response. How can this contradiction be resolved? The question of whether people are responsible for their actions, or are just the result of causal processes in nature and society, is unavoidable in modernity. Kant wishes to arrive at an adequate answer to it which sustains a basis for moral responsibility. The underlying issue involves what he terms 'dialectic'. This is the use of forms of thought which are only valid for dealing with the phenomenal world to talk about noumenal things in themselves. We necessarily employ metaphysical notions to understand the overall nature of our knowledge of the world. These notions should, however, only have the 'regulative' function of systematizing what the understanding does in relation to particular data, not the 'constitutive' function of telling us about the ultimate nature of reality. The attempt to do the latter leads to 'dialectical' contradictions.

Kant's arguments emerge from his examination of the relationship between two terms that will dominate significant parts of German philosophy for the next fifty years: the 'conditioned', and the 'unconditioned' or the 'absolute'. All cognitive explanations rely upon finding something's condition. The condition of a body falling to earth is, for example, the greater mass of the earth than that of the body. Each such condition will itself in turn be conditioned by something else. In other words, every particular thing is relative to, or dependent upon, what makes its existence possible. Kant terms 'the *totality of conditions* to a given conditioned' (ibid. B 380, A 323) a 'transcendental concept of reason'. It is theoretically possible to think of such a concept, even though we can never arrive at the point where we know we have reached it. This totality is, however, not the 'unconditioned in every respect' (ibid. B 383, A 326). It only refers to the sequence of conditions for *one* thing, and these conditions are themselves in turn conditioned. The unity of everything that could be an object of the understanding, the unity of all possible conditions, is a more absolute concept. This unity is an 'idea', a 'necessary concept of reason'. An idea therefore cannot be apprehended in terms of the understanding, even though it involves a generalization of what the understanding does. The idea is, then, not merely arrived at through idle speculation. It is a *necessary* result of how reason works when it moves from what we can know to trying to know about the complete unity of what we can know. There are three classes of 'transcendental ideas': (1) the absolute unity of the thinking subject; (2) the absolute unity of the sequence of conditions of a phenomenon; and (3) the absolute unity of the condition of all objects of thought. None of these could be termed an object in Kant's terms, and they are therefore the result of a subjective necessity in thought. The three classes lead to three forms of 'dialectical conclusions of reason': the first to 'paralogisms', the second to 'antinomies', the third to the 'Ideal of pure reason'. The first two of these forms make the significance of the argument clear.

In the first form, the paralogism, Kant discusses the transcendental unity of the subject. There is a logical, *formal* necessity to think of the subject as unified. If it were not unified, knowledge would, as we saw, become inexplicable. This necessity is, though, often mistakenly used to argue that the subject can be positively *known* as a substance, thus as a noumenon which is the underlying basis of my consciousness of phenomena. Kant insists, however, that the subject is really only ever accessible to itself at particular moments of apperception, not in a timeless manner in which it would grasp itself as a whole. We cannot assert that we *know* our noumenal self without offending against the fact that knowledge is possible only under the conditions of the understanding. Whether the subject can be said, despite Kant's arguments, to exist in an unconditioned manner will form one of the key questions of the philosophers who follow Kant, especially Fichte.

The antinomies (which means 'opposed laws') arise if one tries positively to think the unconditioned as though it were an object of thought like any other. The result of doing so are claims which are in contradiction with each other, as thesis and antithesis, but which both seem to be valid. Kant's point is once again that one must always avoid using the mode of thinking we use for the world of appearances for thinking about the world as it is in itself. The easiest way to understand this is in relation to the third antinomy, between 'nature' and 'freedom'. The thesis of the third antinomy maintains that there cannot just be determinism in nature. Every empirical cause is also the effect of something else, but this means that there can never be a complete sequence of causes. Any supposedly first cause would also have to be the effect of something else, leading to an infinite regress. The argument is similar to that used to argue that there must be a first cause of the universe, i.e. God. There must therefore be another kind of causality in nature, an 'absolute spontaneity', which is not the effect of something else. The *same* kind of causality is what makes us free when we act in a manner that is not determined by antecedent causes such as the prompting of instinct. On the other hand, the antithesis argues, if we were to assume there is such a freedom in nature, the causal chains which led us to seek the first cause themselves would no longer be a basis for explanation at all. We could not assume that the law of causality was universally applicable. If there is such freedom it must lie *outside* nature itself. There can, though, be no evidence of this, because the source of all evidence for the reality of something is what can be observed *in* nature.

The antinomy is resolved by the argument that as phenomena we are determined like the rest of nature, but as noumena we are free. We are free because we can act in terms of an 'ought', which relies upon an idea, not of how things are, but of how they *should* be. How things should be cannot be derived from what we know of the world as it already is. Think of the issue in these terms. We can perform actions which appear as causally determined events in the world. These can be described in terms of physics, chemistry, etc. The *motivation* for the action is, though, nowhere apparent in these terms. The action *may* actually be prompted by my pleasure or self-interest, thus by inclinations based on natural causality, but it may also be that an action causes me considerable difficulties and no pleasure at all. In the latter case the action could be construed in terms of my awareness that I *ought* to do what I do, not for any benefit that accrues to me, but because I think there is more to life than self-preservation and the increase of pleasure. This fact will be what leads to the key element of Kant's moral philosophy. The remainder of the first Critique is concerned with the demonstration that the arguments of previous metaphysics do not offer what they promise in terms of proofs of the existence of God, or of accounts of the nature of reality as a whole, because they repeat the confusion which Kant seeks to avoid in his account of the antinomies. The complexities of these later sections of the Critique cannot be adequately dealt with here, though they do contain a wealth of insights into the problem of how to resolve the need of thought to think beyond what is finite without making unjustifiable positive claims about the infinite.

Morals and Foundations

Kant's solution to the third antinomy dictates the structure of his thinking about morality, and gives rise to many of the attempts by his successors to get beyond what he achieved. The attempts are generated above all by the way Kant establishes divisions between the empirical world and the 'intelligible' world. The problem is that actions based on 'causality through freedom' must take place in a realm wholly divorced from the realm of appearing, deterministic nature. Free decisions are therefore located neither in space nor in time. The point of Kant's argument is to avoid the situation where practical reason, the capacity of rational beings for self-determination, becomes, like everything in the appearing world, subject to something else which determines it. If practical reason were dependent in this way, one would then have to ask what determines what practical reason is determined by, and so on. The result is the following alternative. Either what practical reason depends on must itself be absolute, in the way traditional authority based on God and his representative, the monarch, is supposed to be absolute, or practical reason is itself absolute – in the sense of not being relative to anything else in the world. Kant refuses to allow appeals to divine authority in any sphere, because they entail a claim to know more than we can justify. At the same time, he also insists that reason must transcend the given world. The demand to act in terms of how things *should* be cannot be made in terms of what is already the case. The difficulties Kant attempts to resolve in his practical philosophy are the kind of difficulties which arise with the transition to modernity from societies based on traditional authority.

Kant makes the startling claim at the beginning of the *Foundation of the Metaphysics of Morals* that only a good will can be regarded as good without qualification, and that happiness, well-being, etc., cannot be considered to be unconditionally good. He argues that regarding any particular attribute, such as good health, as unconditionally good must confront the fact that a healthy mass killer is hardly supremely desirable. His concern is, then, to establish the '*supreme principle of morality*' (1974: BA xv). Moral philosophers make the distinction between 'consequentialist' and 'deontological' theories. The former, such as utilitarian theories, regard the results of an action as deciding its moral worth; the latter, in contrast, regard the moral value of an action as being intrinsic to it, so that certain actions, which may have good consequences for the majority, are still just plain wrong. Kant belongs to the latter camp.

The fact that Kant is seeking a 'supreme principle' makes evident how important he thinks his view of morality is to the modern world, where there can be no appeal to transcendent authority. Morality is to depend upon 'the idea of another and much more worthy purpose of existence' (ibid. BA 7) than the purposes of nature governed by natural causality. He is, then, talking about the goal of life lived in accordance with reason and without divine guarantees.[7] The good will

7 Kant does argue in the first and second Critiques that it is rational to think that good behaviour will be rewarded in the long run, but he later comes to realize that this is a cop-out, and that serious moral argument can only appeal to human self-legislation.

manifests itself most obviously in relation to duty (*'the necessity to act out of reverence for the law'*: ibid. BA 14), where the individual's interest and desire can easily be in conflict with what they know they *ought* to do. Furthermore, duty is only present when an action cannot be understood to follow from a desire to perform the action because it brings one some benefit, even including the benefit of avoiding the sanctions the law may demand. The crucial factor is the maxim, the general rule, in accordance with which the act is carried out. Because the result of following the maxim is subject to the contingency of the causal events which follow in the empirical world, and so can turn into disaster, the moral worth of an action depends solely upon its being motivated by the highest principle, not on its consequences.

There is therefore no empirical content to Kant's foundation of morality. Instead of there being Ten Commandments that one should follow in order to be moral, Kant has one wholly abstract imperative. This is the categorical imperative: 'I ought never to act except in such a way *that I can also will that my maxim should become a universal law*' (ibid. BA 17).[8] This imperative is perhaps the most criticized aspect of Kant's moral philosophy. Why this is becomes apparent in relation to Kant's remark that 'it is . . . absolutely impossible for experience to establish with complete certainty a single case in which the maxim of an action in other respects right has rested solely on moral grounds' (ibid. BA 27). On the one hand, then, Kant offers a criterion for making moral decisions; on the other, he takes it away again by denying that we can ever know if we are really following the criterion.

Think of Kant's position like this. If I am to justify something I have done I can try to do so in terms of it being a necessary means to an end. I would then, in Kant's terms, be following a hypothetical imperative. What, though, makes the end I seek legitimate? I cannot justify it as being right because I want it, because I will at some point inevitably come into conflict with what others may want. The alternative here is between my assertion of my prior rights over others, and the acknowledgement that others have rights in the same way as I do. In a post-feudal society, where there is no reason to assign moral status in terms of one's God-given position in the social hierarchy, the demand for some kind of universal principle is inescapable. Empirically it is, of course, obvious that people are not equal in talent, health, etc. In the West and in large parts of the rest of the world it *is*, though, now largely impossible to argue for a morality which takes

8 There are other formulations of the imperative, but this one will suffice for explaining the main argument.

these inequalities as the basis for decisions about the rights of individuals. This does not mean that this equality actually exists, but it can mean that we accept the *idea* of such an equality. Think of the way people feel when a double standard is applied and they are the ones who are negatively treated: on what is their sense of outrage based but something like what Kant intends?

A further aspect of Kant's refusal to accept empirical grounds for morality is the following. Observation of the actions of others in the world gives one no criteria for judging that they are or are not behaving morally. Only if I *already* possess some sense of what it is to perform a moral action, a sense which I cannot derive from observation, can I attribute the same kind of sense to others. If there is a highest good, our awareness of it cannot be derived from looking at the world, and thinking, for example, that happiness is that good. Any empirical good will be likely to entail confusion and difficulty as to how it can be attained, and it will depend on the individual's aims and desires as to what it consists in.

The a priori status of the categorical imperative is therefore the result of the impossibility of founding morality either on what we know about the empirical world or on the information we derive about others from that knowledge. Instead, the imperative rests upon granting to others an autonomous status which we grant to ourselves. It may be, as Kant admits, that we never are autonomous in this way, but the *idea* of seeking to be autonomous gives us the possibility of having a shared aim as rational beings. The problem of how it is that we ever come to grant others that status is not answered by Kant. His successors, Fichte and Hegel, are not the least significant for their attempts to give an account of the genesis of the mutual acknowledgement required for a post-theological morality. Why did human beings not remain in a state of mere antagonism to each other, without developing what is required for acknowledging the rights of others? It is often argued that this acknowledgement comes about simply in the name of self-preservation. Constant aggression against the other would mean that I will only last as long as I do not encounter a foe stronger or more cunning than myself. This account does not explain, though, how the more differentiated kinds of moral feeling become possible. These feelings seem to transcend what would come about for mere pragmatic reasons of survival. Whatever one may think of this difficult issue, the direction of Kant's argument does find an echo in questions which still concern the contemporary world, for instance in the realm of human rights. The vital factor in his argument is autonomy, self-legislation, not heteronomy, obedience to the law for some extraneous reason, such as the fear of the consequences of disobedience. Whereas everything in the realm of nature is subject to its condition, what takes us beyond this state is the ability to decide what we will be conditioned by in performing our actions.

This ability has the vital consequence of undermining a still very commonly employed notion of freedom. The liberty to do whatever I want if I can get away with it, or if it is legal, is not seen as the highest form of freedom by Kant. Instead, we are free if we give the law to ourselves because we accept that this is what we *ought* to do: 'Thus a free will and a will under moral laws are one and the same' (ibid. BA 99). The reason for this attempt to square freedom and necessity is simple, and was given by Rousseau. Merely following one's desires is not the ultimate form of liberation, because one can become a slave to one's passions. How, in any case, does one decide between two apparently equally compelling desires? Deciding what one ought to do is, then, to be achieved in terms of the categorical imperative: do I think all people should have the right to decide to do what I decide to do in this situation?[9] If I think in this way I must regard others not as means to my ends, but as 'ends in themselves', as beings who share the capacity for self-determination. The consequence of this conception is the 'ideal' of a kingdom of ends in which we are both members and subjects. Kant makes the prophetic distinction, which will re-emerge in Marx's thought, between that which has a 'price', and that which has what he terms a 'dignity'. What has a price can be substituted for by something else as its equivalent; what has dignity is above all price, because it has an intrinsic value and cannot be substituted. Autonomous rational beings are to be regarded as possessing dignity. For Kant, the acknowledgement of the existence of beings which are 'ends in themselves' becomes the basis of a just society.

Kant's vision may sound like a woolly liberal utopia. The power of his moral vision in the later part of the eighteenth century lay, though, not least in its rendering feudalism and slavery impossible to legitimate at a time when they were still very much part of the real socio-political world. Despite Kant's own contingent, historically determined failures in his attitudes with regard both to women and to some other races, the impetus of his moral theory is towards thoroughgoing democracy. The weakness of the theory lies in how such a vision is to be translated into concrete politics, and many of the

---

9   The problem which Kant does not really deal with in this context is that in most morally difficult situations we are confronted with competing moral imperatives, rather than a decision about the universalization of just one imperative.

thinkers we shall be considering are concerned precisely with the gap
between moral theory and the political and legal world.

Nature and Freedom: The Third Critique

The arguments of Kant's moral philosophy serve to reinforce the separation between the determinism of the appearing natural world, and
the intelligible world of human freedom. Kant later comes to ask
whether this division is as absolute as it is seen as being in the works
we have considered so far. In doing so, he endangers the strict distinction between the receptive and the spontaneous sources of our
knowledge. The problem he faces will recur in much post-Kantian
philosophy. The separation of the sphere of freedom from a wholly
deterministic nature leaves no way of understanding how it is that we
can gain an objective perspective on law-bound nature and at the
same time can be self-legislating. How, moreover, does the spontaneity that is the basis both of knowledge and of action affect nature,
if spontaneity exists in a *wholly* different realm from nature?
Schelling, for example, will argue in the 1790s that the only way
to avoid an implausible split between mind and nature is to accept
that nature itself must be understood to be inherently subjective and
spontaneous. Otherwise, explaining how something supposedly
wholly objective can give rise to self-determining subjectivity
becomes impossible.

Kant's *Critique of Judgement*, the 'third Critique', considers nature
and our relationship to it in terms not of knowledge, but of pleasure.
Our pleasure in aspects of nature is in one respect subjective, but it
also involves judgement in the same way as do knowledge and morality. I can judge that this particular flower gives me pleasure in a
manner that another flower does not, as I can judge that it is wrong
to steal someone else's flowers. The pleasure the flower gives me is
occasioned by the way in which its parts form a unified whole that
cannot be understood just as the sum of those parts. The relationship
between part and whole, and the relationship between particular and
general, form the focus of the third Critique. One of the problems
Kant tried to solve in the first Critique was how to move from the
particular phenomenon to its classification under a general concept.
The problem of induction is the problem that moving from particular phenomena to a general law can always involve bringing the particulars under a general law which may not characterize what they
really have in common. Furthermore, there seems to be no way of
finally deciding when the generalization is the right one, given the

contingency of the data used to confirm laws. Think of the explanations by the Church of the movement of heavenly bodies and those
given by Galileo. In both cases the theory and the data were regarded
as fitting each other: indeed, the Church's account of the heavens
was apparently more accurate than Galileo's initial attempt at a
new theory. There is, moreover, no cognitive reason in Kant's terms
to assume that nature is a unified system whose particular laws fit
together. At the same time, knowledge does, he maintains, require the
assumption that what is being investigated is not merely a 'labyrinth
of the multiplicity of possible particular laws' (Kant 1968b: 26) if the
move from particular to general is to be plausible. Kant therefore
claims that it is rational to look at nature 'as if an understanding contained the basis of the unity of the multiplicity of its empirical laws'
(ibid. B xviii, A xxvi). This apparently theological claim – the understanding in question would seem to be that of a deity which guarantees that the laws of nature cohere – is both qualified by Kant's saying
we should only look at nature *as if* it were so, and supported by arguments concerning the relation of parts to wholes in nature. The
central aspect of the third Critique is what Kant terms reflective
judgement. In reflective judgement we move from particular to
general via assumptions about the systematic coherence of things
which do not have the status of knowledge in Kant's sense. When
reflective judgement is freed from the task of establishing cognitive
laws it can also combine parts into wholes in a non-directed manner.
This gives rise to a pleasure which Kant thinks was initially attached
to cognition's synthesizing of different phenomena. The same pleasure also allows us to enjoy the different ways that parts of a work
of art can be interrelated. Kant connects ideas about the systematic
constitution of nature to the capacity for aesthetic enjoyment.

   The fact is that all sorts of aspects of nature both obey particular
laws and yet cannot be explained as just the result of the blind interaction of these laws. Organisms seem to show nature as functioning
in terms of 'purposes': '*An organised product of nature is that in which
everything is an end and on the other hand also a means*. Nothing in
it is in vain, pointless, or to be attributed to a blind mechanism of
nature' (ibid. B 296, A 292). A plant is not just an amorphous paste,
made up of the chemicals of which it consists: it seems to function in
terms of an 'idea' that gives it its form. We now can explain the transmission of this form in terms of DNA. However, we are not able to
explain why it is that nature gives rise to organized forms at all, rather
than remaining in a chaotic state. Kant's thought is that we need to
understand how the capacity of the mind to organize phenomena into
coherent systematic forms is linked to the fact that nature itself orga-

nizes its elements in ways which are not merely the result of particular laws. He tries to connect the pleasure nature gives us in aesthetic judgements and the way in which nature seems to function in terms of goals that are not accessible to cognitive judgement. Aesthetic judgements look at nature as though nature itself *aimed* at being appropriate to our cognition. Kant talks of the 'subjective purposiveness of nature for the power of judgement' (ibid. B 237, A 234). The key word, though, is 'subjective': the idea of nature outlined here relies on what takes place in the subject, not on something that could be said to be inherently part of nature. It might be argued, of course, that the basis of our pleasure is very clearly part of *our* nature, which is not separate from the rest of nature. Kant insists, though, throughout the *Critique of Judgement*, that we have no right to cross the boundary between the sensuous and the intelligible. At the same time, however, he suggests it is right to think as though we might, via the non-cognitive pleasure nature can give us, have a kind of access to nature that takes us beyond what we can know.

The significance of the idea that nature might communicate with us beyond the bounds of cognition becomes apparent when Kant ponders the question of artistic creation and appreciation. Two factors are important here. One is the contention that aesthetic judgements are not randomly subjective. Saying something is beautiful is not the same as saying it simply pleases me (Kant calls this the 'agreeable'), because it entails a validity-claim to which I think others should assent. Kant therefore ponders the possibility of a 'common sense', a shared capacity for feeling, which would unite rational beings, despite their empirical differences in matters of taste. He also contrasts 'the pure disinterested pleasure in the judgement of taste' (ibid. B 7, A 7) with judgements based on an 'interest' in an ulterior purpose, of the kind generated by sensuous appetites. The common sense is not something which can be said really to exist, but is another regulative idea that orients our thinking when we accept that it is worth arguing with others about beauty. The other important factor is the way in which Kant talks about the significant artist, the genius. In a striking formulation, he says '*genius* is the innate aptitude [*ingenium*] *through which* nature gives the rule to art' (ibid. B 181, A 178–9). One cannot produce art simply by making something in terms of the rules of a particular form: art involves moving beyond existing rules. The source of new rules has to be another kind of spontaneity, otherwise the rules would just reproduce what has already been done. This spontaneity seems to come from nature itself. In the first two Critiques Kant had argued that *we* give the law to nature in knowledge, and to ourselves in ethical self-determination. Now, though, the aesthetic 'law' actually emerges as a consequence of *nature* acting in the subject.

The further importance of this strand of argument becomes apparent in Kant's famous characterization of an aesthetic idea as 'that representation of the imagination which gives much to think about, but without any determinate thought, i.e. *concept* being able to be adequate to it, which consequently no language can completely attain and make comprehensible' (ibid. B 193, A 190). He gives 'the invisible Being, the realm of the blessed, hell, eternity, the creation' (ibid. B 194, A 191) as examples of such ideas. Aesthetic ideas are means of trying to make the 'intelligible' concerns of reason available in an empirical form. Otherwise the danger is that they will be merely abstract and we will be unable to connect them to the reality of our lives, which are lived in the sensuous world. The intelligible sphere of reason and the empirical world of nature are therefore seen as potentially connected, albeit in a way which is only manifest in symbolic form.

In notes written at the time he was writing the *Critique of Judgement* Kant says that 'The general validity of pleasure [in beauty] and yet not via concepts but in intuition is what is difficult' (Kant 1996: 137). This difficulty goes right to the heart of his project. The first two Critiques relied on the strict separation of the sphere of receptive intuition from the sphere of intelligible spontaneity. In the third Critique Kant works with the fiction that we can regard the world as if these spheres were not wholly separate. Reflective judgement regards nature as a work of art, rather than as a 'labyrinth of particular laws'. In consequence, the idea of a unified system of nature is not relinquished and science can assume that the laws it arrives at do cohere. Similarly, if morality is not to be wholly separated from the empirical world, it must be manifest in things that appear in that world. Kant's ultimate aim is to find a way of showing how the existence of rational beings who can transcend nature by their self-determining freedom is the final purpose of creation. If it were possible to show this, then the regulative ideas, both of nature's systematic coherence, and of a unifying common sense shared by rational beings, would become constitutive. The philosophy of German Idealism will attempt to make this move from regulative to constitutive, but Kant remains wary of the move.

Kant bequeathes a fundamental question to modern philosophy. How much is what the world is taken to be determined by the data we receive from the world and how much is it a product of the actions of the human mind? Any answer to this question will be likely to locate the foundation for knowledge either more on the side of the world or more on the side of the subject. This contrast is sometimes described at the end of the eighteenth century as between 'realism' and 'idealism'.[10] The problem with any division of this kind is that one seems to have to find ways of overcoming it, if basic facts about our knowledge and experience are not to become incomprehensible. In Kant's case, the problem lies in explaining how it is that the spontaneity of the subject emerges from a deterministic nature. If the subject is itself in some sense part of the natural world, it cannot be the case that the subject is wholly independent of the way the world is. Does that mean, though, that the subject is ultimately to be explained in the same objective, scientific terms as the rest of the world? Kant's arguments do give strong grounds for doubting that one could turn the subject into something that can be described in completely objective terms, in the manner of contemporary computational approaches to the mind. This is most apparent in his moral philosophy, where the idea of how things *ought* to be cannot be derived from the account of how we establish how things are. Fundamental aspects of the way we understand ourselves are at stake here, and they play a role in the way the modern period develops socially and politically. This is, after all, the time of the French Revolution, much of which took place under the banner of a new conception of the centrality of reason in human life. There is, though, a complicating factor in the attempt to understand the status of reason in this period, which will form the subject of the next chapter. This factor is language.

SUGGESTIONS FOR FURTHER READING

Allison, H. E. (1983) *Kant's Transcendental Idealism* (New Haven, CT: Yale University Press). *Important defence of Kant's contentions in the Critique of Pure Reason.*

Allison, H. E. (2001) *Kant's Theory of Taste: A Reading of the Critique of Aesthetic Judgement* (Cambridge: Cambridge University Press). *Sympathetic, detailed reading of key aspects of Kant's Critique of Judgement.*

Ameriks, K. (2000) *Kant and the Fate of Autonomy* (Cambridge: Cambridge University Press). *Excellent defence of Kant against objections in German Idealism and since.*

---

10 Given the problems concerning the definition of 'realism', it is important to remember that its meaning at the end of the eighteenth century in Germany is often closer to materialism, in contrast with idealism. The former position is often associated with Spinoza, the latter with Berkeley. Kant's transcendental idealism is, of course, an attempt to get beyond such a division.

Beck, L. W. (1965) *Studies in the Philosophy of Kant* (Indianapolis: Bobbs-Merrill). *Lucid approach by major Kant scholar to important issues.*

Beck, L. W. (1969) *Early German Philosophy: Kant and his Predecessors* (Cambridge, MA: Harvard University Press). *Accessible account of Kant's relation to his predecessors.*

Cassirer, E. (1982) *Kant's Life and Thought* (New Haven, CT: Yale University Press). *Classic biographical and philosophical account of Kant by major neo-Kantian philosopher.*

Chadwick, R. (ed.) (1992) *Immanuel Kant: Critical Assessments*, 4 vols (London: Routledge). *Very extensive collection of major essays on Kant: a useful research tool.*

Gardner, Sebastian (1999) *Routledge Philosophy Guidebook to Kant and the Critique of Pure Reason* (London: Routledge). *Detailed and accessible account of the first Critique.*

Guyer, P. (ed.) (1992) *The Cambridge Companion to Kant* (Cambridge: Cambridge University Press). *Good selection of essays on many aspects of Kant's work.*

Henrich, D. (1994) *The Unity of Reason: Essays on Kant's Philosophy* (Cambridge, MA: Harvard University Press). *Demanding but insightful series of essays by major contemporary German philosopher whose work has had a big effect on both Kant and Hegel studies.*

Höffe, O. (1994) *Immanuel Kant* (Albany: SUNY Press). *Good introductory account of Kant.*

Kemp Smith, N. (1923) *A Commentary to Kant's Critique of Pure Reason* (London: Macmillan). *Classic commentary on the first Critique by major scholar and translator of Kant.*

Scruton, R. (2001) *Kant: A Very Short Introduction* (Oxford: Oxford University Press). *Lively general introduction.*

Strawson, P. F. (1966) *The Bounds of Sense: An Essay on Kant's Critique of Pure Reason* (London: Routledge). *Influential analytical account of Kant, which is, though, not reliable in its interpretations of some key issues.*

Walker, Ralph (1998) *Kant* (London: Weidenfeld & Nicolson). *Good general view of Kant's philosophy.*

2

THE DISCOVERY OF LANGUAGE: HAMANN AND HERDER

Origins of Language

Even before Kant publishes the first Critique in 1781, certain thinkers in Germany become aware that the significance of language for philosophy has not been adequately appreciated. To begin with, this issue is best approached not so much from a philosophical as from a cultural and anthropological point of view. These days, language is such an obviously political matter that it is easy to forget that this political status has a specific modern history. When the present-day Turkish government, for example, tries to ban Kurds from using their own language, this is rightly seen as an illegitimate attack on the very essence of what those people are. How, though, does such a sense of language and cultural identity develop? If the order of the world is thought of as being inherent in the world, because it has been made that way, language can be seen as merely a means of reflecting or representing that order. In this case the question of the origin of language is answered in theological terms: it originates with God. Differences between languages are, in consequence, not necessarily of deep philosophical significance because the essential order of things transcends these differences. However, once doubt is cast upon the world's ready-made status, the status of language changes as well and differences between languages themselves become a vital issue. At this point the question of where language comes from becomes pressing. The fact is that the asking of this question is a significant feature of both the Enlightenment and of thinkers who criticize the Enlightenment. The response in the Enlightenment itself tends to be based on one of two new ideas, both of which involve language as in some way a product of reason. Either language is the result of consciousness coming to make animal sounds into meaningful signs, or the social nature of humankind leads to the establishing of social conventions which give agreed meanings to certain signs. Neither of these positions is able to give wholly plausible answers to the main questions, and the reasons why are connected to wider criticisms of the Enlightenment.

Perhaps surprisingly, the role of language for rationalist philosophers who believe in an inherent mathematical structure of things can remain within a theologically inspired framework, even when theological assumptions are dropped. This is because in the rationalist view differences between languages will be overcome by universally valid scientific knowledge. Such knowledge can, of course, be applied to language itself. Language is therefore supposed to be causally explicable like the rest of the world, on the assumption that the unity of human reason reflects the inherent order of the world. Part of the origin of modern linguistics is a result of this kind of rationalist thinking. The underlying idea here also persists in approaches which assume that computers can, in principle, achieve what we do when we understand and produce utterances. In such approaches the complexities and confusions within natural languages – and even more between differing natural languages – are to be overcome by the establishing of a 'universal language' that is conceived of in analogy to mathematics. Such conceptions of language are 'representational': they regard language as 're-presenting' what is already there – hence their link to a theology which sees God as guaranteeing the order of the world. These conceptions are often associated with the science-oriented side of the Enlightenment, and, in later versions, came to dominate large parts of twentieth-century Anglo-American philosophy.[1] Their strength lies in their connection to the success of modern science, and the success of that science seems to be underpinned by the fact that it can potentially be conveyed in any natural language. Why, then, did this view of language come to be put in doubt at precisely the same time as the science which it accompanies becomes more and more reliable?

The main innovations in conceptions of language in modern Germany take place in the work of two figures, both of whom knew and were influenced by Kant, who were friends, and who also lived

---

1 The Enlightenment is, however, a term with too many varied uses to be reduced to such a model, as we shall see: even thinkers like Hamann and Herder who are critical of the Enlightenment thinkers of their day do not reject much that is associated in a wider sense with Enlightenment thinking.

(at least some of the time) in Königsberg (now Kaliningrad): Johann Georg Hamann (1730–88), and Johann Gottfried Herder (1744–1803). The questions raised by Hamann and Herder, and developed by their successors from Schleiermacher to Heidegger, are germane to the most fundamental divisions in modern philosophy, not least to the perceived division between 'continental' and 'analytical' philosophy. Recent developments in Anglo-American philosophy have brought some of the ideas of this tradition back into the mainstream of contemporary thinking, so it is important to get straight why they are so significant. It might seem odd to make Hamann into a central figure in this context, because, after undergoing a spiritual crisis on a business trip in London in 1758, he became a deeply committed Christian. However, the theology he advocated was directed against the kind of Enlightenment rational theology that could be made commensurable with a view of language oriented towards the sciences. What also makes Hamann so significant is the fact that, besides influencing a large number of his contemporaries, his *texts* pose an often underestimated question for modern philosophy. This question has become familiar in the work of Derrida and those influenced by him, but its history is rarely traced in an adequate manner.

Hamann's texts do not always consist of clearly expressed arguments for the positions he advocates and against those he rejects. Instead, the crucial aspect of his texts is that they self-consciously *enact* the conception of language and the world he is attempting to convey. This means that Hamann's texts cannot be assessed just in terms of whether the arguments they propose are valid or not. Hamann is, then, a 'performative' writer. He aims to affect the reader by the way he writes, not just to convey the propositional content of his texts. We shall encounter the issue of performative writing later in relation to Nietzsche. What, then, is it about Hamann's texts that makes them, even today, so resistant to many assumptions of the dominant ways of doing philosophy?

Irrationalism

The standard edition of Hamann's works, edited by Joseph Nadler (Hamann 1949–57), took thirty years of work by the editor, who provides a 'Key' to the texts by tracing the huge number of allusions in them. The Key constitutes a substantial volume in its own right, and Hamann was not a prolific author. Nadler undertook this monumental task because Hamann is often wilfully esoteric. He is also, though, routinely presented as an enemy of the Enlightenment, and so becomes linked to questionable traditions in German thought, which are often put under the catch-all heading of 'irrationalism'. Membership of this group has become a touchstone of many thinkers' relationship to the subsequent development of Nazism in Germany, as suggested in the subtitle, 'From Schelling to Hitler', of the Hungarian Marxist Georg Lukács's book *The Destruction of Reason*. Lukács, though, does not see Hamann as part of this tradition (and Schelling does not belong to it either, as we shall see).

What, then, is irrationalism? If reason were something universally agreed upon, the label irrationalist would simply apply to those who reject reason in the name of something else. Examples of a rejection of certain conceptions of reason are, of course, legion in modern German philosophy. In the 1920s, for example, Ludwig Klages opposed 'Soul' to '*Geist*'/'Mind', privileging the former, which involves a non-conceptual, intuitive contact with the world, over the latter, which involves analysing things conceptually and scientifically. Other writers at that time privilege 'Life' over reason in related ways. The structure Klages relies on derives from an opposition we shall encounter in Romantic philosophy (which is already adumbrated by Hamann, and is probably first established by the Romantic thinker Friedrich Schlegel) between the 'Dionysian' and the 'Apollonian'. The former is the force of creation and destruction, the latter that which makes possible form and order. The problem is that any characterization of the Dionysian must rely on the Apollonian. A conceptual account of the force of creation and destruction has to rely on language, and language depends on formal rules and structures to make sense. There is, then, an inherent contradiction built into the attempt to *say* anything about the Dionysian: by fixing it in language one misses its essential nature. Invocation of the Dionysian consequently requires an appeal to 'intuition', which is accessible only to non-conceptual modes of thinking. This will be why Nietzsche links the Dionysian to music, which cannot be fully explained in conceptual terms. The question of the tension between intuition in this sense (which is obviously very different from Kant's notion) and conceptual thinking is vital throughout the history of modern German philosophy.

The further important point here is that the Apollonian is itself generally regarded as deriving its formative power from the Dionysian, rather as Freud's rational ego derives its energies from the irrational forces of the id. The potential for the human desire for order to become rigid and destructive, which Freud sees in terms of the neurosis occasioned by the repression of libidinal energy, is already apparent in Euripides' play, *The Bacchae*, from which the idea of the Dionysian derives. In the play, the result of trying to control or exclude the god Dionysus is a terrible revenge, a 'return of the repressed', which destroys the social order. Dionysus' destructive effect on human society makes clear the need to integrate the power of the Dionysian into how societies deal with the world, because excluding it will eventually lead any human form of order to destroy itself.[2] It should be clear, therefore, that there is nothing per se irrational either about examining the motivating sources of the ways in which we order the world and ourselves, or about attending to the dangers of limiting our attention to what can be ordered, be it by scientific knowledge or by other symbolic forms. A conception of reason that is limited, for example, to what can be scientifically established may not itself be very rational at all. Only if the idea of integrating the Dionysian and the Apollonian is abandoned in favour of the Dionysian dissolution of human forms of conceptual thought can a position justifiably be termed irrationalist.

Hamann: Language and Reason

Hamann does not, then, belong under the heading of irrationalism, which complicates the idea that he is an enemy of the Enlightenment. He sees his task as being to reveal the limits of a narrow Enlightenment conception of reason via his very particular conception of language. The easiest initial way to understand his position is by linking the metaphor of Dionysus and Apollo to language. Rationalist conceptions rely on the 'Apollonian' idea of a rational order inherent in the world, and true language reflects that order. Hamann contests this conception by considering how we arrive at the notion of reason in the first place. He sees this as inseparable from the acquisition of language. Language is essentially *creative*, and it is inseparable from the capacity to reveal new aspects of existence which we often associate with art. In consequence, attempts to fix an order of things in language fail to appreciate language's 'Dionysian' aspect, which allows it constantly to refashion the ways in which the world is revealed to us. This view introduces a thoroughly historical dimension into language. Hamann's allusions to and citations of texts from antiquity to the present create a sense of the contextuality of thinking at the same

---

2   The Dionysian is closely linked to carnival, in which the dominant order is mocked, with, for example, a beggar being crowned king for the day. Carnival is therefore both in one sense subversive of the established order, and a means of stabilizing it.

time as they establish new contexts and meanings for the material he employs. The philosophical motivation for this approach derives from his peculiar appropriation of British empiricism.

Hamann's epistemological claim is that our primary contact with the world is in terms of 'feeling'/'sensation' ('*Empfindung*'), not in terms of ideas. This is the core of his objection to Enlightenment conceptions which, like Kant, assume that we possess rational capacities without explaining how it is that we arrived at those capacities. For Hamann, we have a fundamental belief in or conviction of the reality of things which are prior to any abstract philosophical attempt to establish the nature of that reality. Such belief is not supported by reasons and is 'immediate', in the sense of 'non-inferential', not relying on its relationships to any other thoughts: '*belief* happens as little in terms of reasons as *tasting* and *smelling*' (Hamann 1949–57: ii(1950). 74). Despite his indebtedness to empiricism, Hamann does not, though, concern himself with the empiricist idea that will dominate much modern philosophy. This is one reason why his insights have come back into contemporary discussion, where this empiricist idea is now largely rejected. The idea in question is that if our only contact with the world is via the sense-data in our organism, out of which we form ideas, we cannot be said to be really in touch with things, because they will always be hidden behind the 'veil of ideas'. Hamann, in contrast, is interested in the fact that the world is revealed to us at all as something which is always already intelligible: 'The first eruption of creation and the first impression of its historian; – the first appearance and the first enjoyment of nature unite in the word: Let there be light! with this the feeling of the presence of things begins itself' (ibid. 197).[3] Hamann's Enlightenment is, then, intended to sustain the importance of our sensuous relationship to things in a way that the rationalist Enlightenment did not. Following the unorthodox Jewish tradition of the Kabbala (the essay *Aesthetica in nuce* of 1764, from which this remark is taken, has the subtitle 'Rhapsody in Kabbalistic Prose'), Hamann regards creation as a becoming-manifest of the Word.

The intelligibility of things and the intelligibility of language are inseparable, because things are created by God's Word, and they are reflected in the different kinds of articulation used by human beings. Language does not primarily identify things, because that would limit their possibilities. The word is instead what creates things *as* things in ever-renewed ways. While God's Word actually brings what is said

---

3   Note the reflexive 'begins itself', which means there is no separation between creation and created.

concretely into existence, human language reveals the endless ways in which what God has said can be translated into new forms:[4] 'Speak that I see you – This wish was fulfilled by the creation, which is speech to the living creature by what is created' (ibid. 198). The priority of immediate sensuous contact with things is underlined by Hamann's theology, which sees us as involved in a constant interchange with nature: 'Every impression of nature in humankind is not just a reminder but a guarantee of the basic truth: Who the LORD is. Every counter-effect of humankind on creation is a letter and seal of our participation in divine nature' (ibid. 107). Elsewhere he claims against Herder's account of the human origin of language that 'Everything which humankind heard at the beginning, saw with their eyes, looked at and touched with their hands, was a living word; for God was the Word' (ibid. iii(1951). 32). If we lose sight of this connectedness to an intelligible world, as he thinks Enlightenment philosophy has, we will be led to 'unnatural use of abstractions' (ibid. ii(1950). 107). This will 'mutilate' our conceptions of things by rendering them dead and immobile. The danger is that things become mere examples of generalizations, rather than revelations which manifest the diversity and specificity of what matters to us. Hamann can be seen, therefore, as attempting to counter what the sociologist Max Weber will refer to at the beginning of the twentieth century as the 'disenchantment' caused by the rationalization characteristic of the modern world.

The questions Hamann raises as to why the world is intelligible at all, and why humankind possesses language as the means of articulating the world's intelligibility, can hardly be said to have received definitive answers in the interim. God might seem a better explanation of the origin of language than the mythical 'language gene', even to many paid-up atheists. Hamann demonstrates the fundamental difficulty for any philosophy which would give a definitive explanation of language. The explanation of language depends upon its fulfilling criteria demanded by reason. Reason, though, itself requires language. The character of any natural language has a great deal to do with the history of the interactions with the world of the people whose language it is. Even if we can no longer accept a theological story of creation, the immediacy of human contact with things and the development of language do go hand in hand, as the primacy of practical vocabulary before abstractions in the history of languages suggests. Any attempt to generalize about language without taking this historical basis into account will lead to a conception of language

---

4   This conception will be adopted and adapted by Walter Benjamin, as we shall see in chapter 11.

in which an abstract conception of reason is prior. Hamann's polemic against such positions is often couched in sexual terms: revelation is most powerful when it occurs through the body's libidinal link to other parts of the universe. The very fact that languages sometimes divide the world up in terms of genders is therefore one key to understanding how language is attached to the world.

Hamann's views come into sharp focus in his critique of Kant, the 'Metacritique on the Purism of Reason' of 1784, which he himself did not publish, but which became known in intellectual circles at the time. In his review of Kant's first Critique that was published in 1781 the direction of Hamann's later critique is already apparent. He attacks Kant's separation of the two sources of knowledge, receptive sensuousness and spontaneous understanding: 'why such a violent, unauthorised separation of what nature has joined?' (ibid. iii(1951). 278). The two must, Hamann argues, have a common root. In the later essay the objection to this separation is made clear by his consideration of language in Kantian terms. Given the strength of his attachment to theology, it might seem surprising that he is so anti-metaphysical in much of his argument. He first criticizes the Enlightenment attempt to rid reason of any dependence on tradition, as though reason could purify itself of everything it owes to its origins in specific histories. He then wonders at Kant's claim to solve the problems of reason 'after reason spent more than 2000 years looking for, one knows not what? *beyond* experience' (ibid. 284). This leads him to his key arguments, based on the claim that 'the only first and last organ and criterion of reason' is language, which he sees as based on nothing more than tradition and use. The attempt to make the core of language a timeless logical structure ignores the wholly different ways in which language is used and has developed in relation to human beings' practical and libidinal experience of the real, sensuous, historical world.

Kant's attempt to make synthetic judgements a priori the basis of warrantable scientific knowledge provokes this rhetorical flourish from Hamann, which epitomizes his approach: 'Finally it is, by the way, obvious that if mathematics can arrogate to itself the privilege of the nobility because of its universal and necessary reliability, then even human reason itself would be inferior to the unfailing and infallible *instinct* of insects' (ibid. 285). Heidegger will also later claim, in the late 1920s, that, just because mathematics is reliable because of the limitation of its subject matter, it does not mean that using maths is therefore inherently superior to other ways of dealing with the world. If that were the case, as Hamann argues, the mere mechanism of stimulus and response would be superior to what human thinking

– and the freedom it entails – can achieve by relating to the world in the diverse ways it does.

Hamann's main question for Kant concerns the status of the categories: 'words are both pure and empirical *intuitions* as well as pure and empirical *concepts*: *empirical* because the sensation of sight or sound is affected by them, *pure* in so far as their significance is not determined by anything which belongs to those sensations (ibid. 286–8). Language 'deconstructs' Kant's separation of the sources of knowledge into receptivity and spontaneity because it is both sensuously manifest and dependent on logical structures. This separation is often the source of sceptical attacks on Kant's arguments because it is hard to know how the two sources could connect. For Hamann, we can only *acquire* the means of thinking *receptively*, by taking up repeated noises and marks from the empirical world. What makes those noises and marks into meaning-bearers is the *spontaneity* of thinking. The two sources therefore cannot be separate, because each depends on the other for its functioning.

Hamann's attempt to get over philosophical dichotomies between what depends on the world and what depends on the mind will be vital in German Idealism and early Romanticism. The manner of Hamann's writing here is also part of the argument. The rhetorical aspect cannot, as we saw above, just be subtracted in order to arrive at 'the argument'. Hamann enacts his suspicion of the reduction of philosophical language to abstract foundations via his rhetorical verve. It should be apparent, then, that Hamann's position cannot be regarded as questionable just because of its employment of rhetoric. Whatever else one may think of it, the position is internally consistent. The attempt to rid philosophy of rhetoric falls prey precisely to the fact that what is involved in rhetoric is inherent in what is built into all natural languages by their genesis in the real historical world.

An extreme version of this position can, of course, lead to an indefensible cultural relativism, in which languages are 'incommensurable' with each other because of their differing origins, but Hamann's objections do not lead in this direction. An appeal to the diversity made possible by the historical situatedness of languages need not entail the denial either of the possibility that they can be translated into each other, or of the possibility of arriving at shared truths. Instead, that diversity can show the value of what each language may reveal that another language may not reveal. Hamann's own counter to relativism is, of course, the God whose one creation is reflected in the diversity of natural languages. An assumption of this kind can, moreover, be sustained in a variety of ways that do not require theology. The 'regulative idea' of objectivity which the difference of languages leads us to strive for because of our shared *understanding* of the fact that we diverge relies on the same kind of assumption. The ideal here is the sustaining of a universalizing notion of objectivity along with the recognition of the importance of individual diversity.

Hamann's critique of Kant sets up a paradigmatic alternative, between attempts to establish transcendental arguments which we must assume underlie any valid cognition, and the claim that we cannot ultimately do this because all our cognition takes place within a natural language. The structures and practices involved in a natural language cannot all be reduced to general rules which we *know* to be valid for all languages. This alternative will be manifest in conflicts between philosophers oriented towards the natural sciences as their model, and philosophers who suspect that this orientation is missing a whole dimension of existence that cannot be reduced to scientific explanation. The insufficiency involved in an approach based on natural science is seen as evident in the fact that we can only ever begin scientific investigation if we already understand the world in terms of the first natural language or languages which we acquired as children. This language forms the ineliminable background without which scientific judgements themselves would not be intelligible. A scientific explanation of language will always need to employ pre-understandings that it is supposed to be explaining. We shall encounter this issue at various points in the coming chapters, and Hamann has a significant influence on those, like Heidegger and Gadamer, who make it central to their thinking.

Herder

Herder's work helped to establish modern literary scholarship, hermeneutics, anthropology, linguistics, philosophy of history, and a great deal more. The essential motivation behind his work, which had such a radical effect on the intellectual horizons of his era, was again a suspicion of the constricting effects of a narrow Enlightenment view of the world. Herder's relevance for our era is a result of his posing questions about the differences between cultures and about how those differences should be responded to. He arrives at many of his most significant explorations of these questions via his reflections on language. Matters are complicated here by the facts that Herder does not articulate his view of language in one definitive text, spreading his reflections throughout his work, and that he is not always consistent in his claims. At the same time, Herder already arrives at so many insights that he, perhaps more than Hamann – who admittedly had a decisive effect on Herder's thinking – must be regarded as the more influential initiator of the 'linguistic turn' in modern philosophy.

In his *On Recent German Literature. Fragments* (1766–8) Herder makes his groundbreaking initial assumption clear: 'If it is true that we cannot think without thoughts and that we learn to think through words: then language gives the whole of human knowledge its limits and outline' (Herder 1985: 373). Kant thinks the limits of human knowledge are dictated by the necessary mental forms in which it takes place. Before Kant even formulates his main ideas, Herder already suggests how these limits may be interpreted in terms of language as the condition of possibility of communicable knowledge. This idea, of course, now dominates large parts of contemporary philosophy. For Herder, then, 'thinking is almost nothing else but speaking' (ibid. 375). He stresses the cultural development of a language, which he links to the literature of a culture: 'The literature grew in the language and the language in the literature' (ibid.), making clear his distance from the Enlightenment view which regards language simply as the representation of pre-existing ideas. Language is instead 'the tool, the content and the form of human thoughts' (ibid. 380).

Herder then introduces a vital tension, when he asks about the effect on a language of the fact that, for a particular people (*Volk*), it is 'a tool of *their* organs, a content of *their* world of thinking and a form of *their* manner of designating'. In short, he ponders the effect of what happens when a language 'becomes a national language' (ibid. 381). The two-edged nature of this conception is important. On the one hand, a language is a means by which a culture symbolizes its identity, binding the members of a social grouping to each other. On the other, the people who do not speak this language are excluded, both because they cannot speak it and because the language will not express their world anyway. Read positively, in the manner of Hamann, Herder's conception means that people are able to explore other worlds by acquiring other languages. Read negatively, it means that one's language can become a factor in a nationalistic exclusion of 'the Other' who does not share one's language. Herder is writing, of course, at a time when there was no real political entity called Germany, so it is understandable that he concentrates on the until then largely ignored ways in which language can build culture and identity. The German language itself is by no means highly developed at this time, and Herder is one of those who helps to develop it in its modern form. However, although Herder himself has a cosmopolitan interest in linguistic diversity, conceptions of exclusion of the other on linguistic grounds will play a role in the rise of nineteenth-century nationalism. At the same time, there is an essential difference between the linguistic nationalism of an oppressed people attempting to assert themselves, and the linguistic nationalism of the kind that played a role in Nazism's attempts to 'purify' the German language of foreign words. Herder himself was thoroughly liberal and progressive, which suggests how complex an issue the relationship of language to national identity can be. Ideas which in one context are thoroughly progressive can, in a different historical context, be anything but progressive.

Herder also historicizes language in a new way which again has its positive and negative aspects. Languages function, he claims, in the manner of nature. Science and art 'germinate, bud, bloom and fade' (1964: 116), and languages do the same. He omits this metaphor in another version of this text, and concentrates instead on the idea that a language is like a human being who goes through the 'ages of man'. In the childhood stage the language is determined by affective reactions to the environment, and consists of 'tones and gestures'; it is based on feeling and instinct rather than thought. We can therefore never fully understand what this stage was like, because we have moved to the more developed stage of thought and writing. The next stage, as nature becomes less threatening and more familiar, is that language becomes 'song', by modulating the more uncontrolled sounds of the first stage. Language later becomes more able to deal with abstract concepts, but it does so on the basis of concrete sensuous experience: 'For this reason language must have been full of images and rich in metaphors' (Herder 1985: 440). This phase is followed by the time in which language reaches its youth, the 'poetic' age of language. Herder cites Greek poetry as the example of this. As language develops more rules, however, it becomes 'more complete' but also 'loses the pure poetry of nature' (ibid. 441). This is the era of 'prose' and 'philosophy', the mature era of language.

Stories like this sometimes play a disturbing role in European thought, although, once again, Herder's version of such a story is less open to question than later versions. The equation of natural processes with the development of human social characteristics can lead to biologically based conceptions which assume an inevitability or necessity where there is none. Oswald Spengler's *The Decline of the West* (1917 and 1922) relies, for example, upon the idea of human cultures as organisms which grow and then inevitably die, having lost their vitality. Herder's own conception connects more to ideas that will play a role in Romanticism, for which the modern era is characterized by the loss of a more naive relationship to language and the world. This idea is also two-edged. On the one hand, it can play a valuable role in helping generate new kinds of expression, particularly in music, which seek to overcome the perceived inadequacy of modern forms of articulation. Although this perception is oriented towards an almost certainly mythical past, it can still generate new possibilities for the future. On the other hand, the orientation towards an origin from the point of view of which the present is regarded as having 'fallen' translates something formerly expressed in religious myths into a questionable secular form. On what basis is this evaluation made?

Herder claims that 'Whatever literature (*Poesie*) may be in all eras: since prose *had* to come into existence it was definitely no longer one thing: the song of nature' (ibid. p. 470). Battles over the interpretation of modernity in Germany will be fought over such invocations of an origin which has been corrupted by modern developments, be that origin poetry, nature, the *Volk*, or something else. Herder opens up this difficult territory in his desire to emphasize the need to value particular cultural forms because they imbue the lives of the people within them with meaning. Modernity is notorious for the ways in which it can suck the meaning out of such forms and so destroy them. Natural science is a better explanation of many of the threats posed by nature than local myths which offer no real control over those threats. These myths may, though, be part of a whole web of beliefs which enable people to tolerate a world over which they otherwise have very little control. Science itself does not offer new semantic resources to replace the meanings it has disenchanted. Herder aims to defend dimensions of cultural meaning which could never be characterized in scientific terms, and which are sedimented in the history of the language of a social group. He and Hamann both oppose the Enlightenment tendency to suggest that we could or should seek a 'general philosophical language'.

The contemporary Canadian philosopher, Charles Taylor (1995), has rightly given Herder much of the credit for establishing a tradition of thinking about language that shows why the idea of language as primarily the means of representing a ready-made world may be mistaken. One of Herder's key insights is that language must be understood through its use: 'Not how an expression can be etymologically derived and determined analytically, but how it is used is the question. Origin and use are often very different' (1964: 153). Use of language has a great deal to do with tradition, and is therefore affected by a whole series of ways of acting and reacting which need to be understood historically and socially. The limited idea of language standing for things in the world here gives way to the idea that language can do a whole variety of things, only some of which can be thought of in terms of representation. This idea will be central to the work of the later Wittgenstein, Gadamer, Habermas and others.

The Origin of Language

None of the arguments seen so far, however, explains how it is that there is language at all. Herder returns to this question at various points in his work, and does not give a consistent answer to it. Despite this, his attempts to answer the question lead him to other new insights. The problem about explaining the origin of language is the following. If language is to be language, rather than mere noises or animal signals, it seems to require reason, in the sense of coherent thought, to make the sounds into meanings. On the other hand, if we can only think in language, for reason to exist at all it would require language as its condition of possibility. In that case, though, it is not clear what makes language into language. At this point Hamann's theological argument shows its logical consistency. Without some further foundation, which is itself already meaningful, like the Divinity, the origin of neither language nor reason seems explicable. In the famous, but flawed, *Essay on the Origin of Language* (1772) Herder makes it clear that he understands the problem, but then tries to solve it by decree. The positions he opposes in the *Essay* are Johann Peter Süssmilch's claims for a divine origin, Condillac's claim that language develops from animal cries, and Rousseau's argument that language results from the need to articulate emotions and desires. Herder goes to the heart of the real problem in objecting to Süssmilch's idea that language is needed for the employment of reason. If reason cannot function without language, it cannot be right for Süssmilch to argue that 'no person can have invented language for themselves because reason is required for the invention of language'. The consequence of this is that 'language would have already had to be there before it was there' (Herder 1966: 36). The result is a circle in which 'Without language and reason humankind is incapable of divine instruction, and without divine instruction it has no reason and language ... How can humankind learn language by divine instruction if it has no reason?' (ibid. 37).

Herder's answer to this circle is that 'In order to be capable of the first syllable of divine instruction mankind had, as Herr Süssmilch himself admits, to be a human being, that is be able to think clearly, and with the first clear thought language was already in his soul; it was therefore invented with his own means and not by divine instruction' (ibid.). This answer clearly does not work, because the idea of what can invent something already presupposes thought, yet thought is supposed to depend on language. Herder wants to argue that our very nature is inherently linguistic. The strength of this position lies in the way that he implicitly rejects the premise of 'inventing' language, seeing it rather as something inherent in us. However, this still leaves the question as to why it is part of our species which other species largely lack. Herder was obviously aware of the difficulty because in 1784–5 he argues that all humankind's natural attributes – 'brain, senses and hand' – would be useless 'if the Creator had not given us a motivating force which sets them all in motion. It was the *divine gift of language*. Only by language is the sleeping gift of reason awoken' (1964: 163). In effect, he adopts the position of his friend Hamann, accepting that the circle he shows in the *Essay* does not admit of a non-theological solution.

Despite this serious difficulty, Herder's attempted solution in the *Essay* does reveal a vital problem with the positions of Condillac and Rousseau, namely that they fail to explain the difference between language and what precedes it. Herder introduces the notion of 'reflection' ('*Besonnenheit*'), the ability, as Taylor puts it, 'to grasp something *as* what it is', rather than just react to it in the manner of animals, who respond instinctively to the stimuli in their environment (1995: 103). Taylor refers to Herder's conception of language as 'expressive'. Rather than representing things which are already there as themselves, language makes manifest aspects of things that would otherwise not be manifest. Reflection is the ability to take a 'characteristic' of something; it singles out the object *as* something particular. The world, as Hamann suggested, therefore can be articulated in an unlimited number of ways, depending upon the resources of differing languages. Heidegger (see chapter 10) will refer to the 'as-structure of understanding' which characterizes our essential 'being in the world', where our practical needs and desires lead us to see things as means or obstacles to those needs and desires. This structure is what Herder describes by the notion of 'reflection'. Humankind is able, via reflection, to form hugely diverse kinds of world, from the world in which a tree is the repository of a spirit, to the world in which the tree is where one leaves one's signature in a vain attempt to communicate with a lost lover, to the world in which a tree is a means of producing oxygen for the polluted atmosphere.

The image of language which this entails is 'holistic'. Things do not exist in isolation, but rather within a web of human practices, where what we term one thing affects what we term other things. Language therefore cannot be understood piecemeal, because each piece is only comprehensible in relation to other pieces. Herder's resistance to the idea that we should determine what an expression means 'analyti-cally' is based on the fact that he sees the use of language as part of being in a world. This way of being is prior to the results of the analy-sis of meanings in a given language. As Taylor suggests, then, Herder establishes a model of language which is at odds with the one which came to dominate English-language philosophy for a significant part of the twentieth century. This model was concerned precisely with trying to establish meanings for utterances piecemeal, as though there were separate objects called meanings which theories could identify (see chapter 8).

The tension between these two ways of proceeding, the holistic and the analytical, affects the history of modern German philosophy in a variety of ways. The success of modern science in problem-solving undoubtedly has much to do with the analytical method which Hamann and Herder associate with their criticisms of the Enlighten-ment. There is clearly a danger, then, in laying exclusive emphasis on the idea of language as what constitutes a world in the aesthetic sense seen in this chapter. Without the kind of thinking which Kant maps out, which insists on the analytical dimension of thought that tran-scends particular natural languages, many of the most significant advances in modernity would be inconceivable. At the same time, although the natural sciences are necessary to human survival, they are not sufficient. As Gadamer puts it, echoing the essential insight of Hamann and Herder: 'It is obvious that not mathematics but the linguistic nature of people is the basis of human civilization' (1993: 342). This tension between the ways of disclosing the world which precede scientific forms and the conceptualization of the world in scientific terms will re-emerge in the following chapters.

SUGGESTIONS FOR FURTHER READING

Berlin, I. (1976) *Vico and Herder. Two Studies in the History of Ideas* (London: Hogarth Press). *Lively, if rather shallow, account of two major thinkers about language.*

Berlin, I. (1993) *The Magus of the North: J. G. Hamann and the Origins of Modern Irrationalism* (London: John Murray). *One of the few works in English on Hamann, but suffers from inaccuracy and a questionable conception of irrationalism.*

Clark, R. C. (1955) *Herder. His Life and Thought* (Berkeley: University of California Press). *Standard account of Herder's biography and philosophy.*

German, T. (1981) *Hamann on Language and Religion* (Oxford: Oxford University Press). *Account by Hamann scholar.*

Norton, R. E. (1991) *Herder's Aesthetics and the European Enlightenment* (Ithaca: Cornell University Press). *Readable account of Herder and his relation to his contemporaries.*

Zammito, J. H. (2001) *Kant, Herder, and the Birth of Anthropology* (Chicago: Chicago University Press). *Interesting contextualization of the thought of Kant and Herder.*

3

GERMAN IDEALISM: FROM FICHTE TO THE EARLY SCHELLING

The Limits of Self-Determination

The two directions in the reactions to Kant to be considered in this and the following two chapters offer a model of philosophical alternatives which still affect philosophy today, and which have had considerable social, political and aesthetic effects in the intervening period. The first of these directions, German Idealism, tries to build on the aspects of Kant which, if they could successfully be taken beyond what Kant himself thought was possible, would provide a firm philosophical foundation for modernity.[1] German Idealism aims to demonstrate that our thinking relates to a nature which is intelligibly structured in the same way as our thinking is structured, thus overcoming Kant's division between nature as appearance, and things in themselves. Early German Romantic philosophy, on the other hand, raises questions about some of what German Idealism seeks to achieve, even before German Idealism is fully developed in the work of Hegel. The major figure in this context is Johann Gottlieb Fichte (1762–1814), whose response to Kant was decisive for both German Idealism and Romanticism.[2]

Kant's concern was with the capacity of the subject both to attain knowledge of the world and to be self-determining. The question is how far this capacity for knowledge and self-determination extends.

---

1   I shall capitalize Idealism when referring to German Idealism, but not when referring more generally to idealism.
2   It should be remembered that Kant lived until 1804, so that many of the philosophical innovations at issue here occurred during his lifetime.

Kant makes the spontaneity of the subject the core of his philosophy, but he does so while insisting on the limits of the subject's capacities by his refusal to allow positive, 'dogmatic' claims about the intelligible world. Two schematic alternatives tend to emerge here. Either the restrictions which Kant puts on the subject's thinking are not defensible, because without the subject's activity nothing could be intelligible at all, or the laws of the objectively knowable world determine what we know and what we do. The latter alternative still informs theories, such as 'physicalism', which regard the natural sciences as decisive in the last analysis for all true accounts of the world. The former alternative is what informs the origins of German Idealism. German Idealism is directed against the equivalent of physicalism in its time, the materialist philosophy of some parts of the Enlightenment.

Philosophical 'idealism' can be summed up in Bishop Berkeley's (1685–1753) claim that 'being is perceiving'. Berkeley's idea is that things exist solely as perceptions – how else, after all, do we *know* they exist? Even Kant thinks that being 'real' means being available to be perceived. German Idealism should, though, not be assumed to be another form of Berkeleyan idealism. Its main proponents regard Kant as the source of their approach, and Kant does not accept Berkeley's idealism. Kant's refutation of idealism is, however, not convincing. The basic issue in German Idealism is the extent to which the subject's conceptions are the result of its own activity, or are the result of the effects of the world on the subject. Emphasis on the former view results from doubts about whether the object side of the relationship between subject and world is decisive in what we know. After all, as Descartes discovered, the science of the ancients proved to be largely unreliable when tested with the means developed by the new science of his day, even though its validity had until then been largely unquestioned. These days, Richard Rorty (1998) argues that we are tied to the world causally, but that what we think is true cannot be understood in terms of causal effects. This is because causal effects can be talked about in an indeterminate number of ways, which depend on how different vocabularies divide up the world. In a feudal world assumptions about the nature of objectivity are linked to the transcendent authority of God. When feudalism loses its legitimation, *all* kinds of authority are likely to be called into question, and the ability to ask questions about authority liberates a huge amount of intellectual energy. The danger is, of course, that this new freedom might end up being as arbitrary in imposing a new world-picture as what it replaces turns out to have been, and fear of this consequence has significant cultural effects in Germany. The problem German

Idealism faces is, then, establishing the *extent* of the subject's legislative role. How is the relationship between subject and object to be
conceived, once subject and object cease to be fixed quantities?

In France, what underlies these issues could be said to be played
out in reality, in the Revolution of 1789, which poses vital questions
about legitimacy in modernity. These questions arise precisely
because the assumed bases of knowledge and action can easily
become arbitrary: the Terror is carried out, after all, in the name of
Reason. In Germany the issues are largely only played out in thought,
and, of course, in art. (Think of the way Beethoven's music moves
from the heroic expression of new-found freedom to the more reflective manner of his later work.) As the Revolution in France becomes
more violent, responses in Germany to questions about the subject's
legislative role change. They move from the conviction that the
subject is ultimately decisive, to a sense that the subject may never
be fully transparent to itself, and so could not be an unquestionable
foundation for the new philosophy.

Foundationalism and the Subject

Fichte himself was an enthusiastic supporter of the Revolution and
wrote texts defending it in 1793 and 1794, at the same time that he
was developing his major philosophical ideas. He is, though, also
known for his later 'Speeches to the German Nation', of 1806, which
are seen by some as part of the development of nationalist thought
in Germany that leads to the Nazis. His work illustrates the difficulties in assessing the German Idealist concentration on the prior role
of the activity of the subject. From one perspective, Fichte's making
the subject central to philosophy is part of the modern liberation
from feudal ideas; from another, it is part of an arrogance in modernity which leads to the disasters occasioned by nationalism and by
the conviction that any particular human conception can possess
absolute authority.

In his major work of theoretical philosophy, the '*Wissenschaftslehre*' (the 'Doctrine of Science'), the beginnings of which were published in 1794, Fichte claims to be a Kantian, and reading Kant was
undoubtedly the decisive event in his intellectual development.[3]

3   Fichte use the name '*Wissenschaftslehre*' for the subsequent versions of his theoretical
philosophy, though his ideas later changed in significant respects from those outlined here.
There is no definitive version of the work, and I shall be mainly referring to the earlier versions, which were most influential in Fichte's time. It is only in recent years that attention
has begun to be focused on his later work.

Indeed, the work which first made him famous, the *Attempt at a Critique of All Revelation*, was for some reason published without his name on it, and was initially assumed to be by Kant. However, Fichte's emphasis on certain aspects of Kant to the exclusion of others led Kant himself to reject Fichte's interpretation as untenable.[4] The questions Fichte explores derive from Kant's simultaneous insistence on the spontaneous nature of the subject's cognitive and moral activity, and on the inaccessibility of things in themselves. For Kant, human freedom was situated in the 'intelligible' realm of things in themselves, and was therefore inaccessible to cognition. However, if both theoretical and practical reason are inaccessible to philosophical explanation, their very nature would seem to be in doubt.[5] What is the *purpose* of knowledge and action, that takes them beyond being merely the arbitrary doings of one particular species and makes them morally significant? Kant sought answers to these questions, but his answers did not satisfy his successors.

Fichte claims that theoretical and practical reason have a common source in the subject's spontaneity. Fichte's key thought is actually quite simple, despite the formidable difficulties of his texts. It results from his attempt to explore Kant's claims in genetic terms. If nature is merely the realm of mechanical objectivity based on laws, how does it give rise to beings who are capable both of knowing those laws and of acting against their natural instincts? Even to regard nature as a deterministic system means presupposing something other than determinism, otherwise it is not clear how the concept of determinism is to be understood at all. Why would the world produce beings who seek to *know* about what produces them, if the world were merely a series of arbitrary causal chains? We assume that the objective, material world existed before there were thinking beings. It is, furthermore, true that we would not think at all if we did not have a material brain which developed during the history of the evolution of the species. The question is, though, why brains involve self-consciousness and the capacity for self-determination, which do not seem to be reducible to what they are as mechanisms. Inert, objective matter could presumably have remained in an unorganized, 'mindless' state. There seems to be nothing in the laws of physics, chemistry or biology to show *why* it does not do so. These laws can explain how things develop once there is organization in nature. They do not

4   In his last, incomplete, work, the *Opus Posthumum*, Kant seems, however, to come very close to what Fichte was arguing.
5   This kind of doubt was one reason for Kant's interpretation of beauty as a visible symbol of morality in the third Critique.

explain the fact that nature could itself be seen to entail the condition of possibility of the move from mere material existence to being organized and being an object of knowledge *to itself*. The beings that come to know about nature are themselves part of nature. The choice here is either to attempt to eliminate the 'subjective' aspect, or to give an account of subjectivity which can fit into a defensible account of modern science, and this is one of the aims of German Idealism.

Fichte argues that the 'absolute I', which cannot be construed in merely objective terms, is the ultimate foundation of the world. Whether this notion can really be made intelligible is open to question, as we shall see, but the aim of the term is clear. The point is to counter the idea that the prior aspect of existence is its objective, law-bound functioning. This does not, however, mean that Fichte thinks 'Mind', in some quasi-theological sense, creates the material world. Although some of Fichte's formulations might be understood in this manner, it is more plausible to interpret him as claiming that the fact that there is an *objective* world entails something which is prior to that world if the world is to be manifest *as* objective at all. Something can, in these terms, only be an object if, as the two parts of the German word '*Gegen-stand*' suggest, it 'stands against' what it is not, namely the subject, the I. The question is how *my* individual subjective thinking relates to this essential 'subjective' principle. It is here that significant difficulties arise in the relationship between the individual's particular subjective place in the world and the general principle of 'subjectivity'. Both Schleiermacher, and, in his wake, Kierkegaard, will later object to reducing the individual to such a general principle.

The problem Fichte confronts is a version of foundationalism, the search for a point of absolute certainty from which philosophy can begin to construct a true picture of the world. In theology this is the certainty of God's existence and the impossibility that He is a deceiver. For Descartes it is the 'I think, I am', the one certainty that puts a stop to sceptical doubt. Fichte's position is generated by the following reflection: if everything in the objective world is caused by something else, which is caused by something else in turn, each thing in the world is dependent on what causes it, and so on. This seems to mean that everything is relative and that nothing is absolute. However, Kant claimed in his idea of 'causality through freedom' that freedom is *not* dependent on any prior cause. This gives freedom some kind of absolute status, but interpreting this status is one of the major problems for German Idealism.

Karl Leonhard Reinhold (1758–1823), who was the first to make Kant's work more accessible to a wider audience, tried to suggest that the foundation of Kant's position lay in what he called the 'fact of consciousness'. Reinhold gives a very clear version of foundationalism: 'No proposition which can be completely determined and secured against misunderstanding *only by other propositions* can be accepted in philosophy as an *absolutely first fundamental proposition.*' Such a fundamental proposition 'must not be able or be allowed to receive its sense via any other proposition' (1978: 353). For Reinhold, this proposition is the 'proposition of consciousness': *'the representation in consciousness* [i.e. any idea that is conscious] *is differentiated by the subject from the object and the subject, and related to both'* (ibid. 78). This proposition is a version of what Kant meant by the 'transcendental unity of apperception'. For there to be consciousness at all it must have an object to be conscious of. However, for what is thought to *be* a thought it must both not be the object (because it is a representation of the object) and it must be connected to a subject which thinks. At the same time, however, the subject must be aware that the object is not itself, otherwise there could be no consciousness of an *object*, as that which 'stands against' the subject. Reinhold insists that no definition can be given of this underlying fact of consciousness, because all definitions require what is defined to be related to something else.

In an influential text, *Aenesidemus* (1792), Gottlob Ernst Schulze (1761–1833) pointed out that this supposedly immediately certain 'fact' actually relied on an inference about what must be the case from the nature of our experience. Fichte's response is to argue that what is mistaken in Reinhold's conception is the very idea that there is a 'fact of consciousness'. Facts are what exist in the world of objects, and they are necessarily 'finite', in the sense of being limited by other facts. Consciousness is, in contrast, Fichte argues, a 'deed-action', a *'Tathandlung'*. Its very nature is *not* to be objective like a fact, but rather to resist objectification by being active and by not being determined by anything but itself. This makes self-consciousness irreducible to any explanation of the kind applicable to the deterministic natural world.

Fichte's claim that the I which is the foundation of philosophy is 'self-positing' can be made sense of in these terms. For Kant, 'reality' is the 'position' of something as an object in relation to the perceiving subject. The nature of the thing depends on the conceptual activity of the subject, which itself depends on the transcendental unity of apperception. The subject's own reality cannot be the same as the reality of what it knows, which is always relative, or what German Idealism calls 'mediated'. What the subject knows depends for its intelligibility on the ability to link things to other things that are the same as them or different from them. The subject must therefore be 'immediate' for it to be the ground of knowledge, otherwise it would depend for its identity upon its 'mediating' relations to something else. For the subject to be immediate Fichte thinks it must generate itself, as it would otherwise be part of an endless chain of determinations by other things, like the world of objects. His argument therefore extends what Kant meant by the subject's spontaneity. The argument is, moreover, not as implausible as it might first sound. Even though the resistance of the objective world may feel to us like the prior reality, there could be no such resistance without a prior subjective principle that could feel it *as* resistance. The job of philosophy is therefore to give an account of *how* the I is the source of the intelligibility of the world opposed to it. However, the nature of this opposition involves a crucial further problem, namely the 'thing in itself'.

German Idealism attempts to overcome Kant's separation of mind, and nature 'in itself'. The plausible aspect of this attempt lies in the fact that a wholesale separation of the two sides makes it hard to show how they relate at all. We saw in the last chapter how Hamann criticized the separation in Kant between the a priori and the empirical. It was a friend of Hamann's, the writer and philosopher F. H. Jacobi (1743–1819), who really brought one of the decisive problems home to thinkers at the time. Jacobi's point is quite simple. In his 'On Transcendental Idealism' (1787), he asks how appearances arise in the subject at all. Kant claims that appearances are caused by things in themselves, by what he terms the 'transcendental X'. The problem is, Jacobi points out, that Kant is not using the notion of causality consistently. Causality is a category of the transcendental subject. It is one of the forms of thought without which 'experience', in Kant's sense of intuitions judged in terms of categories and concepts, is not possible. A causal connection is therefore a connection between two *appearances* separated in time, one of which follows the other of necessity, and it is brought about by the active judgement of the subject. It cannot, then, be a connection between something which does not appear and something which does, let alone a connection between the intelligible and the empirical world. The realm of appearances is temporal; that of things in themselves cannot be temporal, because time is the form in which the *subject* apprehends things as appearances. However, without some connection, which would explain the source of appearances in something separate from the subject, the appearances would seem to have to be generated by the subject alone. The route to a strong version of idealism therefore seems open.

The Idealist Claim

Another version of the objection to Kant we have just encountered was decisive for Fichte. While Jacobi formulates his objection to Kant in the name of a realism which sought to avoid the problematic residue of a wholly inaccessible thing in itself, the other objection is made in the name of the *opposite* position, namely a thoroughgoing idealism, which seeks to dissolve the thing in itself altogether. This convergence between opposed positions will be important in German Idealism. Its proponents seek to overcome the division between realism and idealism, but they tend to end up on one side of the divide, despite themselves.

When Kant revised the first Critique for the new edition of 1787 he added a section on the 'refutation of idealism', because too many people had interpreted him as arguing, in the manner of Berkeley, that reality could consist of nothing but perceptions. One needs here to distinguish between what Kant means by 'reality', and what he means by 'being'. Something's being 'real' depends for Kant upon its being given to perception, and this determines *what* the thing is judged to be. 'This x is a table' ascribes a predicate to something perceived, but one could also say 'This x is a series of pieces of wood, a brown object, weighs 30 pounds etc.'. 'This table exists', on the other hand, just posits the existence of something, even if it turns out not to be a table, but something else. Kant argued from early on in his career that saying that 'x exists' is not attributing the predicate 'existence' to x in the way we can attribute 'table', 'brown object', etc. to x. *That* there is something is the condition of possibility of predicating *what* something can be described as, be it as table, wood, or whatever. If the thing does not exist at all, nothing real can be predicated of it. This argument is the basis of Kant's rejection of the 'ontological' proof of God, the claim that without existence God would lack an essential predicate, so that He would not be God at all. It might be argued that there are essential predicates that define God. However, if existence cannot be regarded as a predicate, because without it there can be no predicates at all, then the notion of existence cannot be used to argue that God must exist because he would otherwise lack an essential predicate.

The difficulty for Kant in relation to the question of idealism is that if something's being real depends upon its being perceivable, there seems to be no reason not to accept Berkeley's claim that 'being is perceiving'. Kant, however, rejects this position via the claim that things in themselves, which exist independently of perception, are the

cause of perceptions. He does so because he thinks the realist intuition that things exist in a manner which is independent of what we
think they are must be correct. His actual argument against idealism
is, as he himself seems to have been aware, at best of limited use in
establishing this, and this is part of what opens the door to Fichte and
his successors.

The most acute initial idealist objection to Kant was formulated
by Salomon Maimon (1753?–1800), an intriguing Polish Jew whose
tragic life story did not prevent him from impressing the great
thinkers of his era, including Kant himself. Kant argues that my temporal 'inner sense' depends upon the external spatial world in which
things persist in their existence. However, he does not take account
of the fact that the supposedly independent reality of this external
world is, in his own terms, dependent upon our *perceiving* these
external things. Kant's claim therefore does not refute idealism at all,
because perceptions pertain to the subject and space itself is the form
in which objects appear to the subject. All the idealist needs is now
to assume there are two kinds of consciousness, both of which are
ways in which the *subject* feels things to be: awareness of one's own
existence as thinking ('apperceptive' awareness), and awareness of
things. Neither of these can provide a proof of the existence of independent things in themselves. Kant argues that the former awareness
depends on the latter, but the very continuity of the existence of
things would seem, in the terms of the transcendental deduction, to
depend on the continuity of the *self*, not of the things. It is this idea
that leads to Maimon's version of idealism. Maimon attempts to show
why, despite one's apparently unshakable conviction of the independent existence of things, it may be more plausible to argue for a strong
version of idealism. Even if his overall argument does not finally convince, its assumptions will resonate in many philosophers after him.

Kant was understood as having divided the subject into a wholly
passive receptive aspect, and an active, spontaneous aspect. It is,
however, arguable that even the apparently passive aspect of perception is in fact active, albeit to a lesser degree than when we actively
judge something to be the case. If this is so, argues Maimon, we must
seek the answer to the explanation of apparently external things in
the nature of the subject. Kant's attempt to argue that things in themselves cause appearances actually reinforces the argument. Kant uses
the (subjective) *category* of causality to infer the existence of things
in themselves, and the inference is carried out on the basis of the
sensation supposedly occasioned by the thing in itself, which is *also*
inherently subjective. Why, though, does the world of objects feel
wholly independent of us? If it cannot be convincingly argued that

this is because it really is independent of us – in Maimon's view that makes it impossible to explain how the separate spheres of subject and world could be connected – the apparently objective world must be produced by the subject, even though it is not aware of doing so.

This is Maimon's key contention, which is picked up and developed by Fichte. What appears as the external world is therefore seen as the *unconscious* product of the activity of the I. The conscious, receptive part that feels the resistance of the objects is only the less active mode of action of the subject. If the objective world were not a product of the I, the problem of the causality of the thing in itself would just be repeated. How does the I come to have perceptions at all if causality by external things cannot be used to explain them? How can the activity of the understanding bring things into its power if their source is something wholly alien to the understanding? Kant had tried to get round this problem by introducing 'schematism' as a bridge between the empirical and the a priori, but this is an arbitrary attempt to cross a gap that might better be crossed by dropping the idea that there is any real dualism between mind and world at all. The solution mapped out by Maimon and developed by Fichte might, though, seem bizarre, as though we each created the world by the unconscious activity of our thought.

Before moving to an explanation of how we can arrive at a plausible interpretation of Maimon's and Fichte's claim, it is important note their refusal to accept Kant's division of the passive and the active in the subject. Kant argues for a strict demarcation between the spontaneous contribution of the mind, and the external effects of the world on the receptivity of the subject. Hamann realized that if language was a condition of possibility of thought, and language was acquired receptively but could only *be* meaningful language via the activity of the mind, then this strict distinction could not be sustained. The alternatives to Kant's conception seek to break down any kind of fundamental split between the subjective and the objective, the active and the passive.[6] If the avoidance of such a split is sought in the name of foundationalism, the result is, though, likely to be the kind of idealism we have begun to examine. The other possibility will be the Romantic anti-foundationalist acknowledgement of the impossibility of decisively characterizing where the division between the two sides lies. Instead of plumping for the elevation of the subject to the status of an absolute subject, this position will at times seek

6 Kant insists that the receptive and the spontaneous are always both required for knowledge, but this assumes that we can separate what is receptive and what is spontaneous, which is where the real problem lies.

also to avoid characterizing the issue in terms of subjective or objective at all. How, though, can sense be made of the idealist position of Maimon and Fichte, and why did it lead to the further developments in German Idealism that still have a significant effect on philosophy today?

Fichtean Idealism

If one wants to avoid the incoherent idea of an exclusively objective, causally determined world that mysteriously gives rise to spontaneous subjectivity, the assumption has to be that the world is somehow inherently subjective, and that its objective aspect is secondary and derived. Our individual thinking is in this view a part of 'subjectivity' in a very emphatic sense: part, namely, of the 'absolute subject'. This subject is not relative to, and dependent upon, anything else, because it would otherwise raise the question as to what *its* ground is, which would then itself have to be absolute. A materialist might, for example, claim that this ground is actually material nature, without which mind would be impossible, but the idealist question would then again be: 'But how does material, causally bound nature give rise to non-causally bound subjectivity?' What we have here is a decisive German Idealist thought, namely that the structures of the individual subject's thought are, when properly understood and articulated, the same structures as those which inform the rest of the world.

Consider the living organism. The material of which an organism consists will be replaced over the life-cycle of the organism, so that there may after a certain time be no material part of the organism that is the same as it initially was. The 'idea' of the organism is therefore prior to its material instantiation. Do we not regard ourselves as the same person, even though the material of which we consist will be replaced throughout our lives? A merely material world, in the sense of one governed solely by endless chains of causal laws, would lack the principles of organic life. It would, furthermore, never come to the point of producing that which can know it. The question confronted by Fichte, Schelling and Hegel is how to overcome the resistance of the thing in itself and move beyond the Kantian model.

Fichte's answer is to argue for the absolute foundational priority of the subjective principle. He has, though, to find a way of explaining the resistance of the objective world which does not try to conjure away its independence of the way we might want it to be. It is not that Fichte thinks everything can be subordinated to the subject. He is aware of the resistance of things and the objectivity of natural laws, but he also wishes to insist that without the principle of subjectivity this resistance would not exist *as* resistance at all, so there would be no reason to strive to know things. His very influential idea is that the subject becomes divided against itself. The absolute I splits into an I (consciousness) and a not-I (the objective world) that are relative to each other. The I is thus understood as an 'acting upon itself', something which we can understand via our ability to reflect upon our thoughts and actions. Given that the absolute I is 'infinite', this self-limitation creates the constant demand for it to overcome any limitation.

Fichte claims that the core of our subjectivity is our freedom as moral beings who can transcend the finite world of causally determined things. We do this both by knowing these things, and by action to make things the way they *ought* to be, rather than accept them the way they already are. Quite *why* this self-limitation takes place remains obscure, and things become even more obscure when Fichte introduces the idea that the 'infinite activity' of the I is 'checked' and 'driven back into itself'. His aim is to sustain the idea of the resistance of the objective world to the subject, without falling back into the problems inherent in materialism. The main point is that what he calls the 'check' (*Anstoß*) on the 'infinite activity' of the subject results in an increasingly articulated awareness of objects. This begins with the bare 'feeling' of something, as the lowest form of awareness, then develops into more specific 'sensation', into 'intuition' as a more distinct kind of perception and, finally, into the 'concept'.

All this takes place within something which is itself ultimately undivided, the absolute I. All our attempts to understand this I are, however, made from the perspective of the I of the philosophizing subject. This subject is both limited and yet endowed with what can take it beyond limitation, namely its freedom to be self-determining and to reflect philosophically. Questionable as this may be, the idea that we should understand the nature of things in terms of a constant interaction between expansion and limitation should not simply be dismissed. What is at issue is the understanding of a world which is regarded not as a timeless, objective nature, but rather as what constantly changes and develops. Differing understandings of the relationship between the expansive, free possibilities of self-consciousness and the constraints imposed by the objective world are what divide Kant and the Romantics from the German Idealists. The model of a conflict between two aspects of existence that are ultimately the same will link Fichte, Schelling, Hegel, Schopenhauer, Nietzsche and others. The link comes about because they all wish to understand the conflictual nature of finite existence: the Idealists in the name of a foundational philosophy which seeks to overcome finitude; those who move away from Idealism in the name of coming to terms with the inescapability of finitude.

What still remains relevant to philosophical debate is Fichte's insistence on the irreducibility of subjectivity to what can be said about it in objective terms. Before moving on, we need, though, very briefly to take in a further vital aspect of his work. So far we have looked at the subject–object relationship, which is located within the overall structure of an absolute I. What, though, of the relationship between my subjectivity and that of other *subjects*? How is intersubjectivity possible in Fichte's terms? Any moral thinking worthy of the name has to begin with the awareness that others are themselves subjects, and not merely objects for my ends. German Idealism seeks a way of accounting for the fact that I can become able to regard other thinking beings as the same as myself. Thinking would seem to be something which I can only be certain that I do, because there is no way in which I can have direct access to another's consciousness. The problem of how we can come to take the other as the same as ourselves is therefore not easily soluble.

In *Foundation of Natural Law According to Principles of the Wissenschaftslehre* (1796–7) Fichte examines this issue in terms of the 'demand' or 'solicitation' (*'Aufforderung'*) to free action which can be made in relation to the subject by another subject. What stops this being a relationship between a subject and a merely extraneous object is that, unlike the feeling of limitation occasioned by the objective world which gives rise to knowledge of the necessities in nature, the 'demand' makes the I determine *itself* to act in some manner. The I does so on the basis of its understanding that the 'object' which is the source of the demand – i.e. another subject – also possesses 'the concept of reason and freedom' (Fichte 1971: iii. 36). This process must be mutual: each depends on the other as the condition of its awareness of its *own* freedom. The structure involved here, the structure of reflection, is crucial for German Idealism: in it, something can only realize what it is by its being reflected back to itself by something else. I understand my freedom via somebody else's demand, which brings me to the realization both of my freedom and of the freedom of the other. A reflection occurs via a splitting of something into itself and an other that is related to itself. When you look in the mirror, there is the you doing the looking and the you being looked at. Without the separation there is no reflection, but then the question is: how is it that the other is also in some sense you?

Fichte's conception is clearly appealing as a metaphysical answer to how self and other can reciprocally acknowledge their equality, and it will be crucial to Hegel. However, the problem with this structure, as Schelling already shows in his 1800 *System of Transcendental Idealism*, is that for it to work I would *already* have to be aware of what it is to exercise my freedom *before* the demand. Otherwise there would be no way of *understanding* another subject's demand that I exercise my freedom in relation to the demand. How would I understand what they are referring to, given that freedom is not something that I can learn to understand by observing the behaviour of other beings? Such beings only become subjects for me if I acknowledge their demand, but this is precisely the problem: what makes their demand into what Fichte thinks it is?

This is not a trivial objection. There is a decisive difference between (1) the claim that this reciprocal, reflective relationship reveals that self-conscious beings partake of a universal shared structure, and (2) the claim that any attempt to describe such a structure depends on an awareness or a way of being which is *external* to the structure. In the latter case the structure cannot function as the foundation for claims about intersubjectivity because there is an awareness which cannot be dissolved into the intersubjective relationship. This awareness has to exist before any reflective relationship is possible, so it cannot be made into a *result* of reflection. Think of this in terms of reflecting yourself in a mirror. Knowing that it is your *own* reflection requires knowing something that the mirror cannot convey: how do you decide whether the person is you or not? To learn that the reflected object is yourself requires some knowledge beyond the relationship between your real face and the reflected face. The implications of this rather difficult point should not be underestimated. One way in which Fichte's idea of intersubjectivity will be employed by subsequent philosophers is to regard *language* as the shared structure or 'mirror' via which I am supposed to realize who and what I am. The question just posed concerning the structure of reflection actually hits at the very heart of any attempt to arrive at an Idealist system. Such a system cannot allow anything to be external to the system, as this will introduce the problems of the thing itself in another guise.

Nature and Mind: Schelling

In the *Foundation of Natural Law* Fichte remarks that even if we were to attribute 'intelligence and freedom' to nature, nature itself could not be regarded as being able to grasp the 'concept of purpose'. A purpose is required to change something from one state to another

on the basis of a concept: a tree into a table to eat off, for example.
This is because 'nothing is outside [nature] upon which it could work',
as opposed to what is the case for beings endowed with reason, who
can seek to realize their purposes in the external, objective world of
nature: 'Everything that can be worked upon is nature' (Fichte 1971:
iii. 38), and nature cannot purposively work upon itself. The argument
makes sense if nature is regarded in Kantian terms as the realm of
objects governed by necessary laws. However, this view of nature as
the not-I then seems to entail something like a dualist assumption.
The difficulty always lies in how two sides can be connected if they
are supposed to be of a different order from each other. If nature is
merely objective and deterministic, then its relationship to subjectivity becomes problematic. Fichte's solution to this problem was the
idea of an absolute I which includes both individual consciousnesses
and nature within it, as relative I and not-I, but this raises some difficult questions. The idea that the world is both objective and yet also
somehow subjective can be explored in other ways, and the philosophy of F. W. J. Schelling (1775–1854) is based on that exploration.

The importance of Schelling's alternative conception is evident
from the following pattern of thought, which will later recur in Heidegger and Adorno. If nature is regarded merely as that which can
be worked upon, it becomes completely subordinated to the power
of the subject. Indeed, Fichte sees the aim of practical reason as
making nature into the way it ought to be. However, unless reason
can be completely transparent to itself, so that the purposes it sets for
itself can claim to be unquestionably valid, the possibility cannot be
excluded that reason is actually based on something else, which is not
necessarily 'rational'. When Fichte argues that the 'I cannot be conscious of its activity in the production of what is intuited' (ibid. i. 230),
i.e. in becoming aware of things, he opens up the possibility that the
activity which gives rise to the objective world is beyond any rational analysis and may only become accessible in some other way. One
possibility is that this motivational basis of thought is actually a drive
to overcome anything which threatens the existence of the subject.
In that case 'reason' might be a kind of fig-leaf for what is actually
the self-preservation of the subject. The later Heidegger will stylize
this position into a verdict on modern philosophy as a whole, which
is supposedly all based on the subject as a principle of domination
(see chapter 10).

Schelling's early work is characterized by its ambivalence with
regard to the questions raised here. On the one hand, he is attracted
by Fichte's insistence on the irreducibility of the subject to objective
explanation; on the other, he is convinced that nature must not be

regarded as something merely objective. In one version of his philosophy he seeks an account of nature which gets over the dualism entailed by Kant's separation of appearances and things in themselves, but without this leading to the assumption of an absolute I. The idea is as follows: if the essence of nature is that it produces subjectivity, nature itself can be construed as inherently subjective. This idea can be read either as a version of what Fichte proposes, or as a version of the most controversial philosophy of the late eighteenth century in Germany, the philosophy of Baruch Spinoza (1632–77), the Dutch rationalist of the seventeenth century. To understand why, we must take a look at a further influential idea of Jacobi's.

In 1783 Jacobi had become involved in a dispute, which came to be known as the 'Pantheism Controversy' (see Beiser 1987), with the Berlin Enlightenment philosopher, Moses Mendelssohn. The dispute was over the claim that G. E. Lessing (1729–81) had admitted to being a Spinozist, an admission which at that time was tantamount to the admission of atheism, with all the dangerous political and other consequences that entailed. In his *On the Doctrine of Spinoza in Letters to Herr Moses Mendelssohn* (1785, second edition 1789), Jacobi revealed a problem which recurs in differing ways throughout Schelling's work, and which haunts German Idealism as a whole. Jacobi is concerned with the relationship between what he termed the 'unconditioned' and the 'conditioned', between, crudely, the absolute and the relative. Spinoza's God is that which is not relative to anything else, of which the laws of nature are the result.[7] The laws of nature are all relative to each other: they 'condition' each other; only the whole, God, is 'unconditioned'. Cognitive explanation of any phenomenon therefore relies, as Kant argued, upon finding a thing's 'condition'. Spinoza's essential thought is that saying what something is depends on saying what it is not. He sums this up in the idea that all determination is negation. This idea can be illustrated by the claim in structuralist linguistics that there are no positive terms in a language, each term gaining its distinctness by its relations to what it is not: 'cat' is not 'bat' is not 'hat', etc.

Jacobi asks how finding a thing's condition can finally ground its explanation. Any explanation leads to a regress in which one condition depends upon another condition, ad infinitum. A philosophical system that would ground the explanation of any part of nature thus 'necessarily ends by having to discover *conditions* of the *uncondi-*

---

7 The reason for the accusation of atheism against Spinoza and those who adopted his ideas, is that God is therefore in some sense inseparable from the natural universe, rather than being able freely to intervene in the world.

tioned' (Scholz 1916: 51), and this is obviously contradictory. For Jacobi this problem led to the need for a theological leap of faith, as the world's intelligibility otherwise threatened to become a mere illusion. Kant's 'solution' to this dilemma lay in the division between the world as appearance and the world as thing in itself. We have to assume there is totality of conditions for things in themselves, because the world would otherwise not be a unified whole in any way at all. Knowledge, however, can only be of appearances that are given to the subject at a specific time in a specific place. Arguably, though, all this claim does is to shift the place of the unconditioned from the world in itself to the subject, which takes us straight to Maimon's and to Fichte's idealism. Kant, of course, did not wish the transcendental subject to have an absolute status, but the regress of chains of conditions seems only stoppable if the subject has an absolute, non-conditioned ability spontaneously to judge (and to act). This conception can, then, be understood as leading logically to the absolute I.[8]

The problem Schelling encounters in Fichte was first identified by his friend, the poet and philosopher Friedrich Hölderlin (1770–1843), in the light of Jacobi's formulation of the problem of the 'unconditioned'. Hölderlin's idea recurs in aspects of early Romantic philosophy from the same period, notably in Novalis' own critique of Fichte. For something to be an *I* in any intelligible sense, it must be conscious of an *other*, and thus be in a relationship to that other. Being in a relationship to something means precisely *not* being absolute. The overall structure of such a relationship cannot, therefore, be characterized only in terms based on one side of the relationship. Hölderlin argued that one has, in consequence, to understand the structure of the relationship of subject to object as grounded in 'a whole of which subject and object are the parts' (1963: 490–1), which he termed 'being'. This idea will be vital to Schelling at various times in his philosophy, but he is not always clear about its importance. Implicit in the idea is something which can be seen as undermining the whole German Idealist attempt to found a philosophy on the demonstration that the world can be comprehended via the structures of the subject's thinking.

Schelling's philosophy in the 1790s wavers between an attachment to Fichte and to Spinoza. The effect of the latter attachment leads him to his 'Philosophy of Nature' (*Naturphilosophie*), written in the second half of the 1790s, which was to make him famous and which had a significant influence on the thought of his time, for instance on Goethe. In the *Naturphilosophie* the Kantian division between appearing nature and nature in itself is seen as resulting from the fact

---

8   For the best defence of Kant against this interpretation, see Ameriks (2000).

that nature is regarded as an object, a '*Gegenstand*', in the sense described above. This objectification fails to account for the living dynamic forces in nature, including those in our own organism, with which Kant himself became concerned in the third Critique and other late work, and which had already played a role in Leibniz's account of nature. Nature in itself is therefore thought of by Schelling as a 'productivity': 'As the object is never absolute/unconditioned [*unbedingt*] then something per se non-objective must be posited in nature; this absolutely non-objective postulate is precisely the original productivity of nature' (1856–61: I/ii. 284). The dualism between things in themselves and appearances results because the productivity can never appear as itself and can only appear in the form of 'products' – what Kant terms appearances – which are the productivity 'inhibiting' itself. The products are never complete in themselves. They are like the eddies in a stream, which temporarily keep their shape via the resistance to itself of the movement of the fluid that creates them.

As productivity, nature cannot be thought of as an object, since it is the subject of all possible 'predicates', in the sense of the 'eddies' of which transient, objective nature consists. Think of your own body as a kind of eddy in the stream of nature, whose material is constantly being replaced and which will eventually disappear into the stream altogether. However, nature's 'inhibiting' itself in order to become something, as opposed to dissipating itself at infinite speed, means that the 'principle of all explanation of nature' is 'universal duality', an inherent difference of subject and object which prevents nature ever finally reaching stasis as a completed object. Each object has an identity that makes it what it is, but the productivity constantly leads to that identity being overcome. At the same time, this difference of subject and object must be grounded in an identity which links them together, otherwise all the problems of dualism would reappear. In a decisive move for German Idealism Schelling establishes the following parallel between nature and mind. Nature is the absolute producing subject, whose predicates are the synthesized objects in the natural world. The spontaneous thinking subject is the condition of the syntheses required to produce objectivity, which depends upon predication in judgement, upon saying 'X is such and such'. The problem lies in explicating how these two subjects and their predicates relate to each other.[9]

9 The other problem lies in the way that Schelling tends to use the basic principles of what is actually an attempt to establish a metaphysics of nature – an account of the fundamental principles which give rise to what there is in nature – to speculate on empirical aspects of nature. The resulting theories have generally turned out to be plain wrong in the face of empirically based theories, though some of his speculation did actually lead to empirically warrantable theories.

On the one hand, Schelling wishes to sustain a sense of nature's relative independence of the way we think about it. This, however, runs the risk of surrendering key insights of transcendental philosophy. If nature can only be known under the conditions inherent in thought, what right does one have to suggest that we could have access to nature in itself? Although it may be possible to think of nature as being productive, this does not explain how it can produce the subjectivity which makes knowledge of nature possible. On the other hand, his attempt, in the 1800 *System of Transcendental Idealism*, to approach these issues using Fichte's terminology raises the problem of how it is possible to talk of an absolute I, as well as threatening to reduce nature to being merely the object for the subject. Already in 1801 Schelling attacks Fichte for regarding nature as just being there 'for us', thereby making prophetically clear, in a proto-ecological manner, that this is not merely an abstract philosophical issue. In the *System* he tries to explain the emergence of the thinking subject from nature in terms of an 'absolute I' coming retrospectively to know itself in a 'history of self-consciousness'. Having arrived at the point of being aware of itself, thought is able to trace the unconscious history that precedes this self-awareness. This model introduces a historical element into Fichte's genetic approach to the description of the I, and will influence Hegel's 1807 *Phenomenology of Mind*. The *System* recounts the history of which the transcendental subject is the result.

In the *System* nature's resistance to our knowledge and actions is a result of the fact that its productivity is 'unconscious'. Reality is therefore constituted in an interplay between the 'conscious' and the 'unconscious'. Schelling argues that philosophy must therefore be supplemented by something which cannot be understood purely in conceptual, rule-bound terms, if the role of the unconscious is to be grasped. Art must supplement philosophy.[10] This idea was influenced by his contact with Novalis and Schlegel, who, as we shall see in chapter 5, give a similar role to art at the time. They had, in turn, been influenced by Friedrich Schiller (1758–1805), who developed ideas from Kant and Fichte, arguing in his *Letters on the Aesthetic Education of Humanity* (1795–8) that aesthetic activity was able to unite the theoretical and practical aspects of humankind. Art does not come about just by applying existing rules. It requires something which cannot be learned merely by learning a particular craft or technique. This extra aspect of the subject that creates art is, Schelling

---

10   Remember that for Kant an empirical concept is a rule for identifying an object: because what is at issue cannot be regarded as an object, access to it must be non-conceptual.

maintains, 'unconscious', and therefore involves a dimension which philosophical concepts can never grasp. His argument is similar to that of Kant concerning the genius (see chapter 1), but Schelling gives art a much more emphatic role in understanding reality. Despite not offering final answers to the question of how to understand the relationship between nature and subjectivity, Schelling's early work does point to the idea that *philosophy* may not ultimately be able to give a transparent foundation for modernity that would explain how we relate to the nature we also are.

In the philosophy Schelling writes between 1801 and circa 1807, which is referred to as the 'identity philosophy', he moves more in the direction of Spinoza than of Fichte. The I cannot, he now thinks, be conceived of as the initiating principle of the manifest world that it is in Fichte. Indeed, Schelling begins to direct arguments against Idealist assumptions of the kind Fichte inherits from Descartes: 'The *I* think, *I* am, is, since Descartes, the basic mistake of all knowledge; thinking is not my thinking, and being is not my being, for everything is only of God or the totality' (Schelling 1856–61: I/vii. 148). The structure of his conception is summed up in the following remark on time: 'time is itself nothing but *the totality appearing in opposition to the particular life of things*' (I/vi. 220). Time is both endlessly different, each moment not being the other moments, but for the moments to be 'of time' at all they must also be in some sense identical. Our awareness of the absolute, or the unconditioned, arises because of the relativity and transience of everything particular in the world, including ourselves. Schelling is led to his later conceptions by the difficulty he has in accounting for why the unconditioned, the substance, should manifest itself in the world of conditions at all. Why does the absolute give rise to a subjectivity which is both limited by the transient world of objects and yet seeks to grasp what is beyond the transience of that world? The question asked by Leibniz – 'why is there not nothing, why is there anything at all?' – is not, Schelling thinks, answered by a logical, rational dependence of the finite on the infinite, of the kind suggested by Spinoza. Schelling spends much of his subsequent work both exploring the consequences of the possibility that we can give no reason for the existence of a manifest world, and yet at the same time attempting to understand why such a world exists. We shall look at this later work at times in the coming chapters, but need now to consider Hegel's relationship to the ideas considered so far. In doing so we will break the historical sequence, which ought at this point to take us to an examination of early Romantic philosophy. The reason for this is that the Romantics belong in the tradition of the criticisms of idealism, which we will consider from

chapter 5 onwards, rather than in the tradition of German Idealism
with which they are often associated.

SUGGESTIONS FOR FURTHER READING

Ameriks, K. (ed.) (2000) *The Cambridge Companion to German Idealism*
(Cambridge: Cambridge University Press). *Good collection of essays on
main themes and figures in German Idealism based on the most up-to-date
research.*
Beiser, F. C. (1987) *The Fate of Reason: German Philosophy from Kant to
Fichte* (Cambridge, MA: Harvard University Press). *Major historical and
philosophical study of the immediate reactions to Kant, dealing with many
unjustly ignored philosophers.*
Bowie, A. (1993) *Schelling and Modern European Philosophy* (London:
Routledge). *Detailed study of Schelling's development, relating him to
issues in philosophy today.*
Breazeale, Daniel and Rockmore, Tom (eds) (1996) *New Perspectives on
Fichte* (Atlantic Highlands: Humanities Press). *Essays on Fichte based on
recent developments in research on Fichte.*
Martin, W. M. (1997) *Idealism and Objectivity: Understanding Fichte's Jena
Project* (Stanford: Stanford University Press). *Part of the recent wave of
new research that has transformed the study of Fichte.*
Marx, W. (1984) *The Philosophy of F. W. J. Schelling: History, System,
Freedom* (Bloomington: Indiana University Press). *Reliable, if rather
worthy, presentation of issues in Schelling's philosophy.*
Neuhouser, F. (1989) *Fichte's Theory of Subjectivity* (Cambridge: Cambridge
University Press). *Lucid analytical account of Fichte's best arguments in
relation to the philosophy of mind.*
Snow, D. (1996) *Schelling and the End of Idealism* (Albany: SUNY Press).
*Good historical presentation of issues in Schelling's early and middle
philosophy.*
White, A. (1983) *Schelling: Introduction to the System of Freedom* (New
Haven and London: Yale University Press). *Account of Schelling from a
Hegelian perspective. Clear, but misses the point of some of Schelling's most
original contentions.*
Zöller, G. (1999) *Fichte's Transcendental Philosophy* (Cambridge: Cambridge
University Press). *Detailed study of some key texts by Fichte that rather
lacks an independent philosophical perspective.*

4

GERMAN IDEALISM: HEGEL

Universal Mediation

Attempts to base philosophy on either the subjective or the objective aspect of existence of the kind we considered in the last chapter always leave the difficulty of connecting the two aspects and of establishing the priority between them. This difficulty can be seen as an expression of the tension between what the modern physical sciences tell us about ourselves as part of physical nature and the other ways in which we understand our existence, as well as of the continual opposition in the history of philosophy between materialism and idealism. Hegel offers the most impressive attempt in modern philosophy to map out a comprehensive account of our place within things which is systematically complete and which integrates the subjective and objective perspectives in a philosophically defensible manner. Although, as we shall see later, Hegel's philosophy is put in question by aspects of Romantic and post-Romantic thinking, and although Hegel's influence wanes from the second half of the nineteenth century onwards, new interpretations of his work have made him central to contemporary philosophy. The reasons for this revival of interest have to do with Hegel's treatment of the issue of foundationalism.

In a book written in 1802, *The Difference of Fichte's and Schelling's Systems of Philosophy*, Hegel sums up his view of the relationship between Fichte and Schelling as follows. Fichte has proposed a 'subjective subject-object': hence the notion of the absolute *I* as the whole within which subject and object are related. Schelling, on the other hand, has proposed an 'objective subject-object': the *Naturphiloso-*

phie relates subject and object as part of a whole, but this whole is 'nature'. It is nature, though, in a sense which goes beyond the Kantian and Fichtean idea of nature as merely the world of objects bound by necessary laws. The problem Hegel points to here is a version of the problem of foundationalism: any attempt to arrive at a foundational principle seems to involve an aspect which needs to be self-legitimating. This creates the following dilemma. If the foundational principle is not self-legitimating, it requires legitimation by something else, which prevents it being a foundation at all. If it is not legitimated by something else, it seems to have to be arbitrarily asserted, in the manner of the illegitimate authority characteristic of feudalism, which was what Kant had sought to escape in the name of autonomous reason. Hegel comes to think that Schelling's identity philosophy relies on a version of the second possibility, because it presupposes the identity of subject and object, mind and nature, at the beginning of the system. Schelling then just explicates what he has already presupposed, rather than proving by the system itself that this identity can be legitimated. The kind of foundationalism Hegel seeks to avoid relies on what he terms 'immediacy', the assumption that something can be itself independently of its relations to anything else. Hegel wants to show that immediacy is the source of many of the traditional problems of philosophy. The success of this project depends upon whether he succeeds in getting rid of the need for any kind of immediacy, by revealing how even what appears to exist independently of relationships to anything else does not in fact do so.

Having been influenced by both Fichte and Schelling, Hegel arrives at a developed presentation of his own particular approach in the 1807 *Phenomenology of Mind/Spirit* that he finished in Jena, just as the town was being invaded by Napoleon's army. The title describes what the book aims to do. Hegel sees it as an account of the appearance of mind in history, which makes possible what the text itself then seeks to describe. The aim of the book might seem rather strange. In Kant's terms mind is precisely what cannot itself appear, because it is the condition of possibility of things appearing to the subject. However, it is this model which Hegel aims to overcome. He tries to do so by showing that an abstract account of the forms of thought, of the kind Kant presents in the table of categories, actually creates the problem it is trying to solve. Kant assumes that the forms of thought can be separated from what they are the forms of – i.e. the world that the forms allow us to know – and in this way he creates the gap between the two. This assumption gives rise to the problem of the 'thing in itself', which is always separate from the forms in which we know appearances. Hegel's claim is that the forms of thought arise historically through the interaction of subject and world, from the most primitive form of reaction to a stimulus, to the developed concepts which allow us to carry out sophisticated scientific work and to do philosophy. There is therefore no reason to think of thought and the matter of thought as separate.

This approach is what makes Hegel such a crucial thinker for modernity. The philosopher has to look at areas of modern life both as concrete practices and as a series of conceptions which are inherent in those practices: the two cannot be separated. Hegel's mature philosophical texts include accounts of the law and the state, aesthetics, history, religion and natural science. The *Encyclopedia*, Hegel's only overall presentation of his system, divides philosophy into 'Logic', the account of the forms of thought; '*Naturphilosophie*', which deals with the natural sciences, as the manifestation of the forms of thought in the objective world; and 'Philosophy of *Geist*', which deals with the manifestation of the forms of thought in society, where freedom is most developed. Rather than attempt to condense the ideas of each of these parts of the system into a few words, I shall present some of the basic ideas of the *Phenomenology*. These offer a model of the way Hegel goes about exploring any area of philosophy. Hegel's method relies on the philosopher showing how conceptions develop from more 'immediate' conceptions to increasingly 'mediated' ones. This can be illustrated by an example from the *Phenomenology* that relates to Fichte's account of the 'demand' as the source of intersubjectivity. In the undeveloped stage of the relationship between the subject and the other, the other is merely regarded as a threat to my own existence, so it must be destroyed. When this stage is overcome, the other can become someone that is useful to me. Eventually, at the stage where the subject–object relationship is transcended altogether, the other can be acknowledged as the same as me, because they are a thinking, moral subject with rights I agree they should possess. In the *Philosophy of Right* (which is part of the Philosophy of *Geist*), for example, the same kind of move is seen as occurring in the law. The law moves from forms which give priority to the more particular aspects of society, such as the family, to the emergence of the prior right of the community as a whole over the more limited social units, including the family.

The *Phenomenology of Mind*

The *Phenomenology* seeks to establish the preconditions of a system of philosophy by showing how any attempt to establish a foundation

that, as Reinhold had demanded, sustains the system from the beginning necessarily fails. One key aspect of this approach has proved to
be very significant for contemporary philosophers. A fundamental
assumption of the empiricism which derives from Locke, which dominated much analytical philosophy until recent years, is that uncon-
ceptualized data given directly to the senses must be the foundation
of all we know. What, after all, could be more certain than what is
hitting your senses at this moment? Surely all our knowledge is a
result of then building from the direct evidence of the senses towards
more general ideas? The difficult question is, though: how does one
get from contingent packets of sense-data, caused, for example, by
photons hitting my retina, to the certainty that one is looking at a
printed page? The immediate 'sense certainty' of what is in front of
you is, Hegel argues, not immediate at all. Your certainty that there
is a page in front of you is dependent on the other, i.e. the particular
page, but the page is only certain because you perceive it as a page,
which requires a general concept that can apply to any page. The supposedly immediate particular fact is therefore thoroughly mediated
via a universal. The concreteness of looking at the *particularity* of
what is in front of me can only be asserted *as* concrete because we
use the *universal* notions of 'this', 'here' and 'now' to indicate particularity. These are 'indexical' words, which only gain their meaning
by being applied in concrete contexts. What they apply to is, though,
thoroughly unstable. As I write this, it is now 12.18 a.m., here, in
Cambridge; however, I may revise what I am writing at 3 p.m. in
London on another day. In both cases I will need the notions of 'this',
'here' and 'now', but their content will have changed. Without the
universals the particular has no way of becoming knowable, but
without the particular the universals have no content. Hegel insists,
though, that the *truth* of immediate perceptions lies in the conceptual
universality of the ways in which we talk about them; without this
universality the particular is incommunicable, and so cannot be
talked about in terms of its truth at all.

In some respects this argument just echoes Kant's insistence in
the first Critique that 'intuitions without concepts are blind, concepts
without intuitions are empty', but the specific way Hegel characterizes the issue takes us into the heart of his method. The vital idea here
is the demonstration that things which appear opposed to each other
necessarily belong together, and are thus in a particular sense 'identical'. Schelling argued something similar about mind and nature,
which are linked in 'absolute identity'. Hegel's objection to this conception is that Schelling claims that we have access to this identity in
an immediate manner, via 'intellectual intuition'. This is a term which

plays a significant role in the thought of the second half of the eighteenth century. Kant had rejected the term, because he thought it had to be the manner of thinking of the deity. The point of the term is to cross the boundary between the intelligible and the sensuous. It suggests one can 'intuit' – have direct access to – the inherent nature of things, the intelligible realm. Kant thinks this is because God can be thought of as actually producing the things themselves by thinking them. Schelling, on the other hand, argues in the *System* that we can gain access to the intelligible realm via the work of art. This is both an object available to intuition and something that can only be art if it is also a manifestation of the intelligible, via its combination of conscious and unconscious productivity. Intellectual intuition, then, posits some kind of inherent link between knower and the known. It connects the cognitive basis and the real basis of the subject, linking the subject as that which forms concepts to the subject as that which exists as part of the world in relation to which it forms those concepts.

Hegel also wishes to abolish the gap between thinking and the real, but he thinks that what is designated by the term intellectual intuition is not sufficient to make a philosophical system possible. The *Phenomenology* therefore regards its task as explicating what is implicit in the immediate idea of the unity of thought and reality. If the unity is assumed really to exist at the beginning of the system, nothing determinate can be said about it, because any judgements about the unity divide – 'mediate' – what is supposed to be immediate. Hegel, in contrast, takes this unity to be what should instead orient the system towards its *goal* of explaining how thought and reality relate. It is only by carrying out the mediation of what is initially immediate that the *truth* of that unity can then be shown. The truth can only emerge at the end of the system, as the realization of what was only potentially there at the beginning. The absolute is, therefore, 'to be grasped essentially as a result' (Hegel 1970: 24). Hegel uses the example of an embryo. Although the embryo is potentially a developed human being, and a developed human being cannot be without the embryonic stage, the embryo is merely 'in itself', rather than being 'for itself', which it becomes when it fulfils its potential. The natural sciences begin with crude explanatory theories which then become more reliable as more results are produced and more experiments are done: without this activity there is no developing truth about the world. The alternative is just to assume that some existing system of belief is true without its offering any proof of what it asserts. Despite some claims that this is what Hegel's philosophy does, it is in fact precisely what he is opposing.

How, though, does Hegel avoid just offering another version of a system reliant on a foundation, by covertly presupposing at the beginning what he argues can only come at the end? As we just saw, Hegel argues that foundations of the kind we encountered in Reinhold are essentially *positive*, and so are simply asserted at the beginning. In order to avoid such ungrounded assertion, there is, he thinks, only one alternative, namely to avoid anything positive until the system is complete. At the point of completion the system as a whole itself becomes positive, because it has grasped the truth, and so incorporates all the limited truths required to get to this point of completion. But what exactly does this mean?

The answer lies in what Hegel means by 'dialectic'. Hegel's 'dialectic' is often characterized in terms of the triad of thesis, antithesis, synthesis. This is, however, not the way he presents it. The core of the dialectic is rather what Hegel terms the 'negation of the negation'. We encountered an example of this in his argument against empiricism. Sense-data could never provide us with any truth, because they are contingent and never finally identical with any other sense-data. They are therefore 'negative', requiring concepts to make them determinate. The indexical concepts of 'this', 'here' and 'now' are, though, themselves also negative. It is only when they are applied to what they, as universals, are not, namely particulars in the world, that they can produce truth. They also, moreover, rely on their negative status to be determinate at all: 'this' is not 'that', 'here' is not 'there', 'now' is not 'then', etc. Even the truths they may help produce, such as 'I am writing this at 1.19 a.m.', are themselves negative. They only function as truths within a wider context in which I am defined by my relations to other people who I am not, and in which the explanation of why I tend to write when I should be asleep is given in terms of further contexts, and so on. The idea here is in fact a more dynamic version of Spinoza's idea that determination is negation: no single thing can be 'positive' because it always relies on what it is not to be itself.

Ptolemaic physics claims the earth is circled by the sun, but since Copernicus and Galileo we think the earth circles the sun. Knowledge progresses by refutation, thus by the negation of what was formerly held to be true.[1] There cannot be an absolute beginning to this process, because that would mean we would already have to possess the truth before we had carried out any investigation at all. We can only begin with the idea that anything held to be true is open to nega-

---

1 In this sense Karl Popper's theory that all science can do is to falsify theories, rather than finally establish true theories, is thoroughly Hegelian.

tion, because its truth depends on other truths. Every specific claim therefore depends on other claims for its validation, and all claims are open to revision as they are, in turn, related to new claims. This situation does not make knowledge arbitrary, because what is negated is something *specific* that was itself thought of as knowledge, which is better understood in the new account. Hegel's term for this continual move to new accounts is 'determinate negation', the negation of something already known, which is the condition of possibility of a better account. If we think Zeus causes lightning, we have actually already mediated the threatening phenomenon that an animal also registers as a threat, and this makes possible further mediation which can lead to an improved theory that may protect us better. This process is referred to by Hegel as '*Aufhebung*' (often translated as 'sublation'). *Aufhebung* has the threefold, apparently contradictory, senses of 'negate', 'preserve' and 'elevate'. The initial knowledge of lightning is both negated by the new account, preserved in terms of being what makes the new account possible and elevated because the new account is superior to the old.

Two interpretations of where Hegel's approach leads suggest themselves. (1) The approach may be said to open the way to a pragmatism which sees knowledge, not as a correct representation of what is 'out there', but rather as a means of coping with and controlling the world in ever more effective ways. (2) Why, though, if all knowledge is really just negative, should one not adopt a thoroughgoing scepticism? The sceptic also accepts that there is no basis for holding something as ultimately true, because each belief we hold depends on other beliefs, which depend on other beliefs, and so on. This was precisely what led Jacobi to his arguments about the need for an 'unconditioned' to prevent an infinite regress of 'conditions of conditions'. Hegel's claim, though, is that he can adopt the assumption of the sceptic and yet turn it into the *opposite* of scepticism. For this to succeed he has to show that the negation of the negation is overcome by the demonstration that the negation of particular truths is *itself* the manifestation of the most general philosophical truth, namely that all particular truths are finite. This is why he famously asserts that 'The true is the whole' (ibid. 26). Any part is 'untrue' because its particularity can only be understood by going beyond it towards systematic completion.

Does this final move towards the complete system invalidate the possible pragmatic implications of the basic method? One simple way of suggesting the problem here is to ask if the value of what Hegel does lies (1) in its pragmatic removal of fruitless questions about whether our thought is really in touch with reality, or (2) in having given a definitive answer to the sceptic which results in a complete system of philosophy. Does the former require the latter? Contemporary positions can often be characterized in terms of whether they seek to hold on to some (usually attenuated) kind of absolute position, or whether they maintain we can do without such a position.

Talk of 'absolute knowledge' in the *Phenomenology* suggests that Hegel is predominantly concerned with systematic completeness, rather than a more pragmatic approach. Hegel's recent importance has, though, been based on his influence on philosophers who seek to escape the traps of traditional epistemology without giving up on the central notion of intersubjective justification (see e.g. Brandom 2000). The further interest of the *Phenomenology* lies in its implications for social and ethical thought, which arise from its account of the emergence of specific forms of intersubjective acknowledgement. This enables an understanding of the *social* development of the forms of thought of the subject.[2] Having shown how even very basic forms of consciousness of things are already necessarily endowed with some conceptual content, Hegel considers the vital question of *self*-consciousness. The best way to grasp his approach is to consider his account of 'desire'/'lust' ('*Begierde*', which has a more emphatic sense than '*Lust*', which means something more like 'pleasure'). This aspect of the work influenced Jacques Lacan, among many others.

As the subject encounters the other, it is split into two: into the external world it is aware of, and into something opposed to that world.[3] The two sides have the characteristic negative relationship we observed above. In the initial stage the sides are, however, not separated in any fully specifiable manner. Think of the way a baby is conscious, but is not clear about the boundary between itself and the rest of the world. *Self*-consciousness arises when the subject becomes aware of *itself* via its difference from the other, and at the same time realizes that the other is not in its control. In order really to become itself, self-consciousness has to satisfy the lack which results from its not being in control of the other. If it satisfies the lack, however, it also realizes that it is *dependent* on the other. If this sounds too abstract, think of it in terms of the need to eat. This need reminds you of yourself, because it makes you dissatisfied, and at the same time makes you aware of your dependence on the world. The need for the other can then develop into a more general ability to realize how one's own existence is not wholly independent of the other, so

2 Terence Pinkard subtitles his book on the *Phenomenology* the 'sociality of reason'.
3 It is the exploration of the nature of such splits that make Hegel of interest to Lacanian psychoanalysis.

that one begins to think in advance in order to avoid going hungry. This is one way of accounting for the genesis of memory. Rather than assuming memory is 'there from the beginning' in any developed way, it is accounted for by the recurrence of a lack that becomes imprinted into thinking. The lack then becomes something one can control by remembering the need to overcome it.

The next stage of this development, where Hegel comes close to Fichte's account of the 'demand', is the emergence of the ethical capacity to acknowledge that an independent other can be the same as oneself. Kant's categorical imperative relies on the invocation of a universal principle applying to all rational beings that is located in the intelligible domain. Hegel thinks this is an invalid abstraction and seeks to give an account of morality which sees it as developing historically in particular communities via the kind of process just described. This has the disadvantage of losing Kant's sense that morality should be based on universal principles, of the kind we now seek for international law, but it has the advantage of offering a more concrete account of how morality works in real contexts.

The most famous part of Hegel's account of self-consciousness is his analysis of the relationship between the 'Lord' and the 'Bonds-man'. On the one hand, the argument of the *Phenomenology* seems to be historical, because the key terms are those used to describe power relations in feudalism, relations which change in the wake of the English and French Revolutions.[4] On the other hand, Hegel is describing a stage of consciousness which can always play a role in any relationship between subjects where power is unevenly distrib-uted. Hegel adopts Hobbes's idea that the bottom line in undevel-oped social relations threatens to be a war of all against all, because my desire will conflict with the other's desire. Given that the other may well be stronger than I am, I risk annihilation in seeking to satisfy my desire. The Bondsman is the subject who has subordinated himself to the other in order to remain alive, and who provides for the desires of the other. In doing so he develops his capacity for changing the world, restraining his own desire in order to work on the object that the Lord desires. As time goes by, the Lord's merely consumerist atti-tude means that he satisfies his desire, but at the expense of a growing dependence on the developing capacities of the Bondsman. Instead of gaining total mastery of the other, the Lord in fact moves into an increasingly dependent relationship, so that the power balance begins to invert. The implication is that this is what happens in the French Revolution, when those who did the work seized control from a

4 Hegel does not refer, as many commentaries on this passage do, to 'master' and 'slave'.

corrupt aristocracy. This passage has been read in a whole variety of other ways, such as in terms of a Marxist view of the proletariat which holds the real power because it is producing the wealth of society, or in terms of gender relations, where the dominance of patriarchy may turn out to involve the same inversion. The strength of the passage lies not least in the way in which it reveals that apparently fixed subject and object positions can turn into their opposites. The rest of the narrative of the *Phenomenology* – Lordship and Bondage is only one stage along a much longer path – traces the ways in which the subject's relations to the other change the ways in which it can relate to itself, mixing historical manifestations of these relationships with a presentation of the structures involved as part of the overall pattern of the development of Mind. This culminates in the capacity to write the text of the *Phenomenology*, which emerges because thought has encompassed all its relations to itself and to the objective world.

Questions of Being

The tension between the historical interpretation of Hegel and the interpretation which sees the structures he outlines as constituting the true philosophical description of subjectivity – thus as a version of transcendental philosophy – points to key questions in assessing his philosophy. What is at issue are the kinds of claims that can be made for *philosophy* in modernity. Two major options suggest themselves.

1   Is philosophy to be the all-encompassing discipline which pro-
    vides a truth unavailable to any other science? If so, what Hegel
    provides is a version of Kant's framework for knowledge which
    both avoids the problem of things in themselves, and comes to
    terms with the inevitability of historical change by revealing the
    eternal truth that underlies that change. In this sense Hegel would
    still belong in the metaphysical tradition which seeks the timeless
    essence of things.
2   Or does Hegel provide a demonstration that the authority of
    reason can only ever be validated by a philosophical considera-
    tion of how reason came to be what it is at a particular time, of
    the kind offered in the *Phenomenology*? This would exclude an
    appeal to the existence of supra-temporal authority of the kind
    suggested in the first option, and is the interpretation favoured by
    Hegel's contemporary 'anti-metaphysical' defenders.[5]

5   The term was first applied to Hegel by Klaus Hartmann (see MacIntyre 1972).

Given the system which Hegel went on to construct, which is often described in terms of a supra-temporal view of what philosophy is able to achieve, there is much to support the first option. At the same time, it is possible to argue, either that the second option is, in Kant's dictum about Plato, 'understanding Hegel better than he understood himself', or that the often theological way he couched his philosophy was a means of avoiding political trouble over religious matters.

One possible approach to these difficulties is briefly to consider the vexed question of Hegel's account of 'being'. Can philosophy give an explanation of the relationship between thought and the real without there being anything that has to lie outside the explanation? Hegel is universally agreed to be making *some* kind of claim that there is nothing extra-conceptual, but the problem is interpreting what he means by this. As we saw, Kant thinks knowledge is possible, but that there are limits on what can be known. Kant's idea involves one version of a realist position which insists that reality is the way it is independently of what we happen to think is true.[6] Remember here the two ways in which Kant's notion of noumena could be interpreted: either (1) as the totality of all the possible aspects of the thing that we can only ever apprehend from particular perspectives at particular times, or (2) as the idea of the thing as completely independent of anything we could know about it.

Hegel's argument against the idea of things in themselves is ingenious and may be defensible in relation to the second interpretation of noumena. He argues that we think about things in themselves by abstracting everything we know about an object from the object (i.e. from the object as it is *for us*). There is therefore actually nothing left but 'emptiness'. This result comes about by an act of *thinking*. Instead, then, of arriving somewhere that thought is inherently unable to go, we arrive precisely at the realization that the thing in itself results from a certain way in which *thought* characterizes its relationship to the object. Objects known in experience depend upon their relations to other objects, and are therefore relative, and mediated. The idea of the thing in itself, in contrast, seems to be devoid of all relations, and therefore absolute. The thing is 'identical' because it lacks any kind of differentiation (differentiation requiring relation to something else), and so lacks anything that is empirically knowable. This is why Kant sometimes regards the thing in itself as an 'idea', in the sense of that which transcends what can be experienced. The point is, though, that we here have another version of *immediacy*. This immediacy is, however, a result of an operation in thought. We therefore

---

6 The debate about realism is now so complex that I will not try to explain it here. Various aspects will recur in later chapters.

arrive at immediacy through mediation, rather than beginning with something which really *is* immediate. Hegel's claim is that there *is* in fact nothing immediate, because our very attempts to think about any such thing are themselves mediations. Hegel's claims for philosophy turn on whether this is an adequate description of the way in which thought and being relate.

Hegel's main methodological work, the *Science of Logic* (1812–16), begins with examination of the idea of being as that which *seems* most immediate, with which philosophy thinks it must begin. How, though, are we to understand *any* concept, without relating it to something else, thus by mediating it? Is the concept not otherwise wholly empty and indeterminate, so that we could say nothing at all about it? How do we characterize blue, but by 'not green, not yellow', etc.? One way of approaching this question is via the issue we looked at in Kant, concerning whether existence is a predicate or not. Is it meaningful to say that one of a thing's attributes is its existence? For Kant, existence could not be considered a concept of the same kind as other concepts, because it was itself always required for the true use of a concept. Hegel's argument relies upon the claim that *every* concept depends for its determinacy upon its relation to other concepts which it is not, so that even the concept of being depends, for example, upon the concept of nothing. The contradiction between the two then leads to the notion of becoming, in which something both is and is not, because it ceases to be what it is initially and then is something else, thus 'negating' itself. The process of building up the basic ways in which we think about the world follows this pattern. A concept turns out to involve some limitation which needs to be completed by a further concept that changes what it is, and so on, until there is no further structure of thinking that can emerge from the limitations in other structures of thinking. The point in philosophy at which the contradictions are exhausted is what Hegel means by the 'absolute idea'. Hegel's *Science of Logic* is, then, not a logic in the sense derived from Aristotle, which analyses necessary forms of argument, because it involves claims about the very nature of how reality can be thought about, claims about ontology. It has consequently been described as a 'logic of concepts', in which each concept becomes determinate in relation to other concepts, 'being' in relation to 'nothing', etc.

Those who are critical of this approach argue that being cannot be a concept of this kind. An all-encompassing enterprise like the *Science of Logic* therefore cannot fulfil its aim of revealing how even the immediate is necessarily mediated. Being is, instead, that of which things are predicated, the real itself. It is therefore not the real as a concept expressed by the words 'reality', or 'being', that is then made determinate by its relation to other concepts. The logical importance of this claim becomes apparent in considering how we think of non-being. The point is that non-being cannot just be seen as the polar opposite of being. Ernst Tugendhat (see Tugendhat and Wolf 1986) has suggested that if we doubt the existence of unicorns we do not go around looking at unicorns to see if they possess the attribute existence. Instead we look at objects in the world to see if they can justifiably be characterized by the predicate 'unicorn'. The structure of our thinking about what we consider to be real is therefore the propositional structure of 'something as something', not just 'something'. The world cannot adequately be described as the totality of somethings which are defined by their not being other somethings, but has instead to be described as the totality of 'states of affairs' ('x's as something'), because somethings can always be described in an indefinite number of ways. The something which may get in my way can, for example, be described as a table, the table as wood, as an object weighing thirty pounds, as brown, as protection against an earthquake, etc. (This issue will recur when Frege is discussed in chapter 8.)

Thinking this way avoids the model of thinking about being and non-being which derives from the ancient Greek philosopher Parmenides, namely the model in which thinking is assumed to function in the same way as perception. Tugendhat argues (1992) that Hegel falls prey to this model. In perceiving an object, one either, for example, hears something or one hears nothing, so that there is indeed either being or nothing, which seem to be polar opposites. However, if we take this as a model for thinking about existence and non-existence, the result is that 'thinking x is not' – 'unicorns don't exist' – is falsely equated with 'thinking nothing'. The obvious consequence of this is the unanswerable question 'What doesn't exist, then?' One seems to be assuming something (the existence of unicorns), and denying it at the same time. The wider importance of this issue becomes more apparent if we make the claim, for example, that 'race does not exist', where the racist can accuse us of presupposing what we are trying to deny.

The way to avoid the consequence of asserting and denying at the same time lies in 'existential' statements being expressed in the form: 'there is/is not an x such that it is a unicorn', or 'there is/is not an x such that it divides people into fundamentally different categories called races'. The crucial fact about this approach in the arguments against Hegel is that being transcends what we can say of it. Any particular predicate we attach to 'there is an x such that . . .' can be negated as the thing changes, or as we decide the predicate was falsely applied, or even as x ceases to be something we think exists at all, but *being* is not altered by this. Being is therefore the ineliminable basis upon which we can revise our ideas of what there is. The difference between the model based on perception and the model based on the propositional form of 'x as y' is a version of what Heidegger will term 'ontological difference'. This is the difference between *what* there is ('entities'), and the always underlying fact *that* there is (the fact of 'being'), which is the condition of predicating anything of anything at all. Hegel wishes to deny this distinction. He thinks being is reducible to its concept, to its 'whatness', because its 'thatness' is just what we have so far failed to determine by a concept. The *Science of Logic* therefore consists of an attempt exhaustively to outline all the ways in which things can be, thus to provide, as Habermas puts it, an account of the 'context of all contexts' (1999: 219), which is what Hegel means by the 'absolute idea'. The question is how this idea is to be interpreted.

One recent interpreter of Hegel, Robert Pippin, suggests (1997) that the essential aspect of Hegel's thought is that he makes reason into something wholly internal to what human communities can come to regard as valid. The account of the absolute idea is therefore the demonstration that there is nothing outside our developing of our concepts which would legitimate them, except further critical engagement with those concepts and historical examination of how those concepts came to be regarded as legitimate. There can, therefore, be no appeal to a reality beyond what societies have come to think about in the ways they already think about it. Habermas objects to this conception on the grounds that 'What is rationally acceptable according to our lights is not necessarily the same as what is objectively true' (1999: 218–19). In Pippin's argument the fact that we cannot talk about being except in the ways which real societies have actually come to talk about it means that there is no reason to be concerned about ontological difference. We can only ever work in terms of what justifies itself in real communities. Habermas would concur with such a conception in many respects, but thinks that it excludes the side of Hegel which *does* seek to 'have the last word' by overcoming the contingency of being in a philosophical system. What is, in Hegel's own terms, 'objective spirit', the contingent, socially located historical manifestations of our conceptions, is, Habermas maintains, made by Hegel into 'absolute spirit'. Instead of thinking of truth as the regulative idea of absolute validity, which we are aware of by the fact that being always transcends what we can say of it, Hegel lays claim to absolute validity itself.

The aim of thinkers in German Idealism was to overcome the split between thought and the world that seemed to follow from Kant. They sought to do so on the basis of the conviction that thought is able to grasp the real once it has fully grasped its *own* structures. Hegel offers the most impressive attempt to show how this can be done. However, even before he wrote his major texts, the project of German Idealism had been put into question by the early German Romantics. In the next chapter we shall look at both the Romantic criticisms of Idealism and criticisms of Idealism in Schopenhauer and Feuerbach.

SUGGESTIONS FOR FURTHER READING

Beiser, F. C. (ed.) (1993) *The Cambridge Companion to Hegel* (Cambridge: Cambridge University Press). *Useful collection of essays on major themes.*

Houlgate, S. (1991) *Freedom, Truth and History: An Introduction to Hegel's Philosophy* (London: Routledge). *Excellent, if somewhat uncritical, introduction to Hegel.*

Inwood, M. (1983) *Hegel* (London: Routledge). *Extensive major study of Hegel's philosophy.*

MacIntyre, Alasdair (ed.) (1972) *Hegel: A Collection of Critical Essays* (Notre Dame: University of Notre Dame Press). *Groundbreaking collection of essays that helped change the perspective on Hegel in the English-speaking world.*

Pinkard, T. (2002) *German Philosophy 1760–1860: The Legacy of Idealism* (Cambridge: Cambridge University Press). *Informed, lucid historical account by outstanding Hegel scholar.*

Pippin, R. B. (1997) *Idealism as Modernism: Hegelian Variations* (Cambridge: Cambridge University Press). *Brilliant series of essays using the most plausible contemporary interpretation of Hegel to explore issues in modernity.*

Singer, P. (1993) *Hegel* (Oxford: Oxford University Press). *Introductory account of Hegel.*

Solomon, R. C. (1987) *From Hegel to Existentialism* (New York: Oxford University Press). *Wide-ranging, readable general account of aspects of modern philosophy.*

Stern, R. (ed.) (1993) *G. W. F. Hegel: Critical Assessments*, 4 vols (London: Routledge). *Very extensive collection of major essays on Hegel: a good research tool.*

Taylor, Charles (1975) *Hegel* (Cambridge: Cambridge University Press). *Fine, if rather traditional, contextual account of Hegel's philosophy.*

Wood, A. (1990) *Hegel's Ethical Thought* (Cambridge: Cambridge University Press). *Important text by major Hegel scholar.*

5

CRITIQUES OF IDEALISM I: THE EARLY ROMANTICS TO FEUERBACH

Romanticism and the Critique of Idealism

The story of nineteenth-century German philosophy is often told in terms of the rise and fall of the German Idealists' hopes for a philosophical system. Such a system would both demonstrate the legitimacy of the claims of reason against traditional authority and integrate the cognitive, moral and aesthetic spheres of modern life in new ways. Hegel's system attempts such an integration by establishing a hierarchy of truth. The immediate truths of art, which remain attached to the specificity of the particular work of art, or of religion, which are still reliant on images and stories, are subordinated to the more universal ethical and cognitive truths which emerge via the overcoming of particularity in modern law, science and philosophy. The need for such a system results from the awareness that the decline of religion creates a deficit which must be overcome if a new place for humankind in the order of things is to be rationally negotiated. One of the decisive elements in the demise of the hopes of Idealist philosophy is the success of the empirically based natural sciences. These do not, unlike the philosophy of Fichte, Schelling and Hegel, seek to overcome the contingency of nature by submitting it to a priori principles, but try to find whatever regularities are accessible to empirical observation.[1] The result is that the sciences

---

1 This issue is obviously much more complex than I have made it here, but there is no doubt that German Idealist thinking about nature came to be regarded as invalid by many of the most important scientists, such as Helmholtz.

increasingly arrive at solutions to many questions about the working of nature and to many of the technical problems involved in controlling nature for human purposes. In doing so, they obviate many questions which had previously been regarded as philosophical questions. The adoption and rejection of philosophical positions in modernity is, though, not just dependent upon what happens in the natural sciences. This is not least because one of the major tasks of modern philosophy is understanding the place of the natural sciences in the rest of human culture.

The decline of the Idealist aims in the second half of the nineteenth century does not make the question of the integration of different aspects of modernity go away. This is evident in the fears about the effects of science both on the world of nature and on the ways we think of ourselves, as well as in a growing concentration on the darker sides of human behaviour. These issues have not gone away in the interim. Think of the contemporary debates about how far evolutionary and genetic theories can be used to account for human behaviour, and of what this says about the possibilities of human self-determination. Idealism's desire for an integration of natural science into a wider philosophical picture based on that self-determination contrasts with the critics of Idealism's assumption that such integration is now no longer systematically possible. This is either because of limits on human self-determination posed by our very nature, or because of the difference between the kind of reason required by scientific and technical activity, and that required by communication and action in everyday social life. The nature of the anti-Idealist responses to this situation varies enormously, and this is apparent in the very different political affiliations of the thinkers we shall now be considering.

Most accounts of German philosophy have, until very recently, presented the 'critique of Idealism' as being principally the work of Ludwig Feuerbach, Karl Marx and other so-called 'Young Hegelians' from the 1830s and '40s onwards, and of materialist philosophers and scientists in the second half of the century. The question is complicated by the fact that it is not clear whether the critique applies only to Fichte, (parts of) Schelling and to Hegel, or whether it also includes Kant. Kant's 'transcendental idealism', as we have seen, has a realist aspect. It has, moreover, become clear in recent years that there already was a counter-current to Idealism in German philosophy which arose almost simultaneously with Idealist philosophy in the last decade of the eighteenth century, namely what is usually referred to as 'early German Romanticism'. This current of thought has turned out to be in some respects closer to many contemporary philosophical concerns than the conceptions both of the Idealists and of their later critics.[2]

The names of the initial proponents of the Romantic critique of Idealism are better known for their contributions to literature than to philosophy, namely Novalis (Friedrich von Hardenberg) (1772–1800) and Friedrich Schlegel (1772–1829). The theologian and philosopher Friedrich Daniel Ernst Schleiermacher (1768–1834) can also be said to belong to the group in some respects, as can Friedrich Hölderlin (1770–1843), because they share some of the philosophical concerns we are about to consider.[3] The direct philosophical target of the Romantics was really Fichte, but the reasons for the attacks can also be applied to aspects of Hegel. Let us take a rather crude opposition between structures of thinking, that can be suggested via the metaphor of the journey. An idea which recurs in Hegel's conception of philosophy is the circular return to the starting point. In the *Phenomenology*, the system returns at the end to what was 'immediate' at the beginning, having revealed the truth that was implicit in the beginning. Consider, for example, an adult who looks back at youthful feelings and aspirations, which took no account of the realities of the world, in the light of what experience has taught them about the real world. In Hegelian terms, the aspirations of the person which were mere fantasies have been overcome and their aspirations now gain their true form. This structure can be thought of in many ways. In the *Science of Logic* the complex structures of being are fully articulated and understood, having begun with just the bare, indeterminate thought that anything exists at all. The end mirrors the beginning, but it does so by explaining what was not accessible as such at the beginning. This structure means that philosophy offers what is sometimes referred to as 'closure', a system which is self-contained and complete. The journey of philosophy is therefore one which arrives back at somewhere familiar.

The contemporary German philosopher, Manfred Frank, has suggested (1979) that the difference between Hegel and Romantic philosophy can be understood in terms of the metaphor of the 'endless journey'. The metaphor of homelessness is, of course, very common in the modern period. The point of this metaphor is that if the journey of the mind in modernity is endless, it never really can arrive at home.

---

2   This is in part because the Romantics effect what Manfred Frank has termed a 're-Kantianisation' of philosophy which echoes aspects of the contemporary revival of Kant in the USA (see Ameriks 2000).
3   The group included other significant figures, but they were not decisive for the philosophical developments in Romanticism.

To arrive at home the mind must already know what it is and where it comes from. One objection to Hegel's conception, which is made by the later Schelling in the 1830s and '40s (see Bowie 1993: ch. 6; Schelling 1994), is, therefore, that Hegel's claim to be able to begin without any presuppositions and to rely solely upon the 'negation of the negation' would seem to be indefensible. He has in this view to presuppose some kind of 'intuitive', immediate, but still cognitive contact with being at the beginning of the system. Otherwise there could be no way of recognizing ('re-cognizing', in the sense of 'knowing again') that one had returned to the beginning at the end. This intuitive contact would not be wholly explicable in terms of the conceptions that succeed it, because the intuition with which the system begins is not reducible to the ways it can be conceptualized.

What, though, if there were no certainty of returning to the beginning? What if the only possibility was to keep travelling as long as there seems to be some reason for doing so, even though there is no guarantee that one will actually get anywhere? Home may then become a much more temporary place, which is constantly threatened, and so is never really home at all. This idea expresses something of the difference between Romantic philosophy and Hegel's self-enclosed system. Novalis, for example, says that philosophy is 'really homesickness, *the drive to be at home everywhere*' (1978: 675), and he claims that music enables the mind to be 'for short moments in its earthly home' (ibid. 517). The drive to be at home does not have a definitive goal, and has no certainty of success, whence the idea that a form of art may, albeit temporarily, allow us to be at home, while philosophy merely reveals the lack of an ultimate home.

Not very long after Schlegel and Novalis begin to give up their initial enthusiasm for Fichte,[4] Jacobi wrote a public letter to Fichte in 1799, in relation to the latter's being accused of atheism and being forced out of his job. In the letter Jacobi uses an image which captures a common worry about the Idealist philosophy of his time. Jacobi suggests that Fichte's system, which is generated by the absolute I's self-division, is actually like a sock. Like the absolute I, a sock consists of one thing, the single thread of which it is made, that turns back on itself in complex ways, in order to form itself into something. Jacobi's objection is that the reality of the empirical world is made into something merely derived from a philosophical principle. Instead of the sheer diversity of being always transcending our attempts to grasp it, Idealist philosophy thinks that its own funda-

---

4 Most literature on the early Romantics wrongly assumes that they were and remained Fichteans (see e.g. Berlin 1999).

mental principle is able to dissolve being into the explication of how it must be thought about. Jacobi's metaphor may be a bit unfair, but it is useful for beginning to understand Romantic philosophy. The attempt to avoid the problem of the thing in itself and establish a monist system based on a fundamental principle seeks to conjure away the contingency of reality. In his *On Religion. Speeches to the Educated of Its Despisers*, also of 1799, which he wrote having been prompted to do so by his friend Schlegel, Schleiermacher asks in a similar vein to Jacobi: 'I ask you, then: what does your . . . transcendental philosophy do? It classifies the universe and divides it into this kind of being and that kind of being, it pursues the bases of what is there and deduces the necessity of the real, it spins from itself the reality of the world and its laws' (n.d. 47).

The 'narcissistic' relationship between philosophy and reality suggested by Jacobi and Schleiermacher also comes under attack by the early Romantics. Now the obvious assumption would seem to be that, like Jacobi, they can therefore be regarded as 'realists', for whom the truth of what there is is independent of whatever we may come to know. The matter is, however, more complex than this, even in relation to Jacobi. Jacobi took Kant very seriously and was also enthusiastic about Hume's empiricism, so he does not assume that there is no problem about how we gain access to reality. He adopts his realism on the basis of his religious faith, in which the fact that the world is revealed as knowable at all is taken as a basis for believing that it is grounded in God. Nothing in philosophy, he thinks, can explain why things are intelligible at all – crudely, how does a tree cause us to see it *as* a tree? – so the fact of intelligibility has to be a matter of belief/faith (*Glaube*). The alternative is scepticism, because if the truth is wholly independent of what we think it is, we could never know whether our thought is in touch with reality.

The question here is again how what the philosophy of the period terms the 'absolute' or the 'unconditioned' is to be conceived. Is the absolute (1) philosophy's final articulation of all the interrelated ways in which things can truly be, as Hegel claims? Or is it (2) a 'regulative idea' which can never be realized concretely, but which is necessary for orienting our thinking towards the truth? In the latter case one adopts a kind of scepticism about anything that one holds to be true, because its truth will depend upon its relationships to other truths, in a manner which can never be fully explained. This kind of scepticism can help suggest another way of understanding the difference between Idealism and the ideas of some of those who come to reject it. Hegel also regarded all specific truths as negative. Both positions could, then, be said to be 'ironic', in the sense that any truth claim is taken back, even as it is asserted. The difference is, though, clear. In Hegel's case the irony ceases at the end of the system, because all the negatives lead eventually to the positive recognition that one has exhausted negativity: negativity is the path to the truth. Romantic irony, on the other hand, does not come to an end. The sense that we can never rest with a final certainty becomes the essential fact about our being. Romantic irony is, then, an attitude of mind which tries to come to terms with the finitude of every individual's existence, rather than trying to transcend that finitude by reaching a positive, philosophical conclusion. The scepticism involved in Romantic irony is not the kind of scepticism which worries about whether all our beliefs might be false, but rather a kind of 'fallibilism', which assumes we may always come up with new and better ways of dealing with things, because being transcends what we know of it.

This is why art plays an important role in early Romantic thinking. It is precisely the fact that we cannot come to the end of the significance of a work of art that makes it valuable as a way of understanding the nature of our existence. If we really had grasped a work of art in every way there would be no reason to engage with it further. The history of the reception of art suggests why the idea of complete comprehension of art is the wrong way to look at it. The greatest art is not great because we know all about why it is great, but because it compels us to keep coming back to it. There is, therefore, no 'closure' with regard to art, and this is not a deficiency. In this respect the Romantics come close to certain ideas both in contemporary pragmatism and in post-structuralism. A further notable aspect of their way of thinking is that they adopt forms of writing which are not straightforwardly discursive. Some of their best-known work takes the form of short fragments and aphorisms, which *enact* the sense of incompleteness they are trying to communicate.[5]

The Romantic approach gives rise to new questions about the very point of philosophy. Schlegel suggests that 'In truth you would be distressed if the whole world, as you demand, were for once seriously to become completely comprehensible' (1988: ii. 240). Elsewhere he claims: 'If absolute truth were found then the business of spirit would be completed and it would have to cease to be, since it only exists in activity' (1991: 93). In critical remarks on Fichte in 1796–7 Novalis says that the 'absolute which is given to us can only be known negatively, by our acting and finding that no action can reach what we are

---

5   Too much is sometimes made of this facet of Romanticism: Schlegel also wrote major continuous works of philosophy in a more traditional mode.

seeking' (1978: 181). If we were to be able to arrive at the absolute, then, there is nothing to suggest that we would be in some wonderful new position. Indeed, we might feel that life was now pointless. Perhaps it is the very fact that we cannot cease questioning that is the source of value in our existence, rather than the hope that we will arrive at final answers. Philosophy for Novalis is 'striving' to think an absolute 'basis' (*Grund*) that would allow the completion of philosophy. However, 'If this were not given, if this concept contained an impossibility – then the drive to philosophize would be an endless activity' (ibid. 180). The best medium for this activity may be a combination of art and philosophy. We shall return to this issue in relation to the early Wittgenstein in chapter 8.

The early Romantics have often been understood either as hopeless mystics, longing for an unattainable ideal, or (as Hegel saw them) as cynical ironists, who undermine any attempt at a serious account of our place within things. Aspects of these attitudes are present in some of their work, but the remarks just cited put them much closer to contemporary pragmatism. Schlegel claims, for example, in an anti-foundationalist manner: 'There are no basic propositions [*Grundsätze*] which would universally be appropriate accompanists and leaders to the truth. Even the most dangerous [basic propositions] can be justified for certain stages and for the development of the mind and even the most secure and best can lead into an abyss of errors' (1963: 518). Instead, then, of worrying about how we can give an ultimate philosophical account of what makes our thought true, the Romantics are concerned with what to *do* in a world where the idea of the absolute may, in Schlegel's phrase, be nothing more than an 'identical triviality'. The Idealist systems sought to explicate the 'statement of identity', 'A = A', in order to avoid Kant's dualism. The aim was that A as thinking and A as being be shown to be the same. The question is, though, what value this ultimate knowledge could have, beyond what we already succeed in achieving with the fallible knowledge we generate by our continual search for truth.

What is the consequence if the Romantics are right in thinking that the absolute is inherently inaccessible to finite beings and is therefore only the motivation for continuing to seek better ways of thinking? Novalis asserts that 'There is no philosophy *in concreto*. Philosophy is, like the philosopher's stone – the squaring of the circle etc. – just a necessary task of scientists – the absolute *ideal of science*' (1978: 623). Manfred Frank has argued that the Romantic absolute therefore 'exists as that which, in the divisions and fragmentations of our world of the understanding, yet creates that unity, without which contradiction and difference could not be shown as such' (1989: 340).

The work of art – think, for example, of Beethoven's music – may therefore in some respects be a better resource for coming to terms with our situation than philosophy. Such music both relies on contradiction and difference, and yet also gives a sense of how the world can still cohere, even though we may not finally be able to say why. Knowledge, on the other hand, seems continually to have to be revised and recontextualized, so that it never provides any sense of real coherence, offering only another stage in an endless journey. If the journey is endless we may, then, sometimes be better off with experiences of coherence which are inherently transient, like music, but which also offer more than their mere transience. Science is more likely to solve practical problems, but it may not provide a stable sense of a place within things of the kind culture needs to provide.

What, though, if the notion of the absolute as the regulative idea of truth were just our projection, an attempt to hide from ourselves the merely contingent and finite nature of even our most developed thinking? We shall consider this view when we come to look at Nietzsche. For the moment it is important to note the tension that emerges in the Romantics' objections to Idealism. Are we to hang on to philosophy as the search for an ideal which we should share as honest seekers for a perhaps never finally accessible truth? This idea can come up against the idea that philosophy may be of no real significance in the modern world, either because what it seeks could never be realized anyway, or because it is of no use in solving the problems that matter to real people. The idea of the 'end of philosophy' will concern us both in this and in coming chapters. The reasons for the emergence of this idea are quite varied. One of them is the change away from the positive image of the possibilities for human flourishing which takes place in the wake of the French Revolution. This change is reflected in various philosophical positions in the first half of the nineteenth century.

Reason and Will

At exactly the same time, and in the same building, as Hegel, the then doyen of German philosophers, was giving lectures to huge audiences in 1820 at the university in Berlin, Arthur Schopenhauer (1788–1860) was supposed to lecture but did not do so for lack of an audience. Indeed, Schopenhauer's work remained largely ignored until the 1850s, at which point it began to have an effect on European culture that has continued ever since. Wagner read Schopenhauer's main work, *The World as Will and Representation*, which had first been published in 1818, while composing *Tristan and Isolde* in the 1850s, and it influenced all of his subsequent work. One of the crucial causes of the change in fortune of Schopenhauer's work was the publication of Darwin's *The Origin of Species* in 1859. Despite all the continuing attempts to discredit its findings even today, Darwin's book irrevocably changed the self-image of humankind in the Western world. Darwin made it clear that humankind could no longer see itself as singled out from the rest of nature and as wholly different from the animal kingdom. That kingdom is ruled by instinct, and the question becomes how human reason relates to the instincts that are also constitutive of our nature. Schopenhauer, himself a great animal lover (and misanthropist), had already, before Darwin, suggested an image of humankind which is summed up in his assertion that history is merely the 'zoology' of the human species. History is therefore not a progression to some higher way of being based on the development of reason. Unlike nearly all the thinkers we have considered up to now, Schopenhauer was also a thoroughgoing atheist.[6]

The intellectual accompaniment to the French Revolution had often been couched in terms of the rule of reason and of the perfectibility of humankind if it were freed from superstition. The Terror consequently suggested to some people that such ideas might themselves be the source of the horrors that were taking place. Hegel has a section on this issue in the *Phenomenology*. The difficulty is that a criticism of events like the Terror presumably has to take place in the name of reason, but the source of the problem could be seen to be reason itself. The attempt to subject all aspects of tradition to rational scrutiny can, for example, end up destroying much that helps a society cohere, and so can lead to social disintegration. The difficulties in the process of secularization in the modern world suggest how complex an issue this is. The distortions produced in some contemporary Islamic culture by the secularizing forces of modernity make it clear how important it is to understand this process.

Destroying authority based on belief in a divinity can be seen as leading to a wholesale destruction of any kind of moral authority. At

---

6   Given the assumption that Spinoza's idea of God was tantamount to atheism, it is very hard to say to what extent thinkers like Schelling and Hegel could be said to have religious convictions in an orthodox sense, especially in their youth. Later it is clear that Schelling came closer to aspects of more orthodox theology, albeit with some very unorthodox elements.

the same time, blaming the horrors perpetrated in modernity on the loss of belief in God simply ignores the obvious fact that unspeakable horrors are also perpetrated in the name of God. However, if the attempt to regulate society in the name of reason, rather than of authority and tradition, is seen as failing, what position is there left from which to try to get beyond this failure, which does not just go back to older, themselves discredited, ways of ordering things? The political debates in Germany from the nineteenth century onwards are, for example, often affected by attempts by the Right to re-establish the authority of traditional religion, as a means of stopping democratic reform. What is required to oppose this is precisely what both the Idealists and the early Romantics sought to provide. In the light of the perceived limitations of Enlightenment conceptions, which rely too much on the kind of abstractions which are the basis of the natural sciences, they sought a fuller understanding of reason. The aim was to give a central role to moral and affective dimensions of individual human life which are inaccessible to abstract rationality. These dimensions were otherwise open to appropriation by the defenders of now illegitimate traditions.

The early Romantics argued that art pointed to a more all-inclusive conception of reason which can offer ways of articulating what is not conceptually accessible. The danger of Hegel's approach is what is referred to as 'panlogism', the assumption that being itself is inherently rational. The Romantics' contrasting employment of art as a means of understanding reason is important because it does not rely either on a mystical access to something which is wholly beyond or outside reason, or on an irresponsible, merely ironic refusal to engage with society.[7] However, a further – related – way of considering the limits of reason, aspects of which appear in Schopenhauer, Nietzsche, Heidegger and others, gives rise to much bigger problems. This is the step from suggesting there are limits to *philosophical* rationality, to the claim that there is another way of understanding the world which can *only* be arrived at in some other, non-rational manner.

We touched on some aspects of this way of thinking in chapter 2, when considering the question of 'intuition'. Here is one way of trying to understand the question of intuition, which leads into Schopenhauer's key ideas. Spontaneity was fundamental to what Kant was proposing, and the vital fact about spontaneity is that it is not reducible to explanation. Explanations give grounds for some-

7   This is the point of Walter Benjamin's 1919 PhD on the early Romantics: see Bowie 1997: ch. 8.

thing being the case, and this means they reveal how something depends upon something else. Kant argues, though, that reason 'shows a spontaneity so pure that it goes far beyond everything with which sensuousness can provide it' (1974: BA 109). The will which we can exercise in moral action, as Fichte also insisted, was therefore 'unconditioned', unlike everything given by sensuousness, and so could not be explained. Fichte made the will the source of both the cognitive and the practical aspects of the subject. The problem is, though, that if something cannot be explained, our access to it is removed from the sphere of public argument, relying instead on an appeal to something supposedly shared, but not intersubjectively verifiable. Fichte was inclined at this point to insist that if you didn't intuitively understand your capacity for moral self-determination you weren't really worthy or capable of doing philosophy anyway.

What exactly is it, though, that pushes us to do one thing rather than another? Empirically this is often clear: it comes down to socialization, the prompting of an irresistible desire, etc. Kant, however, thought that the real import of moral behaviour lay in the possibility of our moral will transcending these empirical motivations. This assumption led both him and Fichte to the idea that our highest aspect is the ability to transcend determination by our interests and desires, and to act in terms of ethical goals, via a 'pure spontaneity'. The early Schelling then tried to suggest that this spontaneity must in some way be part of nature itself. Such attempts to harmonize the motivating force of internal and external nature are characteristic of Idealist thinking.

However, in a text of 1809, *On the Essence of Human Freedom*, which clearly influenced Schopenhauer, Schelling moved away from this conception. Instead of regarding the spontaneity of human will as the essence of rationality, Schelling now links it to the driving force which moves the whole of reality: 'In the last and highest instance there is no other being but willing. Willing is primal being, and all the predicates of primal being only fit willing: groundlessness, eternity, being independent of time, self-affirmation' (1856–61: I/vii. 350). His description of willing may sound rather over-dramatic, but it corresponds to Kant's description and to Fichte's appropriation of it. The will is independent of time because time is one of the forms of intuition in which the causally determined world is given to us. If the will were temporal it would be dependent on what conditioned it, like everything else in the appearing world, and it would therefore not be free at all. Similarly, it is groundless because it is its *own* ground: that is the very definition of spontaneity. The difference between Kant and Schelling is now that Schelling regards the will as 'a capacity for good and evil' (ibid. 352), not as the capacity for self-determination in accordance with the categorical imperative.[8] The crucial point here is the move away from the idea of the will as ultimately linked to rationality. Instead, it now becomes the motivating force which is supposed to answer the question of why there is a manifest, but transient, world at all.

The Spinozist account of the nature of the manifest world, which Schelling had largely adhered to until this time, claimed that the world's evidently negative aspects, such as evil actions or natural disasters, were a result of lack of insight into the make-up of the whole. The point of philosophy was therefore to make clear why things were this way and thus enable people to act more rationally by fitting into the rational pattern of the world. Schelling now takes much more seriously the idea that so much of what happens in the world seems to have no rational basis at all. Behaving ethically can therefore only have value if it requires the overcoming of something – evil – which is *positively* powerful, rather than just being based on a lack of insight. Otherwise, he argues, all we are supposed to do is to learn to fit into a pre-existing order of things that we have so far failed to understand. This would mean that there is no real point to what we do, because it is all decided in advance.

There is here a fundamental choice between opposed conceptions. (1) Does one have to accept what Jacobi had referred to as the 'nihilism' inherent in Spinoza's deterministic view of being, in which freedom seems not really to exist? Or (2) does one adopt a more existential sense that our own reality, manifest in our will, involves precisely the capacity *actively* to do evil, rather than doing it through a failure to appreciate what the good really is? This same capacity is, crucially, also what enables us to go beyond existing forms of human activity in new ways, taking us into realms which are unpredictable and potentially dangerous, but also potentially creative. (Schelling is thinking of figures like Napoleon, who seem driven by something which they do not fully understand to achieve extraordinary things.) The limitation on rationality inherent in his position is the following. One could not will evil for a *reason*, because that would then take one back into the domain of giving reasons, which is precisely what the ultimate nature of our will is now seen as contradicting. Schelling draws the startling consequence of this position in his *Ages of the World* from the early 1810s. Nobody, he argues,

---

8 Kant had himself become concerned with this issue in his *Religion within the Bounds of Reason Alone* of 1794, which influenced Schelling.

has chosen their character; and yet this does not stop anybody attributing the action which follows from this character to themselves as a free action ... Common ethical judgement therefore recognizes in every person – and to that extent in everything – a region in which there is no ground/reason [*Grund*] at all, but rather absolute freedom. ... The unground [*Ungrund*] of eternity lies this close in every person, and they are horrified by it if it is brought to their consciousness. (1946: i. 93)

The ultimate ground of our doings is therefore both fundamentally part of what we are, and yet inaccessible to rational explanation.

Thinking of this kind is clearly one source of an 'irrationalism' which proceeds from the conviction that the ultimate nature of things resists philosophical attempts to explain it. However, there are different ways of responding to the sense in which reason cannot explain itself. This situation is both horrifying and yet also the *point* of freedom in the sense that Schelling is exploring. If we had a simply *rational* grasp of freedom the result would be the Spinozist reality, which is already complete in itself and which makes what we do merely illusory, because the real nature of things is not changed by our actions and commitments. Schelling's alternative conception of freedom aims to restore the sense that we are really connected to being by the fact that our existence is ultimately groundless in the same way as the rest of being is groundless. If being were explicable in terms of reasons, we would be back with Spinozism and the unanswered question of why there is anything particular and individual at all, rather than a wholly harmonious, unconscious and unchanging substance. Schelling's idea is that God Himself does not have a *reason* to move from a state of complete harmony to the world of division which is the reality that results from creation. He does so because of a prompting of something like the divine 'id', that side of the self which Freud saw as the irrational motivating basis of the rational aspects of the self. The freedom which is based on the ultimate inexplicability of our existence is bought at the price that we have to take on the burden it entails. At the same time, however, it prevents our existence being merely the result of deterministic necessity. It is this line of thought which will play a role in existentialism, from Kierkegaard to Sartre's exploration of the claim that 'existence precedes essence'. What we are is what we become via what we *do*, not something given in advance that philosophy can describe.

Schopenhauer was certainly familiar with the *Freedom* essay, and he attended lectures by Fichte in which the model of the will as driving force is already adumbrated. He was, though, notoriously rude about all the German Idealists, even as he borrowed some of their ideas. The obvious difference between them and Schopenhauer lies in Schopenhauer's rejection of a teleological conception of history. There is for him no advance of humankind to a more rational way of being, merely the replacement of one way of doing things with another. His rejection is based on a profound pessimism, which is itself based on his interpretation of some of the issues we have just examined. Schopenhauer's basic idea is quite simple. He takes the dualism Kant establishes between things in themselves and appearances, and reinterprets it. The way he does so is contained in the title of his main work, *The World as Will and Representation*.

Schopenhauer's initial assumption is Kantian: we know the world in the forms in which it appears to us as 'representation'. This knowledge is rationally assessable in terms of the principle of sufficient reason, 'everything has a reason/cause/ground'.[9] The difference between this and Kant is that Schopenhauer claims that we do have 'intuitive' access to the world in itself, albeit not in the form of knowledge of the kind present in the sciences. Our access is to the world as 'Will'.[10] The Will is accessible in experiences over which our conscious will has no final control, such as pain, hunger and sexual desire. Note how these are indeed immediately accessible to us. If we did not have the concept of hunger, we would still feel directly what is essential about it, namely a painful lack that demands to be overcome. Aspects of our being like hunger are the non-appearing manifestations of the metaphysical ground of what appears in the form of our body. The 'Will' is, then, the prior reality. The body is secondary, being 'the visible expression' of the desires produced by this prior reality: 'teeth, gullet and intestine are objectified hunger; the genitalia the objectified sex drive' (Schopenhauer 1986: i. 168).

Schopenhauer wants to solve with this principle the problem of why the world is not just one immobile, undifferentiated thing. If being is *inherently* divided against itself, it becomes easier to understand why it keeps changing. Will is precisely the motivation to change one state of being into another. Schopenhauer thinks that any attempt to suggest that this motivation points towards a realization of a higher state, in which the individual's will is subordinated to a common goal, in the manner of the Idealist hopes for a reconciliation between individual desires and the community, is a delusion. For Hegel, as we saw, the truth of desire lay in its immediacy being over-

9 Schopenhauer has a complex theory of the fourfold nature of this principle, which need not concern us here.
10 I will use a capital letter when talking about Will in Schopenhauer's specific sense.

come by mutual recognition between self and other, which enabled mind to develop into higher forms. Desire is not abolished in this process, but is taken up into more all-inclusive forms of interaction. Schopenhauer rejects this conception: in his view nothing can redeem desire, except escaping from it altogether.

Schopenhauer's antagonism to accounts like Hegel's derives from his conviction of the ultimately futile nature of existence. Every particular appearance comes about by the subordination of some other appearance of the Will, such as the food you eat, and will itself in turn succumb in the end to the inevitable victory of the Will. There is no further guiding rationality to this process that would suggest it is leading to a less unkind state in the long run. Something similar had already been suggested by Hobbes in the *Leviathan*, and there seems to be a link between the emergence of this view of humanity and nature, and the incursion of ruthless capitalist competition into societies formerly governed by more traditional values. Marx will say of Darwin, for example, that he projects the world of nineteenth-century British capitalism onto the animal kingdom. Whatever one thinks of Schopenhauer's view as a metaphysical position, the question of how one might respond to it if it were indeed the best description of the way things are is worth pondering.

Schopenhauer himself feels compelled to seek a way out of the bleakness his argument entails. This leads him to a strange combination of a version of Idealism with what seems to be its exact opposite. Involvement in the world of Will-driven desire can only lead to endlessly renewed frustration. If a desire is fulfilled it simply gives way to another one, and eventually it all comes to an end anyway. The best solution is therefore to find a way of escaping the Will. Schopenhauer was one of the first people in modern European philosophy to be interested in Eastern thinking, and he adopts Buddhist ideas of self-transcendence as a means of escaping being a prisoner of a Will-driven, frustrated and painful existence. His other, related, response involves a specific understanding of art, particularly music.

Art enables one temporarily to escape the unrelenting pressure of the Will. It involves a kind of contemplation which is, Schopenhauer believes, in the wake of Kant, devoid of the desire to appropriate the object. The subject therefore moves beyond its dependence on the Will, which locates it in the temporal world, to – and this is the strange part – a timeless world of essences or 'ideas' that are contemplated without a feeling of pain or lack. Schopenhauer introduces a Platonic aspect into a philosophy which seems to be the antithesis of Platonism. Famously, Schopenhauer, unlike Kant, Schelling and

Hegel, gives music primacy over the other arts.[11] One reason for this lies in music's connection to mathematics, which Schopenhauer regards as a realm of pure timeless forms. Music 'does not talk of things, but rather of nothing but well-being and woe, which are the sole realities for the *Will*' (ibid. v. 507). As such, it is 'the metaphysical to everything physical in the world, the thing in itself to every appearance. One could accordingly just as well call the world embodied music as embodied Will' (ibid. i. 366). Music enacts precisely what makes life a torment, namely the temporalized, never-fulfilled lack that is the essence of the Will. Schopenhauer's model for 'music' is a melody which moves away from the tonic note, creating tension, and then returns to it, releasing the tension. However, by doing this, music seems able to transmute the Will into pure forms based on the timeless order of mathematics. Although music takes place in time, the structures of which it consists can only be adequately apprehended by getting beyond their temporal occurrence to their pure form.

Schopenhauer is a symptomatic modern thinker because he tries to combine extremes. The idea of the world as Will fits in with the restless, never-ceasing tension and change characteristic of modernity, in which, as Marx puts it, 'All that is solid melts into air'. At the same time, Schopenhauer seeks a way out of this world. He therefore focuses on the domains in modernity in which there seems still to be the possibility of relying on timeless, stable truths, namely art and mathematics. This combination of philosophical purity with a deep sense of the instability of the world will recur in other thinkers, such as Wittgenstein.

Hegel might be seen as attempting to achieve something similar, in so far as the absolute idea, once achieved, is also understood as 'abolishing' time. Hegel, though, seeks to avoid a rigidly dualistic juxtaposition of a world of time and a world of pure ideas. Our ability to think in terms of the latter develops historically out of the former, because the ideas would otherwise fail to articulate the complexity of the real. Schopenhauer's problem is to explain how it is that the essence of the temporal world is inherently non-conceptual and requires intuitive access, while at the same time using conceptual claims to do so. It is, moreover, anything but clear from his argument why there should be a world of pure forms at all, let alone how it connects to the world as Will. As we saw, Hegel rejected all forms of 'immediacy', and Schopenhauer's claims rely precisely on the immediacy of intuitive access to the Will. Hegel does fail to see that there

11 It is often claimed he was the first to do so, but the idea is already part of Romantic thinking in the 1790s and there are signs of it even earlier.

may be immediate aspects of existence which are not reducible to the concepts we use to articulate them. It is, however, quite another thing to claim that the ultimate ground of being is a metaphysical principle like the Will. At the same time, even though there is much that separates Hegel and Schopenhauer, they do share the conviction that philosophy should be the location of timeless insights into the ultimate nature of things. By the 1830s some thinkers were, in contrast, already beginning to doubt whether philosophy could or should have such a status.

The Young Hegelians and the End of Philosophy

We have already encountered the difficulty involved in establishing (1) whether Hegel is to be understood as constructing the ultimate metaphysical system, or (2) whether he is couching in metaphysical and theological language what is really a pragmatic vision of how we should legitimate our concepts in society. In the wake of Friedrich Schlegel, who probably influenced him more than he admitted, Hegel and his successors brought history into the very nature of philosophy. Hegel did so because he was convinced that the relationship between thought and being could not be understood if the ways in which thought changes over time were not understood within philosophy itself. He seeks, though, to incorporate the dynamic aspects of thought into a system which itself would not change. The question asked by many of Hegel's contemporaries and successors in relation to this enterprise is, therefore, whether the structures he describes in the *Logic* really are the structures of being. Might they not be merely a self-contained series of historically developed concepts that gain their determinacy via their relations to each other, with no guarantee that they really grasp the true nature of being? The crucial new issue is how this philosophical objection gains an explicit social and political dimension, which changes the very notion of the task of philosophy.

This new dimension can be demonstrated by looking at a few details of German philosophy at the time. The introduction of politics into the issues does, however, make things very complex. The key *philosophical* objections to Hegel, which set the pattern for the anti-Idealist thinking of the 1830s and 1840s, were made by Schelling from the 1820s onwards, and were already implicit in the arguments of his we considered earlier in this chapter. By the 1820s the once left-wing Schelling had, though, become a pretty conservative thinker, and was regularly attacked as such by those on the Left from the 1830s onwards. Although both he and Hegel supported the monarchy, Schelling can be construed as making a link between the limits he saw in reason's capacity to grasp being, and the transcendence of the King's authority over merely human legitimation. Hegel, on the other hand, sought to legitimate the King's role in philosophical terms, as part of the development of a specifically modern rationality. Schelling was appointed to what had been Hegel's chair of philosophy in 1841 because he was regarded as opposing the dangerously liberal elements in Hegel's thought. By this time many on the Left had also come to oppose Hegel, for both philosophical and political reasons. Much of their *philosophical* critique was, moreover, influenced by Schelling. The constellation is further complicated by the debates over the nature of theology.

The criticisms of the so-called Young Hegelians, such as Ludwig Feuerbach (1804–72), whose aims were increasingly social and political, were directed *against* established theology. Schelling's critique of Hegel was, in contrast, undertaken with the intention of establishing a philosophical theology in opposition to the perceived Spinozist assumptions of Hegel's thought. The objection that Spinozism was essentially atheism, and so led to nihilism, was to be countered by a rethinking of the idea of God as 'personality'. God is here not the 'deist' totality of the ways in which the world is rationally intelligible, but rather a 'theist' active, creative divinity. The complexities of how this contrast of theological conceptions is played out cannot concern us here (see Breckmann 1999). The decisive issue is how certain structures of thought are shared by Left and Right against Hegel, even though the aims of their thinking are very different indeed.

Hegel's notion of universal mediation gives primacy to the relationships in which things and people are located. The truth about particular things is constituted by structures which are prior to the particulars that are comprehended in those structures. This means that the truth about human individuals is to be understood in terms of their location in structures such as legal and property relations. The hierarchy of truth we observed in Hegel leads to a conception of the relationship of the individual to society in which the individual is subordinate to the family, and the truth of the family is constituted in the state, because the state has to mediate between the particular interests of differing families. This conception was formulated at the time in terms of the state as the 'subject', of which the individuals and their families are the 'predicates'. The fundamental idea in the Young Hegelian critiques of Idealism is that subject and predicate have become inverted by Idealism, and need to be restored to their correct relationship. This can happen in relation to a whole series of issues, from the ontological to the political. One version of such a claim is that, rather than the state being the true reality, of which its subjects are the predicates, without the real, living individual subjects there would be nothing of which the state could be the expression.[12] At the same time, some of the same thinkers, like Marx, who wish to correct the perceived inversion in Idealism, also adopt aspects of Hegel's idea that the individual is primarily constituted by their social relationships. The objection to Hegel in this respect will be directed at his failure to appreciate how distorted social contexts lead to individuals who are themselves distorted.

The underlying *logic* of the anti-Idealist position on subject and predicate is already contained in Schelling's remark against Hegel in circa 1833:

> Concepts as such do in fact exist nowhere but in consciousness, they *are*, therefore, taken objectively, *after* nature, not *before* it . . . abstractions cannot be there, be taken for realities, before that from which they are abstracted; becoming cannot be there before something becomes, existence not before something exists. (1994: 145)

Idealism takes 'predicates' – concepts – as the real subject of being. Rather than concepts being what can be predicated of being, they themselves become the prior reality. The Idealist conception can be seen as going back to Plato's forms, which suggests to some thinkers that Idealism and philosophy may be effectively coextensive. This theme will recur in Nietzsche, and in Heidegger and Adorno in the next century. The further consequence is that the critique of Idealism points in the direction of the 'end of philosophy'. If Idealism is overcome, the point of philosophy in an Idealist sense is also overcome. Once the claim that there is a timeless ultimate structure of truth is put in question, certain conceptions of the nature of philosophy also become problematic. This raises the question, of course, of what will replace philosophy. For Schelling this is not a real problem, because his aim is a new combination of philosophy and theology. However, some of those he influences see the replacement of philosophy in social and political terms because they think philosophy is just secularized theology, and so has the same effects as the theology they oppose.

In a later formulation, from the 1840s, Schelling presents the alternative between Idealism and what he now terms 'positive philosophy'

---

12   The state is often seen in Rousseau's terms as that which is to express the 'general will'.

as follows: 'For either the concept would have to go first, and being would have to be the consequence of the concept . . . or the concept is the consequence of being, then we must begin with being without the concept' (1856–61: II/iii. 164).[13] He realizes that this means we can say nothing determinate about being, but that being, as it was for Kant, must be the necessary real presupposition of its predicates. A Hegelian might then argue that this indeterminacy of being is precisely the point: it is only when being becomes something via social interchange that it is conceptually significant. Hegel's conception would seem compatible with an essentially left-wing conception of the centrality of social and political perspectives, rather than merely philosophical ones. Why, then, do Feuerbach and the other Young Hegelians come to oppose Hegel?

The importance of Young Hegelians' objections to Hegelian thinking should not be underestimated. Jürgen Habermas suspects that 'our point of departure is not essentially different from that of the first generation of the pupils of Hegel' (1988: 36). For the most significant German thinkers after Hegel, from Feuerbach, to Nietzsche, Heidegger and Habermas himself, the very understanding of the task of philosophy in modernity becomes an issue because of the demise of Hegel's emphatic conception of the status of philosophy. If philosophy no longer can, or should, play a decisive systematizing role in modernity, what are the alternatives for dealing with what had formerly been seen as philosophical issues? One way of considering the perceived dangers of Hegel's approach to philosophy is in sociopolitical terms. The idea is that Hegel's philosophy subordinates real people to abstractions. This is precisely what Marx thinks that modern capitalism also does to them, by giving money, the abstract medium through which value is exchanged in society, precedence over people. There would therefore seem to be a homology between the idea of the philosophical system which gives priority to universals over particulars, and the negative effects of capitalism on particular human individuals. The consequence is a demand for philosophy to oppose what gives rise to the abstractions in the real world, including the abstractions generated by philosophy itself, which may play a role in obscuring aspects of human reality. In some respects this demand echoes Hamann's and Herder's critique of the Enlightenment's failure to value the sensuous world. The difference lies in the relationship of Feuerbach and the others to theology.

---

13 Positive philosophy is opposed to 'negative philosophy', an example of which is Hegel: the idea is that such philosophy assumes a 'merely logical relationship of God to the world'.

The main philosophical difficulty Feuerbach and the other Young Hegelians face is the need to take account of the undoubted insights of the Idealists into how structures of thought play an ineliminable role in what we can understand of the real. A rejection of Idealism in the name of 'materialism' and increased attention to the fact that we are sensuous beings fails to answer the Fichtean question of how a merely objective world can give rise to subjectivity. It is clear that this problem is not settled by the Young Hegelians, and philosophy today still exhibits similar tensions between more Idealist and more materialist perspectives. Feuerbach's perhaps most influential idea is summed up in the opening of his *Foundations of the Philosophy of the Future* (1843): 'The task of the modern age was the making real and making human of God – the transformation and dissolution of theology into anthropology' (1983: 35). The God of theism is for Feuerbach, as He will be later for Freud in *The Future of an Illusion*, a 'projection' of human attributes onto an external, non-human authority. Positive human attributes, like charity, do not, in Feuerbach's view, have their real source in this authority. The fact that theism claims that they do is what he terms an 'alienation' of the most essential attributes of humankind. If positive human potential is reclaimed from its alienated form in religion, Feuerbach thinks it can be directed towards the overcoming of real social and political problems.

Just how important the idea of religion as projection is can be illustrated by the example of the rise of nationalism in the nineteenth century. One way of accounting for this new factor in modernity is that the need for self-transcendence via devotion to something higher, which had been focused on God, moves its focus onto the collective in the form of the nation. The desire for self-transcendence can be used to legitimate action in questionable ways, by, for example, encouraging individuals to sacrifice themselves to the supposed higher needs of the nation. Rather than relating to the essence of what is best about human beings, projection can, furthermore, also take the form of paranoia. Insecurities can be projected onto the other in a manner analogous to the way Feuerbach sees positive human attributes as being projected onto God. Such paranoid projection can lead to persecution of the other for what one hates in oneself, and this can easily play a role in the genesis of aggressive nationalism. The solution to false projection might seem to be simply the destruction of delusions by rational criticism, but the borderline between mere delusions and what makes life seem meaningful is anything but straightforward. Without some sense of being part of something greater than oneself, the individual may feel isolated, and so lack any feeling of purpose in their life. It is for this reason that the relationship between religion and ideology becomes so important in this period and beyond. Marx refers at one point to ideology as 'necessary false belief'. What is it, though, that enables people to see through false belief, of which religion comes to be regarded as the main example in this period? Moreover, even if people can be persuaded to see through religion as ideology, what is on offer in its place?

Feuerbach's idea is that the truth of the 'metaphysical and onto-theological [= concerned with the reality of God]' aspects in religion in fact lies in 'psychological or rather anthropological' factors. The essence of humanity is sensuous existence in the form of love, which takes one beyond oneself into real participation in the world. Consequently 'the Christian God is Himself just an abstraction from human love' (ibid. 89): subject and predicate are again inverted. This inversion is the theme of Feuerbach's major work, *The Essence of Christianity* (1841): 'the *secret of theology* is *anthropology*, of the divine being it is the human being' (1969: 400). The critique of religion is therefore the 'destruction of an *illusion* – but of an illusion which is by no means indifferent, but which rather has a thoroughly destructive effect on humankind' (ibid. 406). The idea is not, though, to eradicate the feelings which are the basis of religion, but rather to make the everyday world the location of these elevated feelings, feelings which are connected to sensuous experiences, such as the pleasure we can take in the natural world. However, the idea that the truth of religion can be revealed by philosophy is essential to Hegel's thinking as well. He too sees religion as a form of alienation of human thinking, which projects what is really the result of the activity of thought into something which seems separate from thought. The point of philosophy is to integrate the content of religion in a truly rational form into modern life.

The deeper reasons for Feuerbach's rejection of Hegelianism have, then, to do with other factors. One is quite simply Feuerbach's espousal of materialism in opposition to Hegel's Idealism. He reverses what he sees as the Idealist relationship between subject and predicate, where mind is subject and matter predicate. The dependence of the development of mind on the sensuous apprehension of nature means, Feuerbach claims, that Hegel's idea of universal mediation rests on something immediate, namely 'sensuousness'. Sensuousness is therefore not secondary to thought: we saw something similar in Hamann. This simple reversal is, however, not plausible in this form, as Hegel's critique of empiricism suggested. It is impossible to get to an intelligible, knowable world just from sense-data

from the external world. One of the enduring insights of both Hegel
and the Romantics is that separating what the world contributes and
what the mind contributes to knowledge is an impossible enterprise.
Perception is always in some way mediated. The frequent invocation
of 'materialism' against 'idealism' in modern philosophy, especially in
some Marxist theories which think of knowledge in terms of 'mir-
roring' the material world correctly, fails to take account of this
insight. Hegel's mistake is that he still tries to criticize the separation
of mind and material world from the side of mind, having shown in
the most plausible aspects of his work why it is a mistake to do this.
Feuerbach, albeit inconsistently, repeats the mistake from the other
side. When the Idealist asks 'how can mind emerge from matter?',
Feuerbach simply inverts the question: 'How can matter emerge from
mind?' (1980: 32). Schelling got close to a more defensible view in
his *Naturphilosophie*, when he talked of 'real-idealism' as a way of
getting away from the attempt to resolve mind/matter issues from
one side of the divide. If we assume the self-organizing aspects of
nature are part of what nature inherently is, then nature is always
already in some sense both material and mental.

The most important aim of Feuerbach's critique of Hegel does not,
however, completely depend on this thorny philosophical problem.
The philosophical reduction of sensuous experience to its articulation by general concepts can, as we saw in Hamann's criticisms of
Enlightenment thinking, also be seen as repressing something fundamental about human beings. Feuerbach's main desire is for the
species to realize its potential, much of which depends on the possibilities of sensuous enjoyment and inspiration. Hegel is, for
Feuerbach, the last significant modern manifestation of the attempt
to sustain the inversion of God and nature that is present in religion.
He does so by giving the absolute Idea the same status as God the
creator – both are the subject of which the real world is the predicate. The liberation from theology must therefore also include the
overcoming of Hegelianism; only then will humankind really become
able to realize its potential. The familiar notion in Heidegger and
postmodern thinkers of overcoming 'ontotheology' is, then, if rather
inconsistently, already adumbrated by Feuerbach. The complexities
of this overcoming of metaphysics begin to become apparent when
Feuerbach insists that, instead of connecting itself to religion,
'*Philosophy must connect itself again with natural science, natural
science with philosophy*' (ibid. 190). The nature of this connection will
become perhaps the major focus of German philosophy from this
time onwards. Verdicts on this connection will range from the idea
that philosophy should be dissolved into the natural sciences, to the

idea that philosophy should be the location of criticism of the sciences. The next two chapters will further explore these issues, first in Marx, and then in Nietzsche.

SUGGESTIONS FOR FURTHER READING

Behler, E. (1993) *German Romantic Literary Theory* (Cambridge: Cambridge University Press). *Study of Romantic thinking about philosophy and literature by significant scholar of early German Romanticism.*

Beiser, F. C. (1992) *Enlightenment, Revolution, and Romanticism: The Genesis of Modern German Political Thought, 1790–1800* (Cambridge, MA: Harvard University Press). *Informed, if somewhat tendentious, account of key issues in the origins of modern political thinking in Germany.*

Bowie, A. (1997) *From Romanticism to Critical Theory. The Philosophy of German Literary Theory* (London: Routledge). *Wide-ranging presentation of development of ideas concerning literature and truth from Kant and the Romantics to the Frankfurt School, showing the influence of Romantic thought on such thinkers as Heidegger and Adorno.*

Breckman, W. (1999) *Marx, the Young Hegelians, and the Origins of Radical Social Theory* (Cambridge: Cambridge University Press). *Excellent reinterpretation of the thought of the Young Hegelians in the context of issues in nineteenth-century Germany politics.*

Loewith, K. (1964) *From Hegel to Nietzsche. The Revolution in Nineteenth Century Thought* (New York: Holt, Rinehart and Winston). *Classic account by major German philosopher.*

Wartofsky, M. W. (1977) *Ludwig Feuerbach* (Cambridge: Cambridge University Press). *Good general account of the work of Feuerbach.*

Zizek, S. (1999) *The Indivisible Remainder* (London: Verso). *Provocative reinterpretation of Schelling in the light of contemporary theoretical concerns by major cultural theorist.*

6

CRITIQUES OF IDEALISM II: MARX

The Ends of Philosophy

Two facts about the critics of Idealism on whom we will focus in this and the next chapter suggest some of the new issues that come more to the fore in German philosophy of the second half of the nineteenth century. First, Karl Marx (1818–83) belonged to the political Left; Friedrich Nietzsche (1844–1900), despite his influence on many left-wing thinkers, was politically on the Right. Second, although Nietzsche was appointed very early to an academic post, much of his major work was produced after he left that post, never to take another academic job. Marx never had an academic job at all, his theoretical work being produced during his involvement in the politics of the day as journalist, political activist and independent researcher.

The first fact makes it clear that the relationship of philosophy to social and political issues becomes more fraught, as the tensions inherent in modern philosophy that we have been considering become increasingly manifest as concrete problems in the socio-political world. At the same time, for example, as application of the results of science in modern technology provides more solutions to problems requiring the control of nature, technology often makes the lives of many who use it a misery. The relationship between knowledge and action therefore becomes an ever more contentious issue, to which Left and Right offer very different responses. The perception of philosophy's task consequently also changes for many thinkers, in ways we began to examine in the last chapter. The epistemological task of showing why scientific theories work can, for instance, come to be regarded as merely academic, given the success of the sciences. The philosophical task becomes instead the integration of the knowledge provided by the sciences into the rest of culture.

The second fact points to the questioning of the social status of philosophy at this time. Both Marx and Nietzsche adopt Feuerbach's idea that philosophy may itself be a problem to which the solution is the abolition of philosophy, at least in its existing forms. Hegel and Schelling had begun as defenders of the French Revolution and as radical thinkers who did not initially fit into the institutional forms of academia. They were, moreover, part of a period of new philosophical thinking which is often seen as rivalling that of the ancient Greeks. However, they later became the representatives of established academic philosophy, who were attacked as such by the Young Hegelians. Hegel and Schelling came to be seen as themselves part of the problem, as abstract system-builders who defended an unjustifiable political status quo. This may or may not be a fair judgement, and the contemporary sense that Hegel offers vital resources for overcoming the deficits of philosophy in the analytical tradition suggests just how difficult the relationship between philosophy, politics and history can be. The fact that the most important German thinkers of the second half of the nineteenth century do not work within established academic institutions does, then, point to a significant change in the intellectual climate. At the same time, it should be remembered, as we shall see in chapter 8, that academic philosophy was still pursuing its own agenda.

Marx and Nietzsche share the conviction that the way the existing philosophy of the nineteenth century sees the world, and the way the world actually is, are increasingly at odds. They differ radically over how this is the case, but there is a common consequence of their conviction with regard to academic philosophy. Even if it involves radical criticism of philosophy, the academic pursuit of philosophy considers this criticism as something to be carried out within established institutional forms. However, if the crucial new issue is the failure of philosophy to make any difference to the real world, then the kind of philosophical activity which assumes that arriving at watertight metaphysical arguments is the aim of philosophy may seem incompatible with a conception in which what is *done* in the world is decisive.[1] As the Romantics already wondered: even if one were to arrive at the complete philosophical system, would that really make people's lives more meaningful, or make them act more rationally?

1 Hints of this latter conception were, of course, already present in Fichte's thought and are implicit in Kant.

Might it not instead confront people with the futility of living in a world where things were already settled from the outset?

On the other hand, what happens if the idea that philosophy can provide a new, systematic, post-theological way of integrating the conflicting aspects of modernity really is given up? Might this not lead to a feeling of disorientation, and to the search for other – perhaps dangerous – ways of trying to create a meaningful order of things? The problem with such a search is how its results are to be legitimated, given that the traditional forms of legitimation are themselves put in question by doubts about the status of reason. The search can too easily take place in areas that have nothing much to do with philosophy, so that the goal of shared rationality is abandoned. There is, then, a tension, exemplified by both Marx and Nietzsche, between the idea that one is better off getting rid of philosophy, and the temptation to replace philosophy with something else. A vital factor in this tension are the achievements of the natural sciences and the challenges they pose to the very idea of philosophy as a source of truth and legitimation. Should philosophy sustain itself by doing what the sciences cannot do, or does it increasingly dissolve into the sciences? Let us now have a look at how these issues appear in some of the work of Marx.

Alienation

The theme of social transformation, which recurs throughout Marx's work, is already inherent in the notion of 'alienation' from his work in the 1840s. In Feuerbach, alienation meant the mistaken attribution of something proper to humankind to God. Marx realizes, though, as indeed does Feuerbach, that religion should be properly understood, rather than being regarded as merely a delusion. His famous dictum that religion is the 'opium of the people' should, therefore, not be understood as meaning that religion is merely something which prevents people thinking critically about their situation (though it can be that too). Opium also kills pain and thus can make tolerable a life which would otherwise be intolerable: hence Marx's comment, preceding the remark on opium, that religion is 'the heart of a heartless world and the soul of soulless conditions'. The way to obviate religion is therefore to create a world that is not heartless and conditions that are not soulless. Whatever doubts one may have about Marx's conception, it is worth remembering that in modern societies that have created more stable, hopeful and fair conditions for their members, organized religion has tended to play a diminished role.

This is not the case in societies which become less just and more unequal. The link between concrete aspects of the social world, and the creation, adoption and rejection of ideas will, of course, be one of Marx's major concerns in all his work.

Lurking in the question of religion is an ambiguity, which helps to explain the vexed issue of ideology in Marx. Religion cannot just be a conscious invention of the dominant groups in a society which is used to keep subordinate groups in their place, by promising a life after death that compensates for the awfulness of life on earth, or by suggesting that injustice and suffering are part of God's purpose (although some radical thinkers in this period do tend to see it that way). If that were all religion was, it would be hard to see why it could have so much power over so many people in the first place. At the same time, religion *does* function as an instrument of domination. The potential link between certain forms of Christianity and reactionary politics is present from the beginning of modernity. The feudal orders in Europe were supported by the theological conception of a 'chain of being', with God at the top, the King next in line, and so on, down to the peasants, and then the rest of nature. When the feudal orders come under pressure, the function of religion also reveals itself as oppressive, especially if looked at from the perspective of those lower down the pile. It might seem simple, therefore, to equate religion with ideology, in the sense of consciously produced deception in the interest of dominant social groups. The interplay of the conscious and unconscious aspects of religion makes it evident, however, that it can be very difficult to understand the roots of oppressive thinking and action. Ideology can be both consciously employed as deception and yet can also result from the way in which those who actually hold the power unthinkingly regard their being in power as a natural state of affairs. Oppression need not work at the conscious, intentional level. It can also be the result of more complex structural factors which need not be transparent to those subjected to those factors or to those whose activity produces the structures. Think of how ideas one holds to be true at one time, because of social pressure, upbringing, etc., can later turn out to be merely the result of factors which one could not see were distorting what one thought.

The question for philosophy, as seen by Marx and the Young Hegelians, is how it can play a role in overcoming such distortion, so as to arrive at more just social conditions. Another way of seeing the difficulties associated with the notion of ideology is simply to ask: is the theory that maintains there is systematically distorted thinking in a society not itself ideological? Is there *any* mode of thinking which is not in some way affected by the circumstances of its emergence?

If criticism of ideology is itself not distorted, there must be some way of gaining access to the true way things are. But what is this way? Are not all social groups likely to be biased by their place in the social order, and are not some perspectives on things congenitally resistant to being judged objectively, such as certain sorts of decision about right and wrong? What is Marx's response to such problems?

Marx begins by studying law, but moves to the study of philosophy in 1838, and initially thinks along similar lines to Feuerbach, regarding religion as ideological projection. Marx's early move away from the Young Hegelian position depends on his reassessment of the notion of alienation. He comes to think that Feuerbach's position is too much concerned with philosophy and religion in an abstract manner, as though widespread *philosophical* insight into the theological inversion of subject and predicate would really change the injustices he sees in European capitalism. Marx comes to understand alienation, the separation of human power from the person and its transference to something else, in a more concrete manner. He extends Feuerbach's concern with humankind as sensuous beings to the idea that our natural capacities are made alien to us by the way in which they are appropriated by *society*. Rousseau had introduced the theme of the distortion of human nature by social forms into the Enlightenment, and in some respects Marx belongs to the tradition Rousseau helps to establish. However, attempts to establish where the border between the social and the natural is located are the source of some of the most intractable questions in modern philosophy.

Marx's contribution in the 1840s is to make concrete the idea of alienation in the terms of 'political economy'. Instead of beginning with an analysis of philosophical issues, as he had done in his critique of Hegel's *Philosophy of Right* in 1843, his never-completed *Economic-Philosophical Manuscripts* (*EPM*) of 1844 begin with a study of the assumptions of the major theorists of the capitalist economy, such as Adam Smith and David Ricardo. Alienation here takes on a series of related senses. Importantly, Marx rejects the 'Romantic' sense of alienation as the feeling that we are fundamentally not at home in nature. He looks at the issue in a more pragmatic way, arguing that if the main sources of deprivation are removed, human beings will be able, as Feuerbach hoped, to develop their naturally given capacities to the full, rather than have them work to their detriment.

The key factors here are the concepts of labour and labour-power. The latter is initially given in the form of natural capacities of the species for changing things in its environment; the former is what takes on objectified forms in society, notably money. The relationship between the two is therefore not fixed: the nature of labour power can change as the nature of labour changes, and vice versa. The main point is that labour is an externalization of something proper to the individual. The subject makes something objective by externalizing their own naturally given powers. How and in what circumstances the subject does this is the decisive issue. The inversion present in religion here takes on a new form. In a capitalist economy, where workers labour in exchange for pay from the owners of the means of production: 'The worker becomes poorer the more wealth he produces, the more his production increases in power and scope. . . . The object which labour produces, its product, appears against labour as an *alien being*, as a *power which is independent* of the producer' (Marx 1970: 151). Labour is necessary for the survival of the species, so it would seem logical that the more one works in altering nature, the more one is able to gain control of life. In capitalism, though, the value of what is produced is not returned to those who produce it; even worse, the form in which this value is appropriated has the inverse effect, taking more *away* from the worker the more he produces. Starvation-level wages are not unusual even today in many capitalist economies. Much of Marx's subsequent work will be devoted to trying to explain *exactly* how this comes about, which is not very clear in the early work.

The problem with the conception outlined here lies in the huge scope of the notion of alienation. It seems to include any production of anything for someone else's use or ownership. For the notion to have any critical grip it has to rely on an idea of authentic production, of the kind, for example, that is associated with the work of the artist. Marx sees private property as the 'necessary consequence of *externalized work*, of the external relationship of the worker to nature and to himself' (ibid. 12). The answer to this would seem to be production for mutual need within the kind of context of acknowledgement of the other we looked at in Fichte and Hegel. However, this already rather vague conception does not obviate the fact that much labour is a drag, that has to be done if we are to survive at all. Distributing work more fairly can improve things, but it does not remove the necessity of unpleasant labour which prevents those who have to do it from realizing their essential capabilities. Technology can help here, but it will never be able to get rid of drudgery altogether. Furthermore, work which is intolerable for some people can be pleasurable for others, depending on the kind of life they have led and the kind of person they are. What decides which work does and which work does not involve the externalized relationship Marx criticizes?

It is not that Marx is deceived about the phenomena he tries to grasp via the notion of alienation. The employment of labour in nineteenth-century capitalism involves the most appalling brutality and impoverishment, both material and spiritual, of the working classes. The vital thing is to get the diagnosis right of why this is the case, so that responses to this state of affairs are effective.

The difficulty with Marx's conception becomes further apparent in relation to his discussion of money. Money gives to its possessor qualities which they do not really possess: 'I *am* ugly, but I can buy myself the *most beautiful* woman. Therefore I am not *ugly*' (ibid. 223). The use of inversion here is telling, and too neat to be wholly plausible. Marx regards what is wrong with this situation as the fact that private property, in the form of money, 'alienates' essential properties of human beings, such as love for another person. Now there is no doubt that there is a pathological form of relationship to money, to which nearly all of us may be prey in some measure, and which can and does pervert relationships. However, the advantages of money for enabling all kinds of social exchange cannot be ignored. Without the abstract medium, which allows universal exchange of different things for each other, it is hard to see how many of the positive advances of modernity would have been possible. At the same time, the abstract medium of money also plays a role in massive injustice and brutality by obscuring real human suffering. Think of the appalling wages paid to the people who harvest much of the food consumed in the West without any thought for the plight of its producers.

Kant was aware of the dangers of the effects of money in the modern world. He insisted on the need to sustain a form of value, the 'dignity' of the rational being, which could not be exchanged for anything else. Marx is aiming at something similar, but his way of suggesting how dignity can be defended is problematic. His general antipathy to Kant, as the theorist of liberalism, which is based on the rights and duties of the individual, suggests where the divide lies. Marx thinks dignity has to be arrived at via the organization of society as a whole. The liberal concern with the state and with just laws that protect the individual will therefore always fail to appreciate the need for a transformation of the relationships between the individual and society. In capitalism individuals will always live at the expense of others. Marx consequently underestimates the importance of a differentiated *political* conception of how social transformation can be achieved, and this is arguably one source of some of the brutality later carried out in his name. If the – often unjust and inequitable – laws of the state which protect individuals are not *just* an expression of the alienated condition of society, but also a vital defence against abuse, society cannot simply be transformed by the removal of the sources of alienation in private property. What is there to say that this may not result in worse forms of abuse?

Marx does not just seek a return to a previous condition of society, of the kind that preceded the incursion of the capitalist mode of exchange. One of the most important aspects of Marx's thought, which he shares with Hegel, is the refusal to think it can be rational to turn the clock back. Overcoming a problematic condition of society means trying to develop the aspects of that condition which point to a better future, rather than thinking that the past could be recreated. The real problem lies in the apocalyptic nature of his judgement on 'alienated labour'. In the *EPM* he argues that even if there were a substantial raising of wages above the below-subsistence level characteristic of the time in many parts of Europe, this would not give work 'its human determination and dignity' (ibid. 163). He thinks it is probably impossible to raise wages this way, given the nature of the relationship between worker and capitalist. The history of trade-unionism will, of course, prove him wrong. Because wages are a 'direct consequence of alienated labour, and alienated labour is the immediate consequence of private property' (ibid.), the two must be abolished together. What would result from this abolition would be communism, but Marx is notoriously vague about what it would really consist in.

The difficulty here lies in the characterization of the relationship between the self and society. Marx claims that 'Society' – here meant in the emphatic sense of a justly organized form of collective living – 'is the completed unity of essence of humankind and nature, the true resurrection of nature, the developed naturalism of man and the developed humanism of nature' (ibid. 186). What he is seeking is a unity of aspects – the individual and society – which have been understood to be inherently opposed. He thinks they are only opposed because of the organization of society in terms of the acquisitive interests of private individuals. For Marx the individual can only *be* an individual as part of a social order, and as a member of the species. The conception is very close in this respect to Hegel. Despite the worrying sense that the individual is merely subordinated to the society which makes them possible, Marx's anti-individualistic conception does lead him to some remarkable insights. The indication of the need for a balance between the human and the natural which would be to the benefit of both continues the ecological aspect we observed in Schelling's *Naturphilosophie*. Marx here suggests the need to avoid regarding nature solely as something to be controlled in human terms, which is an idea sorely lacking in his later work.

In a remarkable passage of the *EPM* Marx talks of the 'history of *industry* as . . . the *open* book of *human essential powers*, the sensuously present human *psychology*' (ibid. 192). His insistence on the impossibility of understanding how to transform society if one concentrates on the individual, rather than on seeing how society and psychology are inextricably linked, here takes on a more discerning form. Essential aspects of psychology evidently can be better understood by looking at the material products of a society, rather than at the motivations which people cite for their actions. Think of the way things as diverse as Nazi architecture, the private motorcar and digital technology all can tell us something crucial about what people are when they live in a society in which these things play a major role. However, these insights do not obviate Marx's failure to see that the generalized notion of alienation is dangerously imprecise. It relies on a quasi-theological idea of the real essence of humankind, which can only emerge if the right circumstances are created. This idea can lead to a temptation to do whatever is required to achieve those circumstances, and this is where one of the dangers of the Marxist legacy lies. Given the complexities involved in overcoming religion, it is perhaps not so surprising that hints of Jewish messianism seem to be lurking under the surface of Marx's anti-religious arguments.

Historical Materialism

Marx's comments on psychology and industry prefigure his important reflections on what he terms 'historical materialism'. He begins these in *The German Ideology* (1845–6), which he wrote with Friedrich Engels, and he develops the notion in subsequent texts. The difficulty of interpreting the term 'historical materialism' has had a great effect on the history of Marxism as political practice. The initial issue in historical materialism is, however, itself quite simple. Marx increasingly thinks that the social forms of production and exchange are more important in determining how people think about their world and what they do than anything resulting from supposedly pure scientific or philosophical enquiry. This means the Young Hegelian critique of philosophy becomes extended into the more thoroughgoing claim that the independent existence of philosophy is no longer defensible.

What status, though, does a *theory* have which claims that all forms of metaphysics – in the broad sense of accounts of the way things hang together as a whole – are indefensible? The claim is made because metaphysics fails to register the fact that theories result from the practice of actors in specific societies, not from the purely disinterested attempt to get in touch with the timeless nature of being. But how can one make a totalizing assertion about the impossibility of assertions about the totality? Marx is aware of the problem in some respects, because he stresses that ideas have to prove themselves in practice, rather than be merely theoretically justified. Even here, though, one might ask: is this claim itself a foundational theoretical claim, and, if it is, what makes it valid? However, it can also be argued that the demand for such a legitimation is actually a way of just falling back into the notion of philosophy Marx seeks to reject. Similar ideas are encountered in the work of Heidegger and the pragmatist Richard Rorty, who want us to abandon the conception of ideas corresponding to a mind-independent reality, and to work instead with the idea that thinking is inseparable from practical activity (see e.g. Heidegger 1979; Rorty 1991).

Marx talks, for example, of language as 'practical consciousness', which sums up his position very aptly, making the supposedly internal mental aspect of language part of shared action in the world with other people. (We shall encounter similar ideas in Heidegger.) At the same time, Marx himself does seem to pursue the idea that he can reveal the deceptions involved in dominant forms of thought of his time by analysing their relationship to specific forms of social and economic exchange. This conception would seem to assume a more realist approach, such that the theory reveals the ultimate reality behind the illusion. This is, after all, what philosophers had been trying to do since the Greeks. The fact that this task is now construed in scientific terms is neither here nor there. It is the status attributed to science in relation to philosophy that is decisive. Many people in this period and since think that science will eventually replace philosophy, precisely because it gives a picture of reality that can be tested, rather than merely speculating about the true nature of reality. The question will then be, of course, what this means for the everyday human world, which does not function in terms of the latest scientific conceptions. How do we square our everyday perspective on our moral decisions and actions with the way they appear as part of Marx's analysis of the repressive nature of capitalism, an analysis for which he makes increasingly scientific claims?

The tension between assumptions about abolishing metaphysics based on a pragmatic approach, and assumptions based on the claim to superior insight of science over philosophy are fundamental in the subsequent history both of Marxism and of many other forms of German philosophy. Marx tends to move increasingly from the former, praxis-based conception to the latter. His concern with unravelling the mysteries of nineteenth-century capitalism becomes more reliant on what he thinks are core *theoretical* insights into the relationship between economics, social development and politics. These matters are too complex to be dealt with here, so I will just highlight two aspects of his work which are most significant for the subsequent development of modern philosophy. These are (1) the relationship between material and mental production, and (2) the theory of the commodity.

One of the key factors in the movement of philosophy from Kant to the critiques of Idealism is that the role of the autonomous self diminishes. Marx's conception belongs within this trend. It is not the case, though, that he therefore conceives of the individual as *merely* the result of abstract systems and structures. His aim, especially in the early work, is to allow true individuality to emerge. This is only possible in a society which has overcome alienation, which requires the overcoming of what he sees as the false kind of individualism. At his best, Marx 'decentres' the self in ways which offer deep insights into the nature of our self-descriptions in modernity. At his worst, he does move towards a kind of scientism, by reducing people to the causal factors which determine their behaviour, and providing no account of their possibilities for autonomy.

In the Preface to *A Critique of Political Economy* (1859), Marx gives the classic brief formulation of the method he works out in the wake of his modifications to the conception we looked at above. He describes how the 'social production of life' – note how life is not just naturally 'given', but has continually to be 'produced' in society – takes place on the basis of 'material productive forces'. The production of life changes with history, depending, for example, on the technological resources that are available for producing the necessities of life. The key issue is how the 'material productive forces', the organization of which Marx talks of in terms of the 'relations of production' in 'civil society', 'condition' legal and political relationships in a society. This is the notorious model of economic 'base', and legal and political 'superstructure', in which the former conditions how people think in the latter: 'It is not the consciousness of men that conditions [*bestimmt*] their being, but, on the contrary, their social being that conditions their consciousness' (Marx and Engels 1971: 8–9). The interpretation of this conditioning depends on how the German word 'bestimmt' is understood. It can refer to a causal 'determination', but if it is translated as 'condition' the sense of mechanical necessity is weakened in the direction of a priority of the effect of one factor over another. One can be said to be conditioned by one's relationships with one's family and friends, but not necessarily wholly determined by them.

Lives can depend on such matters of interpretation, as the tortuous history of the reception of Marx's texts in the Soviet Union and elsewhere suggests. It is easy to see, for example, that the idea of enforcing changes in the base, in the manner of 'command economies' which industrialize 'from above', can be understood as also resulting in changes in the superstructure. Those changes are, though, themselves brought about by the superstructure, namely the state. Marx's real point, though, was that technological developments *precede* societies' and states' adjustments to what these developments mean, both in terms of property and other legal relations, and in terms of the concepts used to think about them. Think of the extent to which society is now rapidly being changed by digital technology without our being able to control or fully understand the wider implications and effects of that technology. The way the base conditions things is, however, hardly straightforward, not least because there does not seem to be a one-way relationship between it and the superstructure. Marx sees revolutionary change in terms of his understanding of the French Revolution. If we see it in terms of the way the Soviet Union enforced change, supposedly in accordance with Marxist principles, a very different picture emerges, in which the relationship between base and superstructure is arguably reversed by the very existence of Marxist theory itself.

The next part of Marx's argument is that revolutions result when the forces of production come into 'contradiction' with the relations of production. How this change affects the 'superstructure' is, he claims, a question of ideology. It cannot be established with kind of 'scientific' certainty. As an analysis of the nature of nineteenth-century history and of the move away from feudalism there is much of great value in Marx's account. However, as we just saw, once Marxism itself becomes part of the ideological equation in the twentieth century, things get much more difficult. Marx does succeed in showing that the relationship between material and mental production is not solely dependent on the latter, and often depends more on the former. Part of the argument is another version of the question of ideology. In the *Critique* he claims that, just as one should not judge an individual by what he thinks of himself, one should not judge an epoch by the way the people in the middle of it think about what they are doing.

Perhaps the most *philosophically* influential development of the implications of this idea lies in Marx's account of the commodity. The

account is based on the notion of 'surplus value', which forms the core
of his mature economic theory. This is the idea that the capitalist is
able to accumulate his wealth because those working for him are paid
for less time than they actually work. They therefore generate a
surplus which goes to the person who owns the machines, land, etc.,
which is then used to produce the wealth. Only those who control the
means of production can appropriate such wealth. This fact leads to
another version of the argument for the abolition of private property
and for the return of the wealth produced to those who really
produce it. Whether this is a sound economic theory, or more a moral
case for reorganization of the division of labour and property,
remains in dispute. The crucial element of the theory which Marx
develops out of this idea concerns the *form* which this wealth takes.

Marx argues that there are two kinds of value in a capitalist
economy: use value, and exchange value. The former is simply the
usefulness of something, a coat for keeping one warm, for example.
Each thing can have any number of such uses, and the kinds of use
are also indeterminably diverse. Use value is the 'material content'
of wealth, and it is in one sense independent of the kind of society in
which things are used. However, in capitalism, unlike in previous
kinds of economy, use values are also the 'material carriers' of
exchange value. This has the important consequence that 'As use
values commodities are above all of different quality, as exchange
values they can only be of different quantity' (Marx 1975: 52). A commodity's exchange value is the *relationship* of its value to the value
of any other commodity, not, like its use value, something intrinsic
to it.

In Marx's view the essential factor in capitalism is that the
encroachment of the commodity form into society fundamentally
changes the world. The structure in question here should be familiar.
If the exchange value of something depends on its relationship to
other exchange values in a system (of money), it has the same 'negative' status we observed in Hegel's use of Spinoza's idea of 'determination as negation' to characterize the nature of the finite world.
A thing only has exchange value via its relationships to other things,
and this kind of value is purely quantitative. The thousand pounds I
paid for the computer on which I am writing this text could also be
paid for a bottle of wine costing the same. As exchange values, the
two are therefore *identical*, losing all their particularity by being made
part of a system of relationships which Marx terms the 'total work'
(*Gesamtarbeit*) of society. In a famous section of *Capital* (1864), on
'The Fetish Character of the Commodity and Its Secret', Marx uses
another version of the notion of alienation to discuss the significance

of the commodity form. Religion can make products of the human mind into something supposedly independent of the human mind, in the form of the fetish, the inanimate object which is worshipped for its power. In an analogous manner, the commodity system endows the products 'of the human hand' with a status which they do not have as mere use values. Real things are given a wholly abstract status, which allows them to become interchangeable with one another.

In concrete, economic terms this means the capitalist can become rich via the production of newspapers as much as he can become rich by the production of cars. Recent trends in the world economy reinforce this fact. Multinational companies can switch their production from cigarettes to shoes, or whatever, and they can buy up any kind of production, provided they have the requisite exchange value to do so. Marx sees what is involved in this process of abstraction as the rendering equivalent of all human work. This happens in a form which hides the fact that exchange values could not exist without that work. The vital issue for subsequent German philosophy lies in the link between the commodity system, which obliterates the qualitative nature of things, and systematic metaphysics of the kind we have seen in Idealist philosophy.

The idea to hang on to here is that the capitalist world's concrete production of a generalized equivalence of all things is substantially connected to philosophical questions about the effect of thinking of things as 'identical' in the modern world. Think of the slave trade, which relied on making people into exchangeable commodities, and which was abolished in the name of values – like Kant's 'dignity' – which cannot be reduced to exchange values. Whatever doubts one may have about Marx's wider conception of economics, civil society and the state, the importance of his analysis of the commodity for understanding modern culture will be considerable. Indeed, this issue will affect some thinkers' attitude to philosophy itself. Adorno, for example, makes the link between conceptual identification and the commodity form central to his rejection of metaphysics (see chapter 11), and something similar is the case in Heidegger. The most obvious way this link is manifest lies in the fact that the process of abstraction involved in the spread of commodity exchange seems to function in a similar way to the process of abstraction which enables science to apply general laws of nature to particular cases. The question is whether the reduction of the particularity of the object in both these processes is *necessarily* problematic, and whether there is any real philosophical substance to this connection between the commodity structure and scientific thinking. One of the most influential figures in the emergence of this kind of critique of identification in the modern world is Nietzsche.

SUGGESTIONS FOR FURTHER READING

Avineri, S. (1971) *The Social and Political Thought of Karl Marx* (Cambridge: Cambridge University Press). *Reliable presentation of Marx's ideas.*

Callinicos, A. (1985) *Marxism and Philosophy* (Oxford: Oxford University Press). *Committed defence of Marx's ideas.*

Eagleton, T. (1999) *Marx* (London: Routledge). *Lively and readable text that brings Marx's ideas alive for the present.*

Elster, J. (1986) *An Introduction to Karl Marx* (Cambridge: Cambridge University Press). *Lucid critical account of Marx.*

Habermas, J. (1986) *Knowledge and Human Interests* (Cambridge: Polity Press). *Situates Marx in a wider context of critical social theory.*

Korsch, K. (1970) *Marxism and Philosophy* (London: Pluto). *Influential text by leading Marxist which helped change the image of Marx's philosophy.*

Schmidt, A. (1978) *The Concept of Nature in Marx* (New York: Schocken). *Classic account by pupil of Adorno of Marx's approaches to the question of nature.*

Wood, A. (1981) *Karl Marx* (London: Routledge). *Account of Marx's philosophy.*

7

CRITIQUES OF IDEALISM III: NIETZSCHE

Tragedy and Modernity

In the second half of the nineteenth century the idea that rational thought can obscure the real nature of the world recurs in many differing versions. The new question becomes: can the critique of Idealism can be equated with a more general critique of rationality? A common alternative to Marx's historically specific analysis of distortion of reality by the commodity form derives from the way of understanding Kant's division between appearances and things in themselves initiated by Schopenhauer. In this view human thinking is *essentially* illusory, a projection onto something of ideas which have no substantial relation to that something. The task is to work out what it is that makes thinking into projection rather than true apprehension, so that whatever it is that gives rise to the projection therefore becomes the real basis of philosophy. The problem is that the analysis of what gives rise to the projection cannot be accessible to existing ways of thinking, because they must be part of the projection themselves. One way of understanding the kind of conception in question here is via the idea that our thinking is simply an aspect of what Schelling calls nature's 'productivity': it takes place independently of our conscious will. We don't choose to have thoughts; in one sense they just happen to us.[1] The early Schelling presented this view

1 Nietzsche is often credited with this idea, as well as with the associated criticism of the idea of the subject's transparency to itself. The idea is already around at the end of the eighteenth century in the scientist and aphorist Georg Christoph Lichtenberg, and is developed in detail by the later Schelling, some of whose work Nietzsche read (see Frank 1982: 344–7).

of thought in terms of a parallelism between material nature's productivity and the productivity of the mind. However, the idea now is that natural productivity is never accessible as such to any kind of thinking, because it is what gives rise to 'thinking' in *all* its aspects, including, of course, madness.[2]

The possibility arises, then, that human thinking is fundamentally a repression of something which only emerges in its true form when the controls imposed by reason are abandoned. This may take place, for example, in states of ecstasy or insanity, which supposedly put people in touch with the nature of things that is repressed by conceptual thinking. The basic issue here was touched on in chapter 2, when we looked at the question of 'irrationalism'. The difficulty identified there was that if something is wholly resistant to rationality, it also cannot be spoken about, because speaking about it would bring it into the realm of intersubjective understanding. This meant that some other kind of 'intuitive' access to what reason obscures is required, at the price of this access never being able to be made intersubjectively valid. I cannot successfully *assert* to you that I have access to reality in a way you do not, if we cannot communicate about this access.

It would be a mistake simply to write off approaches which appeal to something not rationally demonstrable. One of the sources of modernist art, for example, which often deals with extreme states of mind or extreme situations, is the conviction that established ways of thinking are repressing some other, more authentic, way of being, which needs to be communicated in new, and perhaps shocking, ways. The obvious other reason for not dismissing such ideas as merely incoherent is that we need to understand why they became a major feature of philosophy and art in the later nineteenth and early twentieth centuries. The answer has to do with modernity's destruction of religious and other certainties. As we have seen, this destruction can be felt either as a liberation that leads in the direction of new possibilities, or as a disorienting threat.

The key further factor in the changes taking place at this time is once again the success of the natural sciences. The sciences invalidate conceptions based on teleology, the idea that the workings of nature have a more general goal inherent in them. The abandonment of teleology in favour of the search for particular laws is the source of many advances in modern science, but these are bought at the price of the loss of a feeling of coherence in the human relationship to nature.

2 Schelling considers this approach in *The Ages of the World*, but his concern is always with how rationality can emerge from madness.

The idea that humanity has its own goal, such as Kant's 'kingdom of ends', becomes more difficult to believe when the usefulness of teleological ideas in science is more and more put into question. If the link between freedom and teleology, which suggests that moral action can be seen as contributing to a wider human goal, is attacked, the idea of freedom itself comes into question. As the terrain covered by the natural sciences grows, so does the need for forms of human activity, such as art, which are both not reducible to what the sciences say about them, and are linked to freedom without having to be connected to teleology.

Nietzsche's first substantial published text, *The Birth of Tragedy from the Spirit of Music* (*BT*) (1872), explores many of these issues. Nietzsche began an academic career as a classical philologist. The German obsession with ancient Greece from the Enlightenment onwards, which was the main source of modern philology, had made Greece the location of an ideal of human existence. What Nietzsche does, which leads to the rejection of the *BT* by many classicists in his time, is to use the idea of the superiority of Greek culture as the means of suggesting what is wrong with nineteenth-century European culture. He does so by trying to destroy the image of Greece then prevalent in the humanities. Instead of the 'glory that was Greece' being associated with its philosophers, particularly Plato, he regards the philosophers as having betrayed the deeper insights of Greek tragedy, in the name of what he thinks is a shallow scientific rationalism. It is important to remember that Nietzsche writes this text at a time when optimism about the possibilities offered by scientific progress was very widespread in Europe and the USA.

Tragedy is fifth-century BC Athenian culture's public expression of its collective beliefs. Athenian culture created things of great beauty, and seemed to produce a fundamentally positive attitude to life. The content of tragedy, of course, is incest, patricide, matricide, fratricide; it involves cannibalism, dismemberment and a whole series of other horrors. In short, tragedy is about all the things that societies and individuals seek to avoid. Nietzsche regards this co-existence of the beautiful and the terrible as a key to rendering modern culture more healthy. In seeking to overcome the dreadful side of existence by explaining it scientifically, modern culture has, he thinks, become self-deceptive.

The conceptual basis of the *BT* is initially just a translation of Schopenhauer's metaphysics into a Romantic topos first used by Friedrich Schlegel and Schelling, namely the relationship we looked at in chapter 2 between the two Greek Gods, Apollo and Dionysus (see Frank 1982). The former stands for the world as 'representation', the latter as 'Will'. The 'Apollonian' is the realm of 'form' in general, which includes dreams, i.e. it involves anything which can be the material of conceptual thought. The 'Dionysian' is the realm of intoxication and madness. Like the Will, the Dionysian destroys the results of the 'principle of individuation', the principle which makes us into something separate from the rest of the universe that needs ways of defending itself against the other. Again like the Will (or Schelling's 'productivity'), the Dionysian cannot appear as itself; only its effects appear. Many of these appearances are actually ways of concealing the destructive and chaotic nature of what underlies them. Tragedy expresses the relationship between these two sides of existence. It is constructed of words which can convey conceptual content, but it is underpinned by music which expresses the essentially riven nature of the world 'in itself'. The conception is 'borrowed', without acknowledgement, from Schlegel's *History of Greek and Roman Literature* (1798) and from Schelling's writings of the 1840s: 'Not at different moments but at the same moment to be simultaneously drunk and sober is the secret of true poetry [*Poesie*]. This distinguishes the Apollonian enthusiasm from the simply Dionysian enthusiasm' (Schelling 1856–61: II/iv. 25).

As an interpretation of Greek tragedy Nietzsche's schema has a lot to be said for it. The theme of tragedy is the way in which human forms of order, such as kinship systems, are undermined by a reality which humans can never fully control. Oedipus unknowingly commits patricide and incestuously sleeps with his mother, producing children who are at the same time his daughters and his sisters – all because he consciously tries to *avoid* doing this, having been warned by an oracle that he would do so. Tragedy presents the destruction of order in a dramatic form which is able to contain the terrible events and articulate them in expressive language that in some respects seems to 'redeem' them. Why else would people wish to go to see symbolic enactments of the worst things they can imagine? Nietzsche's argument about music and tragedy is historically less plausible. We do not know enough about Greek music and we have no access to the way it would have been experienced at the time. The argument actually has more to do with Nietzsche's temporary enthusiasm for Wagner's music dramas, which he regards as the possible source of a '*re-birth of German myth*' (Nietzsche 1980: i. 147).

In the *BT* Nietzsche takes up an influential problem we encountered in Jacobi concerning human knowledge. For Jacobi, any attempt to ground an explanation of something in terms of Leibniz's 'principle of sufficient reason' leads to a regress of explanations of explanations. This means there *is* nothing ultimately to ground a claim, unless, as Jacobi does, one introduces God as what makes nature intelligible, or, as Fichte does, one makes the 'absolute subject' into the ground of knowledge. The alternative to this is, Jacobi thinks, to be confronted with an 'abyss' where reason can hold no sway because it has no foundation. Nietzsche sees those who adhere to Leibniz's principle as holding an 'unshakable belief that thinking reaches into the deepest abysses of being via the leading thread of causality', and he claims they believe that thinking can even '*correct* being' (ibid. 99). For Nietzsche, this belief has no justification, and he argues that science will always eventually lead to a limit 'at which it must turn into *art*' (ibid.). When the sciences try to make the fact of existence itself comprehensible they end up having to have recourse to myth, in order to give meaning to an existence which has none. This lack of 'meaning', in the sense of a justification of the kind that ensues from the world being created by a deity, is what is revealed by tragedy.

The sense of 'art' in the *BT* is quite particular. Without 'art in some forms or other, particularly as religion and science' (ibid. 100) the futility of the attempt to explain and justify existence would render life intolerable. People need a goal which functions as an absolute, even if the goal is really a fiction. It makes no essential difference whether this goal is the pursuit of scientific theories, the creation of works of art, adherence to Christian mythology, or whatever. Each of these is a projection which seeks to imbue meaningless existence with meaning, hence the claim that they are all 'art'. The provocative equation of science with myth arises because Nietzsche, like Feuerbach, looks at the world in terms of the ways it affects finite, sensuous individuals. Feuerbach relied on a sense of the essentially benign repressed possibilities offered by nature. Nietzsche, on the other hand, sees being as fundamentally tragic, and thus in need of redemption. He asserts that we 'have our highest dignity in the significance of works of art – for only as *aesthetic phenomenon* is existence and the world eternally *justified*' (ibid. 47). Music is crucial to this justification. It allows us to understand 'joy in the destruction of the individual' (ibid. 108). We experience this joy by the way music reconciles us to the finitude of our existence, giving pleasure precisely via its communication of the dissonance that is the essence of the Dionysian underlying reality.

The cultural battle in the contemporary world is, Nietzsche maintains, between 'insatiably optimistic cognition and the tragic need for art'. However, these must in his terms both be the same, because the former is just a shallower, self-deceptive version of the latter. The latter has been repressed by the dominant optimism engendered by the progress of the sciences. Nietzsche thinks, though, that the optimism of the sciences is beginning to reveal its hollowness. The optimism does not face the fact that the sciences seem unable to arrive at definitive answers. When the results of the sciences manifest themselves as the technology of mass murder in the First World War, this vision will appear to many people as very prescient. In the later parts of the *BT* Nietzsche tries to argue that Wagner's music drama offers a revival of myth that is the result of rationality coming up against its limits. It is this level of the argument which is most questionable. As subsequent history will show, the invocation of a 'splendid, internally healthy, age-old power' (ibid. 146) that will create the myths needed to transform modernity is merely self-deceptive. How does one recognize what is based on such a power and what is not? When the answer is that a specific nation or race has this power, which is therefore lacking in other races, the bankruptcy of this form of revival of myth becomes very apparent.

Fiction, Rhetoric and Argument

Nietzsche does not endorse the conception of the *BT* in his subsequent work, and he rarely, if ever, returns to the idea that German myth and the associated nationalism are a resource for creating new meaning. The reasons for his change of mind regarding the wider themes of the *BT* are characteristic of ambivalences about modernity we have already encountered. The idea that modernity is more threatening than liberating means that modernity is understood in the *BT* in terms of the revelation of a fundamental horror which needs to be 'redeemed' or 'justified'. Schopenhauer and the Nietzsche of the *BT* reject theology, but they both seek to replace it with something that plays much the same role, hence the vocabulary of 'redemption' and 'justification'. They assume that existence is inherently a problem, to which metaphysics in some form, such as art, must be the response.

An alternative conception of modernity regards it as opening up endless opportunities because it liberates people from superstition and from belief in authorities which have no rational legitimation. There may, in these terms, be no reason to think of modernity as involving real loss, because what was 'lost' was illusory anyway. If the feeling of loss is for something that did not exist, there is no advantage to be gained from using it as part of an argument about a new way of looking at things. The American philosopher Samuel Wheeler has rightly talked in this context about the 'bewailing of a deficiency that is a necessary deficiency in every case, and so a deficiency only relative to an impossible dream' (Wheeler 2000: 118). The concern should therefore be to reveal all the ways in which previous world-views, by promoting other versions of the same kind of illusion, still infect contemporary views. One version of this conception was what fired Feuerbach's and Marx's critiques of religion. Nietzsche comes to think that the *BT* may itself be a symptom of the problems of modern culture which he wishes to overcome, because it demands a metaphysical response which would counter the finitude of human existence. However, his new approaches to these problems, though often echoing both Feuerbach and Marx, are significantly different from theirs. Furthermore, Nietzsche exaggerates the consequences of the failure of foundational metaphysical positions.

The search for a metaphysical foundation to replace theological foundations is often associated with the elevation of the subject to being the new ground of reliable knowledge. At the same time, that foundation is under repeated attack from those who fail to be convinced by the idea of ultimate foundations. Even at the level of practical reason, Kant's apparently foundational idea of rational self-determination can be construed as just a regulative idea. It may be something to be guided by in striving to act morally, rather than something which can really be shown to be the 'intelligible' source of the moral law. What, though, if *all* foundational conceptions, including regulative ideas, are *just* fictions, 'noble lies' which are used to conceal the fact that there is nothing ultimately to back up the demand to think and act in terms of them? From sometime in the later 1870s onwards, Nietzsche sees this possibility in terms of the 'death of God'.

Before we look at how he tries to cash out these new ideas, a fundamental problem must be briefly introduced. The claim that all our beliefs about the world are fictional has to answer the standard objection to scepticism and relativism. If the claim is true it must actually be false, because the claim itself has to be assumed to be *true* as a belief about reality, and therefore *not* to be a fiction, if it is to be asserted at all. This might seem to settle the issue fairly decisively, but things are not quite that simple. The claim that all our beliefs are really fictions itself can be seen as relying on the correspondence theory of truth. In these terms, our ideas or statements fail to 'correspond to' reality because they do not articulate what is there independently of our ideas and statements. What, though, if the correspondence theory is not a plausible theory of truth? The idea of statement and thing corresponding may actually make no sense, because there cannot be any domain of reality which is wholly separate from what we say about it. Even thinking about some domain already inescapably occurs within a language. We cannot then step outside language in order to see if what we say is confirmed extra-linguistically by the world corresponding to it. The reason this may be the case is that the number of ways the furniture of the world can be divided up is indeterminably large. It is therefore unconvincing to assume that every new articulation of things we undertake is already somehow present in the things out there, waiting to be 'corresponded to'. That assumption depends on a God's-eye view of things. Hamann and Herder argued that language is both 'world-disclosive', involving a creative element, rather than merely 'representing' what is already there, and the product of human actions in specific societies. If this is so, the correspondence theory does not help in understanding how we come to think a completely new way of talking about something is true.

Given that we cannot get by without thinking in terms of truth – truth seems to be connected to the possibility of using words to mean anything at all – it may not be such a big problem if we give up the possibly incoherent notion of statement and thing corresponding. Nietzsche's response to these issues in his work after the *BT* is anything but consistent, veering from the desire to tell a major story about the illusory nature of our convictions about truth, to much more interesting attempts to circumvent the very terms of most philosophical debate about truth. At his worst he dramatizes the issues into being epoch-making changes in a Western civilization which he believes to be based in many respects on delusions. At his best his texts enact different possibilities of reacting to the idea that philosophy has failed in its desire for an all-encompassing metaphysics.

As Nietzsche's writing develops during the 1870s the role of style and rhetoric grows considerably. The works which will eventually make Nietzsche's reputation – though it is worth remembering that they had sold very few copies before he went mad in 1890 – are, at their best, remarkable displays of wit, rhetoric and insight. However, they also often tip over into hectoring, obsessive rants, which is one source of justified concerns about Nietzsche's political stances and their effects on modern history. Because the works do not each pursue one exclusive major theme, it is best to consider how certain dominant themes are played out in Nietzsche's work as a whole.

The titles of some of Nietzsche's main works (with first publication dates) can help set an agenda: *The Gay Science* (1882, expanded edition 1887), *Beyond Good and Evil* (1886), *On the Genealogy of Morals* (1887), *The Antichrist* (1894). The role of natural science, the attempt to get beyond existing conceptions of morality and the related opposition to Christianity are explored, in conjunction with a whole variety of other issues, in a non-systematic fashion. The texts generally consist of short sections, which are sporadically inter-spersed with collections of poems or aphorisms. Sections are some-times directly thematically connected to each other, sometimes not. In chapter 2 we considered the fact that Hamann was a 'performa-tive' thinker, because he was more concerned with language as action in the world which reveals creation than with language as represen-tation. Nietzsche clearly follows in this vein. The very fact that his texts do not advance sustained, systematic arguments is part of what they communicate.

Even today, many philosophers assume that the main aim of phi-losophy is complete transparency. Arguments and counter-arguments are to be advanced until a satisfactory, unambiguous answer to a philosophical problem is arrived at. Since Plato, there has been a sus-picion of rhetoric, the 'art of persuasion', in philosophy. Philosophy is supposed to arrive at pure truths, which are self-evident, not at 'truths' which merely seduce the person to whom they are argued. The simple problem, Nietzsche thinks, is that philosophy does not actually seem to arrive at self-evident truths by this method. There is nothing *necessarily* to say that it may not eventually do so (though Nietzsche sometimes argues as though there were), but an inference from the history of philosophy since Plato suggests that the method may be mistaken. Philosophical positions are widely adopted, only to be rejected some time later, and, even later, to be taken up again. Unlike refuted theories in the natural sciences, which generally remain refuted, many philosophical theories seem never finally to be refuted.

The vital question is what to do if one gives up on the kind of philosophy which lives predominantly from argument and counter-argument. One fear is that this may lead to the arbitrary making of unjustified assertions. This can be the position of the religious fun-damentalist, and, at times, it is that of Nietzsche. One cannot, of course, consistently *argue* for philosophical argument to be aban-doned. Trying to do so leads to a 'performative contradiction', in which the making of a certain kind of assertion contradicts the content of that assertion. However, there is nothing self-legitimating about making one's assertions and arguments wholly consistent with each other. Mere consistency can be the hallmark of paranoia, where everything one thinks hangs together, but does so in a way which is dangerously at odds with anyone else's view of how things are. Fur-thermore, we sometimes argue different cases in different contexts, because we are trying to achieve something different in each context. This can be merely disreputable, but everyone is likely to find them-selves doing this at some time.

What is one to make of a *philosopher* who sees the obligation to be consistent as only one of many demands, which may be less important than, for example, being interesting or provocative, or achieving one's goals? Does he lose the status of 'philosopher', and does it matter? The difficulty with Nietzsche's texts is that if one reads them as though he were a philosopher in the argumentative sense, it is quite easy to show him being inconsistent. To concentrate on this fact, as though it were the most important thing, can mean one misses something more significant. At the same time, however, there are plenty of places where it seems vital to say, in the manner of the traditional philosopher, that an argument of Nietzsche's is simply unjustified. There are, then, no easy answers to the questions raised by a thinker who may best be understood in performative terms. Their texts may be trying to provoke the reader to respond by, for example, saying something which the author does not actually believe. In that case, objecting to the argument merely means that one falls into the trap set by the text, in the way one looks silly by taking something seriously that is meant as a joke. One strategy is to accept that much of what is happening in Nietzsche's texts is indeed more performance than argument, but to look very carefully at the moments when performance gives way to assertion of a kind that cannot be construed as ironic or as merely performative. A further strategy is to keep in mind the ideological context of his writing. Although the Nietzsche of after the *BT* cannot be considered as a German nationalist, his élitism and his tendency to regard social issues as though they were biological issues – for example in relation to the idea that societies and cultures can become 'sick' – are very much part of reactionary thought in the second half of the nineteenth century. Such ideas fed into Nazism and other anti-democratic movements in the twentieth century, and are neither Nietzsche's creation, nor of any serious philosophical interest.

Revaluations

The premise that religion is a hindrance to human development, which is central to Nietzsche's major work after the *BT*, echoes the Young Hegelians, but the consequences he draws from it are often very different. The way Nietzsche deals with this premise can be illustrated via section 125 of Book 3 of *The Gay Science*, about the 'madman'. This person is described coming into the marketplace in broad daylight with a lamp, announcing that 'God is dead' and that this is an unmitigated castastrophe, for which humankind is to blame.

The issue in the passage is the response to a world in which nothing is guaranteed by an ultimate authority. The dual aspect of modernity as both threat and opportunity appears here once again. At the same time, the *manner* of the appearance of these issues is decisive.

Interpreting this text shows the challenge posed by Nietzsche. First of all, one has to be aware of the rest of the texts that precede and follow it. Book 3 opens with a brief section reflecting on the fact that when Buddha died 'his shadow was shown for centuries in a cave'. The text then baldly asserts that 'God is dead', but that something similar to the case of Buddha may still happen for millennia, so that 'we must also conquer His shadow' (Nietzsche 1980: iii. 467). This text leaves no doubt that the task is to overcome theology in all its variations, and that it will be a very difficult task. The following section is an attack on all kinds of metaphysical accounts of nature as fitting human ways of ordering things. All these ideas are, it is claimed, shadows of God, in the sense that they presuppose an inherent order in things. This assumption prevents us from drawing really new resources from nature because they will always be contaminated with residues of theology. Nietzsche does not tell us what sense of nature is meant here, apart from insisting that nature consists of 'necessities', rather than 'laws'. Laws are another form of anthropomorphic projection, of the kind that requires a law-giver, and that is precisely the idea of the world he wishes to get rid of.

This passage can be understood in two ways. One way is essentially critical, offering no alternative positive account of nature, because a positive account would repeat the problem of metaphysics, by imposing a framework that limits the ways in which we might come to experience nature. The other way is apparent in the next section, when Nietzsche considers the 'Origin of Cognition' in 'life', the power via which control is gained over other parts of nature. Thought is seen here not as primarily the search for truth, but as the basis of self-preservation. Only if it contributes to self-preservation does truth become significant: 'It is something new in history that cognition wants to be more than a means' (ibid. 480). The passage points in the direction of a positive theory which posits an essential underlying motivation for everything that happens. We will consider this idea a bit later when looking at the theory of the 'will to power'.

By the time one gets to section 125 itself, Nietzsche has – to pick just two further examples of the context which informs the section – also questioned the nature of logic as pure thought, and argued that the notions of cause and effect are further anthropomorphisms for the purpose of control by humans over nature. Section 125 is also immediately preceded by a metaphorical reflection on life without philosophical foundations: 'We have left land and have embarked on a ship.' The ship – echoing early Romanticism – is on an endless journey, and the idea of feeling homesick is a danger, because 'there is no "land" anymore' (ibid. 480). As we saw above, a radical anti-foundational approach cannot appeal to something which is lost, because that would presuppose that foundationalism was ever anything more than a mere illusion or projection. The journey is therefore seen as both exciting and terrifying, because there is no guarantee as to what will emerge. The lack of guarantee can, however, itself be either positive or negative. In the context of the ideas just outlined, it seems clear that the madman's vision of the terrifying con- sequences of our having 'killed' God exemplifies the attitude the text opposes. The people in the marketplace, many of whom are described as not believing in God, do not respond with fear. At first, they laugh, and then, after the man has painted his terrifying vision of a world not supported by God, they are merely 'disconcerted', and this may be by the man's demeanour.

The vision the man paints does, however, summarize some of the consequences of the modern scientific view of the universe, which *are* disturbing from many perspectives. In this view, we are located on an insignificant planet going round an arbitrary star in some galaxy located nowhere in particular. Moreover, the consequences of entropy mean that this universe will eventually become devoid of life and development, running down into a state of stasis. Concern in the second half of the nineteenth century with the 'heat death of the universe' was widespread.[3] The skill of Nietzsche's text lies in the way in which it challenges the reader to respond to this situation. It may feel terrifying, but sometimes it can *help* to think that in the long run nothing really matters. This realization can lead to the demand to live life to the full now, but it can also be a traumatic shock to a believer, who may start to doubt in a way which is wholly disorienting. The latter response is part of what Nietzsche terms 'nihilism', which is the *result* of holding metaphysical beliefs that turn out to be illusory. Avoiding nihilism means never even entertaining such comforting fic- tions in the first place, so that there is nothing to lose. In section 130 Nietzsche maintains that 'the Christian decision to find the world ugly

3 The on-line satirical website *'the onion'* brought a wonderful spoof story of Christian fundamentalists in Kansas trying to get the second law of thermodynamics, which is what points to the heat death, repealed: '"I wouldn't want my child growing up in a world headed for total heat death and dissolution into a vacuum," said Kansas state senator Will Blanchard ... "No decent parent would want that."' http://www.theonion.com/onion3631/christian_right_lobbies.html.

and bad has made the world ugly and bad' (ibid. 485). The question is how we should view the world without the distortions introduced by Christianity. The hope is that it will therefore no longer be made ugly. Its beauty can, though, not be a consoling beauty, because the universe no longer has anything inherently consoling about it.

The problem is that the question of how the world could cease to be 'ugly and bad' is a question of evaluation. Without a foundation for evaluation, of the kind Kant attempted to provide with the categorical imperative, values are very difficult to agree on. The very titles of books like *Beyond Good and Evil* (*BGE*) and *On the Genealogy of Morals* (*GM*) suggest the direction Nietzsche takes. On the one hand, he wishes to transcend the morality associated with Christianity. He talks about this task in terms of a 'transvaluation of all values'. On the other, he seeks to establish why Christian morality is the way it is. It is not easy to make the two tasks congruent with each other. Nietzsche often conflates giving an account of the latter, which involves historical interpretation, with attempting to do the former, which requires a new ground for morality. As Nietzsche himself reminds us, saying how something came about does not suffice to characterize what its nature may be in different circumstances. At the same time as offering important ways of re-evaluating some key philosophical questions, the 'genealogical' account of morality does, then, involve substantial difficulties.

The problem with some of Nietzsche's approach is apparent in a passage from *Dawn* (1881), in which he maintains that 'even our moral judgements and evaluations are only images and fantasies about a physiological process that is unknown to us, a kind of habituated language for designating certain stimulations of nerves' (ibid. 113). Conscious thought is therefore 'a more or less fantastical commentary on a text which is unknown, perhaps is unknowable, but which can be felt' (ibid.). However, he has already told us that this 'text' is the physiology of the nervous system, which is a positive claim to knowledge based on a scientific theory. This claim has, though, presumably to be of the same status as our other conscious thoughts, so it is itself just another interpretation. Interpretation takes place for Nietzsche in terms of a competing for attention of different drives in the organism. What we attend to is dependent on which aspect of ourselves plays the dominant role in relation to a particular phenomenon. We can look at a person as a mass of physiological processes, as an object of sexual desire, of sympathy, of anger, or as a whole host of other things. What decides which of these prevails? Given this problem, which is central to Nietzsche's conception, on what basis does *he* opt for the interpretation he does?

Positions analogous to Nietzsche's ideas about 'physiological process' are encountered in contemporary philosophy, in the arguments of those who think our everyday desires, aspirations, moral torments, etc., are merely part of the realm of 'folk-psychology'. The reality of these desires, etc., actually consists in the functioning of the brain and nervous system, which are conceived of in analogy to a digital computer. Nietzsche's point is somewhat more complex than the one involved in this kind of reductionism – the reference to the 'text' that can be 'felt' makes this clear – but it is at best paradoxical. Our moral judgements evidently would not take place without physiological processes in the brain and the body, but it is quite another thing to say that they are therefore really *just* physiological, so that a necessary condition is also sufficient. Even though Kant may fail to convince us of the complete independence of the ethical realm from the realm of determined appearances, he does show that it is implausible to reduce the former to the latter. If moral dilemmas really did just consist in an indeterminacy as to which of two or more bio-chemical reactions will take place in the organism, we would not even understand what a moral dilemma *is*. Moral predicates are of a different order from physical predicates. Getting from the latter to the former looks an unlikely proposition, unless one declares moral predicates to be merely illusory. Even then one would have to be able to say *what* it is about them that is merely illusory, which presupposes what one is denying, i.e. moral rather than just physical facts, in order for the argument to be comprehensible. Nietzsche uses the kind of problematic argument observed here in *Dawn* in many of his later texts, but another dimension of his contentions reveals something more interesting.

Genealogy and the Will to Power

We encountered versions of the attempt to explain the origin of morality in Fichte's account of the genesis of intersubjectivity, and in Hegel's move from 'desire' to mutual acknowledgement in the *Phenomenology*. These accounts both assume that a general pattern of progress in the development of ethical relationships can be established on the basis of the history of ethical life. Despite all the difficulties involved in reconciling the interests of individuals and society in a post-traditional context, where there can be no appeal to pre-existing authority, modernity is regarded as an advance over the past and as offering possibilities of further moral development. Nietzsche breaks with this whole picture and thereby helps create a fundamental division in modern German philosophy between: (1) thinkers who wish to sustain the rational aims of the tradition of Kant and Hegel, which allows for moral progress, and (2) thinkers who argue that the rationalist tradition is trying to hang on to a metaphysical account of ethics, which either relies on covert theology or on an untenable legislative role for the supposedly, but not really, self-determining subject. The radicality of this division clearly has to do in some respects with very differing responses to historical changes in the nineteenth century. At this time, hopes for new social integration often fall prey to the sense that the development of capitalism, the rapid expansion of urban life and the resultant social antagonisms make such integration impossible. These historical developments produce what is often termed 'mass society', and this is one of Nietzsche's main targets. He refuses to think, for example, that the widespread, democratically supported availability of better education and fairer ways of creating social mobility could produce a better, rather than a more culturally impoverished, society.

Nietzsche's arguments in this context rely on his alternative account of the source of moral ideas. It is here that he makes one of his most striking conceptual moves. Without a metaphysical foundation, morality threatens, as we saw, to become essentially arbitrary. Even talking about the genesis of morality involves the problem that there may be no unified meaning to the term. If one thinks in modern Western terms derived from Christianity, morality, as it does for Kant, Fichte and Hegel, has to do with respect for all other rational beings.[4] Nietzsche, of course, thinks that Christianity is precisely the problem in this area, and this means that one cannot construct a history of the origin of morality on the basis of it. However, without invoking some kind of alternative foundation of value, how can one give an account of the source of values? One of Nietzsche's answers to the problem is in many respects very powerful. He asks what the value of morality itself is. The question might seem paradoxical, because morality and value might seem to be coextensive. One answer to the paradox is, then, to make a separation between what 'value' means and what 'morality' means, the latter being equated with Christian morality as self-denial, kindness to others, etc. Here it does make sense to ask what the value of these attributes may be: they can, for example, quite easily lead to the kind of self-denial that eventually makes people ill. At the same time, the question as to what makes a value into a value is crucial, because the answer requires some kind of ground on the

4 This is one reason why it is these days sometimes questioned for its failure to deal appropriately with beings – animals – which are not rational.

basis of which one thing is preferable to another. Kant's 'categorical imperative' assumes that the moral equality of all rational beings is such a ground. The question is, of course, how far this ground can really be said to be universal. In the *GM* Nietzsche argues that the only way to look at the origins of morality is in terms of the *language* of morality.

Nietzsche's way out of the dilemma just outlined is to consider the etymology of moral predicates in differing languages. There is, he maintains, a common tendency for the word 'good' to change its meaning. Having initially been associated with 'noble', and 'bad' having been associated with 'common', the meaning shifts in the direction familiar from Christian morality, so that good comes to mean 'unegoistic'. Instead of the privileged in society defining 'good' in terms of what they *are*, the word comes to be defined by those who are not noble, privileged, etc., thus in terms of what these people supposedly are. Certain historical aspects of this argument may well be defensible, but this kind of classification of people is always dangerous. Nietzsche's defenders rightly argue that he is not an anti-Semite, though he comes very close in certain respects when talking about 'the Jews'. He does, however, often argue in a basically racist manner, for example, in section 5 of the first essay of *GM*. He concentrates here on the dark hair and skin colour of the 'inferior' race which later gains the upper hand, and suggests that social characteristics somehow have to do with belonging to a 'race'.[5] This kind of deliberate conflation of race with culture is characteristic of the period, but does not support the historical argument about moral predicates.

What, then, is his serious argument about morality's origin? The simple answer is that, in order to skirt the problem of how moral concepts could develop, Nietzsche decides they are initially forms of self-assertion, such that the powerful designate what they value, namely themselves, as morally superior. He talks in this connection of language itself as being 'the lordly right to give names', and as the 'expression of power of the rulers' (1980: V. 260). This is both insightful and questionable. Understanding the origin of moral notions should indeed begin with an investigation into the development of the language of evaluation in a culture. Otherwise one risks failing to understand that culture, because one imposes one's own conceptions of value on it. Moreover, it is unclear what other sources of initial

---

5   In case Nietzsche's argument seems plausible to anybody, it is worth remembering that all the biological evidence points to the very idea of race being a myth. *Homo sapiens* seems to be a species with one source, probably in Africa, so that we are all related. Our differences are a result of culture, geography, etc.

evidence one could cite. If one thinks morality depends on moral feelings, they still need to be communicated in a language. One can ask,
however, how we would ever understand alien kinds of morality if
the kind of feelings they rely on were wholly unavailable to us.
Nietzsche's argument needs, though, to be looked at in the wider
context of remarks like the following. In *BGE* Nietzsche argues, with
no sign of irony, that a 'good and healthy aristocracy' will 'accept with
a good conscience the sacrifice of a host [*Unzahl*] of people who will
have to be repressed and diminished to incomplete people, to slaves,
to tools *for its sake*' (ibid. 206). Unreflective self-assertion is therefore both the source of value and itself some kind of ultimate value,
which justifies the repression of others for its sake. That this stance
runs counter to the aspects of the tradition of modern ethical thinking we have seen so far in Germany is obvious. A simple rejoinder to
it is, then, that Nietzsche remains on one of the lower levels of ethical
development traced by Hegel, failing to reach the point of mutual
acknowledgement. This might seem rather unfair, so let us consider
more of the argument.

Nietzsche contends that modern moral life is a result of the 'slave
revolt in morality' (ibid. 270). This revolt derives from the resentment
of the weak against the strong, and is therefore merely 'reactive', in
contrast to the 'active' naming of values by the aristocratic origina-
tors of values. The historical substance of this claim is an interpretation of the Graeco-Roman, as opposed to the Judaeo-Christian
world-view, in which the latter wins out. The strong are persuaded
by the weak to feel guilty about what they are. Nietzsche's rhetoric
makes it clear that the idea of culture as the taming of the 'predatory
animal man' is what he opposes, because culture becomes a repression of what we essentially are. Contemporary culture, he argues, is
contaminated by this repression, which makes people tired of life. The
idea of civilization as repression becomes a commonplace of German
critiques of culture from this time onwards. It is worth remembering,
before one gets too enthusiastic about the idea, that many young
people went willingly into the First World War thinking (often having
read Nietzsche) that the war was a way of breaking free from a
suffocating culture. It is obviously mistaken to deny that cultural
forms can, at certain times, become destructive of the well-being of
members of a particular society. Nietzsche's view of this is, though,
an indication of the weakest side of his work.

Two positions tend to be characteristic of the questioning of
the nature of modern morality. One highlights the problem of the
sheer diversity of evaluations which cannot be reduced to a common
denominator. This view then seeks ways of coming to terms with the

fact of ethical differences which cannot be reconciled in terms of an agreed foundation. The other view seeks to establish a general theory about what has gone wrong with modern morality. Nietzsche at his best forces us to confront the former position; at his worst he proposes a pernicious version of the latter.[6] This duality affects not just his approach to morality, but also to other philosophical questions. Much of the difficulty is summed up in his doctrine of the 'will to power'.

In section 13 of the first essay of *GM*, Nietzsche very entertainingly contrasts the birds of prey with the lambs who think the birds are 'evil'. The birds say they are not annoyed with the lambs: 'we even like them: nothing is more tasty than a tender lamb' (ibid. 279). The point is to mock the idea of expecting the strong not to behave as the strong. The actual argument is as follows. Strength is characterized in terms of 'quanta' of power. Power just manifests itself. There is no 'subject' which determines whether power is manifested, because that subject is *itself* just another manifestation of power. The spontaneity of the subject which Kant regarded in terms of the possibility of rational self-determination is therefore now just another aspect of the power which constitutes the very nature of the whole world: 'there is no "being" behind doing, effecting, becoming; the "doer" is just made up in addition to the deed' (ibid. 279). All is, then, much as it is in Schopenhauer, 'Will'.

The consequence of this position is, of course, just nonsense, as though there were no essential difference between an eagle being its kind of power by eating the lamb, and Himmler being his kind of power by killing Jews despite the fact that he has encountered moral notions in his education. Nietzsche's contentions simply rely upon an absolute, called 'power', or 'will to power', whose manifestations can only be differentiated in terms of their *quantity*. The only way morality can appear in such a view is in the form of power which is turned against itself, thus as repression, such that the strong become aggressive towards themselves by feeling guilty. Similar structures can be observed in Freud's account of the 'id' and its relationship to the 'ego'

---

6   Another version of a metaphysical position occurs in the doctrine of the 'eternal recurrence of the same'. Here the idea is that the universe will eternally repeat itself, so that one's life will keep recurring in the same way in the future. Nietzsche does not provide any argument that shows why this should be the case: the idea seems to be suggested by some aspects of the physics of his day. Nor does he deal with the fact that identical recurrence would be wholly unknowable, because otherwise something new would have happened. The point of the doctrine is that one should affirm life, whatever it may throw at one. The experience of the persecuted in the twentieth century should be enough to suggest the doctrine is less than persuasive.

and 'super-ego', which are generated by the id turning back on itself in the name of self-preservation. The structure in question was already suggested in Fichte's notion of the I's 'self-limitation', but Fichte used it to try to develop a rational account of morality. Nietzsche's historicization of the source of moral notions poses very difficult questions for the rational approach, but is this historicization necessarily fatal to that approach?

The argument that there are no inherent moral qualities to the species *homo sapiens* can indeed be defended in the light of the tortuous history of the development of moral notions. The collective circumstances, language and practices of particular social groupings are, as Hegel argued, part of what moral development is, and we can anyway never know what people would be like without the effects of social contexts. In this sense one cannot simply argue from some absolute basis that Himmler is just evil, whereas the eagle is just being itself, however much one might wish to. At the same time, the Kantian notion that there is a universal aspect to what morality is, which gives rise to at least the aim of equality before the law, seems to grow rather than diminish in power in the light of modern history. The difficult issue is what to do if one gives up on the notion of an absolute philosophical basis for morality. The need for an absolute basis is a metaphysical need, and Nietzsche is, of course, attacking this need. At the same time, though, he relies on his *own* absolute – power – whose only aim is self-manifestation. The real problem in Nietzsche is the reductive nature of this approach.

Even if Nietzsche's metaphysical argument were defensible, would this mean that the complex moral life many people actually live, in which the racist comes to see the error of their ways, or in which people overcome their temptation to cruelty, is *mere* self-deception?[7] What exactly does Nietzsche think people in his society should *do* with his revelations about the ground of what they thought was morality? Is it only those who are strong enough to throw off their moral illusions who can fulfil what he is suggesting? How would things look if they did? What is the 'superman', who is one consequence of his argument for the transvaluation of values, going to do?[8] Nietzsche

7   The same kind of objection made here to Nietzsche could be made against contemporary socio-biology's attempt to explain morality away in terms of evolutionary development. Both assume a metaphysical thesis which prejudges all the evidence, making the position circular.

8   Despite the fact that many people object, the best translation of *'Übermensch'* does seem to be 'superman'. The suggested alternatives nearly all rely on trying to make Nietzsche less problematic in this respect than he actually is.

does very little to answer such questions, and subsequent history might be construed as suggesting that the answers implied by his attitude to 'conventional' morality are anything but inspiring. In the light of twentieth-century history we now know that there is nothing generally inherent in people that can prevent the worst. It simply has to be fought in real terms, but the Nietzsche of the will to power does not seem much of a resource in relation to that history. It is a better idea to look at the real stories of those who did resist, and at why they resisted. Although this may reveal that some of Nietzsche's objections to 'sympathy' and other Christian virtues are perhaps on occasion quite apt, it is highly unlikely that his *overall* vision gets to the heart of what a real modern morality without substantial absolutes might be.

This might seem an overly harsh account of Nietzsche's writings on will, but texts like *BGE* are full of assertions which are now simply morally unacceptable in many societies because they really do just show contempt for the supposedly weak. The very decision as to what counts as weakness is deeply controversial in almost any social context, and Nietzsche's texts leave little space to take account of this. However, when Nietzsche goes into the *detail* of moral life, and considers such phenomena as the self-hatred caused by some kinds of Christian education, he does often provide remarkable insights and jolts the complacency of any easily held moral convictions. Like Freud's attempts to diminish the effects of the super-ego, Nietzsche's attacks on the paranoid aspect of 'God is watching me' are important counters to the cultural repression that results from many forms of religion. However, his wholesale onslaught on our supposed denial of our 'natural inclinations' depends on the metaphysical illusion that we really know what they are. Nietzsche regularly mocks the Kantian and Romantic traditions, but their suggestion of the inextricable ways in which the mental and the physical, the cultural and the natural, go to make up what we are is far more insightful than Nietzsche when he attempts to reduce everything to will to power.

In section 22 of *BGE* Nietzsche again examines the notion of the 'lawfulness of nature', suggesting that this is merely an interpretation. Someone could, he suggests, justifiably regard nature's necessities in terms of 'will to power' acting in various directions, without using the notion of law at all. The section finishes: 'Assuming that this as well is just an interpretation – and you will be eager enough to make this objection? – well, so much the better' (ibid. 37). The provocative acknowledgement of a central problem with his own approach makes a change from some of the often dogmatic and unsupported assertions he makes elsewhere. Nietzsche's *theory* of interpretation as based on competing quantities of power in the organism does, though, involve the same problems as the theory of the will to power. As an empirical observation about how we often deal with the everyday world, the sense that interpretation depends on dominant motivations may be revealing, in the way that the idea of 'Freudian slips' is revealing. However, it is hardly an earth-shattering insight. As a *general* approach to interpretation, the theory is, moreover, always subject to the self-referential problem of itself being an interpretation of how things are, and thus being based on the victory of one quantum of power over another. This means that there must be an essential arbitrariness to any interpretation, which could therefore always be otherwise, if a different quantum of power were to win out. Even this claim is itself subject to the same problem of self-referentiality. Nietzsche's theory has, in its own terms, no *reason* to be considered preferable to any other theory, and therefore looks suspiciously vacuous. If everything is power, nothing is power, because there is nothing with which power can be contrasted. Asserting the theory just becomes an arbitrary manifestation of the same underlying principle, not some deep new insight into interpretation.

There is a split in Nietzsche, between (1) a strong defence of a metaphysical argument about interpretation as power, which makes him part of the philosophical tradition he wishes to leave behind, and (2) the enacting of the consequences of what he terms 'perspectivism'. Perspectivism results from abandoning the idea that there could be a central location from which to understand objectivity. The positive claim that there is no central position in relation to which perspectives are located is, though, itself a claim from a central position. However, another way of advocating perspectivism is not to make a general authoritative claim about how things are. One can instead make all sorts of claims which may not fit together in any obvious way. The experience of reading the best of Nietzsche's work, such as *The Gay Science*, is of a constant shifting of perspectives on issues, so that one often comes to new, productive insights, even when a dominant perspective emerges which one cannot accept, or when the perspectives seem to clash. This performative manner of philosophizing can be a source both of philosophical discoveries and of important practical insights for everyday life. However, performativity also runs the risk of becoming as dogmatic as what it opposes when it ignores the possibility that validity may result from something other than the imposition of power. We will return to this issue in relation to Habermas in the Conclusion.

Four Options

It is useful to conclude this chapter with a brief summary of how Nietzsche can be understood as part of a wider philosophical development in Germany. Nietzsche's most important challenge is to the very idea of metaphysics, but he only inconsistently poses a real challenge, sometimes slipping into a version of metaphysics which is less plausible than some of the versions he attacks. In this sense there are two Nietzsches, one who still adheres to the notion that there is an underlying philosophical principle which he is able to reveal and which nobody has yet appreciated, the other of whom 'deconstructs' this sort of notion by insisting on attending to the often contradictory detail of everyday life. The latter Nietzsche is perhaps best summed up by the little section of *The Antichrist* on 'How the "True World" finally became a Fable', which amusingly points to the advantages of everyday life if we stop worrying about whether the world we inhabit is the true one. Even this passage ends, though, with hints of the other Nietzsche, in its final announcement of a great new era of humanity now that metaphysics has been overcome.

The metaphysical Nietzsche belongs, despite himself, to that strand of philosophy since Kant which argues that the absolute is accessible to philosophy (option 1). Heidegger will argue that from Descartes to Nietzsche this underlying principle is in fact 'subjectivity', whether it be in the form of Cartesian certainty, Hegelian absolute spirit, Marxian historical processes of production or Nietzschean will to power. What he means is that all these interpret the world in terms of an essential principle. Heidegger includes Kant in this interpretation, by regarding transcendental subjectivity as having the same status. However, Kant and the Romantics do not necessarily accept that the final truth is available through any version of a subjective founding principle, of the kind the Romantics criticize in Fichte. Instead of thinking that the subject is essentially transparent to itself, and thus absolute in some sense, they think that the absolute is only ever a regulative idea which is generated by our awareness of the relativity of all our attempts to transcend the finite (option 2). Another strand of Romantic thought comes closer to Nietzsche. If truth is a regulative idea to be approached in 'infinite approximation' it may be essentially empty. How would we know if we were getting closer to it, unless we somehow already knew what it *was*? In consequence the very idea of a *philosophical* pursuit of truth may come to be regarded as a delusion, and the ironic deconstructive strategy of undermining attempts to make philosophical claims about truth becomes the best way to engage in philosophy (option 3). Whether this option means philosophy comes to an end will be a theme in subsequent chapters. The other alternative here (option 4) is that we accept that truth is an ineliminable part of what it is to think and communicate at all. In that case the idea of seeking for something we cannot know in advance is no longer a problem because there is no alternative but to assume an intuitive sense of truth as the basis of all thought. Even denying this claim presupposes an ability to understand the denial, which again requires a sense of truth. This last option, which appears in various areas of contemporary philosophy, can be interpreted in a variety of ways whose significance will become apparent in the following chapters.

SUGGESTIONS FOR FURTHER READING

Bowie, A. (2003) *Aesthetics and Subjectivity: From Kant to Nietzsche*, 2nd edn, completely revised (Manchester: Manchester University Press). *Locates Nietzsche in the context of modern German thought from Kant to the Romantics, placing particular emphasis on the issue of music.*

Clark, M. (1991) *Nietzsche on Truth and Philosophy* (Cambridge: Cambridge University Press). *Analytical account of Nietzsche which helped his work gain greater acceptance among analytical philosophers.*

Deleuze, G. (1985) *Nietzsche and Philosophy* (London: Athlone). *Lively study by major French philosopher.*

Heidegger, M. (1979–82) *Nietzsche*, 4 vols (San Francisco: Harper and Row). *Classic, if sometimes questionable, reading of Nietzsche in the context of Heidegger's ideas about Western metaphysics. Difficult, but important.*

Kaufmann, W. (1974) *Nietzsche: Philosopher, Psychologist, Antichrist* (Princeton: Princeton University Press). *Lucid, if too often rather uncritical, presentation of Nietzsche's ideas.*

Magnus, B. and Higgins K. M. (eds) (1996) *The Cambridge Companion to Nietzsche* (Cambridge: Cambridge University Press). *Collection of essays on major themes.*

Nehamas, A. (1987) *Nietzsche: Life As Literature* (Cambridge: Cambridge University Press). *Notable reinterpretation of the significance of Nietzsche.*

Schacht, R. (1985) *Nietzsche* (London: Routledge). *Reliable general work on major themes.*

Tanner, M. (1995) *Nietzsche* (Oxford: Oxford University Press). *Lively brief introduction.*

8

THE LINGUISTIC TURN

Origins

In 1932 the Austrian philosopher, Moritz Schlick (1882–1936), claims that 'the fate of all "philosophical problems" is this: Some of them will disappear by being shown to be mistakes and misunderstandings of our language and the others will be shown to be ordinary scientific questions in disguise. These remarks, I think, determine the whole future of philosophy' (in Rorty 1992: 51). We have already encountered other versions of the idea that philosophy may eventually come to an end. In the coming chapters the ways this end is conceived will be seen to depend on how the relationship between philosophy, language and the sciences is characterized. Schlick's combination of concentration on language and his assumption that real, as opposed to illusory, questions have exclusively scientific solutions are characteristic of the movement in German philosophy generally termed 'analytical philosophy' (although the German designation – 'philosophy of the analysis of language' – is more accurate). This eventually became the most influential movement in twentieth-century philosophy in the English-speaking world, via the enforced emigration from Germany and Austria of many of its main representatives in the 1930s. The so-called 'linguistic turn' that characterizes analytical philosophy in the Anglo-Saxon world has quite specific features, which are, though, *not* captured by the idea that it made language the central focus of philosophy. As we have seen, language is already central to key thinkers in the eighteenth-century German tradition. How, then, does this new tradition of philosophy relate to the story we have told so far? The contrast between the views of science in the *Birth of*

Tragedy and in Schlick's contention could, for example, hardly be greater. Eighteenth-century language-centred philosophy tends to depend on criticisms, of the kind we saw in Hamann and Herder, of the Enlightenment's failure to take account of the ways language is related to sensuous human existence and to history. Analytical philosophy, on the other hand, continues that side of the Enlightenment which seeks scientific certainty as a means of combating metaphysical speculation based on no empirical evidence. What complicates the matter is the status of the empirical world in relation to language: Hamann, after all, was a great admirer of Locke and Hume, who are essential to the analytical tradition because of their insistence on sense-data as the essential source of knowledge.

The claim that the analytical tradition made language the focus of philosophy is not only misleading because of the concentration on language of some eighteenth-century thinkers. The role of language in German philosophy in the nineteenth century is, admittedly, sometimes underestimated. However, F. D. E. Schleiermacher (1768–1834), for example, makes language central to his philosophical project in his work on hermeneutics, which he begins in 1805 and revises throughout his life. In all his philosophical work Schleiermacher maintains that issues concerning the subject cannot be separated from language: 'exchange of consciousness . . . presupposes a mediating term, a universal and shared system of designation' (1839: 372); 'There are no thoughts without discourse [*Rede*] . . . one cannot think without words' (1977: 77). He also sees language as constituted in the form of 'speech acts' (ibid. 80). For Schleiermacher, historically developed grammatical structures take the place of Kant's transcendental structures of thought. Similar ideas are also advanced by the linguist Wilhelm von Humboldt (1767–1835). Importantly, both Schleiermacher and Humboldt attend to the differing cognitive, aesthetic and practical ways language can be *used*, in a manner which will not generally be the case in the analytical tradition until the work of the later Wittgenstein.

Nietzsche too insists on the importance of language. He contends that questions about the metaphysics of the subject posed by philosophers since Descartes are really a result of 'grammatical habit', deriving from the subject-predicate structure of language. There is, he claims, no subject behind doing and thinking, there is just doing and thinking, so the idea of the subject as the 'transcendental unity of apperception' merely obscures an issue which should be understood via the linguistic forms in which it is manifested. Despite his attacks on the Enlightenment, Nietzsche comes close in one respect to what differentiates much of the analytical tradition from other philosophical approaches to language, because he suggests that metaphysical questions are really questions about language and may therefore be obviated by understanding the nature of language.[1]

What really complicates these issues is that so much therefore turns on what language is. Hamann, Herder, Schleiermacher and Humboldt do not, for example, think of language primarily as a means of representing things in the world. Instead they see it as a form of social action which enables things to be revealed or made manifest in the world and in ourselves. However, in scientific usage, where terms may seem to refer unambiguously to the things which scientific laws predict, the main function of language appears to be representational, in the sense that it 're-presents' what is already there. The analytical tradition can be said to develop because of a growing conviction in certain areas that the representational dimension of language is decisive. Given the success of the mathematically based natural sciences in producing reliable scientific laws, it seems clear to the initiators of analytical philosophy that the task of philosophy is to describe how this is possible via an explanation of language. The task is in some respects reminiscent of Kant's search in the *Critique of Pure Reason* for the conditions of possibility of knowledge, which led him to the idea of 'synthetic judgements a priori'. It is, though, in relation to the idea of such forms of judgement that the analytical tradition will often part company with Kant.

The problem with synthetic judgements a priori was apparent in Kant's idea of schematism, in which the differing realms of the 'pure concepts of the understanding' and 'intuitions' are supposedly made to fit together. The necessity associated with mathematical judgements is clearly in tension with the inconsistent ways in which we perceive things. The necessity of Pythagoras' theorem (within Euclidian geometry) does, though, seem to be reliably communicable in the terms we use to discuss triangles, however messy the mental images we have of triangles may be. Do we, then, really need Kant's strange hybrid, the schema, to show how it is that we can talk about pure geometry? At the same time, the idea behind the schema did help to explain something essential about our ability to use a limited number of words for an unlimited number of different things. This issue will return to haunt the analytical tradition's attempts to give a theory of meaning. The tradition begins, however, with the emergence of the conviction that explaining how language makes mathematical and scientific knowledge possible will be the new route to reliable philosophical knowledge.

1   Nietzsche was a significant influence on at least one of the founders of the Vienna Circle, Otto Neurath.

Schleiermacher's notion of 'a universal and shared system of designation' that is the requirement for thoughts to be communicable was elaborated, at much the same time as Schleiermacher is writing, by the Czech philosopher, Bernard Bolzano (1781–1848), into the basic idea of what later has come to be called the 'semantic tradition' (see Coffa 1991).[2] Bolzano's position is summed up in his assertion that the 'objective representation designated by any *word* is, as long as this word is not ambiguous, single' (1963: 66). A subjective representation is whatever occurs in anybody's mind at a particular time, and is contingent. If the meaning of words depends on the psychological content of people's minds, the objectivity demanded by the sciences evidently becomes unrealizable. The apparent answer to this situation is that words must be assumed to have an objective quality, their meaning, which exists independently of what individuals think that meaning is, in the same way as the truth of $2 + 2 = 4$ is not dependent on whether any individual happens to believe or understand it. At the same time, there must presumably be some sense in which 'objective representations' are accessible to thinking, otherwise the possibility of a theory of meaning dissolves: how would anyone understand the theory at all? This access cannot, however, be in the form of certainty at the psychological level, as an immediate, intuitive awareness of objective meaning, because we can be convinced of the objectivity of ideas that are false.

What, then, guarantees that we can be in touch with the 'objective representation' designated by a word? This is one of the questions which the analytical tradition will seek (and fail) to answer, which suggests that it may be the wrong question to ask in the first place. The source of the problem is hinted at in Bolzano's contention that the word must not be ambiguous. This means that at least some words must be assumed to be able to designate in a manner which involves a one-to-one relationship between the word and what it designates. The alternative is that the meaning of any word relies on a series of relationships to other words, so that the choice between the relationships is uncertain or depends on the context of use and on the context within which the word appears.

A great deal of trouble for the project of a theory of meaning lies in the assumption that meaning attaches to words in the manner Bolzano suggests. A one-to-one relationship between the word and what is designated relies on what Hegel would term an 'immediate' grasping of the sense of the word. The early Romantics already maintained, though, that words only gain their meaning in relation to other

---

2 Bolzano's work was not widely available in his lifetime, and it is unclear how much influence he had. He did, though, advance key ideas which will be echoed by Frege.

words in changing contexts. How else can what a word means be established, except by using other words, whose own sense will also rely, in turn, on other words and contexts? An exception here might seem to be when a word is synonymous with another word or words. Kant's 'analytic' judgements, like 'all bachelors are unmarried men', therefore give a class of statements which are 'true by definition', so that the words in them have a one-to-one relationship with each other, unlike words in 'synthetic' judgements. Being true by definition might also apply to mathematical statements, if all the rules of arithmetic can be formulated in terms of necessary a priori truths of logic. If this were possible, Kant's 'synthetic a priori', which sees arithmetical statements as informative (see chapter 1) would become redundant. The problem will be, though, that both synonymity and the purely logical status of arithmetic turn out to be indefensible notions.

A simple way to see the overall problem with the notion of objective representation is to ask where such a representation is located. If we think of the word 'table', a specific table in the world is not the objective representation, because being able to term something a table itself *depends* on the objective representation. This therefore seems to be the 'form' of the table, in a Platonic sense. It is what enables us to designate very different objects as being tables. Think, though, of all the borderline cases where we are not sure if a word is correctly used. Is this because we have not grasped the objective representation, or is it because the objective representation is not adequate to what we encounter in the world? What Bolzano is looking for is not, however, merely absurd, even if his way of looking for it may be mistaken. Many different kinds of philosopher would agree that the truth cannot be established on the basis of contingent psychological facts about what goes on in people's minds. Moreover, even the idea that truth is constituted via a consensus about the correct way to use a word does not capture all the ways 'true' is used: a universal consensus can turn out to be false. Truth does seem, therefore, to be something absolute, and it must have *some* connection to what words mean. The problem lies in establishing what that connection is.

Frege

Gottlob Frege (1848–1925) initiates a new kind of connection between language and mathematics, via his groundbreaking work in logic. For many analytically oriented philosophers, Frege's contributions are of unsurpassed importance, offering conceptual tools which have made a contribution to the sciences, computing and other areas, as well as establishing the agenda of rigorous modern philosophy. For many in the other mainstream European traditions of philosophy, whose predecessors we have examined in the preceding chapters, Frege is undoubtedly significant for his contributions to logic. He is, however, also one of the sources of a conception which excludes too many dimensions that belong to an adequate understanding of language. In certain respects this criticism echoes what Hamann and Herder objected to in Enlightenment philosophy. The paradigmatic division between these conceptions now becomes a division between (1) the idea that natural languages are deficient because they allow ways of talking which do not really refer to anything, and that we therefore need to construct a logically purified language (which Frege calls a 'Concept-Script'); and (2) the idea that this gets things the wrong way round, because understanding the logically purified language presupposes having learned to understand and use a natural language. Very schematically, this difference represents that between a purely analytical and a hermeneutic approach. It would, though, be mistaken wholly to oppose these approaches. Some of the proponents of each share certain ideas – Frege does not always seem to adhere to (1), for example; the early Wittgenstein is ambiguous about (1); and the later Wittgenstein adheres to (2). In recent years there has been considerable convergence between the approaches in the work of philosophers like Donald Davidson, Manfred Frank, Nelson Goodman, Jürgen Habermas and Richard Rorty. Despite these convergences, the distinction just made will later help to clarify some key questions.

The British philosopher Michael Dummett claims in relation to Frege's innovations that analytical philosophy is defined, first, by 'the conviction that a philosophical explanation of thought can be achieved by a philosophical analysis of language', and, second, by 'the conviction that a complete explanation can only be achieved in this way and in no other' (1988: 11).[3] The point of this formulation is to highlight Frege's 'anti-psychologism', of the kind we just encountered in Bolzano, which 'drives thoughts out of consciousness' and into language. If thoughts are constituted via the sounds or marks we use to communicate, the analysis of the structure and functioning of the

---

3   This view is increasingly contested, though would have been widely acceptable not that long ago. The questioning of the view has come about because the linguistic turn may not be adequate to characterize analytical philosophy. Indeed, there may be no strict way of characterizing analytical philosophy at all.

signs embodied in these sounds and marks will supposedly be able to replace the explanation of thoughts as dependent on the subject. The object of the analysis is therefore to establish how words possess a meaning which is independent of what any particular speaker may happen to think.

In his famous essay, 'On Sense and Reference/Significance/ Denotation' (1892),[4] Frege argues that the 'idea' ('*Vorstellung*', in the sense of the 'mental image') linked to a sign is 'to be distinguished from the reference and the sense of a sign. If the reference of a sign is a sensuously perceptible object, then my idea of it is an inner image that has emerged from sense impressions I have had and from both internal and external activities I have carried out' (1994: 43). The idea is therefore contingent upon the history of my particular experience and has no cognitive significance. Frege explains the difference between 'sense' and 'reference' by the image of looking at the moon: 'I compare the moon itself with the reference; it is the object of observation which is mediated by the real image which is projected by the lens in the inside of the telescope and by the retina of the observer. The former I compare with the sense, the latter with the idea or intuition' (ibid. 45). The image on the telescope lens (the 'sense') is accessible to anyone looking through the telescope, whereas the retinal image (the 'idea') is only available to the person doing the looking. We can all use the same word or phrase for something which is accessible in the objective world. Indeed, we have to assume that we can use words with identical meanings if agreed knowledge is to be possible. It is not clear, though, that this means we have access to whatever Frege means by the 'sense' of the word. Indeed, it is not clear what is meant by sense at all. Frege says sense is 'the manner of being given of what is designated' (ibid. 41), but does this help? Frege's aim is complete transparency in the analysis of language, but nobody is sure what the central terms he uses to achieve this transparency mean, because they depend on a series of not always compatible contexts in the rest of his work.

Frege uses the example of the planet Venus, which for a long time was thought to be two different stars, the morning-star and the evening-star, to illustrate what he means. The basic point is that the

---

4   The German is '*Über Sinn und Bedeutung*', for which there is no agreed translation. The problem lies not least in the fact that the translation of the title depends on what the two main terms in it mean, and this depends on how the essay itself is interpreted. What is clear is that *Bedeutung* does *not* mean the object referred to by a proposition, what is often called the 'referent', because Frege thinks predicates describing an object can also have *Bedeutung*. See the discussion of ascribing properties and referring to objects below.

same thing has two different senses, which for a long time were assumed to have two different references, but in fact do not. The example does not give a clear definition of sense, but it does offer an important partial solution to a dilemma posed by traditional forms of logic in relation to the question of identity. Frege defines a 'thought' as 'not the subjective activity of thinking, but its objective content which can be the common property of many people' (ibid. 46). The *thought* expressed by 'the morning-star is a body lit by the sun' is different from that expressed by 'the evening-star is a body lit by the sun' (ibid. 47). The *reference* of the two sentences is the same, namely what we term Venus, so the thought is to be construed as the *sense* of a sentence. What, then, is meant by its reference? Frege explains that 'The striving for truth is what everywhere drives us to move from the sense to the reference' (ibid. 48). The reference is therefore the 'truth-value' of a sentence, which is the 'circumstance that it is true or false' (ibid.). Frege argues that the reference of *all* sentences must either be 'the True' or 'the False', and that the relationship of a thought to the True is that of sense to reference. Senses can, then, be historically variable, having no intrinsic truth-value. As well as being a stage in seeking the truth, the notion of sense therefore has something to do with how we can understand and believe in things that do not exist or believe ideas that are mistaken, which have no reference. In that case, though, it is unclear how sense can be a 'manner of being given', if there may be nothing to be given in the first place. Sense and reference are, then, of a different order from each other: sense is the possibility of reference; reference is what can express 'the True'. We will come back to this in a moment.

A related innovation by Frege is his proposal of an alternative to the Aristotelian subject-predicate model of logic. This alternative model is essential to many of the ways in which analytical philosophy subsequently develops. Frege's model was, though, already adumbrated by Schelling in 1804, when he also considered the question of identity and predication. Schelling says we should take as an example the statement 'this body *is* red' (think of 'the body' as the x that could be the morning- or the evening-star):

> Obviously the quality of the colour red is here what could not be for itself, but is now, via the identity with the subject, the *body*: it is what is predicated. To the extent to which what predicates, the body, is the *Esse* [being] of this attribute it really *is* this attribute (as the statement says); but it does not follow that the concept of the subject *body* is for that reason (logically) the same as the concept of the predicate *red*. (I/vii. 204–5)

If we take the example of 'this person is angry', said of somebody at one time, and 'this person is not angry', said at another, and the person is the *same* person, the logical point becomes clear.

The logical difference between 'is red' and that which is red is formulated by Frege in terms of 'function' and 'argument'. The function 'is red'/'is angry' on its own is logically incomplete – it cannot be made into a meaningful proposition – and requires the 'argument', i.e. something that is red/angry, to be 'satisfied'. The terms derive from mathematics – think of the example of the infinite number of functions, $2 + 2$, $1 + 3$, etc., which are satisfied by the argument 4 – and Frege contends that what is the case in mathematics also applies to natural languages. This is so, he thinks, because mathematics is actually reducible to logic – that is what is meant by Frege's 'logicism' – and logic is also what underlies the meaningful use of language. The idea that mathematics is based on a series of rules of inference that can be *fully* described in a system of logic is later shown by Kurt Gödel (1906–78), a member of the Vienna Circle, to be indefensible, although it still produces some important insights. The other issue is much more controversial: the problem is the interpretation of the idea that logic is the ground of language's being meaningful.

Against the view that logic is merely formal and therefore lacks substantive content, Frege argues that logic is as much an expression of contentful thought as are other kinds of language. Logic's subject matter is whether thoughts are true, and how thoughts relate to each other, in the same way as the subject matter of physics is the truth about laws of motion, etc. The results of his conception are significant, even if the overall conception is implausible. Frege's sense-reference, and function-argument models, for example, show how to distinguish between ascribing properties ('is red/angry') and referring to objects to which the properties are ascribed ('there is an x such that x is red/angry'). (We saw a version of how Schelling's related point could be used against Hegel in chapter 4.) This distinction allows us to understand how knowledge can develop and be extended. The same object can be characterized in terms of descriptions which may contradict previous descriptions: when, for example, what burns ceases to be phlogiston, and becomes oxygen. In this case the logical point is in accordance with a vital fact concerning what human beings successfully do in the world a lot of the time. Is the logical structure, though, the *foundation* of their being able to do it? If so, just what does this mean, and how can it be shown to be the case? Frege deliberately excludes both consideration of the way lan-

guage concretely gets used in society and attention to the 'psychology' of language users. There is no significance attached for him to
how real human beings are in touch with the truth, because the True
must be independent of what they think anyway.

Is it really convincing to argue, though, as Frege does, that people
did not know what numbers *were* until he gave their true definition,
even though they have been able to do mathematics virtually since
the beginning of human thought (see Hacker in O'Hear 1999: 233)?
Frege offers a Platonist conception of mathematics as a pre-existing
series of ideal forms, which still has many defenders because of
the particular non-empirical status of mathematical knowledge.
However, his extension of a version of Platonism to truth as a whole
reveals a major problem. Consider the following. The two propositions, 'Frege was German' and 'Russell was English', stand in Frege's
terms for the same 'object', namely the True. This can be understood
as meaning, as Ernst Tugendhat has suggested, that all true propositions stand for 'reality' or 'the world', because they refer to something, as opposed to failing to refer. There is, then, a timeless true
world. This world is in one sense wholly determinate, consisting of
German Frege, English Russell, etc. In another sense, however, it is
indeterminate, rather like Kant's thing in itself. 'The True' needs to
be specified, but Frege's being German, like all empirical information, may turn out to be false, if new information emerges to refute
it. How it 'really is' transcends all the evidence we could ever gather,
thus making the True into the inaccessible world in itself.

Frege's difficulties can be further suggested by the following. In
1897 he realizes that the correspondence theory of truth causes difficulties because it involves trying to define truth. If one defines an
idea as true 'if it corresponds to reality', one is left with the situation
of trying to see if any particular idea corresponds, 'in other words
whether it is true that the idea corresponds to reality', which means
that one always has to presuppose truth in trying to define it.
Consequently, 'truth is obviously something so original and simple
that a reduction to something even more simple is impossible' (Frege
1990: 39). At the same time, Frege relies, as we saw, on the idea that
all true sentences correspond to the True. However, as Donald Davidson has remarked, 'there is no interest in the *relation* of correspondence if there is only one thing to correspond to since, as in any such
case, the relation may as well be collapsed into a one-place predicate:
"*x* corresponds to the universe"' (2001: 184). In that case it makes
more sense just to say '*x* is true', but this means giving up much of
what Frege argues. Frege ends up with a threefold world:

- of objects as given in perception, which are contingent, have no truth value, and are the result of my perceptual and other psychological history;
- of states of affairs expressed by thoughts: objects *as* something which could be said to be true – Venus as both the morning- and the evening-star; and
- of the True.

How these worlds can be in contact with each other is a mystery, which is why Davidson, Rorty and others these days seek to get away from any such divisions. The basic problem becomes clear when one realizes that there may be no limit to the number of potentially true things that can be said about anything. Moreover, the boundaries of many objects in the world depend on which language one uses to talk about those objects, or on which actions one performs in relation to the objects. As the holist ideas we have encountered in Idealism and Romanticism suggest, there may well be nothing intrinsic to an object that defines its boundaries for all time. Objective existence and 'being truly the case' cannot, then, be said to be logically equivalent. The problem of establishing how these different worlds relate to each other provides a model for many of the directions in analytical philosophy. The directions now to be considered will strive to find a way of describing the relationship between the world as something immediately given as sense-data in perception, and the world as described by science. The failure of this enterprise will be part of what has led to the contemporary convergence between the analytical tradition and the hermeneutic tradition.

The Vienna Circle and Wittgenstein's *Tractatus*

Thus far in this chapter we may seem to have left behind the concrete social and historical world which played a significant role in the development of philosophy in Germany from the Idealists onwards. However, the more technically oriented arguments we have been considering can take on a political resonance. The Vienna Circle consisted of a group of philosophers and natural scientists who began meeting in Vienna in the 1920s to discuss new conceptions of philosophy.[5] One of the strange facts about the Circle is that it would come under attack, almost from the beginning, by some on the Left, for the

5   A similar group existed in Berlin, involving Hans Reichenbach and others, but the Vienna Circle was more influential.

supposedly reactionary political implications of its ideas. Many of its members, though, began as politically engaged thinkers, some being (and in one case remaining) Marxists, although others would later become conservatives after they lived for a time in exile in the USA. The best-known figures in the Circle, which took on its name in 1929, are Rudolf Carnap, Philipp Frank, Herbert Feigl, Kurt Gödel, Hans Hahn, Otto Neurath, Moritz Schlick, Friedrich Waismann and Edgar Zilsel (see Friedman 1999 for details of publications). The combination of a frequently left-wing orientation and being a target of certain other thinkers on the Left – which characterizes the Circle – points to a vital factor in the development of German philosophy in the twentieth century. Apart from the kind of disastrous factionalism which too often divided Marxists and Social Democrats, what divides many philosophers who see themselves as being on the Left is their stance with regard to the relationship between philosophy and the natural sciences. The disagreements about this relationship cut across political differences in important ways.

The notion of 'positivism' plays a notorious role here. The Vienna Circle's philosophy is often referred to as 'logical positivism', though some people think this is misleading and prefer 'logical empiricism'. Positivism is still regarded as a pejorative term by some on the Left, though the term is too often employed in a very vague manner. The term was brought into widespread usage by the French philosopher, Auguste Comte, in the 1830s. For Comte, sciences go through three stages: the 'theological', the 'metaphysical' and the 'positive'. The last stage results from the rejection of metaphysical speculation and from the insistence on basing knowledge on the evidence of the senses. The opprobrium attached to positivism from the beginning has much to do with what it seeks to exclude from the domain of philosophy. Objections to this exclusion link the Catholic Church and many Marxists in their opposition to positivism.

Despite the differences of Comte's conception from the conceptions of the Vienna Circle, its members do share his aim of excluding metaphysics from science by relying on empirical data as the primary source of knowledge. A key influence on the Vienna Circle was the Viennese philosopher Ernst Mach (1838–1916) (who also influenced the novelist Robert Musil). Mach undertakes the kind of radical move which is characteristic of much science-oriented philosophy from the end of the nineteenth century onwards. He restricts what he takes to be real to the 'elementary given' present in the sense-data that are used to construct scientific knowledge by logical inference. For Mach, this construction is not to be seen as the work of a thinking subject, because there is no need to talk about either the subject or the reality which may give rise to the sensations. Predictions can be made from recurrent data organized according to logical laws, and this is enough to form scientific theories, without making the claim that the theories 'reflect' or 'correspond to' reality, and thus having to show how subject and object relate. This refusal to be pinned down to fixed subject and object notions is regarded as particularly advantageous in relation to relativity theory's dissolution of fixed, Newtonian, notions of space and time. Note that at the same time it excludes much of what we feel about what we are from philosophical consideration: the 'self' becomes a fiction in Mach's terms, because it cannot appear as an 'elementary given'.

Mach's approach differs in some respects from the approaches of those he influenced, but his reduction of the concerns of philosophy to empirical data and to logical laws is also characteristic of the Vienna Circle. Logical rules and empirical data are regarded as the only two sources of knowledge, which means that Kant's idea of synthetic a priori knowledge, that seeks to establish a bridge between the a priori and the empirical, is rejected. There are various reasons for this rejection of the synthetic a priori. One of the most important is that Kant's idea of necessary, timeless principles of thought which govern the intelligibility of the perceptible natural world comes into conflict with changes in the conceptions of mathematics and physics associated with the move away from Euclidean geometry and the theory of relativity. Space and time seem no longer to be the same thing in the light of these changes. Philosophy is therefore seen as being better off seeking ways to become part of the scientific conception of the world. This conception is, after all, providing such spectacularly successful new ways of describing nature as the theory of relativity.

It is here that a major source of tension with other versions of philosophy is located. The questioning of the timeless status of the categories is already inherent in the kind of objections to Kant made by Hamann. One version of this questioning therefore leads to Western philosophy's central concern being the interpretation of other cultures and world views, which means that the natural sciences need not be assumed to have a privileged status. In contrast, the analytical tradition often assumes that science's ability to show the untenability of theories like Kant's entails the demand to exclude from philosophy all claims which cannot be confirmed by the methods appropriate to the natural sciences. This radically restricts the scope of philosophy. Science does not, for example, have ways of talking about ethics or aesthetics. The analytical demand for a restriction of this kind is the source of the general aim of excluding 'metaphysics' from philosophy, on the grounds that it is neither empirically testable nor, like logic, a priori. The manner in which the members of the Vienna Circle seek to achieve this exclusion is characteristic of their approach. Logical truths clearly do not depend on evidence of the senses, but the question is what status they have in relation to reality. By accepting Bertrand Russell's and A. N. Whitehead's claim that logical truths are merely conventional, the Circle hopes to avoid getting entangled with the issue of connecting the two sources of knowledge that is central to Kant. How, though, are factual state-ments to be made into reliable theories? Above all, what status do *philosophical* claims about the relation between the logical and the empirical have, if logic is merely a series of conventions? What is at issue is ultimately no less than the question of how language relates to the world.

One way of highlighting the problem here is apparent in Peter Strawson's question as to whether the world consists of 'sentence-shaped items'. Why should the structure of language be in any way homologous to the structure of non-linguistic reality? Kant had seen the problem here at the level of concepts when he restricted knowl-edge to judgements of the way the world appears to us, thus refrain-ing from claims, of the kind made by German Idealism, about structural links between thinking and material nature. The problem facing the Vienna Circle, which will dog the analytical tradition, is that analysing the relationship between language and the world seems to require the making of metaphysical claims in an enterprise which seeks to exclude such claims.

In some early versions of the analytic enterprise the world is simply assumed to consist of discrete objects. Russell (for a time) thinks that language can be divided into 'names' and 'descriptions'.[6] The former designate objects, and their *meaning* is the object thus designated; the latter do not directly designate objects, because they can apply to many different objects, and so have no 'meaning'. This theory fell apart when it tried to deal with words that seem to be names, but which do not designate anything that exists. There is no need to go into the detail of this here. The vital aspect for our pur-poses is the way the notion of 'meaning' gets into trouble if it is attached to discrete things in the world which are the criteria for meaning. One obvious problem is that so much of the language we use thereby becomes excluded from 'meaning' anything. The trouble

6   Russell changed his mind so often and so rapidly that it is difficult to attribute positions to him that he did not reject at some time in his career, but this position was influential on other thinkers.

is compounded if the focus of the investigation of language is on individual words. Russell had begun as an admirer of Hegel, but came, like most of the Vienna Circle, to regard Hegel's work as nonsensical, as well as adopting a position which is precisely the one Hegel opposed. Russell's world has to consist of nameable, discrete entities. Hegel, of course, regarded such a conception as depending on 'immediacy', and as failing to see that things were always mediated by their relationships to other things, and thus could only be wholly discrete at the price of losing their identity (and, therefore, their meaning). Russell's world is the world as dreamt of by a scientist who wishes everything to be unambiguous and to have an identity that is not affected by other things. While this may (or may not) be desirable in the realm of the physical sciences, it does not do much for the world in which we communicate and interact in terms of feelings, values and aspirations. There are, however, still many philosophers deriving from this tradition who think the everyday realm will eventually be wholly explicable in the terms of the physical sciences.

A more interesting version of philosophy of this kind is represented by Wittgenstein's 1921 *Tractatus Logico-Philosophicus*, which responded to aspects of Russell's and Frege's contentions and became a vital influence on the Vienna Circle. This text, written when Wittgenstein was a soldier in the Austrian army in the First World War, is one of the most intriguing works of twentieth-century philosophy. Its avowed aim is to solve 'the problems of philosophy', and Wittgenstein claims in his Preface that he has achieved this. Perhaps not surprisingly, therefore, interpretations of the *Tractatus* diverge very considerably. Because of its attempt to establish a world of discrete objects 'pictured' in language, some people see it as in the tradition of Russell and science-oriented philosophy; others point to its links to the Kantian and Romantic traditions. However it is interpreted, the *Tractatus* is concerned with what can meaningfully be said. There are, it claims, only two kinds of truths: necessary logical truths and contingent factual statements which correctly 'picture' the world. The former are all tautologies, having no content, like the statement 'red is red', because they are necessarily true but wholly independent of anything that can be learned from observing the world; the latter are the propositions of natural science. Wittgenstein maintains that 'Understanding a proposition means knowing what is the case if it is true' (1984: 28).[7] Meaning and truth are inseparable, and truth, as we just saw, can only be logical or empirical. Apart from the idea of lan-

7   The *Tractatus* consists of short paragraphs whose relation to each other is indicated by numbers.

guage as 'picturing' true facts, this conception is adopted and adapted by the Vienna Circle. However, the way in which Wittgenstein presents these restrictive claims takes us somewhere very different, which explains the continuing fascination of the *Tractatus*.

A tautology does not say anything informative, and empirical truths depend on the observation of a world which is contingent – any structure we think the world has therefore derives at least in part from what we happen to observe. Clearly a great deal of what we say does not fit into these categories. Much of what we say about what we value, what we hope for, etc., is, therefore, in the terms of the *Tractatus*, 'nonsense' ('*Unsinn*'), because we cannot claim to know what is the case if what we say is true. The problem is, of course, that the applicability of the notion of nonsense is very extensive if only logic and empirical facts are not nonsense. Wittgenstein admits that the propositions of the *Tractatus* themselves do not come into either of the categories that have truth-value. They are not tautologies and they cannot be empirically confirmed, so they are 'nonsensical' ('*unsinnig*') (ibid. 85). The text therefore appears to be self-refuting: why should we hold its propositions to be true, given what it says about what can be true? Much depends here on how one regards nonsense. There are basically two ways of regarding nonsense in the analytical tradition at this time. Both claim that metaphysics, which involves truth-claims that are neither solely logical nor solely empirical, is nonsense.[8] In the first way of considering nonsense this judgement on metaphysics can be implicitly or explicitly pejorative, as it will be for most of the Vienna Circle. It can, however, as it is for Wittgenstein, also be an indication that the questions which matter most to human beings cannot be given definitive scientific or philosophical answers, because they lead to what is 'unsayable' (ibid. 33). Note that even the claim that metaphysics is nonsense is not itself a logical or empirical truth. Such a claim is not permitted in the terms which govern what can be said. In the light of the basic issue here, Richard Rorty suggests that philosophers 'are continually tempted to say, "The conditions making an expression intelligible are . . . ," despite the fact that the proposition itself does not fulfil the conditions it lists' (1991: 91). The question is how one responds to this situation.

Wittgenstein sees his enterprise in the *Tractatus* as 'drawing a limit on the expression of thoughts' (1984: 9). This is not the same as

---

8 It is worth already noting here that metaphysics is therefore only identifiable in these terms if the distinction between the logical and the empirical, the a priori and the synthetic can be upheld.

'drawing a limit on thought', because that would mean being able to 'think both sides of the limit' (ibid.). Claiming to do this leads to 'nonsense' because one is supposedly *thinking* about what cannot be thought. The issue here can be elucidated by looking back at an earlier manifestation of the problem involved. The structure in question recalls one of the ways in which Hegel sought to interrogate Kant's idea that what we know is always known under certain conditions, so that we cannot know things in themselves. For Hegel, drawing a limit on thought in this manner inherently takes one beyond the limit one draws, because *knowing* that something is a limit means one has already moved beyond it. The point of Hegel's dialectic is the realization that every particular thing we know is limited, and that limits on thought can be transcended in philosophy by showing how everything particular relates to everything else in a total, self-enclosed system. The 'absolute knowledge' this leads to is clearly not the same kind of knowledge as is involved in knowing something specific to be the case. In the wake of the ideas of the early Romantics, the later Schelling argued that one can indeed build a self-consistent complete logical system, but that this does not explain how that system relates to reality. Such an explanation requires something that cannot be part of the system. Describing how thought and reality relate requires a perspective which could encompass thought and reality, and this is precisely what is seen as impossible: to which side – thinking or reality – would the perspective belong?[9] This is what Wittgenstein means when he thinks it is nonsense to 'think both sides of the limit', given that the limit is the limit of *thought*. The early Romantic conviction that a complete conceptual understanding of being is impossible led to their concentration on art as the place where what philosophy could not say was *shown* in the way that works of art cannot be exhaustively interpreted. Works of art do not positively overcome the problem of thought's relation to reality, but they do make us aware that any attempt to transcend our finite perspective is both bound to fail and yet can give us an 'unsayable' sense of what is not finite.

Wittgenstein seems to suggest something similar concerning what can be said and what must be shown in the *Tractatus*, though the nature of what he is suggesting remains very contentious. By insisting on the utmost rigour concerning what can be said, which he con-

9 There are many attempts to show that Hegel avoids this problem by the way he construes being in the *Logic*, but the arguments about being suggested in chapter 4 do pose serious problems for any Hegel interpretation of this kind.

strues in terms of logic's being 'transcendental' (in the sense of being
a 'condition of possibility' of meaning) and 'not a doctrine but a
mirror-image of the world' (ibid. 76), he restricts what can be said to
what obeys 'logical syntax'. In relation to the confusions which are
inherent in our everyday use of language, where the same word can
perform very different roles, he claims, in the manner of Frege's
'Concept-Script', that we must use a language with a logical syntax
which will exclude the confusions generated by the syntax of natural
languages. At the same time, he does not diminish the role of everyday language, which 'is part of the human organism and no less
complicated than it'. This means that 'The tacit agreements for understanding everyday language are enormously complicated' (ibid. 26).
His target here turns out not to be, as it tends to be for Russell and
Frege, the ways in which we use everyday language, whose propositions are 'really, just as they are, logically completely in order' (ibid.
66), but the confusions that arise when using language for asking and
answering *philosophical* questions whose 'linguistic logic' (ibid. 26) is
not transparent.

In the Preface Wittgenstein maintains, as we saw, that he has solved
'the philosophical problems'. Crucially, however, he goes on to say
that 'the value of this work . . . consists in its showing how little is
achieved by having solved these problems' (ibid. 10). What, then, is
the significance and scope of philosophy, if its questions can be
answered, but the answers do not achieve a great deal? Part of the
proposed solution to the philosophical questions is the picture theory
of meaning (which he would later abandon). The picture theory is
best elucidated by Wittgenstein's remark that 'The gramophone
record, the musical thought, the score, the sound-waves all stand in
that representing internal relationship to each other which exists
between language and world. They all have the logical structure in
common' (ibid. 27). In consequence, there is 'a general rule' which is
the 'law of projection' of a symphony into the language of notes and
of the 'translation of the language of notes into the language of the
gramophone record' (ibid.). The translation from one form of articulation to another does not produce something unintelligible, but
rather something that is as intelligible as what it has been translated
from. The grooves in the record reproduce the music recorded, and
do not produce mere random noise. Moreover, 'The possibility of
all similes, of the whole pictorial nature [*Bildhaftigkeit*] of our means
of expression resides in the logic of representation [*Abbildung*]'.
A 'proposition' (*Satz*) is, then, an 'image of reality' (ibid. 28), and
the proposition is made possible by 'the principle of the representa-

tion of objects by signs' (ibid. 29), which functions in the manner of the relationship between the record and the music that it can be used to play.

Wittgenstein seems, therefore, to assume that there must be a shared principle, which he terms 'logical form', involved in all intelligible relationships between a language and the objects it represents. Logical form cannot *itself*, however, be represented. How is this to be understood? The Romantics were convinced that the transcendental I, Kant's principle of the world's intelligibility, could not represent itself to itself, and they used the image of the painter who can paint an image of himself painting but cannot paint what makes the objective image of the I the same as the I that does the painting.[10] Wittgenstein seems to be saying something similar. The principle in question is, in both cases, the main concern of philosophy, but it escapes representation within philosophy. Novalis already claimed that 'the true philosophy could never be represented' (1981: 557) and saw philosophy as 'an endless activity' (ibid. 180). Wittgenstein maintains that 'Philosophy is not a doctrine, but an activity', namely the 'logical clarification of thoughts' (1984: 32). The decisive point is that even though language can 'represent the whole of reality', because anything meaningful, i.e. the empirical propositions of natural science, can be stated in language, the proposition 'cannot represent what it must have in common with reality in order to be able to represent it' (ibid. 33). The proposition '*shows* the logical form of reality' (ibid.), but therefore cannot *say* what that form is. This is why there cannot be a science of meaning, and why philosophy is fundamentally different from natural science.

The most questionable aspect of Wittgenstein's argument becomes apparent when he says that 'empirical reality is limited by the totality of objects. The limit shows itself again in the totality of the elementary/atomic propositions [*Elementarsätze*]' (ibid. 66). The approach critical of metaphysical claims we have seen so far gives way in this aspect of the text to the assumption of a world which consists of an unchanging totality of objects pictured in 'elementary/atomic' propositions. Wittgenstein gives no examples of what he means by such objects and propositions, even though he makes clear in the early parts of the *Tractatus* that they are central to his overall account of the nature of the world. The *Tractatus* seems here to take us back to a pre-Kantian, Leibnizian world of 'monads', discrete, indivisible, self-identical entities, that are somehow in harmony with the

10 Wittgenstein read at least some Novalis, who uses this image in his reflections on Fichte.

elementary propositions that picture them, but Wittgenstein gives no
indication of what this really means, or of why his contentions should
be believed.

Another, more interesting, dimension of the work actually seems
reminiscent of Kant. Given the limitation of what can be said to 'the
propositions of natural science' (ibid. 85), and the fact that 'all happening and being-thus is contingent' (ibid. 83), there can be no value
in the world. Values are, therefore, *non*-contingent reasons for something being so, of the kind that theology claims would justify the existence of the world or that people adduce for their actions. There can
therefore not be 'any propositions of ethics', because empirically
based propositions are about the contingent world, and 'Ethics and
aesthetics are one and the same' (ibid.). As in Kant, then, the world
of scientific propositions is separate from the realm of values. Kant
is explicit about the existence of an 'intelligible' realm, though he
does insist that we have no cognitive access to it. Wittgenstein is much
less explicit about what lies outside the empirical world, but he suggests the direction he is taking when he claims that 'We feel that even
if all possible scientific questions are answered the problems of our
life are not yet at all affected. Admittedly no question remains any
more; and precisely this is the answer' (ibid. 85). Philosophy cannot
state the answer to the meaning of life. Possessing the meaning of life
would instead mean no longer needing to ask the question, and this
takes one into the realm of silence. It is, though, a highly significant
silence, which means one can leave philosophy behind, because life
would no longer be a problem. Wittgenstein himself did leave philosophy behind for a time after writing the *Tractatus*, only to return
to it later in the 1920s after he became convinced that the conception of language and reality he had proposed was mistaken. Discussion of the *Tractatus* has revived recently in the light of attempts to
show that it is more congruent with the ideas of the later Wittgenstein than had previously been thought. The idea is that by settling
some core issues in logic in the *Tractatus*, he left the space for the
new exploration of the language we actually use in the world in his
later work. This approach does not, however, deal adequately either
with the questions concerning the 'totality of objects' or with those
concerning nonsense, philosophy and ethics that conclude the work.
The other important aspect to note here is the limitation which
Wittgenstein puts on what philosophy is, which he derives from the
narrowly analytical focus of Russell and Frege in particular. The
consequences of this limitation of focus will be very significant for
twentieth-century philosophy, not least because of the development
of the Vienna Circle.

Scientific Philosophy

The assimilation of the *Tractatus* by the Vienna Circle was largely confined to its rejection of the synthetic a priori as nonsense, its empiricism, and some of its answers to logical issues which argued, against Frege and Russell, that logic consisted of tautologies, rather than saying anything contentful. Significantly, they almost wholly ignore the issues that can be linked to Romantic thought. What, then, was the specific contribution of the Circle? Recent research (see e.g. Friedman 1999; Cartwright et al. 1996; Bowie 2000, 2001) has made saying this much more difficult than it used to be, revealing that the actual texts of the Circle are far more diverse than their historical influence would suggest. However, the historical influence of the Circle does tend to rest on one or two ideas that challenged many existing approaches to philosophy, which had an enormous effect on academic philosophy in the English-speaking world, but which are now generally regarded as discredited. From being the defining figures of American philosophy in particular, from the 1940s to the 1950s and 1960s, the work of the Circle has ended up as merely a part of the analytical philosophy of science.

The grand aim of the Circle, before it was forced to abandon Vienna because of the incursion of the Nazis, was 'scientific philosophy', philosophy which is congruent with the results of the sciences. In the political climate of the 1920s and 1930s this was rightly thought to be a way of countering various kinds of reactionary irrationalism in philosophy, which made the sort of negative claims about reason we observed in chapter 7 and were often antagonistic to the natural sciences. For the Circle, if cognitive science comes up with reliable predictive theories concerning perception of the external world, these, together with clarification of the logical status of statements about objects, seem a better basis for talking about how we are able to know than such notions as the mind's ability to make synthetic a priori judgements. It is of course important for philosophers to take account of well-confirmed scientific theories, but what is the contribution of philosophy now to be that cannot be better achieved by the sciences? One answer, the Circle thought, is that its task is to give criteria for what can and cannot be scientifically valid, in order that we could, for example, assess the theory of perception that would replace traditional epistemology. This presumably requires an account of scientific validity which cannot be provided by any science itself, but this sounds suspiciously like what they mean by metaphysics. The Circle's adherence to the two sources of logic and empirical data is, after all, intended to offer a way of achieving an account of science which avoids metaphysics.

The temptation of empiricism is that it seems to be based on what scientists do when they investigate the world by collecting data. If one accepts that knowledge depends on sense-data, the question is, though, as Kant realized, how those data can result in meaningful propositions. One view of this issue, proposed by Carnap in *The Logical Construction of the World* (1928), involves 'phenomenalism', the radically empiricist idea that the only certainty we have about the objective world is what appears to us as phenomena. Such certainty is radically private – Carnap talks in this connection of 'methodological solipsism' – and the challenge is to get from private certainty to publicly available knowledge. The difficulty is that private sensations and public language are not obviously translatable into each other. Which part of the sensations is cognitively relevant, and how do particular bits of private sensations map onto bits of language, given that language is public and general? Is there a way in which certain kinds of experience give us a certainty which we can build on which other kinds do not? How do we know this without requiring something which the objections to metaphysics preclude, namely an aspect of thinking which is neither simply logical nor simply empirical? In chapter 3 we considered the problem of 'foundationalism', which Reinhold summed up when he says that a fundamental proposition 'must not be able or be allowed to receive its sense via any other proposition' (1978: 353). The alternative is a regress in which any proposition depends on another proposition, and so on, with no possibility of a foundation. Much of the history of analytical philosophy has turned out to be a rerun in linguistic form of the problems of foundationalism which we have observed in the wake of Kant, and this is certainly the historical fate of the Circle.

What the Circle wanted, then, was a reliable means of saying how to make the data of experience into propositions which convey knowledge – they had no doubt that this *could* take place: how else did science arrive at theories which made reliable prediction possible? The problem was that philosophy's search for foundations just seemed to lead to this certainty dissolving. Their most famous attempt at getting over this problem was the verificationist criterion of meaning, which states that the meaning of a proposition is the way in which it can be shown to be true. The aim is essentially negative, seeking to exclude as meaningless statements which have in principle no way of being confirmed by anyone's experience (the links to the *Tractatus* should be clear). This leads, though, to a classic foundationalist dilemma. Is the verifiability criterion itself verifiable? If it is not, there is no reason in the terms of the Circle to accept that it means anything, as Wittgenstein realized with regard to his own attempts to describe conditions of possibility of meaning. But how could the criterion be verified without the verification leading to the vicious circle of having to understand what one wishes to verify, whilst supposedly making what one wishes to verify the *criterion* of understanding? Despite some notion of verification being evidently important to any conception of scientific knowledge, the Circle was unable to give an account of it that avoided this problem.

Another attempt to find a way of establishing criteria for meaning is that of Schlick, who claims that, in order to avoid a regress of words defining words, 'we must eventually attach words directly to experience in acts of ostension [pointing], and all meaning ultimately resides in the given' (cit. in Friedman 1999: 29). However, pointing something out directly so that it is clear to another person what is meant can only successfully be done by using words: remember the chair which can be a brown object, something that weighs thirty pounds, etc. Both versions of radical empiricism simply do not work, and Carnap and others are consequently pushed towards a new version of Kant's synthetic a priori. The simple reason is that the borderline between what the world contributes and what the mind contributes to knowledge cannot be strictly drawn in philosophy, not least because language seems to belong on both sides of the mind–world division. If that is so, all attempts to rely just on logic and the empirical 'given' as the foundation of knowledge are doomed to failure: bringing the two together ends up revealing that neither can be said to exist in a pure form anyway. Otto Neurath came to appreciate this fundamental misapprehension and advanced many arguments which point in a much more productive direction, of the kind we shall observe in thinkers in coming chapters (and which were already outlined by Romantic philosophers like Schleiermacher and Schlegel: see Bowie 2000, 2004). However, an adequate assessment of the Vienna Circle cannot be arrived at by pointing out the number of exceptions within it to its historically influential doctrines.

Two related aspects are important in this context. The standard story of the demise of the Circle's dominant ideas is that, along with Gödel's revelation in 1931 that mathematics could not be reduced to logic, the American philosopher W. V. O. Quine revealed in the 1950s that the very distinction between analytic and synthetic propositions, which underpins the insistence on solely logical and empirical truths, cannot be defended. This is because analytic propositions depend on words being able to be strictly synonymous, and this cannot be demonstrated because of the holistic nature of language, in which the

meaning of one word always depends on the meanings of an indeterminate number of other words. However, it is rarely, if ever,
pointed out that Schleiermacher already made this point some time
in the 1820s:

> The difference between analytical and synthetic judgements is a fluid
> one, of which we take no account. The same judgement (ice melts) can
> be an analytical one if the coming into being and disappearance via
> certain conditions of temperature are already taken up into the
> concept of ice, and a synthetic one, if they are not yet taken up. . . . This
> difference therefore just expresses a different state of the formation of
> concepts. (1839: 563)[11]

The point of this historical fact is that the likelihood of people
looking back at the 'metaphysical' Romantic tradition when they are
convinced, as the Circle was, that philosophy is successfully working
in tandem with revolutionary new conceptions in the natural sciences,
is minimal. When there are hopes of a revolutionary rethinking of
philosophy, the past is largely jettisoned, although it is likely to return
at a later date. This leads to the second aspect. The tendency of the
Circle, despite its often laudable progressive political aims, was
towards a scientistic conception of philosophy. The focus of the analysis of language is on scientific propositions and how they represent
reality, and this focus is used to discredit other ways of talking about
things. The tradition to which Schleiermacher belongs had, though, as
should be apparent from what we saw concerning Hamann and
Herder, already advanced very convincing arguments to suggest that
such a limitation on the analysis of language involves a fundamental
misrecognition of the nature of language. The fact that the hermeneutic tradition failed to have any impact on the major developments of
analytical philosophy until very recently is, however, a complex story,
which will begin to be explained in the next chapter. Once again, the
relationship between philosophy, politics and natural science will be
crucial.

SUGGESTIONS FOR FURTHER READING

Beaney, M. (1996) *Frege: Making Sense* (London: Duckworth). *Excellent
study of issues in Frege's thought.*

---

11 Schleiermacher's version of this argument actually has the advantage of being less
dogmatic than Quine's: it is not that the distinction is useless, just that it cannot be a
fundamental logical distinction.

Canfield, J. V. (ed.) (1986–8) *The Philosophy of Wittgenstein*, 15 vols (New York and London: Garland). *Collection of major essays on Wittgenstein's thought.*

Coffa, J. A. (1991) *The Semantic Tradition from Kant to Carnap* (Cambridge: Cambridge University Press). *Outstanding historical account of the sources and early development of analytical philosophy.*

Currie, G. (1982) *Frege: An Introduction to His Philosophy* (Brighton: Harvester). *Useful introductory volume.*

Dummett, M. (1981) *The Interpretation of Frege's Philosophy* (London: Duckworth). *Major work on Frege's philosophy by his most influential contemporary interpreter.*

Friedman, M. (1999) *Reconsidering Logical Positivism* (Cambridge: Cambridge University Press). *Significant reinterpretations of the work of the Vienna Circle, based both on historical research and philosophical argument.*

Kenny, A. (1973) *Wittgenstein* (London: Allen Lane). *Useful general introduction.*

Kenny, A. (1995) *Frege* (Harmondsworth: Penguin). *Good general introduction that underlines the importance of Frege for analytical philosophy.*

Sluga, H. (1980), *Gottlob Frege* (London: Routledge). *Historically informed study of the work of Frege.*

9

PHENOMENOLOGY

The Continental/Analytical Divide

In discussions of contrasting approaches in modern philosophy, the difference between the 'continental' and the 'analytical' traditions of philosophy is often referred to as the difference between the 'phenomenological' and the analytical traditions. It is sometimes justifiable to make such distinctions with regard to the philosophical arguments of each notional tradition. However, this can also easily obscure both the complexity of the distinctions in relation to the socio-historical world and the sometimes tenuous nature of the distinctions themselves.[1] Had there been no Nazi take-over in Germany and Austria, the nature of this divide would, for instance, have been very different, because the communication between thinkers with conflicting philosophical and political viewpoints would not have been distorted to the same extent. Take the following extreme examples. Moritz Schlick was murdered by a Nazi student in 1938, and his friends from the Vienna Circle and from Berlin, who survived by fleeing, influenced the philosophy of other countries, like Britain and the USA, much more than that of their own, as did Wittgenstein. On the other side, Martin Heidegger was a member of the Nazi party almost from the beginning, in 1933, to the bitter end in 1945, and yet he continued to influence German philosophy even when he was banned from holding an official academic post after the Second World War. The extent of his influence was, moreover, certainly

---

1   As we have seen, it is not possible, for example, reliably to describe the division in terms of the analytical tradition's concentration on language.

increased by the initial absence from post-war German philosophy of some of the conceptual resources developed by and in the light of the Vienna Circle. However, there was also opposition, from the 1930s to the 1960s and beyond, by many who saw themselves as on the Left, like Adorno and Horkheimer, *both* to Heidegger *and* to the ideas and effects of the Vienna Circle. Furthermore, perhaps the most significant development in German philosophy in the 1970s was the taking up by Adorno's pupil, Jürgen Habermas, of key ideas from the analytical tradition. In this, he was influenced by Heidegger's pupil, Ernst Tugendhat, who had, in turn, come to reject many of his teacher's ideas in favour of arguments from analytical philosophy.

Such complexities in the supposed division between traditions take us further back in history. Until the advent of the work of Edmund Husserl (1859–1938) at the beginning of the 1900s, and of his pupil Heidegger in the 1920s, academic philosophy in Germany after the demise of Hegelianism in the 1840s was dominated by what is broadly referred to as 'Neo-Kantianism', which sought to find ways of revising the ideas of Kant in the light of new developments in the natural and social sciences. Many of the representatives of this movement, though, often seem closer to what is now regarded as the analytical tradition. They are concerned with logic and scientific validity, in a way that what is now regarded as 'continental' or 'European' philosophy sometimes is not. At the same time, these thinkers also addressed, in a manner not typical of the analytical tradition, the question of how the knowledge provided by the natural sciences ('*Naturwissenschaften*') relates to that provided by the humanities ('*Geisteswissenschaften*'). It is this issue, in which many of the ambivalences that play such a role in the development of modernity in Germany are manifest in philosophy, that will be crucial to much of the rest of the story told here.[2]

We have repeatedly seen how the growing success of the natural sciences and the effects of that success change German philosophy. The extreme versions of positivism lead, for example, to the idea that only scientific propositions are meaningful, and that ethics and aesthetics produce propositions which have no real claims to meaning or validity, because they are based on merely subjective feelings. The work of Kant, the Romantics and Hegel had been concerned to integrate the cognitive, ethical and expressive dimensions of modern life

2   I shall not include an account of Neo-Kantianism because presentation of the diversity of positions it involved would take up too much space. This is regrettable, as the work of Ernst Cassirer, in particular, still has much to offer the debate over the relation of science to modern culture: see his *Philosophy of Symbolic Forms*.

into an overall picture which would locate us in a coherent, meaningful world. Positivism is an extreme result of the perceived failure of this integration, and this is a major source of the desire of so many German thinkers to oppose it. The Neo-Kantian philosophers tended to see this failure of integration as being the result of philosophy not providing an adequate 'grounding' for the differing spheres of human activity. A key aspect of this grounding was to be an account of the relationship of science to the rest of culture which was able to show how science – '*Wissenschaft*' in the sense it has in German, which includes both natural science and the humanities – could be 'unified'. The point of this unification was to establish the nature of the claims in the differing areas, for example, of physics and history, and thus to see how they related to other aspects of human culture. One just needs to think of the Nazis' combination of the use of the most advanced technology with their propagation of the most barbaric conceptions of humankind and society to see why this issue might be so important.

Attempts by Neo-Kantian philosophy to respond to the perceived disunity of the sciences tend to result in elaborate systematic constructions based, for example, on the idea, characteristic of the work of Heinrich Rickert (1863–1936) (see Rickert 1986), that all forms of knowledge must be grounded in some – never adequately specified – essential 'values'. These values transcend the contingency of the historical and empirical worlds, and make true judgements possible. Various versions of the distinction between the physical sciences, which are inherently universalizing and produce general laws (what the Neo-Kantian philosopher Wilhelm Windelband termed 'nomothetic sciences'), and the historical sciences, which are concerned with the particularity of historical events and actions ('idiographic sciences'), are produced, none of which is wholly plausible. The significance of philosophy for actual research in either realm is, moreover, unclear. The choice of philosophical approach in the first third of the twentieth century often comes, then, to be seen as broadly between:

- the 'positivist' or logical empiricist idea of 'scientific philosophy', which excludes much of human life from philosophical consideration;
- philosophy which still regards itself as essentially concerned with the grounding of scientific knowledge and with its relationship to the rest of culture; and
- a new option which begins to emerge with Husserl and really develops in the work of Heidegger.

It is the third option that will have the most effect on the analytical/continental divide and on the subsequent development of German philosophy.[3] The importance of this option lies not least in the attempt to establish philosophy's independence from the particular sciences.

The Central Concepts of Husserl's Phenomenology

(a) Varieties of experience

The widespread appeal of Husserl's phenomenology lies in its initial move away from the attempt to give big answers to philosophical questions, towards a detailed description of our experience of the world in which such questions arise. The description of the ways the world is manifest to us constitutes what Husserl means by 'phenomenology'. The crucial issue is the status of this examination of experience. Is the examination merely descriptive, as Husserl always insists? If it is, how is it that Husserl wants to use the results as a means of establishing a new kind of foundation for philosophy? By doing so he can be interpreted as moving towards the kind of grand metaphysical conception his initial project need not entail. The problem with foundationalist approaches is, as we saw, that if the founding principle cannot be firmly established, the rest of the philosophical edifice is threatened. Furthermore, if the beginning of philosophical enquiry is supposed to be absolutely established, there is a danger that the initial principle will invalidly exclude important questions, even as it enables a system to be constructed. The appeal of empiricist approaches, as against rationalist ones, lies in the idea that empiricism will avoid this problem by being open to the reality of whatever we encounter. However, as Hegel already showed, empiricism itself cannot be said to work merely from the data of experience, because even the most 'immediate' sensory experiences turn out to involve universal concepts, like 'this', 'here' and 'now', if they are to be intelligible.

The problem with many kinds of empiricism really lies, then, in the idea that the primary 'given', via which the world is manifest, consists of unprocessed sense-data. Nothing can be said about such data, because that would mean their particularity was already subject to

3   The role of some of the various versions of Marxism will be considered in chapter 11.

general concepts. The route from raw data to a world of intelligible things articulated in concepts therefore becomes inexplicable. Pointing to the identifiable causal impacts of the world on the organism – photons that can be demonstrated to have a causal impact on the retina, for example – does not tell us about how sense-data can be a basis for knowledge, including, of course, knowledge of the impact of photons on the retina. Having photons hit one's retina is not the same as *knowing* about it. Light has to be experienced *as* something by a subject, and this cannot be said to be a causal process, not least because our very notion of causal process depends on our ability to think. We do not actually *experience* a world of raw sense-data, but rather a world of things and meanings. An indeterminate patch of light is seen as indeterminate because we want to know how it fits into a world where light has all sorts of determinate significances. The real problem is whether what may abstractly be described in terms of 'raw data' is *made* by the mental acts of the subject into a coherent world, or whether the world's coherence is constituted in some other way. Husserl's aim is, in one sense, an empiricist one. He wishes to attend to the world as it is experienced, in order to analyse how its intelligibility is constituted. At the same time, his position often seems closer to both Kant and Fichte. The tension between the empiricist and transcendental aspects of Husserl is vital in understanding the impact of his philosophy.

In phenomenology the starting point is the fact that the world manifests itself as phenomena. However, this need not mean that there is another world, the world as it really is, rather than the one which merely appears. The 'phenomenalist' assumption that there are two such worlds is one way of understanding Kant's split between phenomena and noumena.[4] Phenomenology will admittedly still involve the problem of the 'ultimately real', and some critics argue that it leads to phenomenalism. However, phenomenology begins with the undeniable everyday experiences of the world of things, noises, smells, etc., a world of immediate significances. These experiences were thought by Husserl and others to have been obscured by the mistaken idea that what we experience are only images of things. This would mean experience is of an intermediary between us and the things, rather than being an experience of the 'things themselves'. When we see a tree, though, Husserl insists, we do not see a tree-image, or a packet of sense-data that we make into a tree, we see the tree itself. The task is to describe how this is the case.

---

4   It only fits one interpretation of the thing in itself – the one in which the thing is wholly unknowable (see chapter 1).

Husserl continues to influence contemporary philosophy because
he combines an intense concern with subjectivity with an insistence
on the importance of scientific objectivity. He therefore links the
Romantic and the positivist aspects of modern philosophy in a new
way. There is no definitive version of Husserl's philosophy, and there
are some significant differences between the texts from differing
phases of his work that he did publish – a large amount of his work
was not published in his lifetime. Perhaps the most significant of these
differences lies in the move to an explicitly transcendental perspective in *Ideas towards a Pure Phenomenology and Phenomenological
Philosophy* (1913). The earlier *Logical Investigations* (1900–1) has
recently come to the attention of some thinkers in the analytical tradition for the ways in which it suggests dimensions of the notion of
meaning which the dominant approaches from Frege to Wittgenstein
had tended to exclude. However, it is the conception which develops
in the *Ideas* and is elaborated in subsequent texts that has been most
influential for German (and much European) philosophy. The most
instructive texts are the volume of the *Ideas* Husserl published in
1913, *Cartesian Meditations* (1931) and *Crisis of the European Sciences and Transcendental Phenomenology* (1936).

(b) Pure phenomenology

Husserl refers to his enterprise as a 'pure phenomenology', which is
to be shown to be the 'grounding science of philosophy' (1992: v. 3).
This could seem rather odd, given the aim of phenomenology to
provide a description of experience. Such a description might be seen
as belonging in the realm of scientific psychology, in which the nature
of perception can be experimentally studied by, for example, considering the way optical illusions occur. Husserl, though, consistently
maintains that what he is investigating is essentially different from
the scientific investigation of the workings of the mind, and that philosophy cannot be dissolved into natural science. One of the reasons
for this lies in his rejection of 'psychologism', the idea that logical laws
are explicable in terms of empirical laws governing the functioning
of the mind discovered by psychology. The problem here is that the
results of any scientific investigation must be logically consistent if
they are to be intelligible, so that psychologism has to presuppose
what it sets out to prove. At this level there are good reasons for
rejecting many forms of psychologism, because they invalidly seek
to use empirical data to justify a priori forms without which the
empirical data would not themselves be intelligible. Whether logic's
foundational status or its relationship to reality can be adequately

explained by philosophy is another matter, as we saw with regard to Wittgenstein's *Tractatus*, and Husserl poses interesting questions in this respect.

The difficulty of philosophical concentration on experience is that each concrete experience is inherently particular and never strictly identical with any other experience (we saw this in chapter 1, in relation to Kant and Leibniz). At the same time, we rely on identities between things and thoughts to be able to negotiate the world around us, and the everyday world is experienced as, in the main, directly intelligible. There is an instructive tension in Husserl between the intuitive certainty with which we are able to function in the contingent world, and the conviction that this involves structures which themselves cannot be contingent. His assumptions are therefore close to those of Kant, but the difference lies in the way in which he investigates experience.

If this investigation were psychological, the method would involve taking concrete examples of how the world is given to us and making empirical generalizations that lead to concrete laws governing perception. However, such an investigation itself relies precisely on what Husserl is aiming to uncover, namely the *basis* of the ways of thinking which allow us to move from experiential data to laws governing that data. What allows us to make this move cannot simply be derived from specific cases in which we actually make the move. First of all, these cases themselves depend on what we contingently encounter in the world for their content. They also depend on the fact that the data in question are intelligible, rather than being arbitrary sense-data. Because what we encounter is contingent, an analysis of it cannot function as a *foundation* for claims about what makes judgements of experience valid. The whole point of philosophical foundations is, of course, to overcome contingency. This situation is the source of Husserl's claims concerning a 'pure' phenomenology, which has to be based on an account of subjectivity, because the objective world of facts cannot provide complete certainty.

(c) Eidetic science

Husserl's project is, he asserts, not a 'science of facts', but a 'science of essences', which he terms, following the Greek word for essence, *eidos*, an 'eidetic' science (ibid. 6). A science of facts could not attain philosophical status, for the reasons we just saw. How, then, does one arrive at 'essences'? Each individual thing, Husserl argues, is contingent and could be otherwise, but a thing also is the bearer of predicates which it has in common with other things. It is these that can be investigated as 'essences'. Husserl gives the example of a musical note, which, in order to be a note at all, must share something with all other notes, such as, at the most general level, the essence of 'being something acoustic at all' (ibid. 13). This locates it in a particular 'region' of things, and Husserl talks of 'regional ontologies' as circumscribing such essences. The note can be part of an ontology of acoustics, but it could equally be part of a social ontology, if it functioned as a nuisance by being a noise that disturbs a community.

Each concrete object in the world is the potential source of an infinity of experiences, depending on which of their aspects comes to the fore. The 'intuition' of what there is, which Husserl sees in terms of its 'being originally given', can take the form of the experience of the particular thing in front of me, but it can also take the form of an 'intuition of essence'. Geometry is, for example, a 'science of essences', because the pure forms of space it deals with cannot be encountered as facts of experience in the objective world. The 'finally founding act' present in a geometrical proof is an 'intuition of essence' which cannot be contradicted by experience. How, though, do the two kinds of intuition relate? The empiricist insists on the principle that all knowledge of facts must be legitimated by the immediate data of experience. Husserl agrees. How else can new science come about, but by beginning with evidence that is directly experienced and taken as 'originally given', rather than merely deriving from what is already known? However, he insists that this principle cannot *itself* be established in terms of experience, because there can be no data of experience that could confirm the principle itself as the sole basis of knowledge. (The problem is similar to that facing the verification principle we saw in the last chapter.) It is this failing in empiricism that phenomenology seeks to overcome. The principle that would overcome this failing must itself have absolute status. Otherwise it would be subject to the contingency encountered by the sciences for which it is trying to provide the foundation.

(d) Epoché

All sciences depend on the 'natural attitude', by which Husserl means the way we are absorbed in the reality that is 'there', which has to be taken as it 'gives itself' to us – we shall see how he later develops this notion into the idea of the 'life-world'. We may be mistaken about what actually happens to be there at a particular time, but this only makes sense on the basis of the assumption of the natural attitude. How else can error, illusion or hallucination be understood, except in contrast to that which is not error, etc., i.e. to what is 'originally given'? The claim that experience may be nothing but illusion has to presuppose some prior sense of what is therefore not illusion to be intelligible. In the *Ideas* Husserl next makes the decisive move of 'suspending' or 'bracketing' anything that we accept as 'adequately given' to our intuition, in what he terms the 'epoché'. He defines this as *'a certain abstention from judgement which is compatible with the unshaken and perhaps unshakable, because evident, conviction of the truth'* (ibid. 64). The idea is to exclude any evidence from the sciences or from everyday experience, as part of his project of arriving at philosophically solid foundations. This does not mean he doubts scientifically established truths, merely that they must play no role in what he is trying to establish.

The aim is, therefore, to be able to describe what is particular to consciousness alone, by excluding everything which is not internal to consciousness. He also terms this exclusion the 'transcendental reduction' (ibid. 69). The content of the description are those aspects of consciousness brought to bear on the world which are essential to the way in which the world is constituted for us. Experiences are manifest in the 'stream of experience', which includes everything of which we are actually or potentially aware. Husserl maintains that in looking at the page in front of you there are two crucially different aspects: one is the being of the material thing, the paper, the other is the way in which you experience its being given to you, in terms of the way the paper feels to the touch, the way you see the light reflect off it, and so on. Furthermore, you are also aware of other things surrounding the page, even though your concentration may be on the page itself. These different things involve different modes of attention. Such modes of attention do not rely on the specific being of whatever material objects happen to be in front of you: they can apply to an indefinite number of other cases. They function as a kind of 'space' that can be filled by different things which also fit that kind of space. Without this general applicability of modes of attention, experience would dissolve into a chaotic multiplicity. The modes of attention can themselves in turn become the object of a reflection on their nature. This is an essential part of the task of phenomenology, which describes the different characteristics of modes of attention such as memory, fantasy, direct perception, etc.

(e) Intentionality, immanence and transcendence

Husserl relies on the notion of 'intentionality', which he adapts from the Austrian philosopher Franz Brentano (1838–1917). The intentionality of consciousness means that it is always consciousness *of* something towards which it is 'directed' (from the Latin '*intentio*'). Whereas Brentano assumes that every act of consciousness involves an object in the world towards which it is directed, Husserl wants to be able also to deal with aspects of consciousness which do not have such an object. This means differentiating the ways in which consciousness is 'about' whatever it can be about, which includes fantasies, etc., as well as the real things we encounter in daily life. If we evaluate an object, for example, there has to be a distinction between the thing evaluated, and the 'complete intentional object'. The latter includes the *way* our evaluation directs its attention to what is evaluated, when we look at a painting, for example. This aspect clearly does not belong to the thing as a part of the objective world. Instead of claiming this aspect is 'merely subjective', Husserl sees it as essential to the nature of the world we experience.

The difference between '*being as experience*' and '*being as thing*', between what can be within consciousness and what cannot be – the evaluation of the object and the actual material object of the evaluation, for example – leads to the essential difference between 'immanence' and 'transcendence'. The latter means the existence of the object beyond the ways it is actually apprehended. Perception of transcendent objects always involves only seeing aspects and degrees (what Husserl calls 'shadings', '*Abschattungen*') of the thing, and these can be given in a variety of manners. The aspects cannot all be apprehended at once, even though they are all of the same object. The crucial point about the immanent apprehension of experiences of the world, though, is that they are *absolute*, because the experiences do not exist in the manner of objects in the world. Each experience may be more or less clear, but the fact *that* it is more or less clear is completely *transparent* when one has the experience. The transcendent object, on the other hand, may appear more or less clear, but this fact involves an incompleteness, a relativity, that is essential to the very notion of a transcendent object. The vital further consequence of this difference is that '*The way of being of experience is to be in principle perceptible in the manner of reflection*' (ibid. 95).

Reflection is, as we have seen, the capacity of thought to think about itself. The absoluteness of immanent perception comes about, Husserl argues, because it makes no sense to deny that what one is thinking about – be it a crazy fantasy or a mathematical equation – exists when one thinks about it. Its certainty is of the kind Descartes claimed for the ego that doubts its own existence, and therefore must exist in order to doubt itself. The contingency of the objective world is contrasted with the indubitable necessities of the 'pure I' (ibid. 98), and this I is the focus of 'pure phenomenology'. Not surprisingly, this is the most controversial aspect of Husserl's argument. In some respects his position comes close to German Idealism, because the reality of each thing is dependent on other things and thus is in no way absolute. The only absolute is consciousness which is completely transparent to itself: 'Existence of a nature *cannot* condition the existence of consciousness, because nature reveals itself as the correlate of consciousness; nature *is* only as it constitutes itself in regulated contexts of consciousness' (ibid. 109). What is the significance of this Fichtean approach in the context of Husserl's very different historical world? The answer has to do with Husserl's sense that the sciences need an absolute ground that only philosophy can provide. Without this, both the contingency they necessarily entail, and the lack of unity between the sciences, cannot be overcome. The interpretation of the cultural consequences of the lack of a unity in the sciences will be decisive for many aspects of twentieth-century German philosophy.

(f) Noesis and noema

The I's ability to reflect upon its own mental acts forms the core of Husserl's analysis. The analysis therefore depends on the plausibility of the notion of the 'pure I', whose continuity between different mental acts, like that of the I of Kant's transcendental unity of apperception, is the condition of possibility of experience. Husserl talks of the 'strange duality and unity of *sensuous* hyle and *intentional* morphe', which he, more accessibly, puts in terms of the 'matter' (*Stoff*) of cognition and its 'form'. His analysis of the relationship between what consciousness does to its material and the material itself is couched in terms of what he calls, following Greek terminology for the mind, the 'noetic' and the 'noematic'.

The 'noema' can be explained by Husserl's example of a tree. The tree as 'thing in nature' is fundamentally different from 'this *tree-perceived as such* [*dieses Baumwahrgenommene als solches*]' (ibid. 205). The latter, 'as the meaning [*Sinn*] of a perception', belongs inextricably to perception, not to the world perceived. Whereas the tree can burn down or 'be dissolved into its chemical elements', the meaning 'cannot burn down, it has no chemical elements, no forces, no real properties' (ibid.). The meaning of the perceived object is its noema. Belonging to the noema are 'the ways of being like certainly being, possibly or supposedly being, etc., or the subjective temporal ways: being in the present, past, future' (1992: viii. 38). The noema therefore has something – though there is widespread disagreement about what exactly – to do with the meaning of linguistic expressions.

Its relationship to the object of which it is the noema involves something like the relationship that Frege's sense has to its reference.

Husserl's construal of meaning is, though, much wider than Frege's and could, for example, include the meaning of a piece of music, inasmuch as it matters to us and concerns us, even if we cannot *say* exactly in what this meaning consists. The noetic aspect of consciousness concerns the ways in which this 'meaning' is apprehended in concrete cases, and it relates to the fact that the mode of attention to a noema can be shifted by the move to a different apprehension of the object. The noesis is the specific act that gives a new or different meaning to a noema, and this means the two cannot be separated. The noema is a structure which anticipates ways an object, like the tree, could be experienced, and the noesis is what determines which experience is actually fulfilled. The famous duck/rabbit figure involves one noema as a duck and another as a rabbit, and the change from one to the other takes place on the level of noesis. By differentiating different kinds of anticipation and the ways they are fulfilled, Husserl is able to give an account of both experience of objects in the world and of imagining, remembering etc., where a concrete object is not present.

Foundational Problems

Husserl's analyses of this kind, which he pursues with remarkable tenacity throughout his career, raise many questions concerning the relationship of the noema to the real object of which it is a noema, and thus of the degree to which this may actually be a kind of Berkeleyan or Fichtean idealism. The value of the kinds of distinction he makes is, though, now firmly established, however controversial they may be, as the growth of interest in Husserl in the Anglo-American tradition of philosophy makes clear. Much more problematic is Husserl's conception of his philosophy as a 'strict science' which works on the basis of 'absolute foundedness'. The difficulty lies in the way in which Husserl insists on the purely interior nature of the essential acts of consciousness. The problem with this conception has been pointed out by philosophers as different as T. W. Adorno (1970), Jacques Derrida (1967) and Michael Dummett (1988). The pure interiority of consciousness may actually be a myth, because without the acquisition of language, which is clearly acquired from the external world, the content of consciousness is indeterminate. The linguistic turn would seem, therefore, to invalidate the whole notion of pure transcendental subjectivity. The interiority of consciousness must in some measure be affected both by the historically determined language the subject acquires and by its being located in historically determined contexts of social action. The epoché seeks to exclude these kinds of determination, but it cannot exclude the prior need for language if the results of epoché are to be intelligible at all.

In terms of the *foundational* status of the subject, these objections are powerful, although it can be argued that the complete transparency which characterizes consciousness at a particular moment does involve some kind of absolute certainty. However, the simple linguistic objection from analytical philosophy, to the effect that meaning cannot be explained in the terms of acts of the subject endowing words with significance, has increasingly come to be seen as inadequate to Husserl's claims. A notion of meaning which sees it, in the manner of Frege's 'sense', as something which a word 'simply has', does not do justice to the complexity of how we understand and employ words, and experience 'meanings' in Husserl's wider sense of the word. This understanding would seem to have a significant psychological component which is not accessible to experimental psychology, and which plays a vital role in our relationship to language. Despite Husserl's own aspiration for his philosophy to avoid any link to psychology and to sustain philosophical purity, his account of ways in which the world is understood is invaluable in this respect, whatever he himself aimed to achieve. Nor does the narrow analytical approach take sufficient note of his insights into the way in which our embodied existence makes the world what it is for us, rather than our world being, as it is in some of the analytical tradition, just the set of our statable beliefs.

One consequence of the objections to Husserl's account of the absolute status of the self-transparent I will be a general neglect of self-consciousness by thinkers, like Derrida, who regard his project as a failure. This neglect comes about because the notion of the subject as absolute foundation is linked, via Heidegger in particular, to claims like Descartes's that we can become 'lord and master of nature' on the basis of the foundation of certainty in our thinking. The idea is that, as the project of absolute foundations has failed, *any* philosophical concern with the subject will simply repeat problems that Husserl, like Descartes, was unable to overcome. Indeed, as we saw at the end of chapter 7, Heidegger will come to identify concern with the founding role of the subject with metaphysics itself. We need now to look at a further dimension of Husserl's work which will lead, in the next chapter, into the work of his pupil Heidegger, and which will further elucidate the question of foundations in German philosophy.

Mathematization and the Life-world

Husserl begins the 1936 *Crisis* with reflections on the history of
modern philosophy and its relationship to the natural sciences of a
very different kind from the largely a-historical mode of argument of
texts like the *Ideas*. Husserl's awareness of the disastrous political and
social developments in Europe forces him overtly to consider questions which had often only been implicit in his earlier work. Two
related aspects of the *Crisis* highlight themes that are vital to the next
part of the story to be told here. The first is the way Husserl links the
foundational aims of his philosophy to what he sees as a crisis of
meaning in the modern world; the second is his notion of the 'life-
world'. Husserl admits that claiming that the natural sciences are in
crisis might seem an odd thing to do, given their success in this period.
His concern, though, is with the narrowing of philosophical focus we
have observed in relation to the Vienna Circle, and with the resulting failure of philosophy to address 'questions about the meaning or
meaninglessness of this whole human existence' (1992: viii. 4). The
underlying theme here should be familiar from aspects of Nietzsche,
and is perhaps best presented in the sociologist Max Weber's 1919
essay, 'Science as a Vocation', where he asserts that 'No science is
absolutely without presuppositions, and no science can ground its
own value for him who rejects these presuppositions' (1998: 610). By
renouncing the idea of a foundation of human thinking which goes
beyond what the particular sciences can explain, Weber accepts as
inescapable precisely the situation which Husserl seeks to oppose.
The structure of the problem of grounding human knowledge is the
one we saw Jacobi establish in chapter 3. The tension resulting from
this structure, which formed the focus of much thinking in German
Idealism, is between what can be explained in terms of the sciences
and the *value* that explanation has for human beings, which would
make it part of a meaningful existence. The scope of what can be
explained is infinitely large and can easily lead to Jacobi's regress of
explanations of explanations. There is in these terms no inherent
reason for explaining and exploring one issue rather than any other
issue. Why, then, do the dominant kinds of scientific explanation
develop in the concrete directions they do, and can this development
be given a philosophical justification?

 The essential factor in Husserl's account of the origin of the
modern natural sciences is what he terms the 'mathematization of
the cosmos', which begins with Galileo. Clearly, mathematics was

employed to understand natural phenomena well before Galileo. The decisive change is exemplified, Husserl claims, in the change in the status of geometry. In the everyday world we experience spatio-temporal objects as the particular things they happen to be. This means that the identity of one object with another is only ever approximate, and each particular thing's sameness with itself over time is also never total. Pure geometry, which develops via Galileo, on the other hand, works with a 'self-enclosed world of ideal objec-tivities' (1992: viii. 23), which permits complete exactness and the *'absolute identity'* (ibid. 24) of the figures it works with. In the wake of Galileo, this self-enclosed world, which emerged from the refine-ment of the practical use of geometry for technical purposes, itself begins to become the ideal of technology. Technology now seeks to get as close as possible to the geometrical ideal that it had itself gen-erated. (Think of how more and more domains of life involve forms of technology which are the result of ever more exact measurement.) There is, then, a gradual elimination of the sensuously experienced world from the increasingly mathematized world of science. This is evident, for example, in Locke's development of the notion of 'primary' as opposed to 'secondary' qualities – of colours as degrees on a spectroscope, as opposed to colours as what we enjoy and use for all sorts of purposes in the life-world. The whole of nature thus becomes 'a strangely applied mathematics' (ibid. 36). The 'arithmeti-zation of geometry' leads to the *'emptying out of its meaning'* (ibid. 44) as part of the way we experience the sensuous world. What had begun as a concrete means of mapping terrain becomes something 'idealized' that is not tied to a specific practice. The same kind of development takes place in every domain of the scientific investiga-tion of nature.

A similar account of the nature of the modern sciences will occur in Heidegger (whose work influences the *Crisis*), and in Adorno and Horkheimer (see chapter 11), among others. The vital question is how this account is related to the rest of the philosophical vision of the thinker(s) in question. Husserl's major innovation in this respect lies in his concentration on the idea of the life-world. The concept of the life-world offers a way of suggesting how an exclusive philosophical concentration on the methods and claims of the natural sciences may obscure something fundamental about human knowledge and existence. In the light of the dominating effects of the mathematiza-tion of the world by the modern sciences, the essence of things might seem to lie precisely in the way they are amenable to investigation by the sciences. However, the way Husserl tells the story entails precisely the opposite conclusion, because he insists that any attempt by the sciences to take the role of *philosophical* foundation involves a crucial deficit.

The simple point is that most of humankind has lived (and still lives) with virtually no serious understanding of the discoveries of modern science. Furthermore, this is increasingly the case as the sciences produce more and more differentiated and complex theories and the ensuing technologies in each particular area. At the same time, people are capable of understanding the world and each other with little or no scientific knowledge. This means one of two things.

1   People may therefore be interpreted as functioning in terms of 'folk psychology', i.e. of a series of everyday beliefs and attitudes which have no serious claims to scientifically provable truth, whereas the *real* world is the one that is described by the sciences. This view dominates key areas of contemporary analytical philosophy, particularly those concerned with 'cognitive science'.
2   On the other hand – and this is the idea that plays a vital role in many important aspects of German philosophy since Kant, being first clearly formulated by Schleiermacher – the sciences themselves would be inaccessible if people did not already have pre-scientific ways of understanding themselves and the world. One becomes a scientist having first learned to understand the world in a practical, rather than a theoretical, manner. The ways of understanding in question cannot themselves be scientifically explained, because such an explanation would entail a vicious circle, in which the truth of the sciences would have to be invalidly presupposed. People must already share very many beliefs and attitudes if they are to understand each other and the world, and thus have the potential to engage in scientific activity at all. This means that the priority must lie with these beliefs and attitudes.

Husserl's account of the life-world explores the kind of understanding involved in the second position.

Husserl talks of the 'pre- and extra-scientific life-world which includes within it all actual life, including the life of scientific thought' (ibid. 60). The idea of the life-world therefore relates to the natural attitude. It is a more developed version of the idea that philosophy must begin by looking at the world we undeniably share and cannot conjure away, even if we disagree on the descriptions of some of what that world contains. Think how impossible it would be to live in society if there were no base-line agreements about the majority of facts of everyday life.[5] The underlying question Husserl seeks to answer is what sort of 'mental achievement' makes 'pre-scientific experience' of the life-world into something which can become objectively valid science (ibid. 97). As we have seen, this would be impossible if the primary data were mere sensations, rather than experiences of the already significant objects of the life-world. The crucial point is, then, that the already-constituted kinds of validity, in terms of which we all live, are the '*constant presuppositions* of scientific . . . thinking' (ibid. 112). Without the presupposition of an undeniable pre-existing, shared, meaningful world, about which there is what Habermas calls a 'massive background consensus', the sciences could not come to the point of formulating their questions in terms of mathematical idealizations. The 'theoretical practice' of science is a 'historically late' form of human practice (ibid. 113), and depends on '*what is a matter of course* . . . which all thinking, all activity of life in all its purposes and achievements presupposes' (ibid. 115). Husserl thinks that the epoché can be employed to exclude all scientific accounts of the world and thus to explore the founding structures of the life-world. This would be a 'scientific' exploration, but not in the sense of an objective science like physics. Instead, it would seek to give an account of the necessary 'subject-relative' life-world which makes possible the objective scientific world.

What Husserl proposes is another version of transcendental philosophy, because the life-world is the 'subjective' condition of possibility of the sciences. However, a whole series of new questions arises from this exploration of the ground of the sciences, which Husserl was aware of and which he did not definitively answer. Are the structures of the life-world essentially the same for all human beings, despite historical changes within societies, and despite essential cultural differences between societies? Our ability to understand other cultures and cultural artefacts from the past seems to suggest this is the case, but there is always the danger that our understanding is actually just an imposition of our perspective on the other. However, without a grounding background consensus, it is hard to explain how we can learn other languages and communicate across

5   A recent version of this idea is Donald Davidson's notion of the 'principle of charity', the methodological principle that one should assume that most of what people say is true, as otherwise interpretation becomes impossible. Davidson's point is that without this principle we would never even get to the point of doubting some of what people say, because we can only understand what we doubt against a much larger background of shared assumptions, many of which we are not even aware of.

cultural divisions at all. The division between positions which maintain, like Husserl, that philosophy must try to overcome such differences and formulate a universal conception of rationality, and those
which see this universalization as obscuring vital resources of
meaning, is fundamental to the development of twentieth-century
German philosophy. Why this is the case is very apparent in the work
of Heidegger.

SUGGESTIONS FOR FURTHER READING

Adorno, T. W. (1982) *Against Epistemology: A Metacritique, Studies in
    Husserl and the Phenomenological Antinomies* (Oxford: Blackwell).
    *Adorno's critical assessment of Husserl: provocative, if not always wholly
    fair to Husserl.*
Bell, D. (1990) *Husserl* (London: Routledge). *Tightly argued analytical
    account of Husserl.*
Bernet, R., Kern, I. and Marbach, E. (1993) *An Introduction to Husserlian
    Phenomenology* (Evanston: Northwestern University Press). *Good
    general introduction by major Husserl scholars.*
Mohanty, J. (1989) *Transcendental Phenomenology: An Analytic Account*
    (Oxford: Blackwell). *Lucid analytical assessment of phenomenology by
    leading Husserl scholar.*
Smith, D. and McIntyre, R. (1982) *Husserl and Intentionality: A Study of
    Mind, Meaning and Language* (Dordrecht: Reidel). *Influential detailed
    account of a central issue.*
Smith, B. and Woodruff Smith, D. (eds) (1995) *The Cambridge Companion
    to Husserl* (Cambridge: Cambridge University Press). *Excellent volume of
    essays which takes in many of the most significant perspectives on Husserl's
    work.*
Spiegelberg, H. (1982) *The Phenomenological Movement: A Historical
    Introduction* (The Hague: Martinus Nijhoff). *Reliable historical survey of
    the development of phenomenology.*
Ströker, E. (1993) *Husserl's Transcendental Phenomenology* (Stanford:
    Stanford University Press), *Good general account by major Husserl
    scholar.*

10

HEIDEGGER: BEING AND HERMENEUTICS

Understanding Being

It might seem strange, but probably the most politically and morally compromised major philosopher of the twentieth century, Martin Heidegger (1889–1976), devoted his philosophical life to the exploration of what is meant by 'being'/'to be' (*Sein*). Why, though, would someone who is obsessed with what it means for things to be become so embroiled in the most evil political movement of the twentieth century, and why do many people who are rightly revolted by the actions and ideas of this movement still think that Heidegger is such a significant thinker? The relationship to his philosophy, both of Heidegger's membership of the Nazi party from 1933 until 1945 and of his refusal ever to apologize for what he did, is too complex to be dealt with properly here (see e.g. Safranski 1997). However, the difficulty of understanding that relationship is an indication of how issues considered in the preceding chapters play a role in the disastrous history of Germany in the first half of the twentieth century. The case of Heidegger provides a focus for the new ways in which these philosophical issues relate to the historical world.

Heidegger's key ideas have to do with the tension between the account of the world and ourselves produced by the law-based modern natural sciences, and other, non-scientific, ways of understanding the world and ourselves. His concern with the meaning of 'being' can initially be understood in relation to the following kinds of question. Do the propositions of natural science describe the only true way in which things are? Or is what is described by the sciences secondary to another sense of being, without which we could not even

arrive at the point of doing natural science?[1] In a world where the
rapid changes occasioned by the technological application of the new
sciences lead to increasing social disruption and to the horrors of two
world wars, these are not abstract questions. Both Right and Left in
Germany seek new ways of understanding these changes and of relating philosophy to both science and politics. Their aim is to get to the
root of the crises of modernity. It is not self-evident, though, that a
philosophical diagnosis of what is happening is always the most apt
way to do this. Regarding the problems as essentially the preserve of
philosophy, rather than, say, of sociology, politics and economics,
might itself turn out to be part of the problem, as Marx had already
suggested about the philosophy of his time. Given Heidegger's
political trajectory, this is a fundamental issue.

In the last chapter we considered the view of Heidegger's teacher,
Husserl, that philosophy lacked the grounding needed to enable
humankind to locate itself in the modern world. Husserl was
insistent that the natural sciences could not provide such a grounding. Husserl's ideas are crucial for Heidegger, but Heidegger also
draws (among many others) on the concerns of Wilhelm Dilthey
(1833–1911). Like Husserl, Dilthey is worried that philosophy has lost
touch with the real nature of human experience. However, Dilthey
does not see the response to this situation in the transcendental terms
we encountered in Husserl. Instead he sees it in terms of seeking an
adequate philosophical method for the understanding of history, in
what he already termed in 1867 a 'science of the experience of the
human mind' (1990: 27). Whereas the natural sciences, including psychology, try to explain their object in terms of predictive laws, the
human sciences try to understand human actions and thoughts (this
is even referred to in English as 'Verstehen'). Understanding does not
seek to establish explanatory laws. This is because understanding
wishes to gain access to the particularity of the experience of people
which is the source of the meanings that inform their actions. As
Dilthey puts it: 'We explain nature, we understand the life of the soul'
(ibid. 144), because 'only what the mind has created does it understand' (1981: 180). Dilthey wants to produce a 'Critique of Historical
Reason', based on the interrelations between 'experience (*Erlebnis*),
expression and understanding' (ibid. 99). These three elements are
the basis of significant cultural and historical phenomena. The first,
'experience', which Dilthey sometimes sees as 'life', involves the
'psychic act', which 'is because I experience it' (1983: 98), and which
motivates 'expression'. Expression is the manner in which the inner

1   Husserl's account of the life-world is intended to raise much the same questions.

act, for example a feeling, thought, act of will, etc., becomes objectively available in a culture, be it as a poem, a philosophical work, a piece of music, etc. The third stage constitutes the hermeneutic attempt to understand this objectification as the manifestation of the primary experience. This understanding cannot, though, be achieved in relation to a single experience, but depends on grasping the contexts of the mental life in question, which involve a complex network of linked significances. Hermeneutics, as it did for Schleiermacher, its modern founder, relies on the interplay between part and whole, phenomenon and context, which means that each cannot be understood without the other.

However, unlike Schleiermacher, whose work Dilthey helped bring back to public attention, Dilthey often fails to appreciate the fact that 'immediate' inner experience is only accessible to others via the public medium of language. This puts the foundational status he wishes to attribute to 'experience' in doubt. The supposedly immediate inner element cannot be said to be self-sufficient because it will always require the external resources of language. Despite this problem, Dilthey's concern with the context and particularity of historical forms of expression did highlight the need to establish the status of knowledge in the human sciences by giving them their own kind of validity in relation to the natural sciences. The problems of establishing this validity are, however, considerable.

Dilthey's reliance on the immediacy of individual experience as a source of cultural and historical meaning comes into conflict in his later work with his sense that 'The individual is only the crossing point for cultural systems, organizations, into which the individual's existence is woven: how could they be understood via the individual?' (1981: 310). An analysis of cultural systems (which can also include language) that enjoy at least relative autonomy from the individuals within them would seem to promise a more objective account of the nature of experience in history. It might do so, though, at the risk of failing to grasp what motivates individuals' investment in cultural meaning. A number of problems become apparent here that are germane to Heidegger's ideas. How can one get to grips with the meaning of the experiences that matter to people? This has to be achieved in a manner which does not adopt the method of the natural sciences, because law-based scientific explanation cannot provide an account of motivation. Motivation depends on evaluative interpretation. Such an approach would, at the same time, have to avoid Dilthey's psychologism, which does not always take account of the fact that individual experience involves collectively shared languages and other shared practices. It would also have to come to terms with the historical, time-bound nature of experience, while still offering a *philosophical* approach to that experience. The crux of Heidegger's approach lies in his rejection of the tendency of the thinkers in Germany of the period to work with a model in which the natural and the human sciences are seen as inherently distinct, and thus in need of differing kinds of philosophical investigation.[2] He conceives of his approach in terms of a new version of hermeneutics.

Heidegger's basic concern is with how we understand what it is for things to be, but the exact meaning of this concern is controversial. At one level it can be regarded as a linguistic matter. Verbal forms concerned with 'being' can be employed in a variety of ways. Saying that something exists – when a believer says 'God exists', for example – involves being in the sense of 'existence'. Saying 'God is all-powerful' involves being in the sense of 'predication' (remember that Kant denied that existence could be a predicate). If we say, in the wake of Spinoza, that 'God is Nature', we are saying God is the same as nature, and using 'is' in the sense of 'identity' (think also of Frege's example in which we can say 'The morning star is the evening star'). This involves a different kind of 'is' from the predicative sense, because we can also say 'Nature is God'/'The evening star is the morning star', but we cannot say 'all-powerful is God'. (The reasons for this relate to Frege's distinction between the different roles of function and argument in a proposition.) Any of these ways of talking about being might also be said to involve the idea that 'It is true that – God exists, God is all-powerful, and God is Nature', if we wish to assert all these propositions. This is termed the 'veritative' sense of 'is'/'exists'. It has been argued that these differing senses of being cannot be unified into an overall meaning of 'being', and this may mean that Heidegger's main aim is simply unfulfillable (see Tugendhat 1992). They do, however, all seem to have something to do with truth, and this will be important for Heidegger. All these verbal forms can, significantly, be used both to deal with the everyday world, and as the means of formulating causally based predictive theories. To this extent they do not involve a fundamental methodological distinction between what can be said in one area and what can be said in another, merely differences in the ways in which we take things to be in dealing with them in the world.

Let us take an example to illustrate this. We can say of a sunset that 'the [colour of the] sun is a beautiful orange', but we can also say that 'the rays of the evening sun are refracted through a larger

2   The extent to which this tendency is really shared by Husserl is, though, open to question, and Heidegger owes even more to Husserl than he admits.

amount of the atmosphere, so they belong to a different part of the
light spectrum from those of the midday sun'. The second of these
statements entails a whole series of inferences involving theories of
light, the atmosphere and colour. Both, though, say something about
how the sunset is, the first as a part of the life-world, the second as
a phenomenon dealt with by physics. Heidegger looks at this issue
in terms of what he calls the 'as-structure of understanding'. Why
should seeing the sunset as an object of physics have priority over
the everyday apprehension of it as an object of beauty, given that
this is the way the phenomenon is initially manifest? A decision on
such a priority can be made on a whole series of opposing grounds.
Why is it that phenomena which may exist for many cultures in a
whole variety of ways – think of mythical stories associated with
the going down of the sun – come to be explained in the unique way
that modern science explains them, which is then assumed by many
people to be the real truth about them, as opposed to the merely
apparent truth of the everyday judgement?[3] The underlying issue
here is, of course, the old Platonic difference between appearance
and essence.

The two main directions of Heidegger's thought relate to differing
possible answers to these questions. One answer – that of the earlier
Heidegger, until around the mid-1930s – is basically pragmatic. The
meaning of things is constituted in the ways in which we practically
encounter them in the world. If our way of dealing with something
ceases to work, we are likely to develop a more explanatory, objectifying approach to it. This approach can, though, as the later Heidegger maintains, itself come into question as we gain control over more
and more of the natural world by the adoption of objectifying
methods. In the earlier approach, the locus of the meaning of things
is the practical subject that deals with them. In the later approach,
after what is called Heidegger's 'turn' in the 1930s, a perspective is
sought which goes beyond the actions of the subject to the exploration of the fact that the world is manifest at all. Vital aspects of how
the world can be manifest may actually be obscured by the merely
pragmatic concerns of the subject. The later Heidegger's view has
much to do with the fact that the language spoken by the subject
cannot itself be explained as the product of the subject. Subjects are
located in languages which pre-exist them and which are the condition of possibility of their inhabiting a world of meaning. In both the
earlier and the later approaches the question of being has to do with

3   It is not that Heidegger wishes to dispute the scientific account. His aim is to ask what
kind of understanding of being it depends on.

how things are revealed, or 'disclosed', but the location of disclosure shifts from the subject to language.

The main point about this disclosure is that it is prior to any attempt to theorize about whatever it is that is disclosed. Only because there already are sunsets in our world can physicists attempt to give an objective account of why they appear as they do. Heidegger's conception of hermeneutics extends the scope of 'understanding' beyond utterances or cultural phenomena supposedly 'created by the mind' to the world itself. He does so because he thinks explaining anything always already relies on having understood that the thing in question is *significant*, if only as something we do not understand. It is only against the background of an already intelligible world that things can be unintelligible. That background cannot itself ever be fully described or objectified. We live *in* the world and cannot step outside of it and make the world itself into an object of the kind that exists in the world. Heidegger's ideas have an immediate plausibility to many people that contrasts with the kind of philosophical approach which worries about the 'existence of the external world'. His claims are, though, often highly controversial. Carnap, for example, tried to claim (1932) that some of what Heidegger was saying was nonsense. Heidegger's claims are, admittedly, often couched in very difficult language. Part of the reason for this is that he thinks he has to avoid traditional philosophical vocabulary if he is not merely to repeat certain philosophical problems.

Being and Time

Heidegger's *Being and Time* (*BT*) (1927) is thought by many people to be the single most important philosophical work of the twentieth century. Its influence continues unabated, not least on thinkers in the analytical tradition, who until a few years ago largely ignored it. *BT* is actually more conceptually and linguistically demanding than Heidegger's often extremely lucid lectures on the same themes from the middle of the 1920s onwards, which have been published in recent years. It is, though, the major text which he published at the time, and was a considerable success, affecting not only philosophers but also artists and scientists. Its effect is related to the intellectual climate created by the First World War, in which optimistic ideas about humanity were so brutally undermined, and demands for a radical rethink of what human beings are became widespread. The 'provisional goal' of *BT* is 'the understanding of *time* as the possible horizon of every understanding of being' (1979: 1). One source of this goal is

Kant's account of schematism, which linked 'reality', in Kant's sense of that which can be 'given in intuition', to schemata as '*determinations of time* a priori according to rules'. Kant links questions about what is real to questions about the nature of time in the way we saw in chapter 1. Kant's schema is located in the subject as the source of the connection between the empirical world and the subject's forms of thought. For Heidegger, time is not regarded as a 'form of intuition', but rather as the condition of possibility of understanding, in the specific sense that we will further explore in this section.

Heidegger stresses that he could not even ask 'the question of being' if we did not in some respect already understand being. A key source of how he conceives this understanding is the notion of 'categorial intuition' from Husserl's sixth *Logical Investigation*. The notion is intended to show that we do not just think of what we perceive as some kind of image 'in the mind'. Our perception would not be the way it is without a whole series of meanings which structure what we perceive, and these meanings are not themselves perceivable objects. As Husserl says, 'I can see the colour, not the being-coloured' (1992: iv. 666), and 'I can paint *A* and paint *B*, can also paint both in the same pictorial space; but I cannot paint the *both*, *A and B*' (ibid. 688). One cannot 'taste the difference' between one thing and another, one can only taste one and then the other, and relate the taste of one to the other. 'Sensuous intuition' sees the white paper, and A and B; 'categorial intuition' is the 'seeing', or, better, understanding of the paper *as* white, the grasping of the relationship or 'state of affairs' 'both A and B'. What is expressed by words like 'one', 'the', 'and', 'or', 'if' and 'then', 'thus', 'all' and 'none' cannot be perceived, but without these words we could not understand the world we do perceive. The same applies to 'being': 'Being is nothing *in* the object, not a part of it', it is not a predicate: it is '*absolutely not something which can be perceived*' (ibid. 666). However, the different ways things can be, suggested in the different uses of 'is' and 'exists', are essential for our comprehension of them. At the same time, categorial intuitions are *not* operations of the mind brought to bear on external perceivable objects; they are in fact part of how things *are*.

Heidegger regards the notion of categorial intuition as essential because it moves beyond the model of mind and world which stems from Descartes's separation of extended and thinking things. However, the very division between sensuous and categorial intuition still threatens to reintroduce the model that causes such problems for empiricism when it tries to explain how one gets from sense-data to intelligible objects. Heidegger therefore claims that categorial intuition is present even in the most basic perceptual experiences.

He does so because our primary relationship to things is a practical relationship in which we cope with a world which is always *already* significant, precisely *because* we have to cope with it. This relationship is not a primarily cognitive relationship, of the kind which requires an account of a transcendental subject. Husserl's conception of intentionality involves the idea that our knowledge comes from the subject's mental acts directed at transcendent objects. Heidegger thinks this kind of 'transcendence' – in the sense of that which takes the subject beyond itself to the world of knowable objects – relies on a more fundamental kind of transcendence. He terms this transcendence 'being-in-the-world', which is essentially practical.

The aim of this reorientation is to give an account of being which neither falls prey to sceptical arguments about whether thought is in contact with the world, nor cedes everything to the specific sciences. It is because Heidegger rejects theories based on the notion of sense-data, that he has come to influence the analytical tradition which for so long unsuccessfully tried to explain how sense-data could result in reliable cognition (see chapter 8). The very theory of sense-data is itself always secondary to our immediate understanding of the meanings of things in our world, and cannot be a foundation for that understanding. We first see tables and chairs, not 'packets of sense-data'. Heidegger's concern is, then, with 'an a priori condition of possibility', not only of 'ontic' sciences, meaning sciences, such as biology, physics, etc., that are concerned with particular kinds of entities, but also of the 'ontologies which lie before and found the ontic sciences' (1979: 11). For Heidegger, a particular science 'is only a science to the extent that it succeeds in delimiting in advance the essential constitution of the entities which it has as its theme' (1996: 188). The sciences are part, but only a part, of the behaviour of the entity humankind, which he terms '*Dasein*', 'being there/being here'. The term is intended to circumvent habitual philosophical connotations attached to the notion of the subject, by giving the most basic sense possible of what it means to 'exist' as a conscious being. Stones are not 'there/here' in the sense we are.

The first task is therefore to understand *Dasein*. Rather than conduct an anthropological investigation into dominant features of humankind (which he might, though, be said to do later in the book), Heidegger begins with the most general fact that *Dasein* is, like other things in the world, an entity. However, it is the entity that 'is concerned in its being *with* this being' (1979: 12). Instead of determining the investigation in advance by offering a definition, then, Heidegger takes the bare fact that our very being consists in a concern with itself and with the being of other things. This concern is part of what we *are* in relating to our world. What we are 'shines back' to us from our involvement in that world. The vital aspect of that involvement is understanding things *as* what they are. The understanding of being therefore depends on first arriving at an adequate ontological account of *Dasein*. *BT* provides Heidegger's version of this account, but he never writes the planned third part of the book, which was to move from the understanding of *Dasein* to the understanding of being in relation to time. His later work will therefore move away from the concentration on *Dasein*, but it will never give a satisfactory answer to the question of how being and time relate.

Heidegger insists that he is interested in *Dasein*'s 'average *every-dayness*' (ibid. 16). The project is influenced by the way Husserl's phenomenology begins with the immediacy of experience. It aims, though, to replace transcendental phenomenology with a 'phenomenological ontology'. The task of 'ontology' for Heidegger is to distinguish between being ('*Sein*'), and the 'entities' ('*Seiendes*', in the sense of specific things which are 'in being', like animals, rocks, chemicals, or whatever) that form the object of investigation of a particular ontic science. The difference between *Sein* and *Seiendes* is what is meant by 'ontological difference'. His essential claim is that the '*being* of entities' (ibid. 35) has been forgotten by philosophy, and that remembering it is the task of the 'hermeneutic of *Dasein*' (ibid. 38). What he means is that philosophy has failed to ask how it is that things are intelligible at all. This involves issues like those raised by Husserl's categorial intuition, which does not deal with entities, but rather with what makes entities part of a world of meanings. To understand that world we have to interpret *Dasein* – hence the 'hermeneutic of *Dasein*'.

One way of understanding what Heidegger seeks to do is to regard it as a way of dealing with the problem for Kant of how conditions of possibility of knowledge come about in the first place. We saw one response to this problem in Fichte, Schelling and Hegel. Heidegger offers an account of practical ways of being which make possible an understanding of what gives rise to what we know and what we are. Instead of knowledge resulting from the 'effect [*Einwirkung*] of the world on a subject', it is 'a mode of *Dasein* which is founded in being-in-the-world' (ibid. 62). The formulation is intended to move one away from a model in which the subject is the inside and the world the outside, to a model in which, as the notion of intentionality began to suggest, we are always already 'outside', because our being is *in* the world. This is not like 'being in a bottle', because that suggests a perspective which could see the bottle and what is inside it from outside the bottle. For Heidegger there can be no such perspective, and the attempt to establish it just repeats the basic error of trying to make philosophy into an objectifying, ontic science. One cannot, Heidegger argues, objectify what is the prior condition of possibility of there being objects at all. The implicit suggestion is that philosophy which tries to give a wholly objective account seeks an impossible God's-eye view, for which the truth of things exists in the form of a timeless 'presence'. Being-in-the-world is, in contrast, inherently temporal: all that we know and do takes place in a temporal horizon which we cannot step outside.

Heidegger is sometimes talked about as an 'existential' philosopher. Existentialism is generally thought of as the idea that, because the brute fact that we exist precedes whatever we make ourselves into, and because we can no longer invoke God to explain our existence, we are left with the puzzle of how to make meanings in a universe that has no reason for its existence. Heidegger is, however, not best understood in these terms. He sees us as located in a world which only *is* a world *because* it is full of meanings. We are always already familiar with meanings because that world is 'disclosed'. The idea of the meaninglessness of the world can only come about for beings who are already familiar with meanings. His real interest is in how the primary meaningfulness of our environment becomes the source of other kinds of knowledge, such as that arrived at in the sciences. The relationship he describes to account for this is between what is 'zuhanden' ('in hand'/'ready to hand'), and what is 'vorhanden' ('at hand'/'present'). The former refers to what he terms '*Zeug*', 'stuff' or 'equipment', which is unreflectively part of the world we inhabit. The latter can refer to the same things as are *zuhanden*, but only when they have changed their status and have become something we think about as an object. Heidegger gives the example of a hammer, which we do not primarily think of as an object, but rather as part of a 'totality of involvements' (ibid. 84). The term 'involvement' ('*Bewandtnis*') conveys the sense that we do not generally regard things as inert objects, but rather as what concerns us. Things exist in a whole context of other things in which they are there *for* something. A hammer is part of a context in which we need to mend roofs, hang pictures, etc., not an isolated object. How often do you think 'Now I am holding a hammer' when hanging a picture? The primary meaning of things is therefore holistic, depending on relations to other things and to possible actions. It is only at the moment when the hammer is broken and one needs to mend the roof before a storm that it may change its status and become the object of a reflection. At this point it becomes *vorhanden*, in the sense of 'objectified'. This distinction can be questioned: don't we deal with things in both ways a lot of the time? Is it clear, then, that the distinction is a fundamental one at all?

Heidegger argues, however, that the essential change involved here is the basis of the understanding of being that is characteristic of modern philosophy. Being in Descartes, whom he regards as paradigmatic for that philosophy, is understood as 'constant presence' (ibid. 96). Descartes's world consists of objects which are already there *as such* before they are investigated, which means all thought can do is 're-present' them, rather than disclose new aspects of the world. This is why Descartes's conception of ontology is the basis of the mathematization of the world by the modern sciences, which aim at a timeless, law-bound description of the way the world really is. The idea of the 'forgetting' of the question of being here takes on a more developed sense. Heidegger argues that an ontology which assumes that its basis is the material objects of natural science fails to understand that this is a historically specific understanding of being as 'presence', not the ultimate answer to the question of being.

Heidegger's question is how the primary world of 'involvements', in which *Dasein* always lives because it is always oriented to the future of its projects, comes to be seen as secondary. He takes the example of space, in which distance is first constituted in terms of our purposes and needs (Husserl was influenced by this example in the *Crisis*). In a world of jet travel someone in New York can be closer to someone in London than someone in the Scottish islands. For the scientific world-view this is a merely subjective state of affairs in relation to the distances and times that the sciences can measure ever more accurately. Heidegger's question is: why should this be taken as the real being of space, rather than as just another way in which space is manifest? At the same time, he might be seen as simply inverting the priority in favour of what fits his overall aims, rather than accepting a pragmatic plurality of spaces where the priority of one over the other depends on the context. The nature of space for *Dasein* has always been constituted in terms of its being in a particular world where distance has to do with what it is, from the distance of the prey from the hunter, to the distance of the mother from the child. This being is, though, not something merely 'subjective', because it only exists as the relationship between the entity *Dasein* and the entities of its environment.

The subject for Heidegger is what it is because of what it does and because of the world in which it exists. The subject of Kant's 'transcendental unity of apperception' that 'must be able to accompany all my representations' depends on being in a world where there are others, and is therefore only a manner of being of *Dasein*, not the

ultimate foundation of *Dasein*. Heidegger tends to diminish the role
of the subject and this means he fails, in much the same way as Hegel
does, to take account of those forms of self-knowledge which cannot
be said to be reflected back to the subject from the world and other
subjects. The power of his argument lies, though, in the way it
suggests a problem with philosophical explanations of subjectivity,
namely that they try to isolate something which cannot be finally separated from the world it is in. *Dasein*'s main orientation is, moreover,
necessarily to the future, which means that a theoretical characterization of what it is cannot fully circumscribe it.

The power Heidegger also stresses the central role of moods in what we are.
In moods '*Dasein* is brought before its being as here/there [*da*]' (ibid.
134). The point is that moods are not something chosen, they are what
we *find* ourselves in, and they determine much of how we are. The
German word '*Stimmung*' retains the sense of musical 'mode' and
'attunement' which has got lost in English. Moods are prior to our
knowing about the way we are; they are how we happen to be
attuned. Even if we can change and get control of moods, they are
always already there by the very fact that we exist: 'we never gain
mastery of a mood without a mood, but via a counter-mood' (ibid.
136). Moods are also not something internal, because they are a
primary way of being in the world.

The culmination of these strands of argument is Heidegger's
account of understanding as 'the basic mode of the being of *Dasein*'
(ibid. 143). In contrast to Dilthey, understanding is not seen as one
kind of cognition which is contrasted with explanation in the sciences.
Understanding is in fact the ground of the possibility of scientific
explanation, which is *derived* from primary understanding. Only if
something has been understood as a problem do we need to seek an
explanation of it by making it *vorhanden*. Understanding is 'always
mooded/attuned ('*gestimmt*')', because it must exist prior to reflection upon what has been understood. It takes place as a 'project' in
which *Dasein* understands itself in terms of its possibilities (ibid. 145).
Heidegger then introduces the 'as-structure of understanding' in relation to some of the most crucial contentions of *BT*. The first is that
understanding something as something need not be conceived of as
necessarily expressible in a proposition. Taking some object as a
hammer in order to use it for something already gives the thing a
meaning in the context of a world, and is a prior condition of possibility (but not the necessity) of the proposition: 'This will do as a
hammer.' Such meaning derives from the projective character of
human activity, which discloses things in terms of the future actions
we will perform. This leads to the second key contention, namely that

understanding involves a necessary circularity. This is, Heidegger admits, a common contention in disciplines concerned with the interpretation of texts from the nineteenth century onwards: without an understanding of the whole text, one cannot understand the parts, but the understanding of the whole depends on understanding the parts. Such circularity was, though, regarded as the reason why the claims of interpretative disciplines, such as history and literary study, are generally excluded from scientific status. They have to presuppose what they are supposed to establish. Heidegger sees this argument as getting things the wrong way round, by subordinating understanding to explanation. Explanation is, though, itself only a *derivative* of understanding in Heidegger's sense. It relies on our already having understood something as a problem in the world, to which we need to seek an answer. Both mathematics *and* history involve this circular structure, so mathematics is only stricter than history if one presupposes that strictness depends on reducing things to their most simple elements. History would not be history if it were to do this, because it would exclude vital aspects of understanding which cannot be reduced in this way and which enable it to seek the true understanding of its object.

This is a very contentious position, but it does confront an issue that plays a role in German philosophy from Herder and Hamann onwards. How does one ever understand what the sciences do, if they do not rely on a prior shared understanding given to us by the acquisition of language and by the necessities of being in the social world? What, though, of the clearly more reliable truths produced by the natural sciences? The questions raised by Heidegger concerning truth are some of the most interesting and argued-about in German philosophy. Nietzsche asked about the value of truth, on the grounds that knowing the truth may not always be a good idea, because other things may be more valuable, like discretion, not hurting people unnecessarily, self-assertion, etc. Furthermore, scientists will tell you that one can produce endless completely pointless truths by doing arbitrary experiments and recording the results. This can even become very sinister indeed, if one thinks of Nazi medical experiments, which confirmed the truth, for example, that injecting people with noxious chemicals means they die in agony. In recent philosophy truth has come to be related more to normative issues concerning the *justification* of what one asserts in a linguistic community. That justification is not solely concerned with the question of whether one's assertions correspond to what is in the world, not least because it is, as we have seen, not clear if one can make sense of the notion of correspondence. Heidegger does not concentrate on the norma-

212 Heidegger: Being and Hermeneutics

tive nature of communication, and he also fails to say much at all that
is interesting about ethical issues. However, his account of truth in
BT and later does seek to open up the issue beyond the semantic
question of the truth of propositions.

The other later parts of *BT* will not be dealt with here, because,
despite their effect on the culture and tone of much German and
other philosophy, they often lack the plausibility of the arguments we
have examined. The attempt to give a wholly new account of time,
for example, rejects the 'traditional' conception of time as constituted
in terms of 'later than' and 'earlier than', and past, present and future,
while actually surreptitiously relying on it. Heidegger also seeks to
extend the issues we have examined into a critical account of modern
culture which deals with socially and politically conditioned phenomena like fear and 'being to death' as though they were in the same
way part of phenomenological ontology as things like the 'as-
structure of understanding'. This is clearly not the case, and laid
Heidegger open to justified objections which sometimes led to the
other parts of his arguments being neglected. It is, moreover, these
parts of *BT* which signal some of Heidegger's reasons for joining the
Nazi party. He does so in the name of a radical new approach to the
demands of modern culture that is based on a totally inadequate
social and political assessment of what was wrong in Germany. His
use of philosophy to diagnose cultural and political problems is at
best inept, even when he gives insights into the experience of the
modern world which are still of value.

Truth

The 'as-structure of understanding', which plays the vital role in the
argument of *BT*, is also termed by Heidegger the 'existential-
hermeneutic "as"', in contrast to the '*apophantic* "as" of the proposition' (ibid. 158),[4] which derives from it. The relationship of the two
is that of understanding to explanation. A simple way to explain this
is via the fact that language can itself be regarded both as a *zuhanden* means of being in the world, which goes along with other such
means, and as a *vorhanden* object of analysis in linguistics. Analysis
in linguistics is the attempt of language to describe itself in objective
terms. However, the language required even to begin to explain language cannot itself be wholly objectified. That would require a language which stood wholly outside the language being analysed, and

---

4   'Apophantic' is just the Greek word for what has to do with propositions.

there can be no such language.[5] The problem is familiar from
Hamann and Herder in their dispute over the origin of language:
what first makes a word a word, rather than just a noise? In *BT* Heidegger's answer is that 'Words accrue to meanings' (ibid. 161), and
meanings are part of the 'disclosedness' (ibid. 162) of the world. This
disclosedness cannot be objectified: objectification depends on first
having understood, and understanding is itself what is supposed to be
explained here.

Heidegger extends the notion of being-in-the-world by saying that
it is 'essentially care/concern ["*Sorge*"]' (ibid. 193). The objectivity
demanded by the sciences is secondary to the fact that their object
becomes of concern to us in the first place. It is in this context that
Heidegger analyses truth. He maintains that truth has always been
understood in relation to being. The 'traditional' conception of truth
assumes that its locus is the proposition or the judgement, and that
the essence of truth is 'correspondence/agreement' of judgement and
object. The problem is, once again, that of joining what is assumed to
be mental and what is assumed to be physical. Instead of proposing
a new theory of how to do this, Heidegger, following Husserl's
rejection of intermediaries like images between ourselves and things,
claims that truth is not an agreement between two sides at all, but is
'the being disclosed/discovered of the entity itself' (ibid. 218). The
assertion 'lets the entity be seen in its disclosedness. *Being-true* (*truth*)
of a proposition must be understood as *being-disclosing*' (ibid.),
rather than as failing to be disclosing. This is a 'way of being of
Dasein' (ibid. 220). If the very nature of something existing means
that it is disclosed as intelligible for *Dasein*, and if assertions rely on
disclosure, then truth and the being of *Dasein* are inseparable. This
does not, however, mean we always know the truth, because if things
are disclosed they can also be hidden: 'Entities are torn away from
being hidden' (ibid. 222), but it does mean that without *Dasein* there
would be no truth. Heidegger, as we saw, rejects the Cartesian view
of a world whose truth is timelessly present. Instead, truth emerges
in time by our being in the world. Whatever truth there is emerges
through the interactions we have with each other and with the world.
One aspect of this seems obvious – if truth relies on understanding,
there have to be beings who understand for there to be truth – but
the question is whether truth can be appropriately characterized
in terms of time in the way Heidegger claims. Moreover, is *Dasein*

5 This does not mean there cannot be metalanguage – 'language about language' – but
there is no essential difference in this respect between understanding the language used
metalinguistically and the language it is being used to talk about.

not playing a transcendental role as the condition of possibility of truth?

The issues raised here are some of the most contentious in philosophy, and it is not always very clear exactly where Heidegger stands on them. The strength of his account lies in the claim that an explanatory analysis of truth will, as Frege realized (see chapter 8), always have to presuppose what it is analysing. How would we know if the analysis were true, if we did not already understand what truth is? Truth therefore has to be presupposed as part of what we are. This opens up interesting questions concerning the differing ways in which the world can be manifest that Heidegger explores in later texts, like *The Origin of the Work of Art* (1935). In that text he suggests that artworks reveal the truth of what they are about by making apparent what would otherwise be hidden: a painting can enable us to see things in the world differently, for example. Note how the locus has therefore shifted away from *Dasein* to something that reveals truth to *Dasein*.

The difficulty here lies in the relationship between truth as a semantic issue relating to propositions, and truth as world-disclosure which is prior to propositions. Heidegger's former pupil, Ernst Tugendhat, claims that his concentration on world-disclosure obscures the issue of 'bivalence', the fact that assertions have to be assessed in terms of their being-true or being-false. In the wake of Husserl, Tugendhat argues that an assertion's being true of something must mean that the thing is brought to light 'as it is in itself'. This is the vital function of assertions in social life, where we need this kind of discrimination for knowledge to progress, by showing when things are brought to light in a way which is not 'as they are in themselves'. Heidegger's blurring of the true and the false – can't things be falsely disclosed? – by making a generalized notion of disclosure prior to propositional truth and falsity therefore has questionable social and ethical implications (see also Lafont 1994 for an important account of this issue). Tugendhat also contends that the suggestion that the issue of truth has to do with time mistakes the nature of the meaning of being in propositions. In Heidegger's example of 'the sky *is* blue' the assertion is evidently only true for as long as the sky is blue on a particular day. However, the truth of the assertion about the sky's being blue at that time is itself timeless. Otherwise one is not using the sense of 'true' which we must rely on in everyday communication, which seems inextricably connected with meaning. We don't mean 'I think the sky is blue, but I may be wrong about this at some point in the future' when we say 'the sky is blue'.

The second of these arguments seems plausible, and puts into question at least one interpretation of the overall project of making time the horizon of the understanding of being. The first is, though, not necessarily adequate to Heidegger's claims. It relies on the assumption that we can only discriminate in propositional terms (on this see Dahlstrom 2001). What, though, if propositional discrimination is only one of the ways in which we discriminate by being in the world? The fact that language can mean anything at all depends on things being apprehended *as* things, in a context of 'involvements', and this need not be propositional (remember the hammer). Animals evidently live in the world in this way to some extent. What differentiates animals from language-users is that language-users can offer different descriptions of things. They can make 'metalinguistic' statements about what somebody says something is, of the kind: 'you say it is an x, but I say it is a y'. This capacity does, though, rely on the more fundamental hermeneutic as-structure inherent in being-in-the-world, upon which the apophantic as-structure depends. How would we arrive at differing descriptions if previous linguistic usage wholly determined what we could think? But does the *assertion* that the basis of propositions that can be true or false is a prior hermeneutic disclosure involve a vicious circle? Presumably the assertion itself has to be true, rather than false. What establishes its truth cannot, though, be of the same order as what may establish the truth of 'the sky is blue'. There seems to be some kind of condition of possibility of speaking truly which itself cannot be analysed in the manner of the kinds of inferential knowledge we use to learn the meaning of 'the sky is blue'. For Heidegger's position to work there has to be such a condition of possibility. This condition cannot, however, be further analysed, because, as we saw above, it is itself the condition of possibility of analysis. Heidegger can in this respect be interpreted as being close to semantic theorists like Donald Davidson, who think truth is an unanalysable concept because it has to be presupposed in any analysis. On the other hand, as Lafont (1994) argues, he can be construed as making a rigid distinction between world-disclosure as a general condition of possibility, and everyday pragmatic experience of things which opens the path to some of the questionable aspects of his later philosophy.

The 'Turn'

These questions continue to concern Heidegger throughout his work. What, then, of the 'turn', and his later philosophy? The simple way to describe the turn is that Heidegger comes to think that locating truth in *Dasein* just repeats the pattern of post-Cartesian transcendental philosophy, in which the source of truth is located in the subject. In this interpretation *BT* replaces the necessary structures given by Kant's synthetic a priori judgements with an account of the structures involved in the practical relations to the world of *Dasein*. The reason that the third part of *BT* was not completed is that the move from the temporality of *Dasein* to the account of the meaning of being as time comes to seem impossible to make. In 1962 Heidegger suggests that in *BT* 'The name "time" is the pre-name for what was later called "the truth of being" ' (1969: 30). Time stood for what he comes to see as the essential way to understand being that we will encounter in a moment. It is a pattern in some modern philosophy that when the attempt to use the subject as the foundation of philosophy reveals its limitations, the next move is to seek the ground of subjectivity itself. Schelling, Schopenhauer and Nietzsche make versions of this move by seeing the Will as this ground, for example (though Schelling eventually sees the issue in terms of being in a manner which influenced Heidegger). Heidegger comes to argue that the very search for a ground for the understanding of being as a whole is the essential characteristic of what he means by 'metaphysics', whether the ground be Descartes's cogito, Kant's transcendental subjectivity, Hegel's movement of absolute spirit, the forces of production in Marx or Nietzsche's will to power. All these foundations seek to make present the truth about the way things really are in the same way as did philosophies based on the subject.

Heidegger concentrates on those aspects of *BT* which already begin to point away from the idea that *Dasein* is the ultimate basis of truth. He suggests that if being itself were not already disclosed by time, *Dasein* would have no access to truth. One way to understand his change of perspective is in terms of the fact that *Dasein* relies on the meaningfulness of a language which is always prior to its individual existence and which is connected to the meaningfulness of the world. Nobody can be said to have 'invented' language or meaning, and the later Heidegger claims that it can be construed as a kind of 'gift' from being which changes over time. This is why he becomes so opposed to the idea that there could be a scientific explanation of language. The very possibility of science depends on language as the prior revelation of being, and scientific claims are only one of the ways in which truth 'happens' in the world. It also happens in the form of 'literature' or 'poetry' – '*Dichtung*' – which can say things that the sciences could never say.

The later work comes to see '*Dichtung*', particularly the poetry of Hölderlin, as a possible indication of how one might arrive at a way of thinking that could reveal what is hidden by the dominant ways of 'enframing' what can be true that result from modern science and technology. Enframing occurs when a method is established which determines in advance what can be accepted as true. It can therefore exclude other ways of understanding things. The argument can be linked to the problems we saw in the Vienna Circle's exclusion of much of what we say from serious consideration as to its truth or validity. Heidegger associates enframing with the idea that the activity of the subject is the ground of truth. His idea is that in modern science and technology being becomes what can be made into an 'image' by the subject's projection of it as an object to be manipulated in terms of a method (see the essay 'The Age of the World-Picture'). The theme of the hiddenness of being becomes central to this reformulation of his earlier ideas. This is one of the reasons why he ceases to regard his task as providing philosophical foundations. Foundational thinking seeks to reveal what is absent and has to be made present by philosophy. That was essentially what the phenomenological ontology of *BT* sought to do via the hermeneutic of *Dasein*. Another example would be Marx's claim to reveal the role of the forces of production in what may otherwise be thought of as truth generated by disinterested enquiry. Marx's claim does indeed reveal important new aspects of history, but it may also conceal other aspects of truth that cannot be manifest in terms of this particular foundation.

The point of the idea of being is now precisely that it involves a constitutive 'hiddenness', which could never be overcome: 'Being with regard to entities is what shows, makes visible, without showing itself' (ibid. 39). However, the problem is now how one talks about being at all, and Heidegger often suggests that it is actually impossible to do so. This leads him to employ more metaphorical resources, such as the idea of the 'clearing' ('*Lichtung*', in the sense of a clearing in a forest), in which things become manifest, 'unhidden'. The clearing is what makes the presence of things possible, so it cannot itself be made present to thought. If thought is considered as a kind of light, Heidegger suggests, it can only illuminate if an opening, a free space, is cleared, in which things can be illuminated. Light itself cannot create this free space; it has somehow to be given to us. Being is therefore to be understood in terms of what it grants us if we attend to it appropriately. Part of what it grants us is, as we saw, language.

Language is the essential way in which the world is manifest as intelligible. Heidegger sees language as the 'house of being', because it can allow things safely to be, rather than their being merely dominated by human aims. How we speak of things has deep consequences for whether we respect them. The key issue is therefore what kind of language dominates at differing times in history. It is admittedly rather hard to swallow arguments like this from a man who must have been seduced by the obscene ranting of Hitler, but the kind of thinking he is seeking has echoes in many other contexts which are not subject to the same reservation. Given that being can never be finally comprehensible to the kind of philosophy which looks for foundations, Heidegger now sees it as something which 'happens'. It does not do so in the causal sense in which one thing happens because of another thing. That would mean that we should seek reasons for why it happens in the way it does and so would result in the regress which Jacobi describes (see chapter 3). (Heidegger writes a whole book on Leibniz's 'principle of sufficient reason' ('nothing is without reason/cause/ground').) Seeking reasons in this way would again be 'metaphysics'. Heidegger uses the term '*Ereignis*', which usually means 'event', but which also has the sense of 'appropriation', of making one's 'own' ('*eigen*'), to characterize being. What he seems to mean (though it is far from clear) is that being somehow 'sends' what becomes present to us as a gift. The crucial aspect is that being is not seen as in any way objectifiable in a theory, because it is itself the source of theories.

The difficulty of Heidegger's later work lies not least in the fact that he becomes ever more radical about the attempt to escape the foundational concern of philosophy with 'presence', which he terms 'Western metaphysics'. This means he often seeks to avoid the kind of logical argument that relies on the structure of inference from initial assumptions to what follows from those assumptions. For Heidegger, such an approach is always faced with the problem of validating the initial assumption, which is therefore another form of subjective imposition. The interesting side of his approach – which too often leads to mere obscurity – lies in the idea that instead of seeking to determine things we should 'listen' to what they may have to say to us. This might seem highly implausible: things don't speak, language-beings do. Think, though, of the case of ecology, in which the natural sciences arguably reach their limits, because in their own terms they cannot offer a conception of how to understand the complex interrelatedness of the human and the non-human. One of the ways ecology has to work is on the basis of the feeling that nature may be 'telling' us things when we abuse it. A scientific proof that environmental destruction may render human life unbearable or destroy it altogether would strictly entail allowing the 'experiment' to continue, which would only provide decisive proof when it was too late. The sort of thinking required to heed the message that may be manifest in the ecological crisis cannot allow this to be the case. One has to appeal to another conception of what nature is, of the kind

Schelling sought in his *Naturphilosophie*, and which Kant pointed to in the *Critique of Judgement*. This conception cannot be established in scientific terms based on predictive laws. The problem is that what Heidegger offers is not an argument which could be validated in the manner of a testable theory or even of a conventional metaphysical argument. It is here that things get very difficult, as they always do when claims to truth are made which are supposed to be beyond what can be explicitly stated and argued about. We looked at this issue in relation to 'intuition' in chapters 2 and 5.

Heidegger's later work is also hard to assess because the texts in question, from around 1934 to his death, are written either while he was a member of the Nazi party until 1945 or when he subsequently failed to acknowledge his guilty role in relation to Nazism. Habermas (1990) has suggested that the move away from *Dasein*, whose projects could still be construed in terms of the situation of the individual faced with ethical decisions, to the truth of being, conveniently makes world-historical changes into something which far transcend the individual subject. Heidegger can therefore tacitly excuse himself for being on the wrong side, in the name of a higher truth of the kind that is not available to public discussion as to its justification. There is some validity in this criticism, but it is not in itself a decisive argument (see Lafont 1994, who suggests how the position is already latent in the earlier work).

Heidegger comes to regard the 'truth of being' as what is revealed in the work of the major Western philosophers from Plato, to Descartes, to Kant, to Nietzsche. Their works do not consist in the 'subjective' viewpoints of their authors, but are rather a series of occurrences that reveal the essence of the history from which they emerge. Philosophy itself speaks the 'words of being', in the dual sense of words which are about being and of words which come from being itself. The idea, though very questionable, should not be simply dismissed. The decisive influence on modernity of Descartes's search for a foundation of truth in the subject is not a result of his subjective intentions. Something essential about humankind's new place in the world is articulated in his texts rather than other texts of the time. However, the danger here, which occurs in various ways in modern German philosophy, is that history becomes subordinated to the history of philosophy. Philosophy is therefore supposed to articulate the essential truth about history as a whole. When that history involves the enormities of the Nazi period, one has to be very careful in looking at it through the eyes of philosophy. The question is what could possibly legitimate Heidegger's contention that the truth of being is spoken through the essential thinkers. How does that truth relate to the Holocaust, which might seem, as it does to Adorno, to be the key to understanding the dangers of modernity? On the latter issue Heidegger himself, unsurprisingly, has little to offer, though there are elements of his thought which others have tried to use to arrive at a new conception of what it is to be human in the light of the Holocaust. Part of the problem for Heidegger's own thought, even forgetting his personal failings, is that ethics plays almost no role at all in it.

After the turn, Heidegger tells a story about the essence of philosophy since Plato which becomes ever more monolithic, and so ever more distant from any kind of detailed historical analysis of events in his time. The way to understand this story is by looking at its conclusion: 'The development of the sciences is at the same time their separation from philosophy and the establishment of their independence. This process belongs to the end/completion [*Vollendung*] of philosophy' (ibid. 63). His claim is based on the idea that metaphysics, now in the sense of Western philosophy since Plato, has been concerned with revealing the ground of 'presence'. This task has now passed to the natural sciences, whose very nature is derived from philosophy's search for foundations. The sciences will, he asserts, come to be 'determined and directed by the new basic science which is called cybernetics' (ibid. 64). Cybernetics – which now would include 'artificial intelligence' and the related digital technology – seeks to explain the nature of thinking and behaviour in terms which derive from the initial methodological assumption that thinking can explain and control itself. The Cartesian grounding of thought in its own certainty about itself is therefore continuous with the increasing domination of nature by science and technology, and now even extends to the idea that thinking can artificially create thinking. The task for Heidegger is therefore to arrive at a new kind of 'thinking'. This would no longer be philosophy, because philosophy is itself the source of its own demise in the face of the rigour and effectiveness of the sciences. Just what 'thinking' would be is anything but clear. However, the concern which underlies his contentions is not absurd: if certain conceptions of natural science are to be believed, there will ultimately be no other kind of true description of the world except that provided by the sciences. What that does to human culture is, of course, the big problem, and Heidegger's own failure of judgement in relation to modern culture suggests how difficult an issue this is.

Heidegger's later contentions are a mixture of absurd exaggeration and distortion with deep insights into the price that may be paid for being's domination by the methods of the sciences. He does not condemn what happens: who or what would he condemn, given that it is not *Dasein*'s intentions that makes things the way they are, but the fact that being 'happens' in this manner? Rather than attempt any kind of judgement here on Heidegger's overall claims, we will consider a similar version of the story of modernity in the next chapter, that of Horkheimer and Adorno in *Dialectic of Enlightenment*, which comes from the opposite end of the political spectrum. Consideration in the Conclusion of criticisms of this version by Habermas will then allow a more appropriate assessment of the role and function of philosophy in Germany in the light of twentieth-century history.

SUGGESTIONS FOR FURTHER READING

Dahlstrom, D. (2001) *Heidegger's Concept of Truth* (Cambridge: Cambridge University Press). *Very detailed and extensive examination of a key issue in Heidegger's philosophy.*

Dreyfus, H. L. (1991) *Being-in-the-World: A Commentary on Heidegger's 'Being and Time,' Division I* (Cambridge, MA: MIT Press). *Excellent detailed and lucid commentary on Heidegger's most influential work.*

Dreyfus, H. L. and Hall, H. (eds) (1992) *Heidegger: A Critical Reader* (Oxford: Blackwell). *Collection of essays on major topics.*

Inwood, M. (1997) *Heidegger* (Oxford: Oxford University Press). *Good introductory volume which makes sense of some of Heidegger's most contentious ideas.*

Makkreel, R. A. (1992) *Dilthey. Philosopher of the Human Studies* (Princeton: Princeton University Press). *Reliable historical and philosophical study of the work of Dilthey.*

Mulhall, S. (1996) *Routledge Philosophy Guidebook to Heidegger and Being and Time* (London: Routledge). *Very clear, detailed and readable introduction to* Being and Time.

Okrent, M. (1988) *Heidegger's Pragmatism. Understanding, Being, and the Critique of Metaphysics* (Ithaca: Cornell University Press). *Outstanding analytical account of Heidegger's work.*

Rée, J. (1999) *Heidegger* (New York: Routledge). *Accessible account of Heidegger's work.*

Richardson, W. J. (1963) *Heidegger: Through Phenomenology to Thought* (The Hague: Nijhoff). *Good general account of the development of Heidegger's thinking.*

Safranski, R. (1998) *Martin Heidegger: Between Good and Evil* (Cambridge, MA: Harvard University Press). *Brilliant intellectual biography, as good on the life as on the philosophy*

11

CRITICAL THEORY

'Metaphysics' and Modernity

The Frankfurt School of Critical Theory is the name used for the group of thinkers who developed the most influential ideas of the Institute for Social Research, which was founded by Felix Weil in 1923. In the 1930s the Institute was forced by the Nazis into exile in Switzerland and then in the USA; it returned to Frankfurt in 1949. The most well-known members or associates of the School are Theodor W. Adorno (1903–69), Walter Benjamin (1892–1940), Erich Fromm (1900–80), Max Horkheimer (1895–1973), Herbert Marcuse (1898–1979) and, later, Jürgen Habermas (1929–). The School starts out with an explicit commitment to Marxist politics, but many of its members later come, in the light of Stalinism and the rise of Nazism, to reject such direct political involvement. They do so, though, on the basis of ideas which will turn out, despite their very different political aims, not to be so far from some of Heidegger's. This leaves progressive thinkers in post-war Germany in a difficult situation. The attempt of Jürgen Habermas, from the late 1960s onwards, to suggest a way beyond this situation, and some of the reactions to Habermas, will form the object of the Conclusion.

The dilemma that will be faced by Habermas already becomes apparent if one looks at the contrast between Heidegger and the Vienna Circle. Heidegger, a former member of the Nazi party, wrote in the 1960s of the 'end of philosophy' as a consequence of his failed attempts to find a way of answering the – probably unanswerable – 'question of being'. Heidegger's sense that 'Western metaphysics', which aims at a universal principle for making present the absent ground of truth, will have to give way to new ways of thinking is not, though, by any means the sole preserve of the political far Right. The Marxist tradition always involved conceptions which were suspicious of 'metaphysics', as we saw in Marx's critique of idealism. Marx sought to analyse the politico-economic basis of philosophical ideas in the 'superstructure'. For the later Heidegger, however – who at the same time expressed his admiration for Marx – this critique did not allow the possibility of understanding being because it still depended on a grounding principle. Heidegger's later attempts to overcome metaphysics involved the claim that the natural sciences had taken over as the basis for the understanding of ourselves and the world from metaphysics. Metaphysics cannot, therefore, just be abolished. Metaphysics in the form of science and technology now determines the world in an unprecedented manner. The question is what other kind of thinking there could be which does not 'enframe' the world as metaphysics does.

Importantly, this claim puts Heidegger in almost exactly the *opposite* position to that of the Vienna Circle with regard to what 'metaphysics' means. For the Circle, claims about reality which could not be verified by means of the procedures of the natural sciences were 'metaphysical'. This startling antithesis between conceptions of metaphysics points to the deeper issue for philosophy. The sciences are the source both of unparalleled new capacities to control the natural world, with the enormous benefits which accrue from them, and of the kind of problems for the future of humankind exemplified by the atom bomb and the ecological crisis. The differing conceptions of Heidegger and the Vienna Circle relate to the tension between these aspects of the sciences. Heidegger admittedly does not dispute the results of the sciences or suggest it would be possible to return to the past, but he does have an investment in a highly questionable idealized conception of rural traditions. At its best, though, his work does help to show what 'scientism', the exclusive reliance on scientific method for our dealings with the world and each other, may obscure. The members of the Vienna Circle, on the other hand, are generally unconcerned about whether there may be a darker side to the sciences which would require serious philosophical investigation. They make a strict distinction between scientific theories, and how the theories are applied as technology. One of the major questions in philosophy in the wake of Heidegger and others is: how should the separation of science from the ways it is employed be conceived? The Frankfurt School attempts to develop a Critical Theory that would address the sort of questions posed by both Heidegger and the Circle from a position informed by the ideas of Marx, and it ends up attacking both Heidegger and logical empiricism. Whether the attacks are adequate to their targets is, though, open to question. Habermas's criticisms of the earlier members of the Frankfurt School and the reactions to the School in contemporary German philosophy suggest that the criticisms fall short in certain respects.

The detailed history of the Frankfurt School and the diversity of the views of its members are too complex to present here. A simple framework can, though, suggest the direction of their concerns. The mass destruction and appalling loss of life in the world wars would not have been possible but for the rapid development of technology, which, in other spheres, can make life much better for many people. The capacity for technological innovation becomes more and more divorced from moral and social advance. One response to this situation is to hope for improved moral education of the kind that ensued from the ideas of Kant and Schiller. The root of the problem is here seen to lie in individuals' ethical failures in a world where theology no longer gives a clear lead. However, the very application of technology *itself* seems to lead to an increase in barbarism. One of the reasons for this is that the technical means often enable those using them not to have to see the results: the pilots who dropped bombs on cities in the war did not experience their effects. The root of the appalling events has also to be sought in the effects of the application of the modern sciences and the organization of society on the individual. This search leads to the demand for new ways of understanding and changing the relationship between the individual and society. The main models for such an examination for the Critical Theorists were Marx, Max Weber and Freud.

Marx did not disapprove per se of capitalism. His claim was that a new division of labour and new forms of ownership could transform individuals in modern societies, creating a more humane world precisely with the means which capitalism had brutally liberated from feudal restraints. Doubts about the more optimistic side of Marx's view of social transformation can, though, be expressed on many levels. Weber was concerned that the rationalization of traditional practices by modern societies was an indication of the extent to which technological advances might be the source of an ever more regimented, bureaucratic way of life. Historical events also give rise to other doubts. The Russian Revolution, for example, was supposed to transform a feudal society into a communist one, without going through the phase of bourgeois capitalism. It presents a whole new socio-political and economic scenario that does not fit into Marx's model of revolution as the motor of the move from feudalism to capitalism. The extent to which individuals can be positively transformed by transforming their social circumstances clashes with the account in Freud of how people are determined by unconscious motivations and repressions that have their source in childhood experiences – though the nature of these experiences is, as the Critical Theorists would point out, itself affected by the kind of society in which they occur. The capacity of technology to manipulate nature may grow exponentially, but the danger that nature may thereby be irreparably damaged cannot, as Schelling already suggested, be ignored. Aspects of the ideas of the early Marx we observed in chapter 6 touch on these issues, and it was only in the 1920s that some of Marx's early work was first published. The interest at this time comes to be in his relationship to some of the concerns of philosophy which had not been invalidated by attempts to make Marxism into a science. The idea of Marxism as a science was regarded by some on the Left as the source of the ability intentionally to determine the course of history. The idea was often associated with Leninist Communist parties of the Third International in the Soviet Union and elsewhere. These parties had emerged in relation to the failure of Social Democratic Marxist parties of the Second International to prevent the First World War because they divided along national lines.[1] The disastrous consequences of the 'scientific' conception of Marxism as the theory that reveals the laws of history would eventually be one aspect of what led to the demise of the governments that saw the Party as the source of insight into those laws. However, as we know, it would take until 1989 for this idea finally to be laid to rest in the Western world, at least.

A work which deeply affected philosophy's relationship to these issues is *History and Class Consciousness* (1922) by the Hungarian Marxist, Georg Lukács (1885–1971). Lukács wanted to overcome the traditional problem of epistemology – the split between subject and object – so that revolutionary action could be rationally achievable. He was at the same time, though, suspicious of the idea of Marxism as a science, and was soon forced to retract many of his ideas under pressure from the Party. The crucial idea in Marxism, he argues, in the light of his interpretation of Hegel, is the notion of 'totality'. Access to the totality integrates the isolated empirical data of social life into the context in which their meaning is apparent. Whereas feudal societies cannot be conceived of as totalities, because their parts are not related in terms of a general connecting principle, the

1   The Social Democratic parties also tended to regard Marxism as a science, but they often used the idea to suggest that the laws of history would inevitably lead to the abolition of capitalism without the need for the revolutionary intervention of the proletariat.

development of capital means that the world begins to function as a concrete whole. The connecting principle is, following Marx, capitalism's making all objects into exchangeable commodities. Hegel saw philosophy's ability to grasp the essential aspects of modernity in terms of the interconnectedness of everything, which was revealed in his account of absolute spirit. Lukács regards this interconnectedness as a concrete historical development based on the material reproductive forms of modern society. In the light of the effects of globalization, the power of this conception should be clear. However, the key characteristic of the changes brought about by capitalism is the subjection of individuals to those changes without their being able to make sense of them. This is the source, Lukács argues, of the split in modern philosophy between theory and practice. He refers at this point to the failure of non-Marxist thinkers in particular to understand how the First World War could have occurred in the way it did.

Lukács belongs to the large number of twentieth-century thinkers and artists in Germany who see a radical divorce in modernity between individual experience and the reality which underlies it. The response to this situation involves a fundamental choice. One option is an 'irrational' renunciation of the attempt to grasp the totality that derives from the idea of the impenetrability of historical processes or of the real nature of being. The other is a rational attempt to explain why the totality is the way it is, despite the ways individuals directly experience it. Lukács reviews the tradition we have considered, from Kant and Fichte onwards, with the aim of showing that 'history becomes the history of the forms of objectivity which constitute the external world [*Umwelt*] and the inner world of humankind' (1967: 206). In the terms Heidegger (who was probably familiar with his text) later introduced, Lukács seeks to move away from an objectified, 'ontic' conception of the world to an 'ontological' conception of a world which is constituted by what we do in relation to it.

The crux of Lukács's approach in the central essay of his book, 'Reification and the Consciousness of the Proletariat', is that individuals will never be able to grasp the truth about modern history because they are faced with an objective world over which they have little or no power. The First World War and the social and economic chaos which follows it make the force of the argument evident. Lukács's answer to the problem is: 'Only the class . . . can relate to the totality of reality in a practical revolutionary manner' (ibid. 211). The class in question is the proletariat. The reason it can transform reality is that it is most subject to 'reification' (meaning 'being made into a thing', from the Latin 'res', 'thing'). The historical development of labour involves 'a continually increasing rationalization, an ever stronger exclusion of the qualitative, human-individual qualities of the worker' (ibid. 99), so that the world of things more and more determines the inner world of people. Marx's remarks on industry as the 'sensuously present human *psychology*' are here concretized in a manner that is vital for the Frankfurt School. The source of the subject–object division in its modern form – the division is therefore not something perennial, but something which depends on history – is this process of rationalization. Its effects are most extreme on the proletariat. The labour of the worker, as Marx argued, becomes something opposed to them. Once the proletariat collectively grasps this situation, it is in a position, Lukács claims, to abolish it. Their impoverishment as subjects will then be able to have positive objective effects, both in terms of their conditions of life and in terms of abolishing the modern sense of dislocation from reality that is abstractly expressed in philosophy. The proletariat does, though – and here the argument becomes sinister – require the Communist Party to organize and represent its 'collective will' (ibid. 324), if it is to abolish what makes it into a mere object, and so become the subject of history. The problems with Lukács's approach are legion. How is the Party's speaking for the proletariat to be legitimated? What happens if workers do not regard themselves as reified? – are they merely deceived? How does what Lukács says relate to the reality of what was happening in the Soviet Union? – this is, after all, the time when the Party was setting off on the road that led to the worst excesses of Stalinism. Doesn't the argument force a philosophical perspective onto a world whose reality is too complex to be grasped so schematically?

Despite all these problems, the structure of thought in *History and Class Consciousness*, which seeks to explain how it is that the collective result of modern human activity is so inimical to individual well-being, is a powerful one, and it plays a vital role in Critical Theory. Critical Theory also adopts the idea that capitalism involves the increasing integration of the world in ways which can obscure the real functioning of the economy and which distort people's ability to act rationally. During the 1930s Horkheimer, who becomes the head of the Institute for Social Research, publishes important essays which seek to establish what he intends by the notion of a Critical Theory. Both the Vienna Circle and Heidegger come under fire in the characteristic essay 'The Most Recent Attack on Metaphysics' (1937). Horkheimer seems to adopt the same line as the Circle when he claims that 'Science is to a large extent itself the critique of metaphysics' (1980: vi. 80). At the same time, though, he also criticizes the Circle for its scientism, and Heidegger and others for their 'trivial-

ization of science as a technique that is conditioned by subordinate
concerns of human existence' (ibid. 8). His main argument is plausible enough, namely that 'Science and its interpretation are two different things' (ibid. 49). However, his own interpretation of scientism
and the trivialization of science as both being responses by the bour-
geoisie to their inability to influence the crises of capitalism merely
illustrates the danger of moving too quickly from philosophical to
sociological questions. Neurath was a politically active Marxist, who,
like others in the Vienna Circle, was essentially on the same side as
Horkheimer. Horkheimer refused to publish Neurath's reply to his
essay, which does not inspire confidence in his argument. The dangers
of a strategy which tries to explain away one issue in terms of arguments of a wholly different order from that issue are here all too
apparent. Horkheimer's essays do not always involve this kind of
invalid reduction, and his best analyses of how philosophical issues
are often really political issues often do exemplify the aims of a
Critical Theory.

There is here, however, a deeper problem for the notion of a 'Critical' Theory. Part of what Horkheimer, like Adorno, justifiably seeks
to do at this time is to find a way of criticizing philosophy for the ways
it can be used for ideological purposes. One has to remember in this
context just how desperate the political situation had been in the
Weimar Republic from the very beginning. What Horkheimer and
Adorno have in mind are the kind of thinkers who purport to offer
a fundamental insight into the 'deep' questions of existence but
whose 'insight' has no consequences for people's critical attitude to
the crisis-ridden world they actually inhabit. This is, after all, the
world where inflation and economic crashes – the cumulative results
of human actions – make it evident that capitalism cannot carry on
in the way it had done until that time. An appropriate analysis of the
failings of capitalism is therefore seen as more vital than supposed
answers to deep philosophical questions. Adorno praised the Vienna
Circle in the early 1930s for its work in separating specifically scientific questions from philosophical questions, but this suggests the
dilemma which both he and Horkheimer face.

Their basic idea is that philosophical problems appear to demand
timeless solutions, but that philosophical problems often disappear
when it is realized that the problem has a practical solution. Lukács
was trying to argue something similar with regard to the separation
of subject and object in its modern form. At the same time, however,
Schlick's comment, cited in chapter 8, that some philosophical problems 'will disappear by being shown to be mistakes and misunderstandings of our language and the others will be shown to be ordinary

scientific questions in disguise' also offers an – albeit less grandiose – version of how to overcome the traditional dilemmas of philosophy and get on with changing things for the better. The difference between Schlick and the Critical Theorists lies, of course, in Schlick's scientism, which is indeed a justified target for Critical Theory. However, a Critical Theory that does not just rely on science revealing the illusions of philosophy, and insists on the 'interpretation' of science, still entails a fundamental difficulty. Adorno and Horkheimer want to give up metaphysical claims about the totality, in order to understand the historical situation in which a specific social, cultural or scientific problem is located. The very need for a critical *theory* would, though, seem to demand an overall view of the totality, of the kind suggested by Lukács, if a philosophical perspective is to be developed that would legitimate the critique. If, on the other hand, one gives up an identifiably philosophical perspective by dissolving theory into political practice, a great deal turns on whether that practice can really produce the results and justify them. When both Adorno and Horkheimer lose faith, in the light of the demise of the Weimar Republic and of the rise of Stalin, in the ability of political organizations on the Left to improve – rather than, in many cases, worsen – the situation of the deprived and oppressed, their dilemma becomes extreme. Horkheimer had in many respects wished to make Critical Theory a criticism of philosophy. His change of perspective will in his later work make him too dependent on a totalizing philosophy of history.

Walter Benjamin: Language and Time

The influences which lead to the later position of Horkheimer and Adorno in *Dialectic of Enlightenment* (1947), and to Adorno's mature work, range from Hegel, to Nietzsche, to Marx, to Max Weber, to Freud, to the figure we need briefly to consider here: Adorno's friend, Walter Benjamin. Benjamin is one of the most perplexing and intriguing figures in twentieth-century German philosophy. His work combines a commitment to Marxism, which resulted in part from his reading of *History and Class Consciousness*, with an interest in Jewish mysticism, particularly with respect to its conception of language as bound up with God's creation of an intelligible world. The cabbala, the main source of Jewish mysticism, maintains that God's Words create real things, so that the world and the true language are ultimately the same. Influential new research into the cabbala is initiated under the influence of Benjamin in the 1930s by his friend Gershom

Scholem. Benjamin's interest in language also links to his concern with the early Romantic philosophy of Novalis and Schlegel which we looked at in chapter 5. He writes a groundbreaking PhD dissertation on the early Romantics in 1919, having already written texts on language and literary topics in the preceding years. The dissertation gives a major role to both literature and the criticism of literature for a conception of philosophy that seeks to create meaning by connecting elements of the world in ever new ways. Benjamin's wider project, which develops quite gradually, is the attempt to come to terms with the secularization of history by seeking what can be salvaged for radical politics from the remains of theology. Whereas even Marx might be seen as retaining elements of a teleological conception of history as the realization of humankind's potential, Benjamin wants to give meaning to history without invoking the idea of a future that relies on a story of human betterment. His concern is predominantly with not allowing the past to become forgotten and meaningless. The past is what can transform the present, rather than something objectively fixed. Benjamin's idea relies on what sounds like a theological notion of redemption. Redemption need not, though, be thought of as something exclusively theological. It could be said that psychoanalysis also aims at the redemption of the past, by the overcoming of the effects of trauma in the present. Benjamin thinks this can also occur on a collective level, when revolution leads to a new relationship to the traumatic injustices of the past. The connection between theological thinking and political thinking in Benjamin's writings is neither constant nor easily comprehensible, not least because arguments about the boundaries between the two play a major role in modern politics anyway. The best way to approach his work is through the themes of language and time.

From his early work onwards Benjamin is concerned with dimensions of language which can be obscured by the dominance of the instrumental language of the natural sciences. In 1928 he publishes *The Origins of the German Play of Mourning* (*Trauerspiel*), which gathers together his previous ideas on language and time, and which had a significant effect on Adorno. Benjamin's book is ostensibly about seventeenth-century German baroque theatre, which is concerned with responses to the inevitability of human transience. It also belongs, though, to a series of texts of the period that are concerned more generally with the nature of modernity and time, to which Lukács's *Theory of the Novel* (1914), written before he became a Marxist, also belongs. Underlying both works is the theme Weber discussed as the 'disenchantment' of the world by the modern sciences and by rationalized modern social forms. Lukács talks of the modern condition in terms of 'transcendental homelessness', which results from the loss of a relationship to a nature which is imbued with meaning because it is God's creation, and from the individual's loss of a stable sense of identity. Benjamin sees the growing domination of scientific truth as leading to the loss of 'the realm of truth which is meant by languages' (1980: I 1. 208), an idea which he finds in Hamann's critique of Kant (see chapter 2). Heidegger's later questions about literature as means of understanding the truth of being of a kind inaccessible to the sciences are already present in Benjamin's investigation. How, then, are the 'nihilistic' consequences of the situation, in which the sciences explain more and more while human life is seen as increasingly meaningless, to be confronted? The key element for Benjamin is the understanding of the nature of language in the modern world.

Benjamin alights on the German baroque because of its use of allegory in a manner which is different from earlier literatures. The point of allegory in this new sense is that 'Every person, every thing, every relationship can arbitrarily mean something else. This possibility passes a devastating but just judgement on the profane world: it is characterized as a world in which details are not strictly that important' (ibid. 350). In common with a whole series of writers at the time, Benjamin is concerned by the idea that language appears to come apart from the world in the modern period. Instead of there being an essential bond between a word and what it means in the world, words are merely arbitrary generalizations. Benjamin's speculations on language rely on the idea that creation was a divine naming and that human language has fallen away from the truth inaugurated at and by the creation. He often critically refers to the 'bourgeois conception' of language, by which he means any conception which sees language as mere convention. The notion of a time when language was substantially connected to the world relies on the idea that words are mapped onto the pre-existing truth of things. However, investigation into the history of language, of the kind begun by Herder, shows that language is always in a constant state of transformation in terms of human needs and desires, rather than moving from some primal, pure state to the modern arbitrary state. The notion of another kind of 'true' language, a language of God's creative 'Word', has little or nothing to back it up historically. Benjamin's conception can, though, be adapted in other ways.

One way in which the language of the modern period can be questioned is, as the Romantics realized, in terms of the difference between instrumental and aesthetic usage. The former relies on ever more precise specification of the use of words, of the kind suggested

by the Vienna Circle's idea of a logically purified language. The latter
seeks to employ repressed resources of language to say something
which has its own truth that cannot be reduced to other truths. This
kind of truth depends on the configuration of language into specific
new combinations. In that way, a text, such as a poem, may transcend
the historical arbitrariness of the linguistic material of which it is com-
posed. The arbitrariness of the signifier is, in contrast, the key idea in
Saussure's linguistics, which tried to put the analysis of language on
a scientific basis. Saussure's idea relates to Spinoza's dictum that 'all
determination is negation' and thus to the Idealist and Romantic
ideas which developed from it. There are, for Saussure, no positive
terms in language: each word gains its identity by not being the other
words within the notional total system of the language. Saussure
himself often linked language to money and his conception can be
related to Marx's conception of money as the universal commodity
which potentially turns all use values into exchange values. This link
suggests the direction of Benjamin's conception of language, and
makes evident how it will influence Critical Theory.

The common factor in these conceptions is that everything is what
it is because of its historically contingent relationships to other things,
not because of something intrinsic to the particular thing. The
problem is that what makes the relationships intelligible cannot be
thought of in terms of the relationships themselves. Relational
systems require a foundation if they are to be connected to the real
world and to be comprehensible. Heidegger would see the relations
as 'ontic' and what makes them intelligible as 'ontological'. Spinoza's
God is the positive One that underlies the negatively determined
Many. The totality of the language is the basis of the decision whether
an element is linguistic or not that is made by seeing if its relationship to other elements gives rise to a meaning. Lukács's proletariat
is what can grasp the totality of the apparently arbitrary relationships
in capitalism and transcend them. In the terms made familiar by
Derrida, each of these foundations functions, therefore, as a 'transcendental signified', which would make sense of all the signifiers in
the system. Benjamin's account of allegory in the *Trauerspiel* book,
where words themselves become arbitrary things that can, like anything else, be related to other bits of the world, relies on the thoroughly metaphysical search for 'Ideas'. These are what constitute
the truth of the contingent phenomena being investigated; in this case
the Idea is that of *Trauerspiel*. *Trauerspiel* functions, therefore, as the
transcendental signified of the book. The transcendental signified is
rather like a Kantian 'regulative idea'. It is not that the investigation
will reach it: rather, it is what orients the enquiry, while never being

fully present itself. However, there will always be a question as to whether such ideas can ultimately be legitimated as the aim of an enquiry.

When Benjamin takes a more politicized and Marx-oriented stance during the 1930s, he translates his conception of language into terms influenced by his reading of *History and Class Consciousness*. He tries to combine a theological view of what the true language would be with a political project that would establish a new kind of relationship of humankind to the modern world. In his work on Baudelaire and nineteenth-century capitalism in the 1930s, he claims, for example, that 'The allegorical manner of perception is always built upon a devalued world of appearance. The specific devaluation of the world of things which is present in the commodity is the foundation of the allegorical intention in Baudelaire' (Benjamin 1980: I 3. 1151). The uncompleted *Arcades Project*, on which he worked until his death, takes the rise of the artificial environment of the shopping arcade in nineteenth-century Paris as the most characteristic manifestation of how capitalism produces a 'phantasmagoria' that hides its brutal reality. This further underlines the idea of allegorization as the fundamental process in modern culture. How, then, are things to be revalued? There is no single answer to this in Benjamin's work. In the *Arcades Project* he often relies on the notion of 'constellation' from the *Trauerspiel* book, and on the use of montage of the most disparate historical material. These are intended to give rise to new ways of contextualizing and rendering significant what may otherwise appear to be insignificant phenomena. His aim is to write history in terms which are not those of the historical victors, who set the agenda for the past in terms of their own domination of the present. Another aspect of this attempt is to see history not as a causal narrative, but in terms of discontinuous links between the past and the present. He cites the way the French Revolution used aspects of the Roman Republic as an example of how the past can be changed by the demands of the present. The idea is to get away from a static conception of an objective past, so that the writing of history becomes a part of action in the present.

Underlying most of Benjamin's later reflections is the conviction that the very notion of culture is compromised by its inextricable links to the barbarity of those who have triumphed so far in history. The problem is that this leads him to an apocalyptic sense of the need to redeem the whole of the past by a complete transformation of the present. Although this need is understandable in the desperate circumstances of the rise of Nazism – Benjamin committed suicide on the French-Spanish border while trying to escape capture by the

Nazis – the impetus behind the idea is a questionable theology. It is one of the major insights of Critical Theory that documents of culture are always in some respects testimony to the repressions that result from the injustices of history. However, there are few serious attempts on Benjamin's part to suggest in terms of a concrete political strategy what the redemption of history would entail. Moreover, such a conception can all too easily ignore the ways in which history does involve aspects of real progress, even if history as a whole cannot be regarded in terms of progress towards an ultimate goal. Who but the worst kind of religious fundamentalist would deny, for example, that we can know from history what progress in the role of women in society is, or what progress is in many areas of medicine, hygiene, etc.? This progress does not benefit sufficient people, and that has to be a key source of radical politics, but it should not be written off as still part of some ongoing total disaster, of the kind Benjamin often sees as the essential nature of history. Indeed, he seems to think that getting the repressed classes to regard history as a disaster will be the motor of revolutionary change. This idea has little foundation in the evidence about what motivates real progressive revolutionary movements in the twentieth century. Benjamin is undoubtedly one of the great prose writers and cultural analysts of twentieth-century Germany. His desire to understand culture in terms of the effects of the technological mechanisms of its transmission, from print to film, as well as to reveal how culture is attached to repression, gives rise to many deep insights. Despite this, his philosophical legacy has to be regarded with some suspicion.

Dialectics and Disaster

The date of Horkheimer and Adorno's *Dialectic of Enlightenment* (*DoE*), completed in 1944 and first published in 1947, places it firmly in the bleakest period of German history. As we have seen, Horkheimer's previous work was a Marx-oriented attempt at a general critique of existing philosophy. Adorno's earlier work in philosophy, as opposed to his important work as a music critic – he studies composition with Alban Berg and has ambitions to be a composer – is initially fairly conventional, relating to Husserl's phenomenology, positivism and neo-Kantianism. His reading of *History and Class Consciousness* and Benjamin's *Trauerspiel* book takes him in a new direction by the early 1930s. Like Horkheimer, he takes a Marxist line, albeit one more linked to Benjamin's ideas concerning the nature of language and modernity. His best arguments at this time involve a pragmatist approach to problem-solving. This approach leads him to praise the Vienna Circle and to criticize Husserl's attempt at a timeless transcendental grounding of philosophy, in the name of an awareness of the ways subjects change with history. The rise of Nazism, Stalinism and the war eventually undermine his and Horkheimer's faith in the possibilities for political transformation, and their despair at these developments results in *DoE*. Two aspects of this wide-ranging text, which also looks at Sade, anti-Semitism and a whole series of other cultural phenomena, are most influential for the development of German philosophy after the Nazi period: the account of how 'Enlightenment' can turn into its opposite, and the critique of the 'culture industry'. It is here that the ideas of Heidegger and of the Frankfurt School tend to converge in certain respects, even though there are key differences.

The task the authors set themselves is 'no less than finding out why humankind, instead of entering into a truly human condition, is sinking into a new kind of barbarism' (1971: 1). They admit, though, that the task was too much for them and that their response is only fragmentary. Their response is informed by a desire to avoid any kind of *naïveté* with regard to the dominant modes of thinking of the time, and this explains their often exaggeratedly critical tone. They argue that thought 'has become a commodity' (ibid.), which locates their core idea in the terms of *History and Class Consciousness*. Thought has come to be a mere exchange value because it is more and more limited to merely repeating what is already the case. The kind of thought they advocate looks beyond the facts in order to understand why things are the way they are, so that it may help to change things. The situation of thought being a commodity is part of the 'self-destruction of the Enlightenment' (ibid. 3). By 'Enlightenment', they do not just mean the historical period which is said variously to begin with Descartes, or in the eighteenth century, but rather the whole attempt of humankind, from the beginning, to overcome its fear of the threat posed by nature.

This already suggests a difference from the approach which Adorno developed in the 1930s, and in some respects adopted again after *DoE*. In the best of these other works, Adorno seeks to grasp the specifics of an issue, rather than relying on abstractions. What greater abstraction could there be, though, than the reduction in *DoE* of the notion of Enlightenment to a transhistorical account of humankind based on the principle of self-preservation? Crucially, though, the authors do stress the paradoxical nature of their enterprise: 'We have no doubt – and there lies our *petitio principii* – that freedom in society is inseparable from thought which enlightens' (ibid.). The attempt to criticize rational thought as determined by self-preservation must itself rely on rational thought. Despite this, they still pursue the idea that there is something in rational thought itself which yet leads to its own self-destruction. Whether it is possible to think in such paradoxical terms is in many respects the question which Adorno pursues for the rest of his life.

DoE works with a mixture of ideas from Marx, Weber, Freud, Benjamin and Nietzsche. The main ideas are:

- the commodity as the victory of exchange-value over use-value;
- the standardization of modern forms of social organization;
- the repression of drives as the precondition of social life; and
- the idea that thinking inherently entails a damaging reduction of the diversity of reality to forms of conceptual identification.

The theme which links all these elements is 'the regression of Enlightenment into mythology' (ibid.). Just how difficult this issue appears to the authors is suggested by their claim that clarity in discussing the problems can itself be a form of 'myth' (ibid. 4), because it will obscure what cannot be stated in the terms current in what they see as a deluded society. Already there are echoes here of the ideas developed by Heidegger from the 1930s onwards, in essays like 'The Age of the World Picture'. These ideas led Heidegger to try to develop a new language for the 'thinking' that is to replace philosophy, which has now become subordinated to the sciences. Horkheimer and Adorno's idea of 'the subjection of everything natural to the arrogant subject' (ibid. 5) is very close to Heidegger's idea of the 'subjectification of being' that is exemplified in Descartes's founding of certain knowledge in the subject. The point is that the source of this knowledge is human activity, which seeks control over the other, be it hostile nature, or other people. Adorno and Horkheimer see this process as producing a new kind of 'second nature'. The potentially more humane and just world which technology makes possible by its ability to control nature does not emerge. Instead, technology itself ends up beyond rational control and can be at least as destructive of human well-being as uncontrolled 'first nature'.

In certain respects this last point is incontrovertible, as is clear from any of the appalling uses to which modern technology has been put. The worst natural disasters in modern history destroy fewer lives than do human disasters. The vital issue is the story one tells in order to understand why this is the case. *DoE* differs from Heidegger because it is motivated by the desire for a reduction of suffering, not by the grandiose aim of recasting the whole of Western thought in

order to overcome the forgetting of being. At the same time, some of
its conceptual moves are very similar. Against the 'positivist' conception that science and the application of its results must be separated – which does little to explain how it is that the application of
science is so often to the detriment of so many people – *DoE* tries to
suggest that there is an *internal* connection between the nature of
science and what it does to the modern world. The basis of the internal connection is the concept of identification, the reduction of the
particular to the general, criticism of which played such a role in
Nietzsche's thinking and which is part of Heidegger's notion of
'enframing'.

DoE establishes a link between the idea that all commodities are
potentially equivalent, at the expense of their particularity, with the
idea that scientific theories aim at reducing the world to as few elements as possible. Both modern natural science and the commodity
structure are just further manifestations of thought's inherent nature
as identification for the purposes of controlling the other, whether
the other is nature or other people. Mythology is just the first historical manifestation of this urge to control. The mechanism of identification functions both in society's relationship to external nature, and
in the formation of the individual self. As Freud claimed, the self's
identity also depends on exclusion of the other, this time in the form
of repression of the desires produced by internal natural drives which
take one beyond oneself into potentially dangerous engagement with
the other. The same mechanism can then function as the projection
of one's own repressed drives onto the other, so that one hates in the
other what one actually hates in oneself. *DoE* plausibly regards this
projection as a key source of racism and anti-Semitism.

DoE's suspicion of the effects of thought's reliance on identification extends as far as language itself. Following Nietzsche, language
is regarded as having become merely a means of reducing the diversity of the world to repeatable identities. This idea relates to the wider
contention that the modern world's 'social, economic and scientific
apparatus' (ibid. 36) has become more and more refined, and more
and more complex. The result is the impoverishment of individuals'
capacity to experience anything which does not fit the forms this
apparatus generates in order to function efficiently: 'the machinery
mutilates people today, even when it feeds them' (ibid.). In the same
way as language pre-exists the individual subject and constrains what
they can say, the accumulated techniques and mechanisms of modern
societies pre-form the individual before they can develop a sense of
autonomy. This may seem fine to the individual in those areas of
society where needs can be satisfied, but these areas live at the

expense of other areas. When you buy the fruit imported by the Dole company, for example, you help create 'banana republics'. In the now even more globalized capitalist world, *DoE*'s picture of the situation in which the freedom of individual decisions and actions is so bound up with processes that are not transparent to the individual is undoubtedly powerful. The very nature of one's supposedly most subjective thoughts and feelings is revealed as always involving objective sources and results of which one is not aware.

The problem is that the text makes this analysis into something 'philosophical'. The domination of nature leads to the denial of 'nature in humankind', the denial that we are living beings who cannot be wholly imposed on by artificial structures. The fact that such structures increasingly dominate modern societies produces distortions in the subject. This Schelling-derived point is clearly important for an understanding of modernity. However, the authors then suggest that the state of contemporary capitalism, which mistakes the means – controlling nature – for the end – a happy existence in nature – 'is already perceptible in the primal history of subjectivity' (ibid. 51). The leap from the very first formation of social individuals at some unspecified point in the development of the species to the attributes of contemporary capitalism is simply indefensible. One of the key aspects of Critical Theory is the insistence on 'mediation', on the awareness of the impossibility of adequate analysis of phenomena without locating them in the appropriate contexts. In this case the mediation is simply lacking.

It may be that *DoE* makes intentionally exaggerated claims, given the authors' despair at people's failure to grasp what is happening in the world at the time. This is, though, unlikely to be an effective rhetorical ploy. People tend to dismiss even valid points if they are made in an exaggerated manner. The same problem is present in *DoE*'s critique of the 'culture industry', which is subtitled 'Enlightenment as Mass Deception'. The thesis is essentially the same as in the account of how Enlightenment becomes its opposite. Culture should promote diversity and innovation: instead it has become a commodity which is no longer its own justification and has to be justified in market terms. The result is increasing standardization, rather than real innovation. This means that mass culture is actually just another part of the apparatus which makes people fit into the imperatives of the economic system: 'Amusement is the extension of work under late capitalism' (ibid. 123). The idea that art should not be used in the service of something else and should be the result of the free activity of the artist and of the recipient of the artwork gives way in mass culture to the situation where artists produce in order to be successful in the market. Already existing expectations determine the work, rather than the artist's attempt to say something new.

Although there is some truth in this account of how the structures of modern societies distort cultural development, many of the specific criticisms made in the chapter on the culture industry, for instance about jazz, are impossible to defend. They are based on a wholly inadequate understanding of the specific history and function of what is being criticized. However, some of the criticisms have come to be more apposite in the intervening period. We live, after all, in a world where the endings of films are market-tested and changed if the test-audience doesn't like them, and where the rock-music industry is driven by the imperatives of multinational marketing rather than by musical judgement. At some level the text does get in touch with many of the most pressing issues in modern culture – but which level is it exactly? The real problem in assessing *DoE* has to do with the relationship between its mixture of acute critical insight and indefensible totalizing judgements, and its philosophical claims. The same problem applies to much of Adorno's subsequent work.

Negative Dialectics

If one regards the world that is dominated by the commodity principle as a 'universal context of delusion', as Adorno does, how can a perspective be gained on that world which is itself not deluded? Adorno is insistent that there can be no perspective either from beyond or from within the social world which could provide a philosophical foundation for seeing through the delusion. Such a foundation would, for Adorno, restrict thought's ability to engage with the real, rather than providing definitive access to it. But this seems to lead to a situation in which all we are left with are time-bound, subjective judgements. Sometimes it seems that this is the case in Adorno's own work. His rejection of jazz, for example, is the rejection of the bourgeois German intellectual who is so convinced of the superiority of his own cultural tradition that he cannot see beyond it to something new with its own value. However, the paradoxical situation created by Adorno's simultaneous claims about the totality, and denial that thought can grasp the totality, is not a result of a logical mistake on his part. Giving up philosophical foundations does not make all the issues they involve go away. The important question is how one responds to this renunciation of what is only one particular conception of the philosophical enterprise.

Hilary Putnam suggests that 'almost every philosopher makes statements which contradict his own explicit account of what can be justified or known; this even arises in formal logic, when one makes statements about "all languages" which are barred by the prohibitions on self-reference' (1983: 226). The need to transcend what philosophy is able to say is a recurrent theme in modern German philosophy. The Vienna Circle sought to restrict what could be meaningfully said to verifiable scientific propositions. For Wittgenstein this meant that the things that mattered most were therefore 'unsayable'. In this he echoed the Romantic idea that what may be shown might in some respects be more significant than what can be said. Given Adorno's concern with the effects of commodification on language, it is perhaps not surprising that his contentions cannot be assessed just as literal assertions, or that music played such a role in his thinking. The paradox of trying to talk about a world of total delusion while belonging to that world means, then, that there is no comfortable *philosophical* place to go. Instead of Hegel's dialectic, which moves from determinate negation to the positive 'absolute idea' as the completion of philosophy, the dialectic here remains 'negative', because there is no philosophical conclusion to it. Much of the debate about Adorno has therefore to do with whether his thinking leads to a kind of covert theology which replaces philosophy, or whether he offers a whole new approach to what Habermas terms 'post-metaphysical thinking'. What is further at issue is the very possibility of a Critical Theory.

In *Minima Moralia* (1949), a collection of short pieces with the subtitle 'Reflections from Damaged Life', Adorno sums up the dilemma for the critical thinker: 'Today nothing less is demanded of the thinker than that he should be at every moment in the things [*Sachen*] and outside the things.' This means he is like 'Münchhausen who pulls himself by his own hair out of the bog' (1978: 91). On the one hand, any general assertion about the totality will do an injustice to some particular aspect of the world by failing to appreciate its unique nature. Mere concentration on particulars, on the other hand, obscures the ways in which they are determined by the general situation. One's sense of one's own uniqueness can depend, for example, on ignoring the ways in which one is made what one is by social pressures. Adorno's claims about the total context of delusion must in one sense be self-refuting. However, the fact that they cannot be positively confirmed does not necessarily mean they are redundant: what they point to cannot be ignored. The world of modern capitalism does have deeply damaging effects which will never be fully transparent even to the most radical critical thinking, at the same time as making life much easier for many people. The historical event which reveals the essence of capitalism for Adorno is the Holocaust. One factor in the Holocaust was the extent to which the barbarism was perpetrated by using the organizational structures characteristic of any modern bureaucracy. Individuals could, consequently, defend their particular role by ignoring how they contributed to the whole. As the film *Shoah* revealed, many of the perpetrators saw what they did in terms of making the trains run on time, etc., not in terms of the mass murder of which the train timetable was a vital part. The mass murders also involved using some of the physical constituents of the victims as material for further production or commodity exchange. Direct and indirect brutality have always been part of human history, and the task is to explain why modern European history, which has produced the means to reduce suffering and some of the best progressive and humanitarian ideas, has been even more brutal than earlier history. Are these phenomena of the Holocaust essentially part of what the modern capitalist 'context of delusion' gives rise to, or should they be seen in terms of the specific history of Germany and Nazism? Is there, as Adorno suggests, something about the very forms of thinking in modernity which makes such events likely, and, if so, what can be done about this, given that revolutionary political action has often added to the barbarism? Adorno does important empirical work to investigate the relationship between individual psychology and the working of power in modern societies, which is published in *The Authoritarian Personality* (1950) as part of the University of California at Berkeley 'Project on the Nature and Extent of Anti-Semitism'. How, though, do these issues inform his philosophical approach?

In his major philosophical work, *Negative Dialectics* (1966), Adorno talks of a new 'categorical imperative' forced upon us by Hitler, namely the imperative that Auschwitz could never be repeated. It is clear from this that the book cannot simply be assessed as a series of philosophical arguments about or explanations of the state of the world in the light of the Holocaust. Its aim is instead to find ways of thinking whose main purpose is the reduction of human cruelty. In this respect Adorno comes close to contemporary pragmatists like Richard Rorty. Rorty sees the new task of philosophy as finding ways to avoid the infliction of pain and to augment the sources of post-theological hope, rather than as grounding epistemology or ethics. Adorno claims that the truth he is interested in should be seen in terms of 'giving a voice to suffering' (1975: 29), rather than in terms of 'reducing the phenomena to a minimum number of propositions' (ibid. 24). The idea underlying the conception is similar to that present in *DoE*: 'Thinking means identifying' (ibid. 17) and is there-

fore intolerant of what cannot simply be identified. The question is
how philosophy responds to the ways in which identification can be
repressive – for example in anti-Semitism's labelling of the Jew as the
other – given that philosophy cannot live without identification.

There is, however, an important ambiguity in the concept of identity, of which Adorno does not always take adequate account. The
contemporary German philosopher, and pupil of Adorno, Herbert
Schnädelbach, has pointed out (1992) that there is a logical equivo-
cation in the notion of identity which has consequences for the
project of overcoming what Adorno terms 'identity thinking'. Identity thinking can be understood via the commodity structure. The
effect of the commodity system is to make things the same that are
really different, so that one commodity, e.g. a particular tree, can
become identified *with* another, e.g. a gun, if they have the same
exchange value. There is here a link between the potentially negative
effects of identification and a certain *kind* of thinking, namely identifying one thing with another. However, this link need not extend to
conceptual thinking as a whole, for the following reason. A tree might
be identified *as* a beautiful oak, the material of a Viking ship, an
endangered species, a unique object, and so on, indefinitely. The idea
of an *inherent* reduction of the object by its being identified simply
has no grip here, because one can always further specify what the
thing can be identified as. No concept has an ultimately determining
role, because it can always be replaced by another concept. It is, of
course, hard to know how one could think at all, if one did not employ
the 'as-structure' of identification. The only possible *fundamental*
objection to the as-structure, as opposed to objections to specific bad
identifications and to inappropriate uses of words, depends on something like Benjamin's notion of the true language that expresses the
essence of the thing, in comparison with which all other language is
mere 'convention', or on Heidegger's idea that there is a 'language of
metaphysics' that must be circumvented if the truth of being is to
emerge. Adorno generally rejects the metaphysical implications of
Benjamin's idea (and has no time for the later Heidegger at all) but
his criticisms of 'identity thinking' seem at times to rely on Benjamin.

The fact that the commodity principle is the source of many of the
injustices of modernity can only be substantially connected to a generalized *philosophical* suspicion of identification by something like
the later Heidegger's conception of metaphysics and the 'language of
metaphysics'. The trouble is that this conception led Heidegger to
some completely grotesque remarks. He claims in a lecture in 1949,
for example, in one of very few remarks that refer to the Holocaust,
that: 'Agriculture is now the motorized industry of food-production,

essentially the same as the fabrication of corpses in gas chambers and extermination camps, the same as the blockading and starvation of countries, the same as the fabrication of hydrogen bombs' (cit. in Adorno 2002: 429) – they all derive from 'metaphysics' as the modern subject's domination of the object.[2] Circumscribing a 'language of metaphysics' is as metaphysical as what it seeks to circumscribe: what language does one use to identify such a language? *DoE* never says anything remotely resembling the passage just cited, but it involves some structures of thought that are not wholly different from Heidegger's. In later texts, like *Negative Dialectics*, Adorno is less prone – though by no means immune – to undifferentiated totalizations.

One more effective response to the suspicion of the effects of identification is to look for those aspects of human production which resist being subsumed into existing forms of thought and action. Adorno's *Aesthetic Theory* (1970) uses this idea to arrive at some very insightful approaches to art and modernity. However much artists may seek to produce something original, they are always also subject to the objective pressures of the world they inhabit. Adorno argues that these pressures emerge in the *formal* difficulties artists face, rather than being the direct theme of their works. The important artists take on the formal challenge in a radical way, rather than seeking compromise. In consequence, their achievements convey more about the nature of social reality than those of artists who directly address social issues, rather than concentrating on the formal problems of medium in which they work. These formal problems are, he suggests, in fact 'sedimented' historical content. This means the key artists are the radical innovators, like Schoenberg, Beckett and Kafka. They confront the state of their art in the world of delusion, in the name of an art that seeks to be true. This idea is linked to Adorno's concerns about language and identification. Art, particularly music, is seen as hinting at the kind of language which would avoid repressive identification. At the same time, *Aesthetic Theory* offers constant reminders that art cannot simply escape the consequences of the social pressures under which it is produced.

The basic pattern of Adorno's thinking is to seek ways out of dilemmas at the same time as revealing why there is no final way out of those dilemmas, at least in terms of contemporary ways of thinking. The desire to avoid reductive identification leads Adorno to the notion of the 'thought model': 'the model gets to what is specific and to what is more than specific' in its object (ibid. 39) but it does not subsume it into a general concept. His crucial idea is of keeping

---

2 Only the remark about agriculture appeared in the published version of the text.

thought open to the possibility of new experience, rather than seeking to control and reduce experience to familiar concepts. At the same time, one has to try to see the general significance of what the model can reveal. Philosophical thinking is, Adorno maintains, equivalent to 'thinking in models' (ibid.): models are not final theories, but means of explaining and solving problems that are always open to revision. *Negative Dialectics* is, like much of Adorno's work, impossible to sum up as solely a series of arguments. The book itself enacts at its best the kind of thinking it proposes: any apparently definitive statement turns out to be relativized by further statements. The idea is that all fixed concepts are likely to block access to other aspects of their object. Adorno does not think that one can get by without relatively stable concepts, but the possibility of their becoming obstructions to the truth is perennial, and philosophy must build this into the way it investigates the world. The interpretation of Adorno's both frustrating and illuminating work is still an object of great controversy. As we shall see in the Conclusion, contemporary German philosophy is in many respects still dealing with Adorno's legacy, and with the legacy of the notion of a Critical Theory, in the light of the catastrophe of the Nazi period.

SUGGESTIONS FOR FURTHER READING

Bartram, G. (ed.) (1994) 'Walter Benjamin in the Postmodern', special issue of *New Comparison* 18 (autumn). *Collection of essays on major themes in Benjamin's work.*

Benhabib, S. (1986) *Critique, Norm and Utopia: A Study of the Foundations of Critical Theory* (New York: Columbia University Press). *Important philosophical study of Critical Theory.*

Benhabib, S., Bonss, W. and McCole, J. (eds) (1993) *On Max Horkheimer: New Perspectives* (London: MIT Press). *Essays on Horkheimer, whose work has often been neglected in recent research.*

Buck-Morss, S. (1977) *The Origin of Negative Dialectics: Theodor W. Adorno, Walter Benjamin, and the Frankfurt Institute* (New York: Free Press). *Historical account of the sources of key ideas in Critical Theory.*

Buck-Morss, S. (1989) *Dialectics of Seeing: Walter Benjamin and the Arcades Project* (Cambridge, MA: Harvard University Press). *Study of Benjamin's unfinished major work on Paris of the nineteenth century.*

Connerton, P. (1980) *The Tragedy of Enlightenment: An Essay on the Frankfurt School* (Cambridge: Cambridge University Press). *Readable study of core ideas in Critical Theory.*

Geuss, R. (1981) *The Idea of a Critical Theory* (Cambridge: Cambridge University Press). *Rather narrow and unsympathetic examination of the possibility of a Critical Theory, though it does offer some significant objections.*

Held, D. (1980) *Introduction to Critical Theory: Horkheimer to Habermas* (Berkeley: University of California Press). *Wide-ranging historical and theoretical account of Critical Theory.*

Jay, M. (1973) *The Dialectical Imagination: A History of the Frankfurt School and the Institute of Social Research, 1923–1950* (Boston: Little, Brown). *Classic historical study of the development of the Frankfurt School by major scholar.*

Jay, M. (1984) *Adorno* (London: Fontana). *A readable introduction to the thought of Adorno.*

Reijen, W. van. (1992) *Adorno: An Introduction* (Philadelphia: Pennbridge). *Lively introduction to Adorno.*

Roberts, D. (1991) *Art and Enlightenment: Aesthetic Theory after Adorno* (Lincoln and London: University of Nebraska Press). *Thoughtful examination of important topic.*

Rose, G. (1978) *The Melancholy Science: An Introduction to the Thought of Theodor W. Adorno* (London: Macmillan). *Demanding but important study of Adorno's work.*

Wiggershaus, R. (1994) *The Frankfurt School: Its History, Theories, and Political Significance* (Cambridge, MA: MIT Press). *Detailed history of the Frankfurt School based on extensive research.*

Wolin, Richard (1982) *Walter Benjamin: An Aesthetic of Redemption* (Berkeley: University of California Press). *Accessible study of major themes in Benjamin's work.*

CONCLUSION

Philosophy and Modernity

It is probably no longer useful to talk of specifically German philosophy. Most of the history of philosophy has relied on cross-fertilization between national traditions, with the particular nature of each tradition influencing the development of philosophical ideas. Now, however, as modern communications make intellectual traditions ever more permeable, and as the English language comes to dominate the philosophical world, national traditions play a much less significant role with regard to substantive philosophical issues. The most striking evidence of this is the fact that at a time when philosophers in America from the Frege- and Carnap-influenced analytical tradition, like John McDowell and Robert Brandom, have turned to the Kantian and Hegelian tradition, many German philosophers have abandoned their own tradition in order to pursue philosophy in the Anglo-American analytical style. We shall return to this odd situation later: for the moment it is important to see how it arose.

Philosophy in Western Germany after the war is initially dominated by the influence of Heidegger, despite his being excluded for a time from an official academic post. This dominance of a figure so compromised by his membership of the Nazi party has to do with Heidegger's undeniable philosophical importance, with the complex reactions of the German population to military, political and ethical catastrophe, and with the division of the country into a Western capitalist state and a socialist state under Soviet control.[1] Similar

---

1 The question of philosophy in the GDR is so distorted by the Party's influence that it cannot be usefully examined here. The valuable work tended to be philological and historical, making available texts from the history of German philosophy. Work was done by dissidents, but this had little effect beyond the confines of the GDR.

cases to Heidegger's were common in many areas of West German public life, which became devoted to an incredibly rapid rebuilding of the country immediately after the defeat, with little real reflection on what had taken place. The energy that went into the rebuilding seems to have resulted from sublimated guilt and the concomitant need to 'move on'. Despite the moves to 'de-Nazify' the Federal Republic after the war, much of academic and other institutional life therefore continued to be controlled by those who had at least been compromised during the Nazi period, if they had not been active Nazis. The reckoning with the trauma, as happens so often – something similar occurs after the First World War – takes place years later. It does so in often oblique ways which are both reflected in and affected by the most important philosophical developments.

It took until the student movement of the late 1960s and early 1970s for a real issue to be made of the continuing role in German public life of ex-Nazis and Nazi fellow-travellers. The criticisms of the student movement were occasioned by suspicion of the new affluence of a society that had not long ago been morally, politically and economically bankrupt. The philosophical focus of the student movement was the Marxist tradition, including the Frankfurt School, which had been suppressed in the Nazi period and neglected in the immediate post-war years. Marxist ideas were rather crudely employed to question the legitimacy of capitalist economies in the West which were involved in supporting repressive regimes in the Third World. Such questioning was supposed to lead to revolutionary change. However, it has since become clear that much of the energy invested in the idea of revolution really depended upon feelings to do with the failure to come to terms with the Nazi period. The fact that the often very repressive German Democratic Republic claimed to represent the legacy of Marx also did not make things easy for those in the West who advocated revolutionary politics. During the period from the late 1960s onwards the institutional dominance of Heidegger and of existential philosophy was broken by an insistence on attention to the socio-political effects of philosophy. This led to the renewed influence of Frankfurt School Critical Theory, to a productive questioning of the traditions of German philosophy, and, eventually, to a growth of interest in the tradition of analytical philosophy which had been forced out of Germany by the Nazis.

The dominant figure in the initial criticisms of philosophy's failure to engage with the historical world that had led to Auschwitz was Adorno. However, Adorno alienated some of those who had been influenced by his work because of his refusal to support the student movement's revolutionary aims. Those who sought a shortcut to

revolutionary political action via a supposedly Marxist analysis saw
Adorno as failing to give a clear political direction. The failure of the
more extravagant aims of the student movement in many ways vin-
dicated Adorno's stance. The successes of the movement in fact lay
more in the liberalizing effect on German society of the questions it
posed than in its active attempts at revolutionary change. Adorno's
work did, though, also give rise to doubts even among those politically closer to him, like his student Habermas. Adorno's lasting
importance lies in his consistent refusal to accept easy answers to the
critical questions he posed concerning modernity, and German
history, society and culture. However, some of the basis of this refusal
brings him, despite his repeated attacks on him, quite close to
Heidegger. What is at issue here is the relationship between
philosophy and modernity.

The differing versions, from Feuerbach and Marx, to Heidegger, to
the Vienna Circle, of the idea of the end of philosophy all depend upon
an interpretation of the relationship between philosophy and the
natural sciences. Adorno's antagonism to 'positivism' derives from his
sense that philosophy which gives primacy to the natural sciences
seeks to exclude questions involving criticism of the socio-political
and cultural status quo. This antagonism, which was not present in his
earlier work, culminated in the 1960s in his contribution to what is
known as the 'Positivism Dispute in German Sociology'.

This was a debate between, among others, Adorno and Habermas
on the Critical Theory side, and Karl Popper and Hans Albert, the
Critical Rationalists, about the status and role of the social sciences
(see Adorno 1991; see also Dahms 1998). Adorno claims that an
adherence to 'positivism', which he erroneously attributes to Popper,
involves a necessary link between identifying social facts by empirical research and legitimating those facts by failing to offer a critical
perspective on them. The positivist limitation of truth to what is
empirically verifiable narrows the scope of enquiry because it cannot
deal with the evaluative nature of social issues. However, his oppo-
nents need not be interpreted as arguing that empirical social enquiry
excludes a critical perspective. Indeed, they actually share Adorno's
rejection of the logical empiricism's verificationism. This situation
in the 1960s echoes what already happened in the 1930s, when
Horkheimer had attacked Neurath's philosophical position, even
though their social and political aims were often very similar. Adorno
now attacks Popper, even though Popper's view that science can only
ever falsify theories, and never finally legitimate them, involves a
refusal to accept definitive knowledge claims which Adorno shares.
The degree of antagonism directed by Adorno at all philosophy that

he regards as science-oriented – and in this he includes pragmatism – is largely a result of his most questionable ideas from *Dialectic of Enlightenment*. This antagonism damaged the development of progressive philosophy in Germany after the War by creating divisions between thinkers whose desire for social justice was generally more important than their philosophical differences.

Adorno too often blurs the distinction between scientism and the justifiable insistence – which can be shared by any number of philosophical positions – that explanatory scientific theories have real predictive power which can be used to make life more tolerable. He does so on the basis of his claim that domination of the other by subject is at the root of the ills of modernity. It is this claim which brings Adorno closest to the later Heidegger and to those influenced by him. A search for the root of these ills is evidently not misguided: the Holocaust and the dropping of the atom bomb are events of such enormity that philosophy has to try to find a way of responding to them. The main questions for Adorno's approach are:

1 Must the subject really be thought of solely in these terms?
2 Does the diagnosis offer any practical ways of responding to those ills, as opposed to inducing a sense that they are beyond what can be influenced by human action?

It is significant in this connection that *DoE* becomes much more popular, especially among younger thinkers, after the failure of the revolutionary aims of the student movement, and in relation to the growing popularity in Germany from the 1970s onwards of Nietzsche- and Heidegger-influenced French thinkers, such as Michel Foucault, Jean-François Lyotard and Jacques Derrida. These thinkers often take up themes which are very close to the ideas of Adorno, even when they are not aware of his work. The concept of the 'postmodern', associated in particular with Lyotard, is, for example, linked to the idea of the philosophical 'death of the subject'. Heidegger claimed that modernity derives from Descartes, for whom the 'certainty of all being and all truth is founded on the self-consciousness of the single ego: *ego cogito ergo sum*'. This assumption leads Lyotard to a general characterization of modernity as the subject's attempt to control or exclude the other, in the name of liberating itself from the threats posed by nature and from its own self-imposed constraints. The result of the failure of what he terms the 'grand narrative' of the self-liberation of the subject are diverse forms of oppression in relation to race, gender and other issues. Lyotard claims that reason has an inherently terroristic element because it always excludes what does not fit its frameworks. He therefore argues that competing ways of talking about the world can now no longer rely on the 'modern' search for a general 'discourse of legitimation'. That discourse would involve imposing identity on what should be seen as resistant to any kind of definitive identification. The proximity of this view to *DoE*'s Nietzsche-influenced account of Enlightenment is evident. Adorno, however, still retains a residual faith in the power of reason, though it is sometimes unclear just what account of reason he wishes to defend. It is the need to establish a more positive conception of reason which motivates many of those in Germany influenced by Adorno.

In *DoE* the relationship between subject and object was predominantly instrumental, as though human rationality were *solely* concerned with controlling the other through technological and political power. Similarly, Heidegger maintained that Western metaphysics culminates with Nietzsche: from Kant's account of the subject's spontaneity to Nietzsche's doctrine of the Will to Power, the metaphysical ground of human knowledge is thought of in terms of subjectivity as the will which asserts itself against the other. Heidegger already saw one response to metaphysics in poetic language. By 'letting things be', poetic language works in a different way from the 'language of metaphysics' which underlies natural science's 'subjectification of being'. Adorno seeks what he terms a 'mimetic' rationality. This is not based on identification of the object in general terms, and he finds it in art's ability to relate to things in non-conceptual ways, for example when music evokes the contours of an emotion. Despite offering important ways of questioning some aspects of instrumental rationality, neither of these conceptions results in an account of modernity which allows for the possibility that there have been changes for the better in modernity that depend on specifically modern forms of rationality.

What is required, then, is a modern conception of reason which (1) acknowledges the failure to ground reason in subjectivity, (2) is still able to offer criticisms of the misuse of technology, but which (3) also takes account of the ways in which the natural sciences can make life more tolerable for those who have access to their benefits. Aspects of Adorno's work move in this direction, but too often he succumbs to the exaggerations resulting from his totalizing verdict on modernity.

In post-war German philosophy there are, broadly, two critical responses to suspicions about the role of subjectivity in modern philosophy and its perceived links to the ills of modernity. One response contends that the model of philosophy which makes explaining the relationship between subject and object the aim of philosophy is mistaken. It therefore seeks an alternative model based on 'intersubjectivity', where truth depends on the shared medium of language, rather than being the product of the individual subject. It is, above all, Habermas, the leading figure in the 'Second Generation' of the Frankfurt School, who attempts to develop a model of rationality and modernity that is more open to the positive advances of modernity. Certain important aspects of Habermas's mature conception develop under the influence of Karl-Otto Apel (1922–), and of Heidegger's pupils Hans-Georg Gadamer (1900–2002) and Ernst Tugendhat (1930–). By changing the focus on language from the concern with how propositions represent reality to understanding language as 'communicative action', Habermas tries to avoid the traps into which the Vienna Circle fell.

The other response argues that the Heideggerian view of the subject is inadequate to a proper understanding of subjectivity in modern philosophy. This response shares certain ideas with the first response – it too wishes to establish an account of rationality that is not prone to the same problems as Adorno and Heidegger – but is prepared to keep open questions which Habermas regards as belonging to a superseded model of philosophy. Dieter Henrich (1927–) and Manfred Frank (1947–) question whether the model of subjectivity as the ground of philosophy really encompasses all the ways in which subjectivity has been thought about in Western philosophy (see e.g. Henrich 1982; Frank 1991). They ask whether even a version of the linguistic turn, like that of Habermas, which does not rely on the notion of language as the mind's means of representing the objective world, can obviate all the philosophical/metaphysical problems concerning consciousness and self-consciousness. In doing so, they suggest new perspectives on the German Idealist and Romantic traditions which offer a counter to Habermas's claim to have moved beyond these traditions. These are only a few of the significant philosophers working in Germany in the last thirty years or so. However, they are probably the most influential. I shall concentrate on Gadamer and Habermas because their work has had the most impact on recent philosophy and social thought.[2]

---

2   I shall not be dealing with the work of the later Wittgenstein because its location is essentially Anglo-Saxon. Wittgenstein's later work now has a considerable influence in Germany, but this is a relatively recent phenomenon.

Hans-Georg Gadamer

As we saw, Heidegger's work encountered considerable opposition in Germany during the 1960s and 1970s, only to have interest in it renewed by its new reception in France by Derrida, Foucault and others. His pupil Gadamer's major work, *Truth and Method*, on the other hand, has sustained its influence from its appearance in 1960 until today, despite the changes in ideological climate. Gadamer belongs on the conservative side of the political spectrum, but his concentration on dialogue and on the importance of art to philosophy make many of his ideas sympathetic even to those who question his conservatism. Although, like Heidegger, he sees his thought as bound up with the ancient Greek philosophical tradition, his is a more humanistic and scholarly approach to philosophy, which pays more attention to the demands of philology. Gadamer's role in the Nazi period, when he worked at Leipzig University, could hardly be termed heroic, but it did not involve the kind of support of the Nazis that irredeemably sullied Heidegger's reputation. After the war he demonstrated an exemplary commitment to intercultural dialogue and had a vital effect in salvaging key aspects of German philosophy for the new democracy in the West. He did so while pursuing themes developed by Husserl and Heidegger which lead him to a reformulation of the notion of hermeneutics.

Like Heidegger, Gadamer questions the modern concentration on truth as the sole preserve of the natural sciences, regarding understanding as more fundamental than the specific forms of explanation provided by the sciences. His task is to 'seek out the experience of truth which exceeds [*übersteigt*] the realm of control of scientific method . . . and to interrogate it as to its own legitimation' (1975: xxvii). This is because 'it is not right to separate the question of art from the question of truth and to deprive art of all the knowledge it can communicate to us' (1993: 203). The problem, as thinkers from Dilthey onwards realized, is the status of this non-scientific knowledge. The key factor here for Gadamer is the understanding of language. Although the natural sciences are indispensable to human survival, 'this does not mean that people would be able to solve the problems that face us, peaceful coexistence of peoples and the preservation of the balance of nature, with science as such. It is obvious that not mathematics but the linguistic nature of people is the basis of human civilisation' (ibid. 342). As a member of the tradition which begins with Hamann and Herder, Gadamer is concerned with the ways in which concentration on the sciences can obscure the primary dimension of language as that which enables us to share a world. He sees language in terms of 'tradition', which takes the form of 'effective historical consciousness'. In speaking and thinking we are subject to the effects of a language and of a world of which we can never become fully aware. These effects occur well before we can reflect on them and so can never be fully grasped by our reflection. Our being is always more than we can know and explain, because we cannot step outside the world which has determined what we have become. If we think we can gain this external perspective, we will make metaphysical claims to an authority no real person can attain. Gadamer therefore questions the role of the subject in modern philosophy in much the same way as Heidegger. Because it is 'historically effected and determined', the subject cannot serve as a foundation for philosophy.

The point of the title *Truth and Method* is to suggest that the natural sciences rely on rule-bound methods which predetermine how the world can appear in them. Art, in contrast, is seen in terms of a 'happening' of tradition which transcends the contingent responses of individual subjects. Art's truth emerges by its being transmitted in differing contexts and giving rise to ever new kinds of understanding that involve a 'fusion of horizons' between the recipient and the work of art. Think, for example, of the way in which Greek tragedy is understood before and after the Romantics revived the idea of Dionysus and Nietzsche published the *Birth of Tragedy*: from being part of the idealized Platonic 'glory that was Greece', tragedy becomes the route to a new modern confrontation with the horrors of existence. Understanding of art comes about by being affected by a work and having one's horizons altered, rather than by being able to state definitively what the work means. This is an ongoing process with no necessary end. Rather than the history of different understandings of works of art and texts being seen as an continual history of error and distortion by the concerns of the present, these understandings are regarded as what a work of art *is*, namely not an object, but something which 'happens' in time in real cultures.

Gadamer makes a link between the idea of natural science as the subject's means of control over the object and the rise of *aesthetics*. Both are interpreted as part of the modern subject's attempt to arrogate to itself the right to determine truth while ignoring tradition. In the aesthetics inaugurated by Kant's *Critique of Judgement*, as Gadamer understands it – his interpretation is highly questionable – the work of art is reduced to the contingencies of the taste of its recipients, rather than being seen as a 'happening of truth' which transcends those contingencies. In the same way as a real dialogue involves the ability to leave behind one's own interests and ideas in order to open oneself to those of another person, real engagement with art takes place when one allows the truth of the work to happen to one, rather than trying to control it. This means that 'understanding is never a subjective relationship towards a given "object", but belongs rather to the effective history, and that means: to the being of that which is understood' (1975. xix). The human subject is therefore not the real subject of art: the work is itself the 'subject' whose truth transcends the contingency of its recipients. This questionable, 'reifying' inversion of the notion of the subject occurs in various ways in Gadamer's work. Equally contentiously, Gadamer does not accept that one understanding of a work is better than another, and thinks 'it is enough to say that one understands *differently, if one understands at all*' (ibid. 280).

This claim leads to a crucial issue that underlies many of the debates in modern German and other philosophy. The decisive contrast is between (1) the idea that truth is primarily 'world-disclosure' which can be understood via the experience of how art lets things be seen in ever new ways, and (2) the idea that truth relies on the fundamental possibility of assenting to or rejecting propositions. Gadamer adheres to (1) because of his view of language and tradition, which are always prior to the 'method' which determines scientific thinking. He does not adequately allow, however, for the possibility that the world-disclosure present in understanding and language-use, and claims to intersubjective validity based on the assent to and rejection of propositions, are not wholly separate. The point is to understand their interaction in an effective manner. If one fails to do this, establishing a critical perspective on cultural forms becomes impossible. The fact is that Gadamer is largely silent on how one is to judge when it is that truth happens in art and when it does not, and this is connected to his counter-intuitive claim that there are only different understandings, not better ones. Apel sums up the difference at issue here in the title of an essay on Gadamer: 'Regulative Idea or Happening of Truth?' (1998). Gadamer's idea of the happening of truth leaves too little space for a critical perspective based on the awareness that tradition can be distorted and can lead to the obscuring of truth. The problem with claims about what obscures truth is, on the other hand, that the location from which the obscuring can be identified is one that modern philosophy has great trouble in specifying. This gives rise to the notion that truth is a regulative idea, rather than something which can be said to be directly present to us. The difficulties Habermas encounters in establishing the place from which critical claims can be made highlight some major issues in contemporary philosophy.

Jürgen Habermas

Habermas's achievement cannot be properly assessed if he is regarded simply as a philosopher. In many respects he has been, and remains, the exemplary intellectual figure in the German public sphere since the 1970s, as social theorist, legal theorist, social critic, political actor and as a philosopher concerned to advocate a new direction for German thought after the Nazi period. Adorno and Heidegger can be regarded as leading, in albeit very different ways, to a move away from philosophically oriented analyses of political and social life that can have practical consequences. Habermas has shown that this is not a necessary move for critical thinkers, even in the light of the Holocaust and the horrors of twentieth-century history.[3]

Habermas's doctoral thesis was on Schelling and looked at the relationship between German Idealism's attempt to grasp the absolute and the ways in which history undermines such attempts. The dissertation therefore already signalled his interest in the 'Young Hegelian' historicized perspective on philosophy (see chapter 5), which he has adhered to for most of his career. His first major published work was *The Structural Transformation of the Public Sphere* (1962), an examination of the emergence of the notions of 'the public' and of 'public opinion', which play a vital role in the development of democracy that accompanies the decline of feudalism. This book testifies to his fundamental concern with issues of communication and legitimation.

Knowledge and Human Interests (first published in 1968) begins with the problems of epistemological reflection we considered in Kant and German Idealism, as a way of trying to arrive at a critical theory of the role of knowledge in modern societies. Here Habermas makes the distinction between instrumental and communicative action that will be fundamental to his work. Under the influence of Apel, he looks to the American pragmatist tradition for alternatives to the subject–object model of transcendental philosophy. Pragma-

3   This is somewhat unfair to Adorno, whose work on questions of contemporary cultural politics is often equally engaged. The difference from Habermas is that Adorno's expressly philosophical work does not always point in the direction of intervention in the present, for the reasons we have seen. Adorno the acute commentator on contemporary life and Adorno the relentless, totalizing critic of modernity often seem hard to reconcile.

tism does not aim at an account of the nature of thought's representation of reality, but rather at an account of human action as the primary way in which we relate to the world. As Apel was one of the first to point out, pragmatism can be connected to German philosophy via the earlier Heidegger's account of being in the world, as well as via the later Wittgenstein's concentration on language as a 'form of life'. In pragmatism, knowledge is generated by social practice. Knowledge is reducible neither to a biological explanation in terms of adaptation to an environment nor to a purely theoretical explanation in epistemological terms like those of Kant. Thinking of knowledge in this way offers a way of rejecting scientism and of establishing forms of legitimation which cannot be subordinated to the 'positivist' methods of the natural sciences.

In some respects, what Habermas seeks is the kind of integration of different aspects of modernity that Hegel had sought in his system. The difference is that Habermas no longer thinks he can rely on a pre-existing philosophical principle of unification. Instead, he tries to show how competing, historically generated forms of human interest can be reconciled. He outlines what he terms, with Apel, a 'transcendental pragmatism'. Pragmatic 'conditions of possibility' are not forms of thought, but 'structures of experience and action' (Habermas 1973: 407). Arguments about validity are carried out in social life via these structures. Without such shared structures it is unclear how disputes about validity could arise at all. The structures do not give priority to the natural sciences because there is no privileged access to the objects of scientific knowledge that can be validated outside of communication about those objects. The crucial factor in all claims to validity is therefore the social process of argumentation. This process necessarily involves questions of truth which cannot be accommodated in a merely instrumental theory of interest-based knowledge, of the kind which would be open to the objections one can make against *DoE*. One can, Habermas suggests against a Nietzschean approach, argue for the objectivity of a claim even if it is against one's interests.

Knowledge and Human Interests also uses Freud's account of the role of repression in the formation of the individual psyche to develop an analysis of how communication can become systematically distorted within a society. Mental pathologies are bound up with ways in which the sufferer comes unconsciously to misinterpret everyday communication. Communication can also be distorted at a collective level, for example in the form of racist talk generated by the mechanism of projection. We saw Horkheimer and Adorno use this idea to understand anti-Semitism, and its roots are already present in Feuerbach's critique of religion as projection. Habermas tries to compare 'the world-historical process of socialization with the socialization of the individual' (ibid. 335). The comparison is supposed to establish that individual neuroses generated by trauma and repression correspond to forms of compulsion in society – of the kind present, for example, in religious laws – that are generated by a society's lack of real control over nature. The illusions generated by the repression of drives are supposed to be the source of ideological beliefs and of 'false consciousness'. At the same time these illusions can become the motivation of social change.

Habermas comes to reject this conception because identifying 'false consciousness' relies on a norm of 'true consciousness' which is impossible to specify. Differing social contexts involve differing criteria of what is merely illusory and of what can be justified. Gadamer's argument that the idea of an objective viewpoint from which to criticize forms of communication and interaction in particular cultures is metaphysical, because it presents itself as being outside any culture, makes Habermas aware of the need for a revised approach. His approach has, then, to take account of the inherently situated nature of communication. The difficulty is that he thinks a critical perspective on distorted social forms is vital, because it is essential to a notion of rationality. The tension Habermas faces, between the need to understand local practices of justification and communication, of the kind Gadamer sees in terms of tradition, and the need to establish more universal critical criteria of modern rationality, is central to his monumental *Theory of Communicative Action* (1981) (*TCA*).

Habermas regards his work from this time onwards as part of what he calls 'post-metaphysical thinking'. He understands 'metaphysics' in terms of the 'reflexive' structure we saw in Hegel and German Idealism, in which 'cognitive reason finds itself once again in the rationally structured world' (1988: 42).[4] There are three essential elements in the farewell to metaphysics in this sense.

1   The modern sciences' successful concentration on detailed empirical research into the natural world invalidates attempts like those in German Idealism to establish an a priori system based on necessities built into thinking.
2   The idea in Kant's transcendental philosophy that there must be synthetic a priori forms of judgement is rejected on the grounds

---

4   Herbert Schnädelbach (1992) has suggested that a more apt term would therefore be 'post-Idealist' thinking.

that what is regarded as a priori changes with history. This is because the linguistic structures on which judgements depend are themselves part of history, not prior to it. The subject–object paradigm of philosophy is also invalidated by the role of language in the constitution of what counts as objective knowledge.

3   The dominant ways in which we understand the world are practical: theories are, in the main, generated and confirmed by active engagement with the material world, not merely by abstract reflection.

Habermas arrives at his most influential conceptions by seeking to move away from what he terms the 'paradigm of subject philosophy' or the 'philosophy of consciousness'. This paradigm assumes that the task of philosophy is to establish what belongs on the subject- and what belongs on the object-side, and then to show how they connect. Kant's transcendental subject which guarantees 'an *antecedent* unity in the multiplicity of appearances' (ibid. 43) exemplifies what he rejects. Habermas's argument relates to Heidegger's claim that from Descartes, to Hegel's assertion that 'the substance is subject', to Husserl's search for the 'principle of all principles', the 'concern [*Sache*] of philosophy . . . is subjectivity' (Heidegger 1969: 70). The route out of the paradigm for Habermas is, though, different from Heidegger's. For Habermas, the attempt to get to the bottom of subjectivity leads to a futile search for a grounding principle (such as the Will) which is likely to end up mystifying the nature of the subject. Consequently, he maintains that 'everything which deserves the name subjectivity' (1988: 34) actually depends upon socialization into the intersubjective language and practices of a society. This view has been effectively questioned by Frank and Henrich in particular, who insist that there are kinds of awareness which are not linguistic, upon which understanding of language depends.

The biggest challenge Habermas faces is to develop a conception of rationality while not relying on the metaphysical assumption that reason has an extra-temporal existence in what Kant referred to as the 'intelligible' realm (see chapter 1). Reason has instead to be located in concrete human practices which are historically contingent. The problem is, though, that if reason does not transcend its location in specific socio-historical contexts, it is not clear what can legitimate claims to rationality. Habermas argues that Horkheimer and Adorno's conception of the subject was limited to the subject of means–end 'instrumental rationality'. What is missing is an account of 'communicative rationality'. The subject's rationality is not just exercised in terms of achieving practical goals (what Kant saw in

terms of 'hypothetical imperatives'). These goals must be legitimated
to other subjects in society. This legitimation depends upon shared
structures of everyday communication which transcend the subjective awareness of those employing them. These structures are
transcendental because they are the condition of possibility of establishing validity and legitimacy in secular societies. However, they are
also contingent, because they arise in historically specific contexts. It
is this which creates the tension between more universal forms of
legitimation and more local forms. The natural sciences demand universal validity, whereas ethical and aesthetic issues may sometimes
justifiably be dealt with in local terms. How are the different kinds of
validity to be related without falling back into the scientistic assumption that only the natural sciences can justifiably claim validity for
their assertions?

   TCA is not intended solely as a philosophy book: its concerns are
in fact primarily sociological. It wishes to look at the 'conditions of
rationality' (1981: 16) in modern secularized societies. The approach
is, though, deeply influenced by the Anglo-American analytical tradition of philosophy, whose importance both Apel and Tugendhat
brought home to Habermas in the 1970s. This focus became a major
factor in the contemporary attention in Germany to the analytical
style of philosophy. The key to understanding *TCA* lies in the differing ways in which 'communicative action' can be construed. The
point of the term is to get away from the idea that language should
be understood as representing the objective world. This distances
Habermas from the tradition of Frege and the early Wittgenstein.
Language functions instead primarily as a way of coming to an understanding with other people in order to coordinate and legitimate
actions. To this extent, language might seem, in the light of Nietzsche,
inevitably connected to power, its main function being strategic, as
the means for getting what one wants. However, Habermas refuses
to regard communication as the same as action undertaken in the
pursuit of goals. Language has a further dimension which he thinks
takes it outside of the means–ends relationship. He therefore opposes
those who wish to reduce communication to being just a means for
the conscious or unconscious exercise of power. The question is how
strong the arguments for a conception of reason not based on power
can be. It is here that some of the main objections to Habermas are
located.

   Habermas argues that the very ability to understand another's
communicative acts already involves fundamental aspects of rationality. The fact that one enters into an argument entails a 'telos of
agreement': 'Coming to understanding inhabits human language as a

telos' (ibid. 387). Involvement in argument therefore need not be merely strategic, because one can be persuaded by the 'peculiarly forceless force of the better argument' (ibid. 52–3) into agreeing with something with which one initially disagreed. This force depends upon commitments which transcend one's own interests, suggesting something like what Kant intended with his idea of the 'kingdom of ends', in which others must not be regarded just as the means to one's own ends. In *TCA* Habermas uses the notion of the 'ideal speech situation', which functions as a regulative idea, to suggest a perspective on communication in which the search for truth is not distorted by strategic interests. However, he later drops this notion: even if one believes in the ideal of non-coercive argument, one cannot claim to know when it is taking place, so the notion can do no real work. Habermas does not, though, give up the assumption that rationality involves a commitment to norms, such as the preparedness to acknowledge that one is wrong. He formalizes his conception in terms derived from J. L. Austin's 'speech-act theory' from *How to Do Things with Words*, which is concerned with the 'illocutionary' aspect of language. The illocutionary aspect of an utterance is not apparent in the overt propositional content of the utterance. It is rather what is meant by an utterance as a 'performative' act in social life, where people say things in order to achieve effects in specific contexts. Claims to knowledge of the objective world are not prioritized in this view. They only form one element of communicative action.

Following Kant's division of the three Critiques between the cognitive, ethical and aesthetic, and Weber's view of modern rationality, Habermas sees modernity in terms of the differentiation between the three value-spheres, of 'science, morality and art' (ibid. 202), which 'each follows their own logic' (ibid. 234). These spheres involve different kinds of 'criticizable claims to validity', namely 'propositional truth, normative rightness, and subjective truthfulness' (ibid. 114). Habermas does not seek a foundation of validity for each of these spheres, of the kind logical positivism sought in empirically verifiable propositions. Instead, he concentrates on how claims to validity can be 'cashed in' in these different areas of human activity. The cashing in of claims is only possible via communicative action because there is no direct, extra-linguistic access to any area of human concern, of the kind sought by 'the philosophy of consciousness'. Even the empiricist claim that our knowledge must derive from sense-data can only be legitimated by *argument* about how this claim could be made valid, not by the circular appeal to the 'given' in the form of sense-data. Habermas proposes a version of the consensus theory of truth, on the assumption that the best chance for objectivity arises from unfettered, non-coercive communication. The problem with consensus theories is, though, that a universal consensus can be false. Even if communication were not constrained by strategic interests, it is not guaranteed that it would lead to the truth. In consequence, Habermas insists that there is no alternative to a thoroughgoing 'fallibilism', because we can always be mistaken even about the apparently most certain truths.

In order to account for the undeniable fact of understanding in social life, Habermas employs a version of Husserl's notion of the life-world. This constitutes the horizon of shared understandings that must form the background of any particular piece of communication. Communicative action relies on many historically established, unexamined consensuses if meaningful disagreement is to be possible. The idea is close to Donald Davidson's 'principle of charity', which states that we must assume that most of what anyone says is true, because we otherwise would not know they were speaking a language at all, let alone understand when we were disagreeing with them. The background knowledge of the life-world is, however, 'not knowledge at all in the strict sense' (Habermas 1992: 39), because it is not fallible and open to debate as to whether it can be validly asserted. This limitation clashes with Gadamer's idea that truth occurs in any domain of human communication that discloses the world. The difference between conceptions of truth as world-disclosure and truth as propositional assertion here leads to a still highly contested problem. Everyday knowledge in the life-world, of the kind we rely on all the time, seems to have its own validity, even though it may not stand up to scientific scrutiny. How is philosophy to deal both with the background knowledge that is, as we saw in Husserl and Heidegger, required for scientific activity to be possible in the first place, *and* with scientific knowledge that tends to *contradict* background knowledge? For Habermas, philosophy must rely on understanding that is grounded in the life-world. That is the point of the notion of communicative action, which analyses what always already happens in everyday communication, rather than relying on timeless a priori structures. The very status of philosophical claims would thus seem to be problematic because they are rooted in something which cannot be made wholly transparent to us. Truth seems to be both part of everyday communication and yet at the same time ultimately beyond it. How is this contradiction to be reconciled?

The basic difficulty is that for beliefs to be asserted as true they must be justified, but fallibilism maintains that there can be no end to justification. Habermas claims that 'It is the goal of justifications to find out a truth which stretches beyond all justifications' (1999: 53).

This suggests that there must be some other way of arriving at truth, beyond justification, but he does not specify what it is. He backs up his claim with the further claim that the 'presupposition of a world which is objective and independent of our descriptions' (ibid. 249) is required if the difference between opinion and unconditional truth is to be sustained. However, he also admits that this presupposition is only 'formal', i.e. it is a regulative idea we use in communication, not something we know to exist. Were it to be assumed to exist, he would have to hold to a version of 'metaphysical realism' – the idea that the truth of the world exists absolutely independently of whether we can know it, and that all our beliefs could therefore be false. Accepting such a theory would invalidate a major aim of the theory of communicative action, namely of getting away from metaphysical dilemmas of this nature, which have no necessary effect on what we do when we establish knowledge. These issues are still the subject of considerable debate, and it is not clear that Habermas has a wholly plausible response to the difficulties.

However, the importance of Habermas's work lies less in his technical contributions to such philosophical questions than in the ways he links the questions to the modern social world. The vital issue in this case is how questions of truth relate to Habermas's conception of modernity. The concrete social effects of the difficulties over the nature of truth become apparent in the question of how the value-spheres relate to each other and how the results of activity in these spheres impact upon the life-world. Whatever difficulties Habermas's theory may encounter, it still offers ways of investigating the issues which avoid Adorno's conclusions about the inherently repressive nature of modernity. In pre-modern societies the spheres which become differentiated in modernity are not separate, so that the validity of knowledge can, for example, be established on the basis of the authority of someone with a superior social rank, rather than on the basis of public argument and proof. Pre-modern societies identify 'the linguistically constituted image of the world . . . with the order of the world itself' (Habermas 1981: 81). For Habermas, the move away from this situation does not involve the loss of a supposedly purer relationship of language to the world, as Benjamin's ideas sometimes suggested. Instead, the perennial possibility of criticizing claims to validity enables the cognitive, moral and aesthetic developments he sees as so important to modernity. Rapid technical and scientific advances, the emergence of democracy and of autonomous art depend, for Habermas, on the specific kinds of validation that develop for the sciences, for modern law and for modern art.

Habermas does not, however, advance a naively positive view of the development of modernity. His work is, after all, also a response to the traumas of German history and is motivated by the need to avoid a repetition of those traumas by making democracy an integral part of philosophy. The development of separate value-spheres in modernity represents an advance on pre-modern forms of legitimation. It is the ways in which the spheres relate that give rise to destructive consequences. This idea helps explain much about the development of modern German history, where the technological results of science often interact disastrously with the life-world. He sums up one of the major concerns about modernity in his notion of the 'colonization of the life-world' (ibid. 10). Specialization in science, politics and other areas of modern life creates systematic institutionalized forms, as Weber argued. These can stifle the ability of people in the life-world to make sense of their lives in their own terms and to resist the domination of their lives by economic and technical developments. Adorno thinks, in the light of the Nazi experience, that the modern 'context of delusion' infects even the most basic aspects of social behaviour and thinking. Habermas, in contrast, thinks that the particular structures of everyday communication developed in the life-world *can* resist being 'colonized'. The idea that validity in communication can depend on a shared, non-coercive search for truth gives him this hope. The problem is again, though, what role philosophy has in relation to the practices of the life-world. The status of the theory of communicative action's analysis of structures of communication in relation to the creative linguistic potential Habermas sees in the life-world is unclear.

Habermas, like Rorty, thinks philosophy 'can today no longer relate to the whole of the world, of nature, of history, of society, in the sense of a totalizing knowledge' (ibid. 15). He asks, though, unlike Rorty, who sees nothing in philosophy that substantially differs from any other critical discourse, what role philosophy *can* play in correcting the distortions occasioned by modernity. His claim is that philosophy might now 'at least help to set in motion again the frozen interplay between the cognitive-instrumental, the moral-practical and the aesthetic-expressive, which is like a mobile that has become stubbornly entangled' (1983: 26). Philosophy can play the role of 'interpreter', rather than of presiding judge, by enabling different specialized disciplines to communicate. At a practical level – in universities, for example – philosophy can play a useful role in breaking down methodological barriers between disciplines, though it too rarely actually does this. But what, in Habermas's terms, would allow philosophy to make a methodological case for this as its new role, if it does not offer some overall conception of how the spheres should interact? The theory of communicative action relies on theorizing the kind of differentiations we always already make in dealing with cognitive, ethical and aesthetic questions in the life-world. These different kinds of question are, however, not as obviously separate as Habermas maintains. What happens when divisions between kinds of validity claims are themselves in dispute? How can the theory of communicative action adjudicate in such disputes? Dieter Henrich cites the case of the neurophysiologist who 'leaves his laboratory, in which consciousness and emotions are just complexes of firing neurones, to return to the circle of the family he loves' (1982: 60). Which description of emotions is to be preferred, and on what basis? Must the theory stand outside the different spheres, so that it can assign problems to their correct sphere? In that case, though, would it not play a metaphysical role of the kind Habermas thinks is now indefensible?

Hilary Putnam suggests the underlying difficulty in Habermas's conception in relation to the way natural scientists actually arrive at theories with predictive and explanatory power. The basic problem for a scientist is that one can in theory arrive at an indefinite number of scientific accounts of any phenomenon. The issue for scientists is therefore often a hermeneutic one. Theory-choice, like other forms of understanding, relies on evaluation based on background knowledge that can never be completely formalized: 'Judgements about coherence, simplicity, etc., are presupposed by the physical sciences. But coherence, simplicity and the like are *values*' (in Wingert and Günther 2001: 310). This means that science itself often depends on 'normative rightness' as much as it does on propositional truth. There already is, then, an interplay between notionally separate spheres – coherence, simplicity, etc. are, of course, also essential to aesthetic discourse. Putnam's point is that values ought to be just as assessable in terms of their truth as claims about the natural world. That was, after all, one point of the move away from the positivist idea of truth as representation of objective reality and towards a theory of communicative action that included all kinds of validity claims. Habermas, a pupil of Adorno, moves at times, then, too close to the assumptions of the Vienna Circle, by implicitly assuming the primacy of the natural sciences. It is Putnam, a pupil of Carnap, who invokes aspects of German metaphysics' attempts to integrate the diverging spheres of modernity against Germany's most influential philosopher.

Prospects

This partial reversal of roles between Habermas and Putnam – the two are in agreement on many other issues, and Habermas's position is clearly also critical of scientism – points to questions about the future of the tradition we have been considering in the present book. We have repeatedly encountered the tension between German philosophy's need to take account of the growing power of natural science and its concerns about science's effects on modern culture. In the light of German history it is not surprising that Habermas is worried that the tradition beginning with Herder and Hamann can lead to 'an abdication of problem-solving philosophical thinking before the poetic power of language, literature and art' (Habermas 1991: 90). For him, the priority must be with the attempt to solve problems in a democratic manner with the most reliable means. This leads him, though, to put a sometimes questionable philosophical view of natural science above the creative resources of the life-world. On the other hand, it is also not surprising that Putnam increasingly sees the philosophical danger in a technology dominated culture like the USA, not as the critical questioning of science's role as the supposed sole bearer of reliable truth, but as the refusal fundamentally to question science's role in public life. Philosophy's role within a culture is, as Habermas himself suggests, often to oppose dominant cultural developments. The question is how firm the *philosophical* basis for this opposition can be made to be, given that the effects of science on culture are so different in different social and historical contexts. The use of science to criticize mythological beliefs is, for example, a justified strategy in relation to inhuman practices in more traditional cultures, though even there, as Habermas makes clear, the practices of those being criticized must be engaged with in an appropriate manner.

These issues are, of course, anything but exclusive to German philosophy, and here is not the place to suggest how they might be resolved. What the preceding chapters have shown, though, is that German philosophy does still offer diverse and developed resources for investigating them. There is, at the same time, no doubt that the contemporary centre of philosophical gravity in the world is the USA, where, with the exception of the Vienna Circle, German philosophy was often ignored until quite recently. One effect of this is, as we saw, the tendency of many philosophers in Germany to regard their own tradition as exhausted and to concentrate on the agenda set by American philosophy. The strange counterpart to this is the growing concentration of many of the most significant American philosophers on ideas from the German tradition. The best way to approach this change of focus is via a very brief concluding characterization of some contemporary philosophical alternatives and their relationship to the tradition we have followed in the book.

English-language analytical philosophy is still predominantly based on the style of questioning that developed in the light of the issues we looked at in chapter 8, which are summed up in Dummett's 'conviction that a philosophical explanation of thought can be achieved by a philosophical analysis of language' (1988: 11). Such philosophy has the obvious advantage of its close links to the natural sciences, and its insistence on logical and conceptual rigour gives it the appearance of echoing the rigour of its main point of reference. There are five main issues in the growing dissatisfaction with the domination of this tradition. Many of these issues are now often incorporated into the agenda of some of those who still pursue the analytical mode of questioning. The crucial point in the present context is that many of the objections to dominant analytical assumptions involved in these issues derive from the tradition we have been examining, much of which was rejected by the analytical tradition until very recently.

1   Unlike the natural sciences, philosophy oriented to the empiricist analytical tradition does not produce theories with empirically testable predictive power, despite the concern with logical and conceptual precision.
2   The sciences do not actually need this kind of philosophical accompaniment to achieve successful results, so it is less and less clear what the attempt to solve epistemological problems by connecting philosophy to the sciences in this way is actually for. This does not mean that there can be no interesting research into how empirical investigation of perception relates to epistemological issues, but the result of this investigation will not be a foundational account of what makes scientific knowledge possible.
3   The widespread conviction that the objections to empiricism made by Kant, Hegel and others, for example in Hegel's account of 'sense certainty' (see chapter 4), are valid even if the wider claims of these philosophers cannot be defended. The pure empirical 'given' that can serve as a foundation for philosophy is now very widely seen as being a myth.
4   The history of analytical philosophy, which itself now forms a substantial area of research, is not the history of clear philosophical progress towards timeless solutions to philosophical problems, but rather a series of often contingent responses to issues which were generated by a particular ideological focus on certain problems in modernity.
5   The adherence to a strict fact/value distinction, and limitations on what is permitted as philosophically acceptable use of lan-

guage mean that questions of ethics and aesthetics receive
often very inadequate treatment. A philosophy concerned with
the pursuit of complete clarity in the analysis of concepts, rather
than with developing more effective modes of criticism, interpretation and communication, does not have the resources to come
to terms with questions that require the latter to precede the
former.

These and other worries about analytical philosophy form part of
a wider concern about the nature and role of philosophy today. It is
here, of course, that the resources of modern German philosophy are
still invaluable. From the beginning, German philosophy sees itself
as an attempt to respond to the challenges of modernity, so that it
is always connected to a critical attitude to all forms of culture.
Although much of his reception in the English-speaking world would
not suggest this, Kant did not just write an epistemology. Instead, he
attempted to locate modern humankind in a world where there were
no pregiven answers to the meanings of life. As such, he already
offered a warning, which is now being heeded in the renewed attention to his work, about what happens when the focus of philosophy
is reduced to the legitimation of knowledge.

Contemporary debates over the role and nature of philosophy
offer different focuses and emphases in relation to the role of language, the nature of metaphysics, the nature of the self, the status of
nature and the consequences of the failure of philosophy to arrive at
final foundations. These differing approaches can be mapped onto
aspects of the thinkers we have been examining. A few examples can
illustrate how this is the case.

1   Dieter Henrich claims, in the light of Kant and Fichte, for
example, that the linguistic turn fails to give a satisfactory account of
self-consciousness: 'We understand ourselves equally primordially as
one [person] among others', in the intersubjective realm of language,
and 'as the One [subject] opposed to the whole world' (1982: 138),
when the resources of language are inadequate for articulating my
particular sense of my existence. If this is valid, what does it do to the
'post-metaphysical' claim that subjectivity must be accessible to language in the same terms as any other aspect of the world? Henrich's
idea is not that the subject can serve as a foundation of knowledge
and ethics, as German Idealism hoped. However, without some elu-
cidation of what it is in us that is able to resist the pressures of established custom and usage, and to arrive at new ways of articulating
things, there seems to be something important missing from our
self-understanding.

2   Although there is widespread agreement that *knowledge* of nature is, as Kant argued, only possible in law-bound terms, the ecological crisis has revived issues we saw in Schelling, Heidegger, Adorno and others concerning other ways in which we relate to the natural world. Are we right to assume that any attempt to arrive at a more substantive philosophical conception of nature, that links the destruction of external nature to the destructive effects this may have on the internal nature of people, is invalidly metaphysical? Metaphysics, in the sense of the attempt to 'hold together a world in thinking' (ibid. 60), seems as yet both unavoidable and unsustainable.

3   The direction of some of the philosophy we have considered was towards a foundational account of the essential principles of knowledge or ethics, and this led to many of the problems we have examined. However, philosophy can also, as we saw in the best aspects of the Romantics and Nietzsche, be employed as a means of undermining foundational pretensions, and of reminding us of what other ways of thinking may have obscured. What, though, prevents this undermining slipping either into the reductionist account of morality and truth we encountered in the worst aspects of Nietzsche, or into the kind of failure to offer any orientation in real cognitive and ethical dilemmas that is too often the result of a deconstructive approach?

4   Putnam thinks the new role of philosophy should be as cultural criticism. The difficulties involved in legitimating critical perspectives have been a major factor in German philosophy, from which a great deal more can be learned.

5   Many of these issues relate to the tension between propositional conceptions of truth and conceptions of truth as world-disclosure. The former run the risk of ignoring key dimensions of human existence, but can sustain the demand for public accountability; the latter run the risk of appealing to something that cannot be publicly justified, but offer semantic resources without which culture cannot survive. Does the propositional conception depend on the world-disclosive conception? Responses – rather than answers – to such issues form the substance of much significant contemporary philosophy.

My final point is a plea that philosophy should remain aware of the historical resources at its disposal by not forgetting traditions like the one looked at in this book. The English-language philosophy of the twentieth century too often conspired with some of the most dispiriting aspects of modern culture because of its limited conception of what life is about. It did so not least because of the mistaken conviction that it had finished with the tradition we have been exploring. Things are now changing, and the German tradition, with all the admittedly serious flaws it contains, still deserves close examination.

SUGGESTIONS FOR FURTHER READING

Here I have included some translations of books by contemporary German philosophers on whom there is little secondary literature in English as yet.

Bernstein, R. (ed.) (1985) *Habermas and Modernity* (Cambridge, MA: MIT Press). *Collection of critical essays.*

Bowie, A. (1999) 'German Philosophy Today: Between Idealism, Romanticism, and Pragmatism', in Anthony O'Hear (ed.), *German Philosophy Since Kant*, Royal Institute of Philosophy Lectures (Cambridge: Cambridge University Press). *Assessment of the legacy of the classical German traditions of philosophy for contemporary philosophy.*

Dews, P. (ed.) (1992) *Jürgen Habermas. Autonomy and Solidarity* (London: Verso). *Series of enlightening interviews with Habermas.*

Dews, P. (ed.) (1999) *Habermas: A Critical Reader* (Oxford: Blackwell). *Collection of good critical essays that approach Habermas from less familiar angles.*

Frank, M. (1989) *What is Neostructuralism?* (Minneapolis: University of Minnesota Press). *Extended study of French post-structuralism in the light of the German tradition by major contemporary German philosopher.*

Frank, M. (1997) *The Subject and the Text. Essays in Literary Theory and Philosophy* (Cambridge: Cambridge University Press). *Major essays on philosophical issues in literary theory. Introduction gives an extensive account of Frank's work.*

Freundlieb, D. (2003) *Dieter Henrich and Contemporary Philosophy* (Aldershot: Ashgate). *First study in English of a major contemporary thinker who is still too little known in the English-speaking world.*

Habermas, J. (1977) 'A Review of Gadamer's Truth and Method', in F. Dallmayr and T. McCarthy (ed.), *Understanding and Social Inquiry* (Notre Dame: Notre Dame University Press). *The best place to begin looking at the relationship between Habermas and Gadamer.*

Holub, R. (1991) *Jürgen Habermas* (London: Routledge). *Excellent study of Habermas as social critic.*

McCarthy, T. (1984) *The Critical Theory of Jürgen Habermas* (Cambridge: Polity). *The standard work in English on Habermas.*

Tugendhat, E. (1982) *Traditional and Analytical Philosophy* (Cambridge: Cambridge University Press). *Based on lectures on analytical philosophy for a German audience: full of insights for both analytical and European philosophers.*

Wachterhauser, B. (ed.) (1986) *Hermeneutics and Modern Philosophy* (Albany: SUNY Press). *Useful collection of essays.*

Warnke, G. (1987) *Gadamer: Hermeneutics, Tradition and Reason* (Stanford: Stanford University Press). *Good account of the major aspects of Gadamer's work.*

Weinsheimer, J. (1985) *Gadamer's Hermeneutics: A Reading of Truth and Method* (New Haven, CT: Yale University Press). *Good account of Gadamer's magnum opus by leading Gadamer scholar.*

Wellmer, A. (1991) *The Persistence of Modernity* (Cambridge: Polity). *Series of seminal essays on modernity and post-modernity by one of Adorno's most interesting pupils.*

GLOSSARY

Philosophers are often rightly suspicious of definitions. The explanations of terms offered here are merely a means of enabling the reader further to explore the term in question; they make no claim to be definitive and I have kept them as simple as I can.

a priori   Latin for 'from the beginning'; refers to what cannot be learned from experience and must therefore already be present prior to experience

absolute   that which is not relative to something else (also referred to as the unconditioned)

aesthetic idea   in Kant, an image or thought which conveys an abstract idea, like goodness or bravery, via something perceptible because conceptual language cannot adequately convey it

aesthetics   until the end of the eighteenth century this means the theory of perception; towards the end of the eighteenth century it comes to mean the theory of art and beauty

alienation   in Feuerbach, the mistaken attribution of something proper to humankind to God; in Marx, the situation of people who are prevented from realizing their human potential, or the situation in which people's labour does not belong to them in any way. (See chapter 6 for further senses of the term)

analytic judgement   a judgement true by definition, as in 'a bachelor is an unmarried man'

analytical philosophy   the philosophy that developed in the early twentieth century which seeks to solve philosophical problems by the analysis of language

antinomy   in Kant, 'opposed laws', for example the opposition between free-will and determinism

antithesis   a claim which is opposed to another claim. To the **thesis** 'humankind possesses freedom', one can oppose the antithesis 'humankind is part of nature and is, like nature, wholly determined'

Apollonian   the domain of form and order, as opposed to the **Dionysian**

apperception   awareness that one is thinking about something, including one's own thoughts

autonomy   giving the law to oneself, rather than having it imposed by others

bivalence   the assumption that assertions must be either true or false

categorical imperative   see **imperative**

categories   in Kant, the 'pure concepts of the understanding', i.e. forms of thought that do not depend upon experience, are a priori, but which are necessary for our empirical knowledge

cogito   Latin for 'I think', used to refer to Descartes's argument that he must exist because he can doubt his existence in thought: 'cogito, sum' ('I think, I am')

communicative reason   reason based on non-coercive argument and discussion in pursuit of the truth rather than on a priori principles

condition   something upon which something else depends for its existence; hence the idea of the unconditioned as that which does not depend on anything else, which is sometimes how God is seen

constitutive idea   in Kant, an idea which purports to describe the ultimate reality of something, as opposed to a **regulative idea**

continental philosophy   term normally used to contrast the traditions from Kant and German Idealism, to hermeneutics, Critical

Theory and deconstruction with the analytical tradition from Frege to the present. This distinction is increasingly redundant

contingency   refers to what cannot be explained in terms of a prior necessity. The existence of the world is contingent if we cannot, for example, use God to explain it; what we encounter in the world is contingent because we can never be sure if our predictions about what we will encounter will turn out to be correct

correspondence theory of truth   the theory that truth consists in the correspondence or adequacy of statements or of ideas to reality

Critical Theory   the theory that philosophy should constitute a critique of the unjust nature of society associated with the Frankfurt School

Dasein   literally 'being there/being here'. Heidegger's term for what previous philosophy refers to as 'the subject' or 'the I'. He employs it in order to avoid the traditional connotations of these terms, which create a split between subject and object

deduction   normally refers to an inference from a principle, such as deducing why something falls to the ground on the basis of the law of gravity; in Kant it also has the older German sense of legitimating a form of thinking

deism   doctrine in which God is conceived of as the initiator of the universe's intelligibility, and rationality, rather than as the **theist** God whom we understand through revelation of how He is also immanent in the world He created. The meaning of deism and theism varies in differing periods

determinacy   having the status of being something specific

determinism   the doctrine that all events in nature have necessary causes, and that freedom is therefore an illusion

dialectic   in Plato, seeking truth by discussion; in Kant, the use of forms of thought which are only valid for dealing with the phenomenal world to talk about noumenal things in themselves; in Hegel, the account of the fact that all particular thoughts are 'negative' because they must relate to other thoughts in a system. The dialectic functions in Hegel by 'Aufhebung', sometimes translated as 'sublation': the word has the threefold meaning of 'negation' or 'destruction', 'preservation' and 'elevation'

Dionysian the chaotic domain of creation and destruction, as opposed to the **Apollonian**

dogmatism in Kant, philosophy which relies on presupposed theological ideas about the inherent order of the world. The 'pure reason' criticized in Kant's first Critique is a form of dogmatism

empiricism the doctrine that all knowledge depends on sense-experience, rather than relying on a priori principles

Enlightenment the philosophical and intellectual movement in the modern period which put its faith in the power of human reason to explain the universe and provide a basis for morality. The term has many other, sometimes conflicting senses

epistemology the theory of knowledge

epoché in Husserl, the exclusion of all mental content deriving from the external world in order to examine the internal structures of consciousness

existentialism the doctrine that existence precedes essence, which means that what we are is what we become via our actions, rather than something already established by our nature. Existentialism also assumes there is no reason why there is something rather than nothing, so the universe is contingent

fallibilism the doctrine that even the best-confirmed beliefs may turn out to be false

foundationalism the assumption that philosophy requires an initial principle of certainty if claims to knowledge are to be legitimate, e.g. the certainty that I exist because I think in Descartes

genealogy an account of the origin of something

German Idealism term used to refer mainly to the philosophy of Fichte, Schelling and Hegel, which sought to explicate the relationship between the structures of thought and the structures of nature as a way of giving a new account of humanity's relationship to the modern world

German Romanticism   in philosophy, term associated mainly with Novalis, Friedrich Schlegel and Schleiermacher, who were critical of some of the aims of German Idealism

hermeneutics   the art, or theory, of interpretation; also, the philosophy developed by Heidegger and Gadamer which regards understanding as fundamental to what we are

heteronomy   being governed by the law of the other, as opposed to **autonomy**, being governed by a law one applies freely to oneself

historical materialism   the doctrine that conceptions of reality are the result of the interaction of humankind with material nature within specific, historically developed forms of society

holism   the idea that no particular phenomenon can be understood in isolation, so that its nature depends on the contexts in which it occurs

hypothetical imperative   see **imperative**

idealism   in Berkeley, the doctrine that 'being is perceiving': because we can only know about what there is by thinking it, we have no right to assume reality is more than just ideas. This must be distinguished from German Idealism (see chapter 3), which tries to show that the structures of thought are identical with those of the world

ideology   a system of ideas; in Marx comes to mean a system of ideas that distorts the perception of reality

idiographic   a science which is concerned with the particularity of things, rather than the general laws governing them

immanence   'dwelling within' something, as opposed to **transcendence**, which takes something beyond itself

immediacy   something is 'immediate' if it does not depend upon its relationships to something else

imperative   a principle in terms of which one ought to act; for Kant there are two kinds of imperative: **hypothetical** imperatives, which are those required for a particular end, and the **categorical** imperative, which enjoins one to act on principles that one would wish everyone else to act on

indexical a word, such as 'this' or 'now', which only gains its meaning when used in specific contexts

induction moving from a series of different particular phenomena to a law which explains them

instrumental reason reason based on seeking the means to an end, which requires what Kant terms a '**hypothetical imperative**'

intelligible in Kant, the intelligible world is the world 'in itself' that is not available to the senses, in which human freedom is located

intentionality the fact that consciousness is consciousness of something, and so is directed at the world

intuition in German philosophy refers to the contact one has with something: our empirical contact with the world takes the form of 'sensuous intuition', for example

irrationalism doctrine which regards reason as the obstacle to true insight

mediation something is mediated by being related to other things

metaphysics an account of the general principles of reality

nihilism in Jacobi, the idea that if the whole world functions deterministically there is no point to human existence. In Nietzsche, nihilism is the result of having believed there is a greater purpose to existence, and then ceasing to believe this

noema the meaning of a perceived object; roughly the ways of being of, e.g. a tree, rather than the tree itself

noesis the way in which an object is apprehended, for example in terms of memory or belief

nomothetic a science, like physics, which involves general laws

noumenon (pl. **noumena**) in Kant, a thing as it exists independently of our apprehension of it

ontological difference   in Heidegger, the difference between 'being' and 'entities', between the fact that things exist at all as something intelligible, and what we think they are in particular contexts

ontology   the theory of what kind of thing there is in the world: an idealist ontology would claim there are only ideas, a materialist ontology would claim that there is nothing but matter

ontotheology   the linking of questions concerning being and existence to questions concerning God

panlogism   doctrine that proposes that the whole of reality is governed by a reason that is inherent within it

pantheism   the doctrine that God and nature are identical, so that everything is God

paralogism   an argument whose form is false

performative   used to describe language conceived of as a form of action, which has effects on the listener. Rhetoric, the 'art of persuasion', is concerned with the performative nature of language

phenomenalism   the doctrine that we only apprehend phenomena, not real things

phenomenology   an account of the ways in which something appears; also refers to the philosophical movement associated with Husserl described in chapter 9

phenomenon (pl. **phenomena**)   that which appears

physicalism   the thesis that everything, even what we think of as mental, is in the last analysis physical

positivism   in Comte, the final stage in science that results from the overcoming of the 'theological' and the 'metaphysical' stages, in the name of knowledge based on empirical observation. Later tends to refer to conceptions in which the only valid knowledge derives from empirical observation that is ordered in terms of logical laws

practical reason   reason concerned with principles for action

pragmatism philosophy which considers the usefulness of ideas to be the primary concern, and therefore rejects the idea that the truth is to be understood as the correct representation of an independent reality

principle of sufficient reason the principle that everything has a reason/cause/ground

proposition an assertion about something: e.g. 'This wine is good'

psychologism the doctrine that all aspects of thinking, including logic, can be explained in terms of the laws of the mind discovered by psychology. The term is more loosely used to characterize the view that cultural and social matters can be understood in terms of the inner life of individuals

rationalism in the seventeenth and eighteenth centuries, refers to the doctrine that the universe has an inherent law-bound structure that is expressible in mathematical terms, thus in terms of a priori principles

realism the doctrine that reality is the way it is independently of how it is thought about (there are many other ways of characterizing realism)

receptivity the capacity to be affected by the objective world

reflection the splitting of something into two related aspects, as when I look in a mirror and see an image of myself looking at the image of myself

reflective judgement judgement which seeks a general rule by abstracting from particulars

regulative idea an idea that orients our thinking without us being able to claim to give an account of it which proves what it refers to really exists. In Kant the idea of nature as a law-bound system is such a regulative idea

reification to make into a thing, for example when people are reified by their individual human attributes being ignored

relativism the idea that all claims to truth are relative to the social or historical context, or the language in which they occur, and so cannot be absolute

scepticism   the doctrine that we cannot know anything for certain

schema (pl. **schemata**)   in Kant, the means by which concepts are connected with appearances

schematism   in Kant, the function of the mind which connects the a priori and the empirical

scientism   the doctrine according to which only explanations involving scientific laws have claims to truth

solipsism   from the Latin for 'self alone': the doctrine that I can only be sure that I exist and that the reality of the rest of the world therefore depends on my consciousness

spontaneity   that which is 'cause of itself', rather than being caused by something else; used by Kant to characterize our faculty of knowing things by active judgement

synthesis   joining together

synthetic judgement   a judgement which is not true by definition and so adds to our knowledge, as in 'all Catholic priests are supposed to be bachelors'

synthetic judgement a priori   a judgement that does not rely on experience but which adds to knowledge. Kant sees mathematics as consisting of such judgements

tautology   a statement which says the same thing twice: 'a man is a man'

telos   goal, aim or end

theism   belief in God as a 'personality' who both created the world and is immanent within it

thesis   a positive argument, to which an **antithesis** is opposed

transcend   to go beyond

transcendence   in **phenomenology**, the move beyond the subject to objects in the world

transcendental argument   an argument about the conditions without which an experience or a kind of knowledge would be impossible

transcendental philosophy   philosophy concerned with the 'conditions of possibility' of what we know; in Kant's case these are necessary forms of thought without which experience would be unintelligible

transcendental subject   the subject as described in the account of the necessities in thought required for knowledge; in contrast to the empirical subject, for which experience is contingent

transcendental unity of apperception   Kant's idea that an 'I think' must be able to accompany all my thoughts

understanding   in Kant, the capacity for knowledge governed by rules and based on intuitions

verificationism   the doctrine that only statements which can be verified by empirical observation can mean anything or be true

REFERENCES

All quotations from German texts are my translations from the original. In the case of easily available translations, I have put an English edition after the reference. I have not done this where, e.g. for Kant and Nietzsche, there is more than one easily available translation. In some cases, English-language selections from an author do not always fully match the German edition. Many of the texts prior to the twentieth century are available in both German and English on the web.

Adorno, T. W. (1970) *Zur Metakritik der Erkenntnistheorie* (Frankfurt: Suhrkamp); *Against Epistemology* (Oxford: Blackwell, 1982).
Adorno, T. W. (1973) *Ästhetische Theorie* (Frankfurt: Suhrkamp); *Aesthetic Theory* (London: Athlone, 1997).
Adorno, T. W. (1975) *Negative Dialektik* (Frankfurt: Suhrkamp); *Negative Dialectics* (London: Routledge, 1990).
Adorno, T. W. (1978) *Minima Moralia* (Frankfurt: Suhrkamp); *Minima Moralia* (London: Verso, 1981).
Adorno, T. W. (ed.) (1991) *Der Positivismusstreit in der deutschen Soziologie* (Munich: dtv); *The Positivist Dispute in German Sociology* (London: Heinemann, 1976).
Adorno, T. W. (2002) *Ontologie und Dialektik (1960/61)* (Frankfurt: Suhrkamp).
Ameriks, Karl (2000) *Kant and the Fate of Autonomy* (Cambridge: Cambridge University Press).
Apel, Karl-Otto (1998) *Auseinandersetzungen* (Frankfurt: Suhrkamp).
Austin, J. L. (1962) *How to Do Things with Words* (Cambridge, MA, and London: Harvard University Press).

Beiser, Frederick C. (1987) *The Fate of Reason: German Philosophy from Kant to Fichte* (Cambridge, MA, and London: Harvard University Press).

Benjamin, Walter (1980) *Gesammelte Schriften* (Frankfurt: Suhrkamp); *Selected Writings*, 3 vols (Cambridge, MA, and London: Harvard University Press, 1996, 1999, 2002).

Berlin, Isaiah (1999) *The Roots of Romanticism* (London: Chatto and Windus).

Bolzano, Bernard (1963) *Grundlegung der Logik* (Hamburg: Meiner).

Bowie, Andrew (1993) *Schelling and Modern European Philosophy* (London: Routledge).

Bowie, Andrew (1997) *From Romanticism to Critical Theory* (London, New York: Routledge).

Bowie, Andrew (1999) 'German Philosophy Today: Between Idealism, Romanticism, and Pragmatism', in Anthony O'Hear (ed.), *German Philosophy Since Kant*, Royal Institute of Philosophy Lectures (Cambridge: Cambridge University Press).

Bowie, Andrew (2000) 'The Romantic Connection: Neurath, the Frankfurt School, and Heidegger', in *British Journal for the History of Philosophy*, Part One, 8 (2), 2000; Part Two, 8 (3), 2000.

Bowie, Andrew (2004) 'Schleiermacher and Post-Metaphysical Thinking' (forthcoming).

Bowie, Andrew (2003) *Aesthetics and Subjectivity: From Kant to Nietzsche* (Manchester: Manchester University Press).

Brandom, Robert (2000) *Articulating Reasons* (Cambridge, MA, and London: Harvard University Press).

Breckman, W. (1999) *Marx, the Young Hegelians, and the Origins of Radical Social Theory* (Cambridge: Cambridge University Press).

Carnap, Rudolf (1932) 'Die Überwindung der Metaphysik durch logische Analyse der Sprache', in *Erkenntnis* 2: 219–41.

Cartwright, Nancy, Cat, Jordi, Fleck, Lola and Uebel, Thomas (1996) *Otto Neurath: Philosophy Between Science and Politics* (Cambridge: Cambridge University Press).

Coffa, J. Alberto (1991) *The Semantic Tradition from Kant to Carnap* (Cambridge: Cambridge University Press).

Dahlstrom, Daniel (2001) *Heidegger's Concept of Truth* (Cambridge: Cambridge University Press).

Dahms, Hans-Joachim (1998) *Positivismusstreit* (Frankfurt: Suhrkamp).

Davidson, Donald (1984) *Inquiries into Truth and Interpretation* (Oxford: Oxford University Press).

Davidson, Donald (2001) *Subjective, Intersubjective, Objective* (Oxford: Oxford University Press).

Derrida, Jacques (1967) *La Voix et le phénomène* (Paris: Presses Universitaires de France).

Dilthey, Wilhelm (1981) *Der Aufbau der geschichtlichen Welt in den Geisteswissenschaften* (Frankfurt: Suhrkamp); *Selected Works: The Formation of the Historical World in the Human Sciences* (Princeton: Princeton University Press, 2003).

Dilthey, Wilhelm (1983) *Texte zur Kritik der historischen Vernunft* (Göttingen: Vandenhoeck and Ruprecht).

Dilthey, Wilhelm (1990) *Die Geistige Welt. Einleitung in die Philosophie des Lebens*, Gesammelte Schriften, vol. 5 (Stuttgart: Teubner).

Dummett, Michael (1988) *Ursprünge der analytischen Philosophie* (Frankfurt: Suhrkamp); *The Origins of Analytical Philosophy* (Cambridge, MA, and London: Harvard University Press, 1996).

Elliot, Anthony (ed.) (1999) *The Blackwell Reader in Contemporary Social Theory* (Oxford: Blackwell).

Feuerbach, Ludwig (1969) *Das Wesen des Christentums* (Stuttgart: Reclam); *The Essence of Christianity* (London: Prometheus, 1989).

Feuerbach, Ludwig (1980) *Philosophische Kritiken und Grundsätze (1839–1846)* (Wiesbaden: VMA).

Feuerbach, Ludwig (1983) *Grundsätze der Philosophie der Zukunft* (Frankfurt: Klostermann); *Principles of the Philosophy of the Future* (Indianapolis: Hackett, 1986).

Fichte, J. G. (1971) *Werke I, Werke II, Werke III* (Berlin: de Gruyter); *The Science of Knowledge* (Cambridge: Cambridge University Press, 1982); *Foundations of Natural Right* (Cambridge: Cambridge University Press, 2000).

Frank, Manfred (1979) *Die unendliche Fahrt. Ein Motiv und sein Text* (Frankfurt am Main: Suhrkamp; 2nd substantially extended and revised edn, Leipzig: Reclam, 1995).

Frank, Manfred (1982) *Der kommende Gott* (Frankfurt: Suhrkamp).

Frank, Manfred (1988) *Grenzen der Verständigung* (Frankfurt: Suhrkamp).

Frank, Manfred (1989) *Das Sagbare und das Unsagbare. Studien zur deutschfranzösischen Hermeneutik und Texttheorie*, Erweiterte Neuausgabe (Frankfurt am Main: Suhrkamp; 1st edn 1980); *The Subject and the Text* (Cambridge: Cambridge University Press, 1998).

Frank, Manfred (1991) *Selbstbewußtsein und Selbsterkenntnis* (Stuttgart: Reclam).

Frank, Manfred (1997) *'Unendliche Annäherung'. Die Anfänge der philosophischen Frühromantik* (Frankfurt: Suhrkamp).

Frege, Gottlob (1990) *Schriften zur Logik und Sprachphilosophie* (Hamburg: Meiner); *The Frege Reader: Selected Philosophical Writings* (Oxford: Blackwell, 1997).

Frege, Gottlob (1994) *Funktion, Begriff, Bedeutung – Fünf logische Studien* (Göttingen: Verlag Vandenhoeck and Ruprecht).

Friedman, Michael (1999) *Reconsidering Logical Positivism* (Cambridge: Cambridge University Press).

Gadamer, Hans-Georg (1975) *Wahrheit und Methode* (Tübingen: J. C. B. Mohr); *Truth and Method* (New York: Continuum, 1997).

Gadamer, Hans-Georg (1993) *Ästhetik und Poetik I. Kunst als Aussage* (Tübingen: J. C. B. Mohr).

Goodman, Nelson (1978) *Ways of Worldmaking* (Indianapolis: Hackett).

Habermas, Jürgen (1973) *Erkenntnis und Interesse* (Frankfurt: Suhrkamp); *Knowledge and Human Interests* (Cambridge: Polity, 1986).

Habermas, Jürgen (1981) *Theorie des kommunikativen Handelns*, 2 vols (Frankfurt: Suhrkamp); *Theory of Communicative Action* (Cambridge: Polity, 1989).

Habermas, Jürgen (1983) *Moralbewußtsein und kommunikatives Handeln* (Frankfurt: Suhrkamp); *Moral Consciousness and Communicative Action* (Cambridge: Polity, 1990).

Habermas, Jürgen (1985) *Der philosophische Diskurs der Moderne* (Frankfurt: Suhrkamp); *The Philosophical Discourse of Modernity* (Cambridge: Polity, 1990).

Habermas, Jürgen (1988) *Nachmetaphysisches Denken* (Frankfurt: Suhrkamp); *Postmetaphysical Thinking* (Cambridge: Polity, 1992).

Habermas, Jürgen (1991), *Texte und Kontexte* (Frankfurt: Suhrkamp).

Habermas, Jürgen (1992) *Faktizität und Geltung* (Frankfurt: Suhrkamp); *Between Facts and Norms* (Cambridge: Polity, 1996).

Habermas, Jürgen (1999) *Wahrheit und Rechtfertigung* (Frankfurt: Suhrkamp); *Truth and Justification* (Cambridge: Polity, 2003).

Hamann, J. G. (1949–57) *Sämtliche Werke*, 6 vols (Vienna: Herder).

Hamann, J. G. (1967) *Schriften zur Sprache*, ed. Josef Simon (Frankfurt: Suhrkamp).

Hegel, G. W. F. (1969) *Wissenschaft der Logik I, II*, vols 5, 6 Werkausgabe (Frankfurt: Suhrkamp); *Science of Logic* (Amherst: Humanity, 1998).

Hegel, G. W. F. (1970) *Phänomenologie des Geistes (PG)*, vol. 3 Werkausgabe (Frankfurt: Suhrkamp); *Phenomenology of Spirit* (Oxford: Oxford University Press, 1979).

Heidegger, Martin (1960) *Ursprung des Kunstwerks* (Stuttgart: Reclam); trans. in *Basic Writings* (London: Routledge, 1993).

Heidegger, Martin (1969) *Zur Sache des Denkens* (Tübingen: Niemeyer); parts in *Basic Writings* (London: Routledge, 1993).

Heidegger, Martin (1979) *Sein und Zeit* (Tübingen: Niemeyer); *Being and Time* (Oxford: Blackwell, 1978).

Heidegger, Martin (1983) *Die Grundbegriffe der Metaphysik* (Frankfurt: Klostermann); *The Fundamental Concepts of Metaphysics* (Bloomington: University of Indiana Press, 2001).

Heidegger, Martin (1996) *Einleitung in die Philosophie* (Frankfurt: Klostermann).

Heine, H. (n.d.) *Sämtliche Werke in Drei Bänden* (Essen: Phaidon).

Henrich, Dieter (1982) *Selbstverhältnisse* (Stuttgart: Reclam).

Herder, Johann Gottfried (1964) *Sprachphilosophische Schriften* (Hamburg: Meiner); *Philosophical Writings* (Cambridge: Cambridge University Press, 2002).

Herder, Johann Gottfried (1966) *Abhandlung über den Ursprung der Sprache* (Stuttgart: Reclam).

Herder, Johann Gottfried (1985) *Über die neuere deutsche Literatur. Fragmente* (Berlin: Aufbau).

Hölderlin, Friedrich (1963) *Werke Briefe Dokumente* (Munich: Winkler); *Essays and Letters on Theory* (Albany: SUNY Press, 1987).

Horkheimer, Max (ed.) (1980) *Zeitschrift für Sozialforschung 1–9* (Munich: dtv).

Horkheimer, Max and Adorno, T. W. (1971) *Dialektik der Aufklärung* (Frankfurt: Fischer); *Dialectic of Enlightenment* (London: Verso, 1997).

Husserl, Edmund (1992) *Gesammelte Schriften*, 9 vols (Hamburg: Meiner); *Ideas Pertaining to a Pure Phenomenology and to a Phenomenological Philosophy* (Dordrecht: Kluwer Academic Publishers, 1990); *Cartesian Meditations* (Dordrecht: Kluwer Academic Publishers, 1991); *The Crisis of European Sciences and Transcendental Phenomenology* (Evanston: Northwestern University Press, 1970).

Kant, Immanuel (1968a) *Kritik der reinen Vernunft* (CPR), Werkausgabe III and IV (Frankfurt: Suhrkamp).

Kant, Immanuel (1968b) *Kritik der Urteilskraft* (*CJ*), Werkausgabe X (Frankfurt: Suhrkamp).

Kant, Immanuel (1974) *Kritik der praktischen Vernunft, Grundlegung der Metaphysik der Sitten*, Werkausgabe VII (Frankfurt: Suhrkamp).

Kant, Immanuel (1996) *Schriften zur Ästhetik und Naturphilosophie*, ed. Manfred Frank and Véronique Zanetti (Frankfurt: Deutscher Klassiker Verlag).

Lafont, Cristina (1994) *Sprache und Welterschliessung* (Frankfurt: Suhrkamp); *Heidegger, Language, and World-Disclosure* (Cambridge: Cambridge University Press, 2000).

Lukács, Georg (1967) *Geschichte und Klassenbewusstsein* (Amsterdam: de Munter); *History and Class Consciousness* (London: Merlin, 1991).

MacIntyre, Alasdair (ed.) (1972) *Hegel: A Collection of Critical Essays* (Notre Dame: University of Notre Dame Press).

Marx, Karl (1970) *Ökonomisch-philosophische Manuskripte* (Leipzig: Reclam); *Economic and Philosophic Manuscripts of 1844* (London: Lawrence and Wishart, 1987).

Marx, Karl (1974) *Grundrisse der Kritik der politischen Ökonomie* (Berlin: Dietz); *The Grundrisse: Foundations of the Critique of Political Economy* (Harmondsworth: Penguin, 1993).

Marx, Karl (1975) *Das Kapital*, vol. 1 (Berlin: Dietz); *Capital*, vol. 1 (Harmondsworth: Penguin, 1992).

Marx, Karl and Engels, Friedrich (1971) *Werke*, Band 13 (Berlin: Dietz).

Nietzsche, Friedrich (1980) *Sämtliche Werke*. Kritische Studienausgabe in 15 Bänden, ed. Giorgio Colli and Mazzino Montinari (Munich, Berlin, New York: de Gruyter).

Novalis (1978) *Band 2 Das philosophisch-theoretische Werk*, ed. Hans-Joachim Mähl (Munich, Vienna: Hanser); *Philosophical Writings* (Albany: SUNY Press, 1997); *Fichte Studies* (Cambridge: Cambridge University Press, 2003).

Novalis (1981) *Werke* (Munich: Beck).

O'Hear, Anthony (ed.) (1999) *German Philosophy After Kant* (Cambridge: Cambridge University Press).

Pinkard, Terry (1996) *Hegel's Phenomenology. The Sociality of Reason* (Cambridge: Cambridge University Press).

Pippin, Robert (1997) *Idealism as Modernism* (Cambridge: Cambridge University Press).

Putnam, Hilary (1983) *Realism and Reason. Philosophical Papers Vol. 3* (Cambridge: Cambridge University Press).

Reinhold, Karl Leonhard (1978) *Über das Fundament des philosophischen Wissens. Über die Möglichkeit der Philosophie als strenge Wissenschaft* (Hamburg: Meiner).

Rickert, Heinrich (1986) *Kulturwissenschaft und Naturwissenschaft* (Stuttgart: Reclam).

Rorty, Richard (1980) *Philosophy and the Mirror of Nature* (Oxford: Blackwell).

Rorty, Richard (1989) *Contingency, Irony and Solidarity* (Cambridge: Cambridge University Press).

Rorty, Richard (1991) *Essays on Heidegger and Others. Philosophical Papers Vol. 2* (Cambridge: Cambridge University Press).

Rorty, Richard (1998) *Truth and Progress. Philosophical Papers Vol. 3* (Cambridge: Cambridge University Press).

Rorty, Richard (ed.) (1992) *The Linguistic Turn* (Chicago: University of Chicago Press).

Safranski, Rüdiger (1997) *Ein Meister aus Deutschland. Heidegger und seine Zeit* (Frankfurt: Fischer); *Martin Heidegger: Between Good and Evil* (Cambridge, MA, and London: Harvard University Press, 1999).

Schelling, F. W. J. (1856–61) *Sämmtliche Werke*, ed. K. F. A. Schelling, I Abtheilung, vols 1–10; II Abtheilung, vols 1–4 (Stuttgart: Cotta); *Ideas for a Philosophy of Nature* (Cambridge: Cambridge University Press, 1989); *Philosophical Investigations into the Nature of Human Freedom* (Living Time, 2002); *On the History of Modern Philosophy* (Cambridge: Cambridge University Press, 1994).

Schelling, F. W. J. (1946) *Die Weltalter*, ed. Manfred Schröter (Munich: Biederstein and Leibniz); trans. in *Abyss of Freedom* (Ann Arbor: University of Michigan Press, 1997).

Schelling, F. W. J. (1977) *Philosophie der Offenbarung* (1841–2), ed. Manfred Frank (Frankfurt: Suhrkamp).

Schlegel, Friedrich (1963) *Philosophische Lehrjahre* (1796–1828) (*Kritische Friedrich Schlegel Ausgabe*, vol. 18) (Munich, Paderborn, Vienna: Ferdinand Schöningh).

Schlegel, Friedrich (1971) *Philosophische Lehrjahre II* (1796–1828) (*Kritische Friedrich Schlegel Ausgabe*, vol. 19) (Munich, Paderborn, Vienna: Ferdinand Schöningh).

Schlegel, Friedrich (1988) *Kritische Schriften und Fragmente*, Studienausgabe vols 1–6, ed. Ernst Behler and Hans Eichner (Paderborn, Munich, Vienna, Zurich: Schöningh); *Philosophical Fragments* (Minneapolis: University of Minnesota Press, 1991).

Schlegel, Friedrich (1991) *Transcendentalphilosophie*, ed. Michael Elsässer (Hamburg: Meiner).

Schleiermacher, F. D. E. (1839) *Dialektik*, ed. L. Jonas (Berlin: Reimer).

Schleiermacher, F. D. E. (1977) *Hermeneutik und Kritik* (Frankfurt: Suhrkamp); *'Hermeneutics and Criticism' and Other Texts* (Cambridge: Cambridge University Press, 1998).

Schleiermacher, F. D. E. (n.d.) *Über die Religion. Reden an die Gebildeten unter ihren Verächtern* (Berlin: Deutsche Bibliothek); *On Religion* (Cambridge: Cambridge University Press, 1996).

Schnädelbach, Herbert (1992) *Zur Rehabilitierung des animale rationale* (Frankfurt: Suhrkamp).

Scholz, Heinrich, ed. (1916) *Die Hauptschriften zum Pantheismusstreit zwischen Jacobi und Mendelssohn* (Berlin: Reuther and Reichard).

Schopenhauer, Arthur (1986) *Die Welt als Wille und Vorstellung*, in *Sämtliche Werke I*, ed. Wolfgang Frhr. von Löhneysen (Frankfurt: Suhrkamp); *The World as Will and Representation* (New York: Dover, 1969).

Sellars, Wilfrid (1997) *Empiricism and the Philosophy of Mind* (Cambridge, MA, and London: Harvard University Press).

Taylor, Charles (1995) *Philosophical Arguments* (Cambridge, MA, and London: Harvard University Press).

Tugendhat, Ernst (1992) *Philosophische Aufsätze* (Frankfurt: Suhrkamp).

Tugendhat, Ernst and Wolf, Ursula (1986) *Logisch-semantische Propädeutik* (Stuttgart: Reclam).

Weber, Max (1998) *Gesammelte Aufsätze zur Wissenschaftslehre* (Tübingen: Mohr Siebeck).

Wheeler, Samuel C. III (2000) *Deconstruction as Analytic Philosophy* (Stanford: Stanford University Press).

Wingert, Lutz and Günther, Klaus (2001) *Die Öffentlichkeit der Vernunft und die Vernunft der Öffentlichkeit. Festschrift für Jürgen Habermas* (Frankfurt: Suhrkamp).

Wittgenstein, Ludwig (1980) *Culture and Value* (Oxford: Blackwell).

Wittgenstein, Ludwig (1984) *Tractatus logico-philosophicus. Tagebücher 1914–1916. Philosophische Untersuchungen* (Frankfurt: Suhrkamp); *Tractatus Logico-philosophicus* (London: Routledge, 2001).

INDEX

Bold entries refer either to a passage involving explanation of a key term, or to a chapter or section on the thought of a particular philosopher or on a particular philosophical direction.